HARDHATS, HIPPIES, AND HAWKS

HARDHATS, HIPPIES, AND HAWKS

The Vietnam Antiwar Movement as Myth and Memory

Penny Lewis

ILR PRESS

AN IMPRINT OF CORNELL UNIVERSITY PRESS

ITHACA AND LONDON

First published 2013 by Cornell University Press
First printing, Cornell Paperbacks, 2013

Printed in the United States of America

Library of Congress Cataloging-in-Publication Data

Lewis, Penny (Penny W.)
    Hardhats, hippies, and hawks : the Vietnam antiwar movement as myth and
memory / Penny Lewis.
        p. cm.
    Includes bibliographical references and index.
    ISBN 978-0-8014-5174-4 (cloth : alk. paper)
    ISBN 978-0-8014-7856-7 (pbk. : alk. paper)
    1. Vietnam War, 1961–1975—Protest movements—United States. 2. Peace
movements—United States—History—20th century. 3. Social conflict—United
States—History—20th century. 4. Collective memory—United States.
5. Memory—Social aspects—United States. I. Title.
    DS559.62.U6L49   2013
    959.704'31—dc23   2012043994

Cornell University Press strives to use environmentally responsible suppliers and
materials to the fullest extent possible in the publishing of its books. Such materials
include vegetable-based, low-VOC inks and acid-free papers that are recycled,
totally chlorine-free, or partly composed of nonwood fibers. For further
information, visit our website at www.cornellpress.cornell.edu.

Cloth printing   10 9 8 7 6 5 4 3 2 1
Paperback printing   10 9 8 7 6 5 4 3 2

Printed with union labor

For Steve, Clara, and Eleanor
In loving memory of Evelyn Dorothy Shtob

Contents

Acknowledgments

I am deeply grateful to all of the wonderful people in both my work and personal lives who have sustained me through the development of this book from its first days. Colleagues, friends and family shared their ideas, criticisms, and advice; sent me sources and helped me navigate archives; supported me in myriad ways to give me space to write; and offered encouragement at every stage. The book that emerged is all the stronger for their support. (Its weaknesses remaining quite my own.)

I worked within the City University of New York (CUNY) throughout this time, where I found outstanding mentors, colleagues, and institutional support. At the CUNY Graduate Center, Stanley Aronowitz, Frances Piven, and Josh Freeman generously shared their wisdom, extended their encouragement, and provided me with models of engaged intellectual work. They served as advisers when this book was first hatched as a dissertation, and I feel profoundly fortunate that they continue to advise me as colleagues and friends. Bob Alford, who passed away before I began this project, contributed to how I initially mapped out my inquiry, and I was buoyed by my memory of him and his dedication to sociological practice throughout the process of writing it.

Faculty and fellow students at the Graduate Center, colleagues at the Borough of Manhattan Community College, and other past and present colleagues across CUNY and the Professional Staff Congress provided years of intellectual fellowship, direct support (thank you reading groups!), and solidarity while I was at work on the successive iterations of this project. My thanks go to Victoria Allen, Debbie Bell, Dorothee Benz, Gay Brookes, Jeff Bussolini, Barbara Bowen, Jonathan Buchsbaum, August Carbonella, Ron Doviak, Ariel Ducey, Hester Eisenstein, Mike Fabricant, Bill Friedheim, Anne Friedman, Maggie Gray, Rebecca Hill, Robin Isserles, Miriam Jimenez, Rati Kashyap, Bill Kornblum, Steve London, Lorna Mason, Rich Meagher, Kathy McDonald, Ananya Mukherjea, Jim Perlstein, Charlie Post, Nancy Romer, Michelle Ronda, Neil Smith, Alex Vitale, Jean Baptiste-Velut, and Betsy Wissinger. Miriam Greenberg and Kristin Lawler have been my steady comrades throughout; their constant encouragement and example, intellectual energy and fearlessness have kept me going from our first days as graduate students.

I have benefited enormously from the intellectual and political community at the Joseph S. Murphy Institute for Worker Education and Labor Studies, and my deep appreciation goes to my students, as well as my Murphy colleagues and those at the School of Professional Studies who have given me such cheering encouragement while I finished writing this book: Mimi Abramovitz, Steve Brier, Nelly Benavides, June Cumberbatch, Debby D'Amico, Suzette Ellington, Naomi Fatt, Paula Finn, Tica Frazier, Zenzile Greene, Larry Jackson, Laurie Kellogg, Kitty Krupat, Linda Levin, Greg Mantsios, K. Maynard, John Mogulescu, Ellie Morales, Kadzi Mutizwa, Kim Ocasio, Padraig O'Donoghue, Daniella Olibrice, Ed Ott, George Otte, Brian Peterson, Walter Romney, Kevin Simmons, Samina Shahidi, James Steele, Ralph Tricoche, and Pam Whitefield. Stephanie Luce and Ruth Milkman have served as both mentors and friends, shielding my time and liberally sharing their own throughout this process; I could not ask for more supportive, inspiring, or committed colleagues.

Junior faculty reassigned time, negotiated between the Professional Staff Congress and CUNY, gave me critical time in the final stages of the book. The PSC and CUNY also oversee the PSC-CUNY Research Grants, and I am very grateful for a 2011–2012 grant that helped me to complete my research. This book draws heavily from the work of many outstanding scholars of class, and writers and scholars of the Vietnam era, including historians, analysts, veterans, and activists whose compelling and insightful histories, memoirs, and stories served to animate the period and help me to make sense of it. I owe an incalculable debt to them, and gratefully acknowledge the imprint their work has had on mine. The staff librarians and archivists at the Tamiment Library and Robert F. Wagner Archives at New York University, the Bancroft Library at the University of California at Berkeley, the Swarthmore College Peace Collection, the George Meany Center for Labor Studies, the Chicano Studies Research Center, the Charles E. Young Research Library of Special Collections at the University of California at Los Angeles, and especially the State Historical Society at the University of Wisconsin, Madison, provided me with friendly expert guidance during my short and long research visits.

Generous readers gave me critical and incredibly helpful feedback on sections and, in some cases, complete drafts of this book. They include members of the Politics and Protest Workshop at the CUNY Graduate Center, especially James Jasper, John Krinsky, and John Torpey; anonymous reviewers at Temple University Press; Anthony Arnove; Aaron Brenner; Miriam Greenberg; Steve Jenkins; Micah Kleit; Carolina Bank Munoz; Charlie Post; Peter Rachleff; Rob Saute; Rachel Sherman; and Mike Zweig. Anthony Arnove, Carolina Bank Munoz, and Corey Robin shared their calm guidance and good sense at critical points of the process of bringing this from manuscript to book. Many other wonderful friends have also brought me humor, sympathy, and encouragement through this long process, including Elizabeth Adams, Sapna Advani, Jessica Blatt, Marnie Brady,

Runit Chhaya, Dan Cogan, Peter Colavito, Nathaniel Deutsch, Liza Featherstone, Liz Garbus, Kim Hawkins, Doug Henwood, Sean Jacobs, Steven Johnson, Annie Keating, Chris Kenneally, Meredith Kolodner, Josh Kranz, Ted Levine, Stephen Lovekin, Dara Mayers, Ora Pearlstein, Tony Perlstein, Alexa Robinson, Ralph Russo, Alex Sierck, Sally Slavinski, and Deirdre Schifeling. Friends across a lifetime helped as well: Courtney Lichterman and Jen Sermoneta generously hosted me during parts of my research, and Wilma and Esteban Cordero offered me extra-parental encouragement.

I have been very lucky to work with the excellent editors at Cornell University Press who patiently guided me through the process of finishing this book. I thank Fran Benson, Katherine Liu, Julie Nemer, and Karen Laun, for helping me to improve this book in its final stages. Rob Saute provided me with help with notes and indexing, but in both cases he served as critical reader for my book as a whole, and I am very grateful for his incisive feedback.

I am indebted to Jenny Castellanos, as well as the teachers at the Park Slope Childcare Collective and Arts and Letters for helping me to raise, teach, and take such wonderful care of my daughters during the time I have been working on this book. I am grateful to Chris and Mary Jenkins, Kevin Jenkins, as well as the extended Zuazua-Bradley-Moore-Jenkins clan, for their love, generosity, and support. Abigail Lewis and Justin Lorts have given me familial and professional support throughout; I am incredibly lucky to be their sister. My parents, Mina MacFarlane and Brian Lewis, have been, as always, unstinting in their love and support. They have been my role models—for the communities they create and sustain in their lives; for the work they do to change the problems they find in the world, both large and small; for finding beauty and humor in all circumstances; and for treating everyone in their lives with fairness, as equals. Their outlook and actions have strongly influenced the direction of this book and made possible its realization.

Steve Jenkins has been the essential element in helping me bring this book to fruition; it could not have happened without his love, patience, humor, and attention to housecleaning. I look forward to a lifetime of returning the favor (likely minus the housecleaning). My final, and immeasurable thanks go to Clara and Eleanor, my greatest joys.

My dear friend Dotty Shtob was an activist during the Vietnam era, just as she had been since the Depression and just as she continued to be in the decades that followed. Dotty was my constant interlocutor on this project, and—along with many others who have spent their lives working and struggling for social change—she was my constant inspiration. With my family, this book is dedicated to her memory.

HARDHATS, HIPPIES, AND HAWKS

This first thing you notice about the antiwar movement is that it isn't your father's. It has a populist, womanly flavor. In the Vietnam era, the male elite were at the head of the parade—*Über*-pediatrician Benjamin Spock, Yale chaplain William Sloane Coffin, Harvard intellectual Daniel Ellsberg, and barefoot poet Allen Ginsberg. The campuses were on fire, and *The New Yorker* had editorials every week telling the privileged how to think.

This time around, the movement's one household name is a mom in straw hat and white shorts, Cindy Sheehan. "In Crawford, you could drive from the [pro-war] rally at the stadium to the [antiwar] rally at Bush's ranch and not be able to tell which one you were at," says David Swanson, and activist with Progressive Democrats of America. "Red-white-and-blue banners and clothing, SUPPORT OUR TROOPS everywhere. It's no longer the good workers of America against the crazy liberal elitists."

—Philip Weiss, "How the Antiwar Was Won," *New York Magazine*, 2005

The film *Forrest Gump*, released in 1994, is widely recognized as a modern classic. In addition to six Academy Awards, including Best Picture, *Gump* appears on the American Film Institute's 100 Greatest American Films list and has been preserved by the Library of Congress. This crowd-pleasing, nostalgic film recasts the social conflicts of the 1960s, 1970s, and 1980s as periods containing within them the possibility of social cohesion and personal redemption, brought together through the whimsical character of Gump, a "mentally retarded" southern white man named after a member of the Ku Klux Klan. Gump's mother's explanation of why she named him after a racist terrorist—to remind him that "we all do things that just don't make no sense"—neatly captures the ethos of the film: people get worked up about all kinds of crazy things in this world, when it would be a much kinder and gentler place if we all just saw that precisely because, as she says, "we're all different," "you're just the same as everyone else."

1

Gump is a simpleton who serves as a foil to the complex events of the era—race relations, Watergate, the "opening" of China, AIDS, and more. While the movie plays with questions of life's meaning—Are we ruled by destiny? Is our time here purposeful?—it functions as a movie about healing, putting ghosts to rest, downplaying when not outright denying fissures in the US social fabric. Gump is himself a liberal character, insofar as he is racially colorblind, nonjudgmental regarding social deviance, and generous with his remarkable fortune (early investment in "some kind of fruit company," Apple computer). But the film's historicity is remarkably conservative.

The trick of the movie is to digitally insert Gump into the videographic historical record, so that the audience now sees him in footage from the 1960s White House, the jungles of southeast Asia, and so on. These canonical scenes, which in turn are spliced into the narrative of the film, create a semi-seamless historical narrative. Watching the extensive archival intercutting, the viewer is encouraged to understand that the background representations of the past are largely factual, even if the fictional Gump is suddenly given an outsized role as innocent catalyst of great events.

What story does *Gump* tell us about the Vietnam War and the protest against it?

To begin with, Gump serves in Vietnam as a soldier. The movie implies that intellectual guilelessness is an asset in the military: Gump "fits in the army like a round peg." His best friend, an African American named Bubba, is similarly sweet and simple, an interracial pairing that, while plausible, obscures the racial polarization and complexity of the Vietnam-era military.[1] Gump describes fellow soldiers as "some of America's best young," whose allegorical names in the movie include Dallas, Cleveland, and Tex. Soldiers and veterans are treated sympathetically, on the whole.

When he returns from the war abroad, Gump stumbles upon one of the massive antiwar demonstrations of the era while visiting Washington, D.C. Like many of the characters and scenes in the film, the antiwar protest is an amalgam, with elements from the November 1967 March on the Pentagon (complete with a ringer of Yippie activist Abbie Hoffman at the microphone), November 1969's March of Death, and the massive multiday protest of April 1971, with its heavy veteran presence. In uniform and randomly finding himself onstage, Gump is asked to speak to the crowd of hundreds of thousands of protesters reaching far back along the National Mall.

As he takes the mike Gump assures us, "there's only one thing I have to say about the war in Vietnam." But an older, distinguished-looking officer has made his way to the controls, and he pulls the plug on Gump. Gump nevertheless speaks for nearly a minute while the audience in the crowd and the audiences in the movie theaters hear only the efforts of the protest organizers to get the mike turned back on. The sound returns as Gump says, "and that's all I have to say about that."

We can assume that Gump said something moving and compelling for the protesters on stage, as the Abbie Hoffman character wipes away tears, offering the affirmation, "That's so right on, man." And we see that the military brass were nervous about the content of a veteran's statement, as they are the ones depicted as pulling the plug. But the movie does not take sides. It is vaguely antiwar, but not clear why it is antiwar. Unlike the other social issues he takes on, a simpleton like Gump can't, it seems, make sense of Vietnam. Gump's presence had managed to bridge social divides stemming from racism, AIDS, even communism. Yet the war at home is the only conflict with which the movie cannot come to terms. It can't be perfectly encapsulated, its divisiveness smoothed over.

Decades following its conclusion, the US war in Vietnam remains an unsettled part of the collective memory and experience of this country. Like *Gump*, politicians, members of the military, veterans, scholars, journalists, and artists continue to revisit and reinterpret the war, still making sense of its historical significance while seeking meaning in it for the wars fought today. Despite the continual efforts of our political elites to put the ghosts of Vietnam to rest, US wars in Iraq and Afghanistan have provided twenty-first-century opportunities to prolong these national discussions. Books and articles with the titles "Is Iraq Another Vietnam?" and "Is Afghanistan Another Vietnam?" abound. The economic and political imperatives that drive US military policy, the appropriate use of force, the domestic costs of war, the treatment and trauma of veterans, whether these wars are "winnable" or "worth it"—these are some of the many points of comparison and concern that surface today.

Whether or not contemporary wars are appropriately compared to Vietnam, to some observers the antiwar movement that quickly emerged (and faded) in recent years was quite a different beast from that of the Vietnam era. "The first thing you notice … is that it isn't your fathers," quipped *New York Magazine*. Surveying the national scene, this reporter observed, "It's no longer the good workers of America against the crazy liberal elitists." "Womanly," "populist," and patriotic, these protesters stand in stark contrast to the "male elite" of the Vietnam era.

To the extent that our memory of Vietnam remains ambiguous, it underscores the incompleteness of any process of historical rendering and the nagging uncertainty that the United States was left with after that war. But amid this incomplete accounting—resting in the death, divisions, shame, and doubt of the Vietnam era—some dominant myths emerged that hold sway in our popular imagination as we remember the war abroad and the war at home. In the pages that follow, I make the case that a particular, dominant narrative of sentiment about and protest against the Vietnam War developed during and after the war itself, one that informs our contemporary understandings of class politics as well as the social sources of support for and protest against war in the United States.

Our collective memory, or the story we tell ourselves and each other in this country, about the social division over the war in Vietnam follows a particular, class-specific outline, fleshed out in numerous movies, TV shows, textbooks, journalist's renderings, histories, memoirs, political speeches, and personal recollections. In these sources the war is typically remembered as having "split the country" between "doves" and "hawks." The "doves" are most often conflated with "the movement," and both are remembered as upper-middle class in their composition and politics. The movement was the quintessential New Left movement, and a big part of what made the New Left "new" was its break from the working-class politics and roots of the "Old Left." Some of the individuals and groups we commonly associate with the era are Dr. Benjamin Spock, Tom Hayden, Jane Fonda, Eugene McCarthy, George McGovern, the Students for a Democratic Society, the various mobilizations against the war, and Weatherman: students, intellectuals, professionals, celebrities; liberal or radical privileged elites. Historical treatments sympathetic to the cause range from being impressed by the strength and passion of the "antiwarriors" to more critical chroniclers who portray them as possibly overly radical and certainly overly entitled—they may have been right, but they went about expounding it in the wrong way. Hostile treatments of the movement, associated with revisionism, focus on the elite and out-of-touch nature of the protesters, antiwarriors as "spitters" and "haters."

And what of the "hawks"? Beyond the predictable military brass, war supporters are often imagined as "ordinary" Americans: white people from "Middle America" (a phrase coined in the 1960s), who supported God, country, and "our boys in the 'Nam." Soldiers and their families, veterans and their communities, they were working-class patriots who insisted that criticism of the war meant criticism of the soldier. "If you can't be *with* them, be *for* them," as the sign read. Many of these "Middle Americans" epitomized moderate middle-class solidity and stolidity, while the workers among them, or members of the lower-middle class, are remembered for having supported George Wallace and Richard Nixon, and their status as Reagan Democrats was imminent, even immanent, as early as 1968.

Most accounts of working-class attitudes, dating from the period and persisting to this day, depict the class as largely supportive of the war and largely hostile to the numerous movements for social change taking place at the time. We need look no further than the most enduring image of the US working class from that period, a certain cranky worker from Queens. The TV character Archie Bunker brought the working class to prime time as a white, bigoted, sexist, homophobic group, suspicious of social change and conservatively yearning for the good old days before the welfare state, when everybody pulled his weight, when girls were girls and men were men. *Joe*, a movie that gained some popularity in 1970, the same year *All in the Family* debuted, depicted a working-class antihero whose distorted patriotism and hostility to the new social movements explode in interpersonal violence and murder. Images of a similarly strident hawkishness flowed directly from the labor movement. "Hardhats," a stereotype based primarily on construction workers in New York City who assaulted antiwar protesters at a rally in downtown Manhattan in May 1970, were the iconic hawks. The most important working-class institution in the post-war era, the American Federation of Labor and Congress of Industrial Organizations (AFL-CIO), is remembered for being virulently anticommunist and vociferously pro-war; big labor's embrace of the Vietnam cause confirmed the image of the working-class patriot who shouts "love-it-or-leave-it" at young, entitled hippies.

Our understanding of the socioeconomic divisions of the Vietnam era thus rests on twin pillars: (1) the antiwar movement was largely an upper-middle-class social movement, led by privileged radicals, with college students serving as its troops, and supported by the sentiment of elite doves; and (2) the working class distanced itself from or despised the movement, mostly supported the war and its makers, and was growing increasingly conservative during the era.

But this memory contains only half-truths, and overall it is a falsehood. Instead, I argue that the reigning assumption of elite dominance within the social groups opposing the Vietnam War has served to obfuscate a more complex story of the class character of this social movement and the antiwar sentiment of the era. Working-class opposition to the war was significantly more widespread than is remembered, and parts of the movement found roots in working-class communities and politics. In fact, by and large, the greatest *support* for the war came from the privileged elite, despite the visible dissention of a minority of its leaders and youth. The country was divided over the war, alongside many other pressing social issues—but the class dynamics of those divisions were complex, contradictory, and indeterminate with regard to what the future might bring.

Many books briefly address the discrepancy between our historical impression of class-based sentiment and its reality in passages similar to this one in *Class Matters*: "Opposition to the war was in fact higher among lower-income than among higher-income Americans."[2] The turn of phrase "in fact" acknowledges the common misperception that the opposite was true. Yet no account systematically explains why such a misperception exists, its extent, or its impact.[3] That is the project at hand, encompassing two overlapping endeavors: an historical revision of the distorted representations of the class dynamics of Vietnam antiwar sentiment and protest, and a theoretical accounting of why such a distorted image developed and persists.

Historical Sociology

This book works within the traditions and problematics of historical sociology. Robert Alford argues that work in this field "combines a search for systematic patterns and an understanding of how contingent and converging events create different outcomes or make alternative scenarios plausible."[4] (The distinction Alford draws echoes Antonio Gramsci's separation of "organic" and "conjunctural" movements of structure.[5]) The challenge for historical sociology is to distinguish the structural from the contingent and then determine the nature of their interaction—a tricky endeavor. William Sewell elaborates on the difficulties in sorting out these "complex temporal conundrums" created by the different temporalities present in historical events:

> How do we handle the problem of sequence when we are dealing not with a chain of discrete and precisely timeable decisions, but the intertwining of long-term with punctual processes? Which social processes, with which temporalities, will emerge as dominant in an event that mixes them together? How, and when, do short-term processes override, deflect or transform long-term processes? How do long-term trends reassert themselves in situations where they seem to have been eclipsed by more pressing political processes?[6]

Much of what has been written and presented about the Vietnam era contains unexamined assumptions about its "social processes." The dominant narrative of the period's class-based political action, of working-class conservatism and liberal elitism, by now has the ring of catechism to it, assuming that such developments are not only true but deeply engrained in post-war US culture. They are understood as long-term processes, overdetermined by how class was structured and experienced in the United States over the course of the twentieth century. What is structural and what is contingent are collapsed, resulting in a myopic story of an inevitably conservative working class and an ineluctably elitist progressivism.

Yet the historical record is more muddied and dynamic than this narrative allows. I first became aware of this buried history a decade ago while working to organize against the US wars in Afghanistan and then Iraq. In the weeks following the terrorist attacks of September 11, 2001, trade unionists in New York City began what seemed to many an anachronistic, and counterintuitive, project: they organized for peace. New York City Labor Against War was one of the first coalitions nationwide to anticipate the probability of an armed response from the United States against the attacks, and it was quick to reach out to other unions around the country as the war efforts shifted from Afghanistan to Iraq. The resulting organization, United States Labor Against War (USLAW), was formed in January 2003, months before the United States began its war in Iraq. Its affiliates drew heavily from public-sector and service-sector unions, but included dozens of central labor councils and other diverse groups, indicating widespread opposition to the imminent war in Iraq. Pressure from USLAW resulted in early criticism of the war effort from the AFL-CIO and in the unprecedented passage of an antiwar resolution by the AFL-CIO in 2005, which called for a rapid return of US troops from Iraq.

I was involved in these efforts as a representative from my union, and I participated in the founding convention of USLAW. Over the months that stretched to years—staffing tables, working on resolutions, and organizing protests, petition campaigns, and other events—I spoke with fellow labor activists about their experiences within the Vietnam antiwar movement. They, too, remembered the college students, the educated and religious pacifists, Eugene McCarthy, and the Weather Underground. But these colleagues, whose days in labor and/or peace politics spanned the three decades between the wars, remembered more: the high school kids from Brooklyn and the Bronx, for whom college was a remote dream, who left school by the thousands to protest the war; their working-class communities, who loved their soldier sons but abhorred the war; the unions (their own or others) that took out advertisements condemning the war, hosted labor education programs about Indochina and the US war, co-sponsored rallies, and started petition drives; the draft resisters, who were often as concerned with the class iniquities of the Selective Service System as they were with the immorality of the war itself; the veterans, most of whom had never protested before, joining and helping to lead the movement when they returned stateside; the working-class GIs who refused to fight; and the deserters who walked away.

I began this project a few years later, working in peace, labor, antiwar, and other movement archives, researching Vietnam antiwar sentiment and action.[7] Collections from movement organizations and the papers of numerous individuals associated with these movements, together with contemporaneous academic studies and media coverage, confirmed the more dynamic story told by the activists. In fact, the history suggested what Alford describes as "alternative scenarios made plausible": a submerged, counternarrative to the familiar stories of Vietnam antiwar sentiment and action. Through this counternarrative, a more realistic picture of the class dynamics of the Vietnam era emerges, one in which working-class people played important roles and antiwar protest was itself shaped by politics informed by class-based experiences.

Class, Collective Identity, and Representation

In many instances, the groups and individuals I identify as working class—due to their relative power; occupations; or, in the case of young soldiers or students, family background—engaged in antiwar protest through other identities that were at least equally important as, if not preeminent to, their class experience. African Americans, Chicanos, students from working-class backgrounds—their antiwar sentiment and action were substantially shaped by their class experiences of exploitation, oppression, and alienation from the war and its means. Our collective memories of the moral and political objections to the war made by many of its more elite opponents misses the moral and political, but also the pragmatic and experiential, frames for protest more commonly expressed within these groups. Highlighting these class-based frames for war protest is a central endeavor of this book.

Yet veterans protested as veterans, Chicanos as Chicanos, and soldiers as soldiers. Class was part of their movement identities, but typically not their defining expression. Why this was the case can be understood both theoretically and historically. The analytical framework through which I understand class accepts that broad relative experiences—of power, ownership and labor, material scarcity and affluence, and control and freedom—shape class categories, along the lines of the classic Marxian concept of class "in itself," wherein workers are structurally situated as "a class against capital."[8] The conditions for solidarity within the working class implied by these shared experiences become clear when we look at the history of working class formation under capitalism. Workers' parties and the labor movement have been built when workers come to common understandings of shared mutual interests and their possible collective power "against capital."

Yet history provides countless examples where such a conscious class "for itself" has either not been realized, or has been directly challenged. This can be explained in part by looking again at the material experiences that workers face under capitalism. Workers are brought together in similar conditions of oppression and exploitation, but they also compete against each other for jobs and positions at work. Such competition in the labor market can help lead to fractious relationships between groups of workers.[9] When viewed from a structural perspective, class thereby constitutes a potential for social cleavages of power and identity, and it can account for solidarities, as well as social divisions and conflict as experienced by people in their everyday lives.

Further, these material predictors of class behavior are situated within cultural, political, and ideological fields that co-determine class formation. This relationship between the objective structural sense of class as place and conditions and any forms of knowledge and behavior we may associate with such objective positioning is therefore always mediated. Classes are groups that, due to their economic lives and livelihoods, occupy similar structural positions, *may* share common understandings, and *may* take similar actions—but they may *not,* for within and between these levels of class are competing, and often overriding, emotional, sociological, and historical considerations. Race, ethnicity, gender, political affiliation, nationality, geography, community history, personal experience, union association, other institutional affiliations, and the nature of the work performed are just some of the most obvious factors that co-determine the self-conscious sense of class that might develop within a group or that might allow outsiders to recognize a collection of individuals as a class.[10]

Among antiwar protesters who were working-class people in the structural sense, other collective identities as well as movement identities frequently superseded that of class. As I explore in detail in chapter 6, this was in part due to the fact that the very category of class as something that helped to meaningfully explain social experience was itself under erasure during this period, and particularly during the postwar period directly preceding Vietnam. It was also because collective identities are themselves created in and through social action. People may come to movement groups, for example, with a preexisting sense of identification with the others who are organizing. But, frequently, the consciousness of oneself as belonging to a group, and acting on interests related to that group, is forged in social action itself.[11] Because veterans worked together as such, and Chicanos, and African Americans, these collective identities were paramount to these movement actors. This capacity for social movement groups to forge collective identities became very important for how antiwar protest was represented at the time and eventually remembered in the class-polarized fashion I describe here.

If black workers, working-class soldiers, or less-than-privileged students were not recognized as workers, who *were* the workers of the day? When any dominant institution of the era conjured a representation of the working class, it was the white, male, goods-producing workers who fit the bill. These industrial and trade workers made up the vast majority of the country's union members, and they had memorably engaged in collective struggle decades before—struggle that had not ended by the time of Vietnam, although its character had changed. Theirs was the working-class identity most commonly recognized, both from within and without. Well before the widespread and more self-conscious public assertions of white ethnic Americans in the early 1970s, a long history of segregation encouraged separate racialized identities among white workers, even among white workers who were not necessarily racist: pervasive segregation in neighborhoods, workplaces, schools, churches, teams, clubs, and other places of daily life cemented this racial cohesion.[12] As I explore later in the book, appeals to this white identity characterized much of the politics of the 1960s; certainly, although not exclusively, from the right.

Exclusive, if at times implicit, focus on the white working class—rather than on a broader interracial set of workers—has tended to distort how both contemporary and historical observers have made sense of the working-class response to Vietnam. First, dominant images of (certain) white workers eclipse the antiwar activities of other (multiracial) workers. Criticisms and active opposition to the war among this broader group that reflect their experiences of social class were not typically counted as such at the time or recorded as such in the histories of the period.

Moreover, dominant images of conservative white workers have also distorted our memory and understanding of white working-class political behavior. Conservative voting patterns do not tell the whole story. White antiwar veterans entered the factories and returned to live inside working-class communities. Union members' children returned from college with antiwar opinions and experiences. Major unions and labor leaders adopted antiwar stands. White workers did not simply move in one political direction—contradictory experiences and interactions meant that a range of political attitudes and actions were expressed by white workers at the time and could be expected to be expressed by white workers in the future.

The overheated class-war rhetoric of the Vietnam era helped create an impression of a chasm between the movement and the working class that served to constrain possible alliances and solidarity. Foregrounding the actual class diversity of the movement and the varied political actions and attitudes of workers—black, brown, and white—should create an analytical bridge between what might otherwise appear to be the contradictory expressions of hard-hat workers raging against antiwar protesters on Wall Street in 1970 and hard-hat workers actively supporting the Occupy Wall Street protesters in the current period; they are not now, and have not been, as far apart as we might think.

Movement-Relevant Theory

My study raises further questions about how we study social movements, particularly within the discipline of sociology. Students of social movements will notice that, with the exception of collective identity, I only on occasion make use of any of the concepts that have organized much of sociological social movement research in the US context over the past few decades. This in part has to do with the movement I'm studying. Incredibly, there are no full-length sociological studies of the Vietnam antiwar movement and relatively few scholarly articles. In "The Forgotten Movement: The Vietnam Antiwar Movement," James Max Fendrich describes the "lack of analysis of the antiwar movement" as a "gaping hole" in the sociological literature.[13] What accounts for this silence? What makes this movement resistant to sociological study?

The Vietnam antiwar movement was a massive, sprawling, multiheaded phenomenon. It is estimated that as many as 6 million Americans actively participated in it in one form or another, with another 25 million close sympathizers.[14] Its scope was often very narrow, if ambitious: for the most part, people were united, quite obviously, to end the war.[15] The overarching goal uniting its many iterations was to leverage whatever power it had to pressure the US government to do so. But, short a revolution, the timing of this eventuality was outside of the hands of the movement—it could push hard for the war to end sooner, but the movement itself could not make the call. Very few activists had any sense that it would take as long as it did for the war to end. For many, the war appeared so untenable at its start that they thought it would be over within months or the year. Official positions of the major political figures abetted this misapprehension of the durability of the war; every politician of the era, with the exception of Barry Goldwater in 1964, ran as a peace candidate of one stripe or another. The movement had a start-stop tempo to it that was largely outside of its control, with horrific bombing campaigns followed by "progress in the peace talks," and an all-or-nothing character—either the war would end or it would not; "no partial victories or breathing spaces could be won."[16] This rhythm led to ups and downs of extreme excitement and agitation followed by extreme disillusion and disappointment, with waves of people feeling their power and then their powerlessness. The extent to which the movement did change foreign policy—and there are many moments at which it did—was mostly invisible to the participants themselves.[17]

For all of its focus, the movement was internally riven, with revolutionary nonreformers battling those who would work within the Democratic Party, proponents of a single-issue orientation fighting those who would broaden its objectives, and full of heated disagreements about demands, audience, and especially tactics. Movement participants ranged from people who belonged to recognizable peace and antiwar organizations, to those who belonged to other social movement organizations for whom antiwar work was not the primary reason for existence (but who devoted some—or at times nearly all—their energy to it), to the hundreds of thousands who pursued antiwar work through other institutions, self-created groups, or even individual actions. The meaning of the primary grievance of the movement—what it meant to be opposed to the war—could range from being opposed this particular war at this particular time to being opposed to all wars at all times, from believing the United States *had made* a mistake to believing that any allegiance to (the imperialist) United States *was* a mistake, and so on. Similarly, the movement's framing processes were so varied and divergent that we can, at best, use this conceptual tool as something through which to descriptively list moments, often overlapping and transitory, of movement self-identity and external presentation. Mobilizing structures, too, can be denoted—and I later use this particular concept to make sense of college and military mobilizations—but they served to bring people into a patchwork of organized and disorganized dissent.

The abundant scope of the antiwar movement perhaps makes it an unsatisfying example of the particular models used in much social movement analysis in the United States. This is to be contrasted with the other major US movements of the 1960s and 1970s—the civil rights/black power and feminist movements—which have not similarly suffered from sociological inattention. Grievances, targets, social movement organizations, political opportunities, collective identities, and other analytical tools used by sociologists to explain how movements work were created largely in response to these movements. Most scholars and people concerned with social change view them as the central movements of the period—but as a result of being so, they are also the prototypes for the types of scholarship that were created about the nature of movements at the time.

Fendrich notes the antiwar movement's ill-fittedness for recent theories of social movements, and this is largely because these theories were precisely making sense of other kinds of movements. The Vietnam antiwar movement did not fit the type. It was not identity based or rights based; it did not draw on any necessary group. The theoretical models that account for more modern social movements—starting with theories of resource mobilization, political process, and the European-based turn to culture—all work to varying degrees with the antiwar movement but their own partiality is underscored by the vast and heterogeneous nature of the movement.

The movement has, of course, received extensive attention from historians, who have examined its roots, its interactions with other movements, and its effects. Although there are important exceptions, for the most part these histories have worked within definitional constraints of what counts as a social movement that tend to exclude many of the elements of the countermemory developed here. Charles DeBenedetti, for instance, whose *An American Ordeal* is rightly held to be the outstanding history of the antiwar movement, takes a classical definition for his own investigation, writing at the outset that "This study assumes that the antiwar movement was a social movement, [using Charles Tilly's definition], 'a sustained *interaction* in which mobilized people, acting in the name of a defined interest, make repeated broad demands on powerful others via means which go beyond the current prescriptions of the authorities.'"[18] "Sustained," "mobilized," "defined interest," "repeated," and "broad" point our attention to the visible or-ganizations of self-identified activists with articulated grievances who engaged in protest over significant stretches of time—in fact, precisely the movement as stud-ied by DeBenedetti and the vast majority of other books written on the subject.

But a broader view is available. As sociologist James Jasper observes, "there is protest ... even when it is not part of an organized movement. Most scholars have defined this kind of action as outside their interests, preferring to examine full-fledged, coordinated movements. This choice renders invisible all the ways that individual acts of protest do or do not feed into more organized movements." In a similar vein, Margit Mayer points out that resource mobilization theorists de-fine social movements in ways that exclude many forms of movement. Rational-ity, formal organization, resources, and professional organizers characterize the ideal-typical social movements for the resource mobilization school, such as labor and civil rights. The success or failure of these social movements (which become synonymous with *social movement organizations*) is measured through their abil-ity to affect policy changes that "culminate in distributional goals." Mayer argues these "tacit assumptions about the polity narrow the scope of movements, which can be perceived as just one type, making others invisible."[19]

Accepting these broader considerations, some have argued, for example, that resistance from working-class soldiers on the front lines of Vietnam and resis-tance of working-class deserters had as great, if not greater, an effect on the US military's ability to fight the war than did the more typical protest actions studied by most scholars.[20] Both the typical movement activists and the GI resisters op-posed the war—yet only one group's actions have been registered as having done so in a proper social-movement way. Among the categories of movement action I consider here that receive almost no attention from DeBenedetti and others are veterans' participation and GI dissent; the role of labor, which receives almost no space in most books; and the Chicano moratorium movement, which astonish-ingly typically gets no mention at all.[21]

How we define *proper opposition* has similarly narrowed our consideration of antiwar sentiment. The antiwar sentiment of the working class had its roots in both morality and pragmatism. As captured in news reports, surveys, interviews and memoirs, questions such as "Why our boys?" "Why our tax dollars?" and "Given our sacrifices, why aren't we winning?" dominated working-class discussions of the war. Should such sentiment be counted as antiwar in the same way as those whose opposition was overwhelmingly political or more traditionally moral?[22] The implicit, and sometimes explicit, answer provided in these studies is no.

Where, then, do we draw the lines around a movement? What happens when we define a movement beyond its own organizational borders, even beyond its own cognitive framework, and place it within a more dynamic historical and cultural context? In recent years, in response to the perceived limitations of academic social movement analysis, there has been a call for movement-relevant theory, defined by Richard Flacks as "useable knowledge for those seeking social change."[23] Douglas Bevington and Chris Dixon, arguing for such an approach, absolve historical studies of movements from their roster of (what they see as) relatively less-usable contributions made by social movement scholars, based on the fact that activists tend to like such historical studies and learn from them. But they argue that sociology should also rise to the occasion, creating a movement-relevant theory that "locates the issues and questions of most importance to movement participants," engages directly with the movements being studied, and offers analytic expertise to compare or summarize the successful tactics or theories generated across different movements.[24]

Moving toward movement-relevant theory would, then, entail taking the movement's social embeddedness into account and recognizing that the clear distinctions that academic analysts might make—between movement and nonmovement, activist and nonactivist; and between different movements, action and theory, grievance and satisfaction—are useful but possibly limiting for understanding the interactive and dynamic relationship between the broader social field and social movement. This immersive reality—the kinds of dilemmas and opportunities they face—is the reality for people making movements. Movement-relevant theory rests in part on the appreciation that social-movement participants themselves theorize their own movements. Their focus is always on the movement inside its real-world conditions, affected by its real-world context, with an eye to change. My focus on sentiment *and* protest makes this tension explicit. The vast majority of Americans opposed the war in Vietnam by the time it was concluded; the movement, although mass, was always a minority movement. What happens at the borderline between feeling and protest is precisely the borderline where a broad understanding of contentious politics, protest, and movement action can be developed.

John Burdick, an ethnographer of social movements who explicitly seeks to make his observations useful to the activists with whom he works, argues that a useful way to do this is "reporting the patterned testimony of people in the movement's targeted constituency who on the one hand held views and engaged in actions very much in line with movement goals, but who on the other hand felt strongly put off, alienated, or marginalized by one or another aspect of movement rhetoric or practice."[25] Examining the tensions between the antiwar movement and the broader social field within which it moved, I do through history here what Burdick does through ethnography: explore the distrust and dislike many felt for the movement, and the extent to which and how the movement itself exacerbated, recognized, or mollified these concerns.

This friction at the borders of movement and nonmovement does not occur only at the moment of movement making. The broader social field in which I make sense of the sentiment and protest against the Vietnam War now extends to our collective memory of this movement. I am examining our collective memory of the movement precisely because of its relevance to social movements today. The dominant, exaggerated, and distorted memory of class polarization has meant that antiwar activists today, and people who desire social change, have not fully understood our history—its shortcomings and achievements, divisions and solidarities, problems and possibilities.

Overview and Main Arguments

In chapter 1, I detail the class-polarized representation as it has come down to us through a close reading of the media and popular and academic texts. In the next set of chapters (part I), I take up the accuracy of the image of an elite antiwar movement. I begin somewhat counterintuitively—with an argument and evidence that supports the dominant view. I do this because, although our perception of the middle-class nature of the movement against the war in Vietnam is half-falsehood, it is also half-truth. Despite being as likely to support or question the war as any other group, workers were not significantly involved in the earliest years of protest. If we limit our analysis to the leaders and earliest mobilizing vehicles of the first days of the movement, we find that the earliest groups drawn into protest were significantly from the middle class. Even more, the organizations, including their strategic foci and tactical repertoires, tended to reflect and reproduce middle-class cultures. In chapter 2, I argue that the middle-class culture of the main antiwar organizations and the social locations of the early antiwar movement together help to explain why, even in the later period of the war, the traditional venues and perceived values of the movement were so often unpopular among many workers.

In chapters 3–5, however, I present a countermemory, as Michel Foucault might describe it,[26] one that both differs from and challenges the dominant memory concerning class politics during the Vietnam era. Drawing from my own archival research and from recent scholarship, I tell a story of the sentiment and movement against the war that highlights their cross-class and multiclass natures. The social movement organizations most commonly recognized as forming the core of the antiwar movement themselves contained much more class diversity and concern with class audience than is typically remembered. Civil rights, black power, nationalist, and self-determination movements were among the first and, in some cases, most active sites of antiwar protest during the period. Antiwar currents within the labor movement grew and gained legitimacy over the course of the war. Thousands of active-duty GIs joined antiwar groups, wrote and disseminated hundreds of antiwar newspapers, and took other forms of dissent, and thousands more engaged in direct disobedience during active combat. Returning veterans formed speakers' bureaus that educated thousands about the war they opposed, and eventually they became some of the highest-profile and most effective members of the massive movement. In its final years, working-class people opposed the war in greater proportions than their more privileged counterparts and joined the movement through these diverse streams.

Yet we are left with the image of the "hardhat hawk." In part II, I turn to accounting for why this image, and other conservative visions of working-class life that buttress it, gained so much traction in our collective memory. The sociologist Maurice Halbwachs argues that our social frameworks of memory exist both external and internal to the passage of time.[27] Outside of time, as representations of the past, their stability and generality frame our personal and group recollections, helping to forge our group identity and a sense of commonality. Our exaggerated perception of political polarization along class lines finds support in stable and general understandings of the nature of class and class politics in the United States—that of an increasingly conservative working class and an increasingly liberal elite—that are distorted and incomplete. The experience of the post-war boom and the accompanying rethinking of class relations in the United States are the proximate sources for these polarized distortions, as I explore in chapter 6. Changes within the labor movement during the 1940s, 1950s, and early 1960s, along with postwar academic scholarship and influential cultural reference points, together helped create this image of political class polarization prior to and during the early years of the Vietnam War.

From 1968 forward, a majority of people in the United States opposed the war and wanted to see the troops come home. Yet, despite this change in actual sentiment and growing working-class involvement in the movement, the media's and politicians' representations of antiwar sentiment and action continued to draw on, and in fact amplify, the earlier anticipations and experiences of class divisions. As I take up in chapter 7, working-class political consciousness was neither strong nor unified in any one direction during most of the Vietnam period. In fact, working-class political attitudes and action—whether measured by the narrow gauge of voting patterns or broader currents of political action, by studying only white male organized workers or extending the study to the "new" working class, which included African Americans and working-class women—were all over the map. Referring specifically to organized workers, social critic Mike Davis describes the postwar working class as "disorganized and increasingly depoliticized," and historian Jefferson Cowie describes the working class of the 1970s as "vigorously left, right, and center."[28] Any extant expectations that the political left might have had of a worker's vanguard were disappointed, but so were those of workers epitomiz-ing virulent reaction or authoritarianism. Yet, just as the early elite nature of the antiwar movement signaled a privileged cast to liberalism, the hardhat rallies of 1970 became the iconic reference point for working-class conservatism.

This hardhat image had "legs" from the get-go, in good part thanks to the longer-term predictions of working-class conservatism that I trace in earlier chapters. But in chapter 7, I argue that the post-1968 period marked a crisis in the public representation of working-class life—economic, social, political, and cultural—that created ideal conditions for the proliferation of these polarized images. In *Language and Symbolic Power*, the sociologist Pierre Bourdieu argues that the working class as a whole lacks the social power of cultural capital, which is of central importance for representing oneself in the public arena. Cultural capital can be understood as the knowledge and cultural values that individuals both inherit from their families and learn over time from their peers, in school, and at work. Educated and professional middle-class people have greater access to forms of public self-representation because the cultural capital they have ac-crued precisely enables such access; they know how to talk the talk, and they know, or are themselves, the people doing the talking. They are the journalists, politicians, and academics; they form the professional associations, community leaders, and spokespeople. The most privileged of the early antiwar activists had precisely this kind of capital, and it accounts for much of their prominence.

On the other hand, Bourdieu argues that, to the extent that working-class attitudes or opinions are represented in the public realm, they get there because workers themselves, or the observing public, assign them to representative bod-ies; workers do not do it alone in the same way. He explains, "[t]he 'working class' exists in and through the body of representatives who give it an audible voice and a visible presence."[29] These labor parties, socialist parties, and—in the US con-text, most important—trade unions have "authority to speak for the class—to articulate its history, political opinions, needs, and demands."[30]

During the Vietnam era, the two dominant institutions that represented the working class in the United States—the labor movement and the Democratic Party—were internally fragmented. Vietnam was a major cause of this fracturing but not the only one. Ultimately, neither labor nor the Democrats spoke for the "left, right, and center" political directions of the working class. Into the opening created by their inability to adequately represent workers' attitudes and actions came two powerful institutions that were able to shape popular representations of workers: the media and the Republican Party.

In the conclusion to this book, I turn to the more contemporary forces that have enabled the Vietnam-era image of class polarization to both flourish and be challenged today, and I consider their implications for our understanding class-based political behavior. For academic analysts, the experience of the Vietnam antiwar movement has contributed to a rethinking of which groups best, or actually, constitute agents of social change within the United States and other industrialized societies.[31] For movement activists, concern over working-class participation in and support for social movements has recurred since the 1960s, today yielding urgent debates about how to create coalitions across the class divide. In my review, I develop a clearer understanding of what prevents—and allows—wider working-class participation in social movements in our era.

Forty years after Vietnam, such a study remains timely. We are a country at war, and images of the social polarization that characterized the Vietnam era remain. Activists have struggled to understand why a promising antiwar movement that began in 2002 all but disappeared within a few short years. Economic crisis, neoliberal policies, and austerity create conditions of scarcity that increase working class competition and can undercut solidarity. Most working people today lack an effective and independent political voice, which means that all kinds of people can still "speak for" workers in ways largely disassociated from what workers might say for themselves.

Perhaps most salient is the question raised by Thomas Frank in *What's the Matter with Kansas?*, which tries to account for why Republicans attract working-class and lower-middle-class voters, against their economic interests. The emphasis in *What's the Matter with Kansas?* (and frequently in other books that take up this problem) is on the positive points of attraction offered by the Republicans to a working-class audience. My book sheds further light on these problems, offering a new perspective. To a much greater degree than Frank and similar studies, I emphasize the inadequacy of meaningful political representation for working-class Americans within the context of the Democratic Party and labor, in particular. But I focus on the problem of representation more broadly, extending it to the stereotyping, simplifying, and hardening of the image of class-based political polarization that most observers, including Frank, are guilty of. The social divisions in this country have within them greater room for maneuverability, for alliances, and for actual solidarity than our dominant image allows. Recently, the Occupy movement of the "99 percent" and renewed efforts of labor and community coalitions suggest that people are discovering in practice the possibilities that I found in history and theory and present here. By entering this troubled discourse of class and politics, these incipient movements are bringing to light submerged narratives and the possibilities opened by them, knowledge of which are the ultimate contribution that I seek to make in this book.

COLLECTIVE MEMORY OF VIETNAM ANTIWAR SENTIMENT AND PROTEST

We [Harvard undergraduates] certainly could have seen that by keeping ourselves away from both frying pan and fire, we were prolonging the war and consigning the Chelsea boys to danger and death. . . . You could not live through those years without knowing what was going on with the draft, and you could not retain your sanity with that knowledge unless you believed, at some dark layer of the moral substructure, that [by getting out of serving] we were somehow getting what we deserved. . . . "There are certain people who can do more good in a lifetime in politics or academics or medicine than by getting killed in a trench"; in one form or another, it was that belief that kept us all going.

—James Fallows, "What Did You Do in the Class War, Daddy?"
Washington Monthly, 1975

The best selling book, *Lies my Teacher Told Me*, explores the deplorable state of history curricula in secondary education, detailing "everything your American History textbook got wrong." The bulk of its chapters are devoted to how particular episodes, people and themes of American history, such as "discovery," Native Americans, racism, and "progress," are discussed in a selection of history textbooks. Throughout, author James Loewen offers multiple interpretations as to why some facts are valued over others, why some distortions are rampant, and why certain stories are absent and others universal. He devotes his concluding chapters to answering, in more general terms, the questions that are implicit throughout: "Why Is History Taught like This?" and "What Is the Result of Teaching History like This?"[1]

Loewen addresses the title question of this last chapter by choosing as emblematic a "Vietnam exercise" he conducted with "more than one thousand undergraduates and several hundred non-students" over the course of a decade.[2] In these experiments, he gave his class or audience a chart that showed the public's overall response to a Gallup poll question of January 1971: "A proposal has been made in Congress to require the US government to bring home all US troops before the end of this year. Would you like to have your congressman vote for or against this proposal?" After he had excluded the "I don't knows," 73 percent of respondents answered "yes" for withdrawal, whereas 27 percent answered "no." Loewen left three columns of the chart preceding this overall breakdown blank, except for the headings of adults with "grade-school education," "high-school education," and "college education." He asked students to fill in how they imagined these opposing attitudes about the war broke down according to education, which, as discussion had made clear, could also be understood as a proxy for class. By a margin that approached 10 to 1, students consistently indicated that the college-educated adults would have been most critical of the war; the nonstudents agreed at the only slightly less-overwhelming margin of 9 to 1. A "typical response" allocated the preponderance of withdrawal sentiment to the college-educated (90 to 10), close to average likeliness of calling for withdrawal (75 to 25) to the high school–educated, and least likely to call for withdrawal to the grade school graduates (60 to 40). Students explained their interpretations in varied but related ways: the better-educated someone was, the more critical and liberal they were likely to be; working-class people in the United States had a self-interest in being pro-war because their jobs were more likely related to war-making (in factories or the military); and other responses indicating that the "archetype of the blindly patriotic hardhat" was alive and well. Antiwar sentiment, the great majority of these college students and nonstudents agreed, was the province of the privileged; the lower down that ladder you were, the more likely you were to have supported the Vietnam War.[3]

But, as Loewen showed these students after they had made their speculations, the education/class breakdown of the "withdrawal" respondents was the opposite of what they had hypothesized. Answering his own question, he argues that the result of teaching history the way it is taught is that we get history wrong—we misapprehend and distort our past. The actual polls are shown in table 1.

The poll results were surprising to the respondents in Loewen's experiment. He notes that they "surprise even some social scientists," who should, he implies, know better. But should they? On a smaller scale than Loewen, I have encountered similar surprise as I described my project to others, who often asked me to explain, again: *How* did the sentiment against the war break down? Because wasn't it the college students who marched against the war? Wasn't it the elite and well-educated—intellectuals, peace activists, creative artists, and eventually prominent political leaders—who led the antiwar movement? Didn't workers *support* the war? Weren't the labor unions especially vocal in supporting the war? Didn't workers beat up activists, proudly display American flags, and confront the students with forceful advice to "love it or leave it"?

Table 1 Antiwar sentiment, 1971

	ADULTS WITH:			
	COLLEGE EDUCATION	HIGH SCHOOL EDUCATION	GRADE SCHOOL EDUCATION	TOTAL ADULTS
Percentage for withdrawal of US troops (Doves)	60	75	80	73
Percentage against withdrawal of US troops (Hawks)	40	25	20	27

Source: James Loewen, *Lies My Teacher Told Me: Everything Your American History Textbook Got Wrong* (New York: New Press, 1995).

These suppositions have only gained greater ground in the wake of the current wars being fought by the United States. A *Law and Order* episode titled "Veteran's Day" neatly captures the contemporary remembrance. In it, a Gulf War veteran who is grieving his son's recent death in Afghanistan kills a young antiwar activist. Brian Tighe, the activist, is from a wealthy family, is "good at pushing other people's buttons," and comes off as a real jerk: blindly moralistic, self-righteous, out of touch with the real world that most ordinary people live in. We are told that Brian combatively argued against a community board proposal to rename a street after the veteran's son, saying that streets should not be named after "murderers." His girlfriend, Rehana Khemlani (who, although an American, is by name and appearance seemingly of Middle Eastern descent), defends Brian's outrageous tactics, saying, "sometimes you just have to make a lot of noise to get people to listen." Brian's privileged WASP-y family, depicted as emotionally distant, nevertheless firmly defends his activism.[4]

Meanwhile, the accused and bereft Gulf War veteran is a letter carrier for the US Postal Service. His friends, other veterans, are similar working-class figures who collectively question Brian's patriotism and priorities. "Guys like Brian Tighe make me sick—driving around with picket signs in his Daddy's SUV, calling us murderers," explains one friend of the accused. Matt, his son, "could have been the first person in [his] family to have gone to college," but chose to be a "soldier like his father" instead. The father explains, "I love my country, and I raised my son to love it, too."

Although the possibility is raised that Brian the activist "was against the war, not soldiers," the city's prosecutor himself asks, "Is it the truth—or is it just what we learned to say after Vietnam?" Brian's antiwar activism is used against him in the trial, which turns on whether his behavior caused the veteran father "extreme emotional disturbance," thereby mitigating the charge of murder. The jury is deadlocked, and a mistrial is declared. Commenting on the clear identification of the jury with the accused, the prosecutor notes there were "too many blue-collar people on the jury," further observing that "the same people that get out of jury duty get out of serving in the army."

Like the responses of Loewen's students, this *Law and Order* story line is based on a dominant cultural narrative that makes sense of the relationships between antiwar activism and class and, relatedly, between the activists themselves and "regular people," especially soldiers. And although *Law and Order* addresses contemporary issues—"ripped from the headlines" is its motto and modus operandi—Vietnam was the clear subtext, serving as a touchstone for the narrative. The figure of the veteran on trial here evokes the hardhats of 1970, whose violent rampages in lower Manhattan became the focus of the anxious response of the nation to the war and protests against it. The fantasy trial in this episode of *Law and Order* parallels a common response to the hardhat demonstrations of 1970, in which the violent aggressors become the righteously aggrieved victims. Prominent ideologues argued throughout and since the Vietnam War that the protesters "stabbed us in the back," sapping the government and military of the will to keep fighting, and turning the public against the soldiers when they came home. This campaign to discredit the movement, placing the US defeat and the problems of veterans on its shoulders, found its grounds in charges of elitism. Those kinds of people—who are cowards, who do not send their sons to die, who avoid the basic duties of citizenship, who live in ivory towers—do not deal with the muck that the rest of us are in. Even more sympathetic observers such as Larry Heinemann, working-class Vietnam veteran and author of *Paco's Story*, express this; Heinemann explains, "I know there were many people who opposed the war for moral and political reasons, but I also know there were many people against it because they were chicken and because their mommy and daddy had money to keep them in the streets."[5]

The story line shared by these events, real and unreal, contains several common elements. Protesters are culturally and economically elite, as well as unsympathetic, bombastic, and insensitive. In contrast, working-class people are less educated but know the world better, are reflexively patriotic, and support the country when we are at war. Soldiers are the working-class victims of both the wars they fight and a culture at home that does not respect them economically or personally. Privileged youth do not carry their weight as citizens, and so regular citizens view these activists with skepticism and hostility, seeing their anger as incongruous to their advantages.

The cultural chasm between these groups is depicted as unbridgeable. In yet another description of Vietnam protest from a more current vantage point, John Micklethwait and Adrian Wooldridge, *Economist* contributors, provide a vision of the period that is similarly rife with stereotypes:

Another divisive force was the antiwar movement. For many activists, the Vietnam War was the greatest evil of the day—and the counterculture was a natural accompaniment to a life of protest. For many rank-and-file Democrats, however, the antiwar movement was an abomination. What did the average workingman have in common with hippies who spent their time taking drugs and squandering their families' trust funds? Or with students who desecrated the American flag? The antiwar protesters, most of whom would be given student deferments rather than being sent to fight, were even more unpopular than the war itself. Far too many of them seemed not just hostile to this or that American policy, but to America in general. The shooting of four students at Kent State in May 1970 may have inspired Neil Young to song, but a week later blue-collar America cheered when a group of hard-hat union construction workers in New York beat up a group of antiwar demonstrators.[6]

Blue-collar America, in fact, disapproved of the hardhat attacks, and other authors argue that it was precisely the over-the-top actions of the construction workers that catalyzed greater antiwar involvement from the official labor movement. Yet these facts do not interfere with the ruling narrative on the subject.[7]

Together these examples provide a basic outline of the conventional thinking that pervades US popular culture regarding the class dynamics of antiwar sentiment and protest during the Vietnam period and afterward. This common wisdom is typically shared, if more implicitly, among academic treatments as well. Many authors have written about the war in Vietnam and the struggles at home. Again and again, among the wars we fought during the Vietnam period, "the class war" figures with varying degrees of prominence.[8]

This historical memory of the class dynamics of the domestic response to the Vietnam War misapprehends the complexity of the class make-up, culture, sentiment, and action of the antiwar forces in the United States. It is this distorted memory, embodied in the students polled by Loewen and "Veterans Day" episode of *Law and Order* that I elaborate on in this chapter. Looking at film and television, history textbooks, academic studies, and mainstream political discourse, I trace the collective memory of the class dynamics of the period that remains with us today.

Collective Memory

Collective memory is a concept used to explain the social nature of our capacity for remembrances at both the individual and group levels. Sociologist Maurice

Halbwachs provides the classic formulation of the relationship between this individual ability to bring the past to mind and the social interactions and group-belonging from which it springs. It is only in our interactions with others, he argues, that we successfully reconstruct the past—we rely on "social frameworks for memory"; "it is to the degree that our individual thought places itself in these frameworks and participates in this memory that it is capable of the act of recollection."[9] Our interactions with and affirmations from the group not only substantiate the memories we hold but, he argues, make possible their recollection. Beyond the commemorations and rituals that Halbwachs invokes to show how these frameworks are sustained, later students of collective memory have argued that collective memory is created through other social texts and spaces, including the educational system, art forms, subcultures, and media of the society.[10] It is, in fact, critical that we locate these specific instances of memory creation and inscription because Halbwachs's discussion of "a" collective memory might too easily lend itself to reification, making memory a stable and complete object hovering outside specific social action and interaction. Memory is created through a process checked by some objective criteria, with periods of relative congealing, but it is ultimately fluid and open to interpretation, reinterpretation, and contestation. Who represents what and where something is said, defended, or refuted, all matter when it comes to constituting memory.

Like history, memories take on narrative form and are embedded within stories we tell ourselves and each other. Yet history and memory have often been counterposed on the basis of reliability. History, integrated from various sources, is considered the more reliable of the two, whereas memory is seen as more apt to discoloration or distortion. This distinction is less secure in recent years in light of the many critical claims made on historical claims of truth, particularly within the fields of social or bottom-up history, and the terrains covered by "memory studies" and history are becoming less distinct. I am, nevertheless, using the idea of memory in this more traditional way to underscore its potential for distortion, which I relate to the relatively more alive sense that memory brings to our sense of ourselves—the active, emotional, and embodied ways that the past affects the present. For the majority of its participants, the US war in Vietnam and the movement against it are, after all, still a living memory.

The Politics of Memory

As our collective memories help constitute our sense of ourselves, they serve "orientational functions," showing us both what we are and what we might be.[11] Since the end of the war, memories about the US war in Vietnam have served as the ground for substantial levels of conflict about what "we," in this country, are all about.[12] First and foremost, memories of Vietnam have oriented US foreign policy; how and in what context we remember Vietnam has set the tone for domestic debate about military intervention. President George H. W. Bush referred to Vietnam in his inaugural address of 1989, arguing, "that war cleaves us still. But, friends, that war began in earnest a quarter century ago; and surely the statute of limitations has been reached. This is a fact: The final lesson of Vietnam is that no great nation can long afford to be sundered by a memory."[13] Bush and his advisers were concerned with "curing" the country of what they referred to as the "Vietnam syndrome." Norman Podhoretz described the syndrome as "sickly inhibitions against the use of military force."[14] In Podhoretz's view, shared by figures such as Jeane Kirkpatrick, Ronald Reagan and others, memories of Vietnam caused the United States to be gun-shy in the face of legitimate threats to its interest and power; conquering that appeasement tendency became a central tenet of neo-conservative policy. Yet, in the case of the syndrome, the very framing of the problem indicates the ideologically charged terrain of competing memories. On the other end of the political spectrum, Noam Chomsky named the Vietnam syndrome as part of a larger crisis of legitimacy for US elites because it represents "the general unwillingness of the population to bear the material costs and the moral burden of aggression and massacre."[15] For Chomsky and other opponents of the war, the experience and memories of Vietnam served as a brake against imperialist adventurism, and forced the use of covert operations during the 1970s and 1980s.

For many conservatives, the first Gulf War of 1991 appeared to be the cure for the resilient syndrome. In its aftermath, President Bush declared, "By God, we've kicked the Vietnam Syndrome once and for all!" Yet the specter of Vietnam was not put to rest. The US invasions and wars in Afghanistan and Iraq have prompted endless comparisons to Vietnam, with evocations of quagmires, mistakes, counterinsurgency, and more. Predictably, contemporary war supporters have generally tried to distance themselves from these comparisons, whereas the war critics have often pointed to the similarities between Vietnam and the new wars.[16]

In the case of Vietnam, therefore, the orientational functions served by our memories point to other political alignments, and opposing ideological ends are served by the particular memories recalled. What is the appropriate role for the US military? Was the war a "mistake" a "noble cause" or "fundamentally wrong and immoral"? Did the Vietnamese "win" the war, or was the United States "betrayed," "stabbed in the back" for its efforts? This is the context in which our memory of the domestic class dynamics of the period has developed as well, in a terrain marked by ideological strife. How we remember the class dynamics of our national response to the war also, therefore, serves orientational functions, situating our political analyses of (1) who participates in social movements, particularly antiwar or peace movements; (2) what kinds of political attitudes can be predicted of people based on their class and educational background; and (3) the extent to which cross-class political action and coalitions are possible. These memories also shape our understandings of the current natural constituencies of the Democratic and Republican parties, the end of the liberal consensus, and the rise of conservative politics in the United States since the 1960s.

Yet unlike questions about foreign policy, the effects of the antiwar movement, and other controversial elements of the Vietnam experience, the memory of its class dynamics is remarkably noncontentious. It is as if left and right disagree vehemently over most elements of the Vietnam period, save one: that the war was opposed by elites and supported, with ambivalence, by the white working class. Unlike in the more obviously polarized or polarizing debates about the war and the movement against it, an unusual degree of consensus surrounds the nature of the class response to the war.

An early, and influential example of how liberal and conservative viewpoints appeared to find common ground in this memory of class polarization is one of the first "memories" of the movement to be published in the mainstream press: James Fallows' article, "What Did You Do In The Class War, Daddy?" which appeared in *Washington Monthly* in 1975.[17] Appearing in multiple anthologies, otherwise reprinted and quoted, its fame is "evidence of how painful a nerve he had struck."[18] To the extent that a "common sense" about the class dynamics of the movement was achieved following the war, Fallows' article is a good place to start.

Fallows' narrative begins in the fall of 1969, when, as a young Harvard graduate, he received his draft notice. Draft resistance, he knew, meant going to prison or leaving the country. He instead sought a physical deferment, which "would restore things to the happy state I had known during four undergraduate years." Along with a significant majority of his Harvard classmates, Fallows succeeds in evading the draft, in his case winning an "unqualified" status; he is overcome with relief. Yet he soon begins to feel a "sense of shame that remains with me to this day." Beyond having lied to the draft board, his shame sprang from witnessing the "boys from Chelsea . . . the White proles of Boston," who "walked through the examination lines like so many cattle off to slaughter." When the cosseted Cambridge collegiates returned to the Yard later that day, there was "something close to the surface that none of us wanted to mention. We knew now who would be killed."

It was in fact working-class men who overwhelmingly comprised the Vietnam-era armed forces, and bore the brunt of the casualties. Fallows' argument, here, rests on sure ground. Yet the thrust of his argument is not that the working class disproportionately served and died. He turns his eye instead to those, like himself, who did not serve. And there he finds the "seedbed" for "class hatred now so busily brewing in the country."

Like Chris Buckley's similar article "Viet Guilt" (1983), Fallows' essay argues that elite students avoided the draft to save their own skin, though they rationalized this decision through various politically correct "theoretical frameworks" that made them feel virtuous.[19] Their political arguments for not serving, however, were "basically fraudulent." In the eyes of the nearly thirty-year-old Fallows in 1975, the underlying insincerity of the political case against the draft should have been apparent to anyone who was being honest with himself at the time.

Fallows is recounting his personal experiences, not setting out to write a history of the movement. Like all our memories, his is anecdotal, selective, and not always accurate. He confuses those who argued for resisting the draft with those who argued for evasion.[20] He supplies caricatures or allows the movement's most caricature-ready elements to stand in for the whole of the anti-draft scene in Cambridge.[21] The particular argument made by many local antiwar activists— that resistance itself was perhaps an elite tactic, and that evasion was more inclusive—is lost on him.[22] He moves between describing the actions and beliefs of all Harvard students and those of antiwar activists as if they are the same group, a conflation he continues as he develops his argument about class warfare, in which he collapses liberals, the antiwar left, and the "highbrow circles" he (self-loathingly) condemns.[23] His overall argument has been taken as evidence of his "neo-liberal" status.[24]

Yet Fallows makes two compelling, and damning, critiques of the movement that deserve attention despite their compromised context. The first finds echoes across the revisionist spectrum: by counseling people to avoid military service, or by following such counsel, antiwar protesters *prolonged the war*. "It is clear by now that if the men of Harvard had wanted to do the very most they could to help shorten the war, they should have been drafted or imprisoned en masse." Criticizing himself and others, "our reluctance to say 'No' helped prolong the war. The more we guaranteed that we would end up neither in uniform nor behind bars, the more we made sure that *our* class of people would be spared the real cost of the war." He explains: "Because their boys weren't being killed," the parents of the elite "opposed . . . the war . . . in a bloodless theoretical fashion . . . the mothers of Beverly Hills and Chevy Chase and Great Neck and Belmont were not on the telephone to the congressmen screaming, 'You killed my boy.'" He concludes, "We certainly could have seen that by keeping ourselves away from both frying pan and fire, we were prolonging the war and consigning the Chelsea boys to danger and death."[25]

It is undoubtedly true that a mass imprisonment or drafting of Harvard men would have had an effect on the war. It was, in fact, precisely the former strategy—of mass imprisonment—that the Resistance and other anti-draft groups were pursuing in the years before Fallows' successful evasion. Yet the government did not oblige them, a fact that Fallows does not communicate. Very few draft resisters were prosecuted largely because of the unpopularity of the war, which increasingly made such prosecutions politically untenable, and the government wisely declined to take the bait. Fallows also dismisses as largely insincere a primary criticism leveled against the draft by the movement: that it behaved in a class-discriminatory manner, disproportionately culling the working class and releasing the middle class to their families and careers. It was concern over the selectivity of the Selective Service that prompted anti-draft groups like the Boston Draft Resistance, operating in Fallows' backyard during his halcyon days as an undergraduate, to focus their work among the area's "proles."[26]

There is debate about the role the movement played in relationship to the duration of the war, and some honest speculation that the credibility gap created by the movement served to restrain Johnson, who otherwise might have authorized extreme measures to "win" the war. (This argument assumes that the Vietnamese could have been bombed into submission, basically, had the movement not put the brakes on the war machine. Given the nationalist support found by the National Liberation Front it's far from clear that this would have been the case.) But most observers agree that the movement served to prevent an even more vicious bloodbath in Vietnam. In Fallows' construction, the blood of the working class casualties is on the movement's hands—it was the movement, not the war policies, that was "consigning [them] to danger and death."[27]

Which leads to the most insidious charge in the piece. Fallows writes, "You could not live through those years without knowing what was going on with the draft, and you could not retain your sanity with that knowledge unless you believed, at some dark layer of the moral substructure, that [by getting out of serving] we were somehow getting what we deserved." We, the elite who didn't serve while claiming opposition to the war, thought this moral calculus made sense. Fallows, in a sense, sees a little of former vice president Dick Cheney in every peacenik who didn't go to jail: the anti-warriors had more "important things" to do than serve in Vietnam.

Here, Fallows attributes a deep, fundamental elitism to a substantial wing of antiwar activity, using a broad enough brush that the answer to the question, "which side were you on?" comes down very simply to the choice of elite protesters or working-class soldiers. This ignores the fact that the movement specifically argued against the class discrimination of the student deferments, and everyone who burned their card or otherwise resisted the draft was directly confronting that system. Evasion was understood at the time by many as an appropriate if less noble response to an immoral and illegitimate war, as was desertion. By taking the actions of the evaders out of context, confusing resistance with counseling, and attributing an elitist cynicism to those who didn't go to war, Fallows creates a highly distorted picture of the class dynamics of the anti-draft movement. Fallows turns history on its head here, history so recent it's barely past.

Many points from Fallows' personal remembrance find echoes in subsequent representations of class connotations of antiwar activity. In movies, shows, and textbooks, the polarized, guilt- and blame-ridden class chasm appears again and again.

Film and Television Evocations

The first sites of memory I explore are mainstream TV and film representations of Vietnam.[28] In the realm of cultural production, the years immediately following the war were marked by a collective silence, and references to Vietnam were rare.[29] Beginning in the late 1970s, and picking up steam through to the mid-1990s, Vietnam emerged as a central site for cultural work. This is not to say that we stopped mining the 1960s after the mid-1990s but that there has been much less attention to the era in our popular culture since. The reasons are probably related to the age and life-place of dominant cultural producers and to the timing of subsequent historical events. Beginning in the mid-1970s and continuing through the 1980s, the country was actively haunted by the lost war, although the nature of that haunting meant very different things to different people. The progression of our cultural reaction to Vietnam can be described as follows. Repressed silence and anxiety reigned until 1978, during which time negative and fearful depictions of veterans appeared in films such as *Taxi Driver* (1976) and the country seemed committed to forgetting. From 1978 through the Reagan years, alongside an outpouring of work from Vietnam veterans themselves, something frequently described as "revisionism" began to take hold in films such as the *Deer Hunter* (1978) and the *Rambo* series (1982–1988), TV shows such as *The A-Team* (1983–1986), and books such as Guenter Lewy's *America in Vietnam* (1978), Norman Podhoretz's *Why We Were in Vietnam* (1982) and Harry Summers's *On Strategy* (1982).[30] Revisionist interpretations of Vietnam tended to defend or justify the war effort against what they saw as liberal orthodoxy on the subject; US defeat was generally attributed to the lack of political will to fight, which was in turn usually blamed on the domestic opposition to the war. Oliver Stone's film *Platoon* (1987) marked a break to a more antiwar, antirevisionist representation, coupled with a large number of new histories and collections of essays by historians and cultural critics who were critical of the war and more sympathetic to the movement, such as Charles DeBenedetti's *An American Ordeal* (1990) and Marilyn Young's *The Vietnam Wars: 1945–1990* (1991).[31] The first Gulf War of 1991 brought the problem of Vietnam front and center, and was credited with "curing" the country of its "Vietnam syndrome."

Many of the students who Loewen polled were the right age to have seen or heard about the Hollywood blockbusters that had brought the war back to popular consciousness: the *Rambo* series (1982, 1985, 1988), *Platoon* (1987), *Hamburger Hill* (1987), *Born on the Fourth of July* (1990), and *Forrest Gump* (1994); perhaps they had seen *Hair* (1979), or *The Deer Hunter* (1978). *The Big Chill* (1983) reintroduced the veterans of the antiwar movement (and their music) to the younger generation; *M*A*S*H* was a mainstay of their child-hoods;[32] Vietnam veterans played central roles on shows such as *The A-Team* and *Magnum PI*; *China Beach* was a prime-time hit.

The specific films and TV shows that I discuss here are significant for their popularity or critical acclaim. Because I am interested in popular perceptions of the war, I have purposefully limited my detailed discussion here to mainstream films and shows that reached a mass audience.[33] Even though these films and shows—and there are dozens more—fall all along the political spectrum, their representations of class are fairly consistent. Questioning the purpose or mo-rality of the war is an elite profession; college students, intellectuals, and the upper middle class are the critics of the war (*Platoon, Big Chill, Hamburger Hill, M*A*S*H*). Most soldiers are working-class "grunts" (*Platoon*) or "blood and soul types" (*Hamburger Hill*), whose loyalty is first to each other and then to country (*Deer Hunter, Hill, Rambo, The A-Team*); when they show ambivalence about the war, their feelings are subsumed by the pressing and concrete circum-stances they face (*Full Metal Jacket*) or they are rising above their group or class (*Hair* and *Born on the Fourth of July*). With the exception of the two films ex-plicitly about the movement (*Hair* and *Born on the Fourth of July*), the antiwar movement is singled out for scorn or remembered with ambivalence.

Films about the Vietnam era have received a great deal of critical attention.[34] Commentators note that films contemporaneous with the war were often criti-cal of the war and sympathetic to the movement (with the obvious and sole exception of *The Green Berets*, the 1968 John Wayne film that attempted to place Vietnam in the tradition of heroic wars). These critical films gave way to the revi-sionist narratives of the late 1970s, and by the mid-1980s, a shift occurred again, with more realist films picking up the burden of representation. *Platoon* was one of the films lauded for its realism.

Genre Constraints and Middle-Class Narrators

It is the middle-class narrator of Oliver Stone's semi-autobiographical *Platoon* who explores the ambiguity of the war, expressing his personal uneasiness and considering its contradictions. College-bound, from the suburbs, Chris Taylor (Charlie Sheen) defied his parent's aspirations and enlisted. In a voice-over letter to his grandmother that opens the film, Taylor describes the typical soldier: "guys nobody really cares about," from the "end of the line," "small towns"; "two years of high school," "job in a factory if they're lucky," and "poor and they know it." He concludes, they're the "best I've ever seen—the heart and soul." He hopes that "maybe from down here in the mud I can be something to be proud of." Taylor is talking about the mud of Vietnam, but also the mud of his poor and working-class compatriots—their genuineness and groundedness is contrasted with his being, as he puts it, a "fake human being": middle-class, inexperienced, someone who lives in abstractions rather than reality. Later, in an exchange with other soldiers, Taylor asks, "Why should the poor kids go to war and the rich kids always get away with it?" and a fellow soldier points out, "You gotta be rich in the first place to think like that." The soldier continues, "Poor always been fucked over by the rich. Always have, always will." Middle-class people ask the abstract questions; working-class people live the concrete realities. Theirs really *is* not to question why but, rather, simply do and die.

Platoon is thematically organized around the conduct of the war itself. Stone focuses on US troops, those who commit or condemn barbarism, and is thus taking up transhistorical questions about the nature of warfare and man's inhumanity to man.[35] Although this theme is apparent throughout the film, a Taylor voice-over again spells it out for the audience: "We did not fight the enemy, we fought ourselves, and the enemy is in us." Two middle-class characters—first the superwarrior and heroic officer Elias (Willem Dafoe) and then Taylor himself—lead the fight against corruption and barbarism (embodied in the character of another officer, Barnes, played by Tom Berenger).[36]

As an immanent critique of war, *Platoon* largely bypasses any concrete criticism of the particular war in Vietnam. Taylor's early voice-over ruminations make him seem the obvious character for such a critique and imply that he might have brought a critical perspective with him. But the movie seems to make the case that Taylor gives up this power of political critique when he decides to become part of the "mud" of the war. Stone dodges the problem of antiwar sentiment in this way, but he implicitly makes the point that asking such political questions comes from outside the experience of the war, from the college-educated or those "rich" enough "to think like that." Yet, by choosing as his protagonists officers and the exceptional grunt, Taylor, Stone reaffirms the idea that middle-class individuals are the ones who both question the ways things are and effect change.[37]

Such individualism is common in the Vietnam films. This is not overly surprising because it conforms not only to the individual warrior trope but also to the norms of classical coming-of-age narratives. As a genre, the bildungsroman journey of self-discovery by a young man striking out on his own does not necessitate a particular class background for its protagonist, but it implies an ideal-typical middle-class free agent. Such a narrative works on the main character to transform him into a man who retains his individuality while conforming to more universal social norms, norms that could be best understood as middle-class insofar as they are not the particular norms of community or group but, rather, norms of the dominant society as a whole. This transformation is obvious in Stone's other Vietnam film, *Born on the Fourth of July* (1990), and it is also true of Michael Cimino's *The Deer Hunter* (1978).

Born on the Fourth of July, based on Ron Kovic's autobiography of the same name, is the story of one man's transformation from gung-ho marine to antiwar leader. Kovic, played in the movie by Tom Cruise, signed up to go to Vietnam believing in the mission. "Communism has to be stopped" and "I love my country" are his articulated motivations for enlisting. According to his memoir, Kovic, like Taylor of *Platoon*, also went to Vietnam to "make something of [his] life." In Kovic's case, however, this was not a spiritual journey but one of climbing out of his class: "I didn't want to be like my Dad, coming home from the A&P every night"—a store where his father worked as a clerk, not a store that he owned.[38] Stone's on-screen depiction of Kovic glosses over his working-class roots, however, making him more like any middle-class guy from the suburbs.[39]

The dramatic tension of the film version of *Born on the Fourth of July* turns on two related axes. First is the question of patriotism, evident from its title, and what it means to serve one's country. The second is the question of what constitutes manhood. In the film, Kovic's decision to join the marines is framed against his patriotism, his love of war games, and his desire to prove himself a real man to his friends and love interest. At war, he sustains devastating injuries that permanently disable him, confining him to a wheelchair. The first shot hit him in the foot, but rather than lie down, he got up, trying to be "the hero," trying to be "John Wayne." It was this effort that paralyzed him and robs him of his manhood by functionally castrating him. Stone emphasizes this point: that it was precisely the effort to be like the fake heroes of the movies that got us into trouble to begin with.

Despite the generational and collective trauma experienced by Vietnam soldiers and veterans that are continually underscored in Kovic's memoir, his struggles as filmed are personal, emotional, and intellectual. His exposure to the ideas of the antiwar movement comes from TV, discussions with orderlies in the hospital, and, most important, his first girlfriend's college activism. In fact, the Kovic in the film appears to be redefining masculinity by adapting a more pacific (i.e. feminine) outlook. As Kovic writes the story, however, it was attending antiwar demonstrations, speaking out at high schools, and attending his first Vietnam Veterans Against the War (VVAW) meeting that together brought him into political activity. In real life, he had no girlfriend during this period, and he left the college he attends on the GI bill to better pursue his activism. In the book, Kovic describes the movement as the way in which thousands of his brothers could collectively redress the wrongs they both committed and experienced. Writing of the few minutes in which he and others successfully disrupted President Nixon's acceptance speech at the 1972 Republican National Convention, Kovic explains:

> this was it, all the pain and the rage, all the trials and the death of the war and what had been done to me and a generation of Americans by all the men who had lied to us and tricked us, by the man who stood before us in the convention hall that night, while men who had fought for their country were being gassed and beaten in the street outside the hall. I thought of Bobby [Mueller] who sat next to me and the months we had spent in the hospital in the Bronx. It was all hitting me at once, all those years, all that destruction, all that sorrow.[40]

But the movie deemphasizes the relationship between personal and collective transformation described in the book and instead spends the bulk of its development on Kovic's isolated battles with his personal demons. It moves rapidly over the antiwar activism that is a focus of the memoir, using it thematically as an answer to the problems of patriotism and manhood faced by Kovic: being a leader against the war is the best way for him to fulfill his earlier identity objectives of becoming an outstanding citizen and real man.

Working-Class Stories

Cimino's fictional working-class characters in *The Deer Hunter* are similarly declassed and individuated through their experience in Vietnam. The movie begins by situating its main characters within a tightly knit, Eastern Orthodox working-class community in Pennsylvania. These white ethnic steelworkers are one another's best friends and hunting companions, and they sign up together for Vietnam. Like its idyllic beginning, the film takes a mythic approach to the war itself, placing its main characters in historically inaccurate and highly improbable situations—for instance, they cross paths repeatedly in Vietnam. Fable-like, heavy-handed storytelling signals that the film is operating on the level of meta-phor rather than reality. Enormously popular at the box office and awarded an Oscar for Best Picture, the film's symbolic story line appears to have resonated deeply with the American movie-going public.

The central protagonist, Mike (Robert DeNiro)—the true "deer hunter" of the group—rises above his buddies to become a member of the Special Forces. It is Mike who manages to rescue his friends when they encounter one another in National Liberation Front (NLF), or Vietcong, custody. Yet, by the harrowing end of the movie, Mike avoids the homecoming party planned for him, and we never see him working in the mills again. By then, each character has at some level broken his ties to family or community. The film is book-ended by oppos-ing visions of community: opening scenes leading to a massive jubilant wedding filled with eastern European folk dancing are replaced by a small gathering of some of the broken men and their friends at a bar, singing "God Bless America." The movie narrates a fall from grace, stipulating a romanticized working-class community at its outset that is then shattered by the experience of the war. But equally romantically, if also tragically, it reintegrates the characters into a na-tional community that transcends the particularities of their locale. Their story becomes America's story.

Although *The Deer Hunter* does not directly take up the movement against the war, it does make important statements about the working class and Vietnam. Leonard Quart and Albert Auster argue that the working-class characters in *The Deer Hunter* are "politically unconscious men and women."[41] They are not people who make things happen but, rather, people *to* whom things happen, who are played on by larger social forces. Like many of the films of the era, the working class is depicted as the victims of social change.[42] And although the men and women of *The Deer Hunter* are not reactionary (as are, say, the characters Travis Bickle in *Taxi Driver* and Joe in *Joe*), by the end of the movie they are positioned much farther from the war critics than they are from its supporters.

The Deer Hunter was noted at the time it appeared for initiating a revisionist interpretation of the events in Vietnam.[43] The US troops, here, were the victims of atrocities, and it is the US culture that has been warped and destroyed by the Asian. This directly reverses some of the main claims of the antiwar move-ment—that the Vietnamese were victimized by the US war and had their culture savaged by us. Much of the potent imagery coming out of the war, including the iconic images of children fleeing a napalmed village, the tiger cages of the South Vietnamese Con Son prison, and the assassination of an NLF prisoner by a South Vietnamese officer allied with the United States, makes clear that the United States and South Vietnam were the primary sources of brutality. But in *The Deer Hunter*, it is the Vietcong, with their (entirely fictional) Russian roulette games and underwater cages, who are unspeakably brutal, and the Americans who are terrorized. Following *The Deer Hunter*, multiple films reversed the narrative of victim-victimizer, underdog-bully, that had developed as a result of antiwar critique. As H. Bruce Franklin has argued, the manipulation and wholesale creation of the problem of prisoners of war was the vehicle through which much of this reversal was effected; going back for "our guys" who had been "betrayed" by their countrymen is the premise of *Rambo* and the *Missing in Action* film series.[44]

Antiwar Movement in Film

These films and others obscure the antiwar consensus achieved in the United States by the end of the war end. The vast majority of people in the United States opposed Vietnam long before its conclusion and had come to agree with many of the main critiques of the war made by the movement—specifically, that the war was "fundamentally wrong and immoral." But in the revisionist retelling, the movement is made foreign or vilified, and the attitudes of typical Americans are made to seem more ambivalent. *Rambo* refers to antiwar activists, whom the title character describes as having spat on him at the airport on his return, as "maggots"; returning soldiers are menaced by antiwar protesters in the film *Coming Home*.[45] Jerry Lembcke's *The Spitting Image* details the absolutely mythic nature of these tales, but they persist to this day.[46]

Hamburger Hill, released in 1988, a year after *Platoon*, is the movie that contains the most potent tropes of the collective memory being traced here. *Hill* is also the film that best represents the realism of the films made in the late 1980s, and its one-sidedness is all the stronger because of its (frequently solid) claims of historical truth. The action of *Hill* is based on the actual battle at Dong Ap Bia in May 1969, a strategically insignificant spot where US soldiers were "chewed up like hamburger." (Dong Ap Bia is often compared to the French pyrrhic victory at Dien Bien Phu, which preceded the Geneva Accords.) It is told from the perspective of the "grunts" in the war—or, as one soldier remarks, "blood-and-soul types." Although it does faithfully represent the working-class status of the typical soldier and is a scathing antiwar film, the selective views attributed by the film to these soldiers fall completely within the revisionist project. The fact that the film was critically and popularly embraced for its realism despite its distortions indicates how solid the collective memory of class polarization had become at that point.

The film is unsparing in its contempt for the movement. The soldiers going home are cautioned not to wear their uniforms when they get back because they may be the target of "dog shit," among other things. Unlike the action in *Platoon*, which takes place before the Tet offensive of January 1968, *Hill* takes place when the domestic sentiment against the war had shifted and the country had decisively turned against the war. Symbolizing the lack of domestic support for the fight, the movie depicts the antiwar movement as having influenced the soldiers' families at home, particularly the women, who are emblematic of a home front that cannot appreciate what is actually happening in the war. Speaking of one man's girlfriend, another soldier says, "Some hair-head has her on her back right now and is telling her to fuck for peace"; another laments, "My girlfriend said she's not going to write anymore—friends at college told her it was immoral to write to me." The antiwar movement even uses women to demoralize the soldiers. Talking about the North Vietnamese radio broadcasts they pick up, one soldier explains, "Sometimes they get American assholes to tell us what assholes we are. . . . No lie man, it's a trip." In what is no doubt a reference to Jane Fonda and her turn as "Hanoi Jane," we then hear an American woman's voice coming over the radio saying, "Embrace the heroic people of Vietnam like so many of your heroic countrymen."

Antiwar critique is fully excluded from the theater of war. An officer shouts at the new arrivals, "Some of you think you have problems because you're against the war, you demonstrated in school, you have peace symbols on your steel and you have attitudes." He continues, "When you get home, grow your beard and become a goddamned hippie protester," but no complaints are permitted at the front. And, from there on out, there are no explicit critiques of the war by any of the soldiers—just the overall, meta-critique of the war made by the meaningless slaughter itself.

While college, gender, and geography mark the distance of the antiwar movement from the soldiers on the front, *Hill* makes it clear that the war is a working-class affair. As such, the collective identity of these workers is created against the rich kids who are not there. Much of the dialog within the troops establishes the men's common identity as working stiffs who at least "showed up" for the war, in contrast to the "long-haired faggots" who did not. Such negative class consciousness unites even black and white soldiers, as in the following exchange:

> White soldier: The smart white people go to college.
> Doc (black soldier): You people must be aware that the brothers are here because they cannot afford an education?
> White soldier: What am I doing? Sitting in some fucking country club sipping on 7s and 7s and eating a steak? I see all kinds of white faces here.
> Doc: OK, the war started for you when you farted and said Good Morning Vietnam. You see now I was born into this shit.

> White soldier: And they pulled the gold fucking spoon out of my mouth so I could come here and see how you low-class [people] live? Is that it?
>
> Doc: Brother . . . [they shake hands]. . . . We all no-good dumb niggers on this hill, blood and soul types.

This particular exchange is interesting for its simultaneous truthful and mythic elements. The solidarity achieved within the troops during Vietnam was similar to that of other wars—men report they were fighting for each other more than they were fighting for anyone or anything else. But historian Christian Appy points out that, unlike other wars, the solidarity "was shaped not only by the common dangers of war but also by a common sense of the war's pointlessness."[47] The instances of troop cohesion described by Appy in the post-1968 period of the war were usually rooted in feelings that survival was the soldiers' key objective, which over time gave way to collective combat avoidances and combat refusals. He argues that "we must resist romanticizing" the unity because it was "a solidarity dependent on the danger and violence of a war that itself had no meaning the soldiers could embrace."[48] Further, the depiction by the movie of a class-based identity overcoming the extensive racial divisions that existed in the increasingly balkanized army is precisely romantic and, although not unheard of, was nevertheless unlikely.[49]

In *Hamburger Hill*, when one soldier ventures to defend people who resisted or dodged the draft—"Some guy doesn't go—you gotta respect that"—he is quickly put in his place. "No way. You don't want to pull on the little people, no sweat, don't use your weapon. All I want from anybody is to get their ass in the grass with the rest of us. You don't have to like it but you have to show up." Many soldiers and returning veterans felt this way about the young men who did not serve, but this is not the only way they felt. The movie also does not reveal one of the more striking facts about the outcome of the battle at Hamburger Hill: the surviving soldiers put a $10,000 price on the head of the officers who ordered the attack.[50]

Representations of the Movement

During the Vietnam era, even while the media became more critical of the war itself, the antiwar movement never experienced especially positive coverage. In Mel Small's exhaustive account, *Covering Dissent*, he sums up:

> From the first major demonstration in April 1965 to the wild Mayday activities of May 1971, the media framed their stories in terms of the size and composition of the crowds attending antiwar events, and

especially the absence or presence of violent, bizarre, or countercultural behavior. Aside from reporting that the protesters wanted out of Vietnam, the media virtually ignored the political discourse that served as the centerpiece for most antiwar activities. They rarely exposed casual readers and viewers, who constituted the bulk of their audiences, to the rationales behind protest activities.[51]

Later fictional representations, even those without any explicit axe to grind, still often echo the revisionist portrayals as they echo the caricatures and simplifications found in the mainstream media. *Forrest Gump*'s portrait of the radical left, for example, resonates directly with Small's synopsis. In one scene Gump, now a returning Vietnam veteran, finds himself at *a* "Black Panther Party" (his understanding), with black radicals barking stereotyped jargon and "No Vietnamese Ever Called Me Nigger" signs all over the walls. But the white left gets the worst treatment. As Jenny, Gump's friend and future wife, leads him into the room, she is accosted by her abrasive boyfriend, who aggressively asks, "Who's the baby killer?" while gesturing at the uniformed Gump. She proudly introduces her boyfriend to Gump as the "President of the Berkeley Students for a Democratic Society" just seconds before we see the boyfriend hit Jenny across the face, presumably for bringing a "baby killer" into their midst. These are the violent antiwar protesters, filled with rage.

A more quiet contempt for the antiwar movement is registered in the depiction of these activists in *The Big Chill*. Here, college veterans of the movement gather fifteen years later for the funeral of their friend Alex, who committed suicide. Alex seems to represent the spirit of the 1960s for the group; he is described early in the film as being both the personification of hope and also its failure. During his funeral, the officiator sets a challenge for the group of friends, asking whether they can "regain that hope" in the face of its dissolution.

The characters are fantastically—absurdly—ideal-typical of the yuppie "Me" generation. *The Big Chill*'s conceit is that these former radicals have all transformed into apolitical, status-, success-, and money-seeking individuals, albeit with some ambivalence about their newly "evolved" state (the film explicitly uses the metaphor of evolution, thereby underscoring this progression as a natural one). Note, however, that such a direct transformation was actually unusual for the "sixties generation." Most people who were heavily involved in the movements of the 1960s maintained their commitment to social justice, with a disproportionate number staying involved in movement-type work.[52] In the movie, however, only the successfully suicidal Alex and the drug-dealing, impotent Vietnam veteran Nick (William Hurt) are depicted as still caught in the 1960s, quite obviously to their detriment. The rest of the very successful group—consisting of a *People* magazine reporter, business owner, doctor, corporate lawyer, affluent housewife, and TV star—are to varying degrees uncomfortable with their new status. They joke about how "property was theft" back then, how they had wanted to "go to Harlem to teach the kids," and how one became a public defender thinking she would be defending "Huey [Newton} and Bobby [Seale]." But this lawyer's turn-around explains that of the whole group: "I didn't realize how guilty [my clients] would be." Their earlier rebellion is framed as idealistic but also as inauthentic and immature. Ultimately, the movie seems to say, it is okay to live for oneself and one's family to the exclusion of nearly everyone else (except your old college friends). If the characters in *The Big Chill* are to be believed, the 1960s really was no more than an adolescent rebellion by a bunch of privileged youth.

Sympathetic Representations

Some mainstream representations of antiwar attitudes and action are more congenial. The television show *M*A*S*H* (1972–1983) and movie version of *Hair* (1979), both filmed in the 1970s, are products of liberal 1960s sensibilities. *M*A*S*H* is based on Robert Altmann's 1970 film, and the stage musical *Hair* was originally produced in 1967. Their generally positive rendering of antiwar sentiment and the movement was in part a product of this earlier genesis, as well as their explicitly liberal orientation. Yet they too reproduce a middle-class-based representation of antiwar sentiment and action, and they tend to soften the anti-war messages of their original versions.

By making the decision to keep the action of *M*A*S*H* in Korea, the TV show, like the movie, was able to deliver its satire and critique of Vietnam as parable, which served to both give it greater artistic license and avoid the difficulties of-fered up by the fighting in Vietnam. The dissidents in the TV show drank home-made hootch instead of smoking dope (or anything stronger), and they tended to be aggrieved and annoyed by their superiors rather than made murderously angry. As doctors and officers, Hawkeye Pierce, Trapper John, and B. J. Hu-nicutt certainly stood in well for a liberal elite, who could have fun with Charles Emerson Winchester III, the Boston Brahmin, and Frank Burns, the incompetent "lifer" (gung-ho military careerist), who continued to support the war. Colonels Blake and Potter were each easygoing in their own ways and were oblivious to (Blake) or generally tolerant of (Potter) the shenanigans of the dissident leaders. As one critic argues, in *M*A*S*H* "the resentment of military bureaucracy in the main characters is a trivializing surrogate for the rebellion and antiwar feeling of the Vietnam years."[53] *M*A*S*H* offers a tamped down, polite, and humor-ous vision of an antiwar army and, (very) inaccurately, mostly confines antiwar sentiment and action to the officer class.

Hair, the film, also plays down the original antiwar critique of its original 1960s version by centering its story line around a love story of Claude Bukowski, an Oklahoma cowboy, and Sheila, a New Jersey Short Hills debutante. This unlikely pairing across class and culture, among others in the film, helps to convey the message that the young generation has cohered in the experience of the counterculture and that remaining divisions within the country are specifically generational. The tension in the film stems from whether the love and freedom experienced by the youth can grow, challenged as they are by the war itself and the elder generation (from "1948," not "1968," as the song "I've Got Life" points out).

In many of its characters and much of its action, the movie significantly departs from the original stage "American tribal love rock musical." In the stage production, members of the tribe were all non-elite hippies—Claude, always a hippie in the play, was from Queens and Sheila was a commuter student at New York University—and the unity of "the tribe" was political: they were united in their strong, active, and loud opposition to the war. From 1968 to 1972 *Hair* was an international phenomenon, playing in numerous locations around the country and the globe while also running on Broadway. *Hair*'s "tribe" regularly performed at antiwar rallies, including the largest of the decade, and many of its songs became anthems of the peace movement.

In the stage musical, Claude's decision whether to not burn his draft card and thereby accept his induction is the sole coherent narrative thread, with the bulk of the second act taken up by representations of the horror of the war. *Hair* the stage musical also turns the bildungsroman narrative on its head. Claude decides not to burn his card and is successfully drafted. He wonders, "Where do I go?" and ultimately answers Vietnam, where he is killed. Rather than finding himself, he is lost. The original production makes the stark political point that war is personal and cultural suicide. The movie, however, perversely uses the character Berger (Treat Williams), who is casually opposed to the war and interested in personal rather than political rebellion, for its dramatic war death. Signaling the trivialization of the movement by the movie, the first scene has Berger burning his draft card with three friends looking on. They laugh and run away, beginning a carefree romp around New York Central Park. But later Berger is accidentally shipped to Vietnam when he impersonates Claude for a few hours at his military base. This outlandish loss reinforces the message that the war was a random and tragic mistake.

Despite their sympathies with the antiwar cause, each of these representations tells a story that minimizes the extent of the real social conflict that took place as a result of the Vietnam War. And to the extent that such conflict is acknowledged, it is usually represented as having happened between opposing social classes.

History Surveys

These ideological frameworks extend beyond the cultural production of the post-Vietnam period. Scholarly considerations also follow their basic outline. Historical surveys are by nature condensations, shorthand narratives of complicated events. They are also the primary way that people are taught history in the US secondary and post-secondary educational systems. The following discussion is based on an analysis of thirteen US history surveys, nine of which have recently been among the most common textbooks assigned in college history classes.[54] Although some of these textbooks are fairly nuanced in their discussions of Vietnam antiwar protest and the class dynamics of the domestic response to the war, many of the stereotypical story lines described thus far appear in their pages.

The majority of these textbooks overstate the extent to which affluent youth served as the base of the antiwar movement and understate the breadth of opposition to Vietnam, particularly the eventual dissent appearing within the armed forces and veterans' communities. In almost all the textbooks studied, the last topics are simply omitted. Some also overstate the conservatism of the white working class, whereas others do not discuss class politics at all.

Anticipating the "triumph of conservatism" and the "end of liberalism," many of these books use stereotypical, iconic images to foreshadow rifts that developed in the coming decades. The splits within the Democratic Party between its "liberal" and "mass" bases and the rise of the working-class "Reagan Democrat" are unproblematically predicted by the responses to Vietnam and other political behaviors of the Vietnam period. This is the inevitability fallacy: because we now know what came of the era, it is easy to find the inevitable signs of the future in the past. Digging up and highlighting these precursors makes for a more successful, linear narrative of clear causal relationships.[55]

These books also underscore the forgotten nature of the Vietnam antiwar movement. With only one exception, James A. Henretta, David Brody, and Lynn Dumenil's *American History*, the antiwar movement receives no investigation into its internal dynamics.[56] We can contrast this to the attention received by the civil rights/black power and feminist movements, both of which are described in nearly all of the books in terms of their leaders, organizations, and specific grievances and goals. Most of these books invoke the antiwar movement in their discussions of Presidents Lyndon Johnson or Richard Nixon (as felling Johnson, and as frustrating or being frustrated by Nixon), or in relation to student protest—but almost never as a movement unto itself. Again, with the same exception, the movement also receives considerably less page space than feminism or civil rights (anywhere from one-quarter to one-tenth the space) and often equal or less space than the other influential movements of the period, including gay liberation, the Chicano/a rights movement, and the American Indian Movement. The primacy given to civil rights and feminism is perfectly reasonable (textbooks have to make choices), but the relative lack of attention to the antiwar movement is nevertheless pronounced.

Social Divisions: Students versus Workers

Typically, the Vietnam antiwar movement is conflated with the "student movement." Demonstrators are referred to as "student demonstrators" and attention is paid to campus unrest at the expense of nearly all other sites of protest. The elite nature of the protesters, usually students but in some cases nonstudents, is repeatedly emphasized. One book begins its discussion, "Many college students and other opponents of the war."[57] Another relates the image, "Children of affluent middle class families . . . burned their draft cards, grew their hair long and joined free living communes where drink, drugs, and sex were readily available."[58] And another: "Well-to-do white youths . . . hippies and flower children . . . became the bulwark of the marching, chanting, peace movement."[59] Robert A. Divine et al.'s textbook limits Vietnam protest to the youth: "the most dramatic aspect of the youthful rebellion came in opposing the Vietnam war"; however, "the *students* failed to stop the war."[60] After writing persuasively about the political aspects of "the student revolt," they go on to make the kind of stereotypical slippage seen elsewhere: "The meteoric career of the SDS [Students for a Democratic Society] symbolized the turbulence of the 1960's. For a brief time, it seemed as though the nation's youth had gone berserk, indulging in a wave of experimentation with drugs, sex, and rock music. Not all American youth joined in the cultural insurgency; the rebellion was generally limited to the children of the upper middle class."[61] Here, the New Left is seamlessly collapsed into the counterculture, and its early upper-middle-class cast is projected onto the entire era, despite all findings to the contrary.

Some of these survey books evoke a broader movement but focus on its typically middle-class constituency. James West Davidson et al., for instance, use the campus and intellectual bases of discontent as their case study for the movement.[62] Enslow Publishing, specializing in K–12 library books, published a series called "In American History," within which *The Vietnam Antiwar Movement in American History* was printed as a stand-alone volume. There an upper-middle-class base for the movement is described up-front, despite the inclusive "every walk of life" description: "College students made up a majority of the protesters. But the antiwar movement included people from nearly every walk of life.

Many college professors, businesspeople, parents of draft-age youth, religious leaders, doctors, lawyers, politicians and entertainers also voiced their objections to American involvement." Henretta et al.'s textbook similarly details early antiwar protesters as consisting of "students, clergy, housewives, politicians, artists, and others."[63]

In these representations the movement is largely middle class, but those who reacted against the movement or supported the war most certainly are not. A number of the books play up the extent of polarization to the point of distortion. The national unpopularity of the war is generally framed against the even greater unpopularity of the "affluent students" who "had no right to insult their nation or squander its educational privileges." Invoking the hardhat rallies of New York City in 1970, this textbook argues, "NY police who cracked heads . . . or the construction workers who roamed lower Manhattan beating up longhaired youths were expressing the feelings of innumerable fellow citizens."[64] (As discussed earlier, the actions of the hardhats were condemned by a majority of people, including the majority of union households.) Another implies blue-collar support for the war, stating that "northern blue collar workers . . . smarting from the repeated setbacks the country had experienced in Vietnam and resentful of what they considered the unpatriotic tactics of antiwar protesters, also approved of Nixon's refusal to pull out of Vietnam."[65] (Nixon, of course, refused to pull out *immediately*, but he consistently promised to end the war, so the plan these workers approved was actually a "peace plan." These same Northern blue-collar workers agreed that the war was a mistake, a point obscured by the emphasis of the book.)

Not every book looks explicitly at the class dynamics of the domestic response to Vietnam. Yet, when it is discussed, the working class is more often evoked as conservative.[66] For example, the main base of appeal of George Wallace, the conservative populist third-party presidential candidate, was lower-middle-class Southerners, and in 1968 he eventually received 8 percent of the northern vote. Yet early in his campaign he was polling much higher among northern blue-collar workers. Because this is seen as anticipating the eventual support received by Nixon in 1972 and Reagan in 1980 from blue-collar workers, these early polls are emphasized in several of the books. Analyzing Hubert Humphrey's challenges in his presidential run in 1968, Divine et al. write that George Wallace "cut deeply into the normal Democratic majority"; specifically, the group that the book sets up as these Wallace supporters is the "urban working classes."[67] Even though the authors soon recant this statement—Wallace's "following declined," and "Humphrey held on to the urban Northeast"—the book leaves intact the impression that the urban working classes were particularly conservative. Wallace's appeal among blue-collar workers is also unproblematically linked to his social conservatism in some discussions: "Wallace, whose calls for victory in Vietnam and 'law and order' at home appealed to many northern blue-collar Democrats."[68] Investigating the events of 1970, Paul Johnson makes the hardhats emblematic of blue-collar sentiments: "Nixon's contrast between privileged students engaged in nihilism and hard-working kids from poor families getting on with life struck home. On May 7 in New York a crowd of construction workers stormed City Hall and beat up students who were occupying it—the first hard-hat demonstration against the New Left. This was Nixon's 'silent majority' beginning to react, adumbrating his historic landslide victory of November 1972."[69]

1968 as Peak

The "climax came in 1968," for Divine et al. Davidson et al. also describe 1968 as the peak of antiwar protest, and most books limit their discussion of the movement to the Johnson presidency, implicitly marking that year as its final meaningful moment. In this, they are following certain historiographic norms. It is repeatedly implied or stated in these books that the greatest achievement of the antiwar movement was Johnson's decision to abandon the race for a second term in office. This, in part, accounts for the 1968-as-peak argument. Furthermore, perhaps the dominant way of periodizing the "long" 1960s begins roughly with third-world anticolonial and revolutionary struggles of the 1950s—and the US civil rights movement—and extends to the mid-1970s, with end of the Vietnam War, the fall of Salvador Allende in Chile, and the oil shocks of 1972–1974.[70] Within that long trajectory, 1968 is the standout year in the United States and, arguably, internationally as well. Tet, the assassinations of Martin Luther King and Robert Kennedy, the Columbia University building takeovers, the Chicago protests at the Democratic National Convention, the Paris May, the Czech spring, and the Tlactelolco massacre and subsequent protests at the Mexico Olympics: 1968 was undoubtedly a watershed. Many have singled out that year in particular in their treatment of the period.[71] So the story of a peak of the movement writ large is echoed in many historical framings, not just for the antiwar struggle in particular.

But there is another contributing factor to the 1968-as-peak framework. The historiography of the Vietnam antiwar movement is often structured with an emphasis on the ascendance and decline of the youthful New Left. The Vietnam antiwar movement is correctly understood as the dominant movement of expression for the white and middle-class New Left, usually seen as synonymous with Students for a Democratic Society (SDS). In a faulty inversion, however, the implosion of the New Left appears to stand in for the end of the antiwar movement.

Todd Gitlin's *The Sixties* can be taken as emblematic in this regard. His book, which he describes as "at the edge of history and autobiography," more often takes the analytical perspective of the latter and devotes much of its critical attention to why "middle class kids from the fifties" became the radicals of the following decade.[72] Gitlin served as an early president of SDS, and *The Sixties* understandably exists within the confines of the lifespan of that organization, beginning with its iconic and visionary Port Huron Statement of 1962 and ending with its sectarian split in 1969. For Gitlin and his immediate contemporaries, the end of SDS brought disillusion and dissolution and, more important, the end of the thing called "the sixties." SDS and the New Left produced a good number of (mostly) men and (some) women whose amazing stories have been told in memoirs, histories, and films, and these activists have also helped shape the stories that are told. To make an obvious point, middle-class activists are more likely than their working-class comrades to tell their stories and are more likely to have landed in professions where they tell such stories and make interpretations of the past for a living. Therefore, the perspective from which Gitlin's story is told is typical of the genre. Judith Clavir Albert and Stewart Edward Albert's *The Sixties Papers*, Sohnya Sayres et al.'s *The 60s, Without Apology*, and James Miller's *Democracy Is in the Streets* all generally follow the same vein.[73] For these authors and collections, it is not that nothing happened after the New Left was broken, it is just that that its particular story was over. Nevertheless, to the extent that the antiwar movement is linked to the New Left youth movement, its own historical arc gets cut short.[74]

The implications of this break in the historical renditions of the movement are twofold. First, the initial character of the antiwar forces overshadows what eventually developed within the growing movement. That character—largely youthful, middle-class, or elite; limited to campuses; concerned with intellectual and policy debates; and increasingly radical and sensationalist—has unquestionably become the dominant image of the movement as a whole. Explorations of the long arc of the movement have been left to a few titles dedicated to the subject, few of which are referred to in the historical surveys discussed here.

Second, in related fashion, the great diversity of the movement and the extension of its claims and influence in the years after 1968, are largely erased. Post-1968 is the period when the movement formed deeper roots among people of color, religious communities, labor unions, the armed forces, veterans, and students attending second-, third-, and fourth-tier college campuses. The post-1968 rationales for opposing the war shifted from the more historically minded policy critiques and moral condemnations of the early years to include more explicitly grounded criticisms of the varied domestic repercussions of the fight. And, after 1968, for all of the unpopularity of the movement, the majority of people polled echoed many of its arguments when asked about the war.

Exceptions to the Rule

Specialized histories significantly redress the lacunae and shorthand distortions found in the survey textbooks described here. The antiwar movement has received strong attention from historians, including a number of full-length studies. These explore the groups and leaders of the movement as a whole,[75] particular groups within the movement,[76] or the movement and its interactions with political elites.[77] There are, of course, many other books about the movements or New Left of the 1960s that focus on the antiwar movement as part of their overall analysis[78] or that compare the antiwar movement to other movements.[79] Numerous anthologies have also been directly concerned with the movement or have considered the movement in light of larger studies of the Vietnam period or the other movements of the 1960s.[80] Some cultural criticism has been written about the movement as well, from both sympathetic and unsympathetic viewpoints.[81] What is important to note here is that none of them has the reach or audience of the survey textbooks nor does as much to shape popular understanding, to the extent that such understanding exists.

One textbook stands out amid the others: the American Social History Project second volume of *Who Built America?*, a social history of the United States. This textbook argues that "although the antiwar movement was initially based in the middle class, it won thousands of working class recruits after 1968," and it describes how "the radicalization of working class youth had a direct effect on the military, where internal conflict undermined the morale of may Vietnam combat units." The tensions between the New Left and labor are also underscored, as well as the apprehension by many New Leftists that the "white working class had bargained away its radical potential." The authors also point out the limited reality of the Archie Bunker stereotype and the resentment felt by white workers against what they saw as affluent college students.[82]

But *Who Built America?* is in many ways the exception that proves the rule. The challenge of the stereotyped polarization is that it is bigger than the sum of its parts. Working-class conservatism and liberal elitism on questions of war and peace contribute to a larger narrative about class polarization along cultural or social issues today. Clearly it is important to empirically rebut the content of our distorted memory of the class dynamics in the response to Vietnam, but the overall memory frame is much harder to dislodge. In part I, I take up the first project; I explore the resilience of the second in part II.

Part I

THE ANTIWAR MOVEMENT

A Liberal Elite?

MIDDLE-CLASS CULTURES AND THE MOVEMENT'S EARLY YEARS

> We call upon all men of good will to join us in this confrontation with immoral authority. Especially we call upon the universities to fulfill their mission of enlightenment and religious organizations to honor their heritage of brotherhood. Now is the time to resist.
>
> —"A Call to Resist Illegitimate Authority," October 1967

> The great failure of the anti-war movement has been in its arrogance toward people who work with their hands for a living and its willingness not only to ignore them, but to go even further and alienate them completely.
>
> —Jimmy Breslin, "One Way to End the War," *New York Magazine*, 1970

In the next four chapters, I review the period of the war itself and trace the growth and development of antiwar sentiment and the many strands of the antiwar movement that developed. In this first chapter of part I, counterintuitive to my main argument, I detail how the movement began and expanded within a middle-class milieu. It is these years of movement activity, 1965–1967, that make the strongest case that antiwar action was concentrated among the relatively privileged sectors of US society. Nevertheless, as I explore in chapter 3, even in this early period, when we look within the movement organizations that grew at that time and among some of the most prominent antiwar activists, there was more economic diversity and attention to issues of class than is typically remembered. In chapters 4 and 5, I further develop this countermemory, one that differs from and challenges the dominant discourse regarding opposition to the Vietnam War in the United States.[1]

Sociological studies often detail the complexity behind what appears simple on the surface, and this countermemory does just that: rather than simply replacing the controlling narrative, I hope to expand, question, reorder, and reprioritize its main patterns and threads. To begin with, if we look at who opposed the war, we see that working-class people did so as frequently as the middle class in the early years, and more so as time went by.

49

Who Opposed the War? The Polls

When we combine the nationwide polling data from the large agencies, such as Harris and Gallup, with the university polls and community studies conducted during the period, a clear trend emerges. Howard Zinn calls it "the most surprising data"—*throughout* the Vietnam War, Americans "with only a grade-school education were much stronger for withdrawal than Americans with a college education."[2]

I will go through the numbers in detail.[3] From August 1965 to May 1971, Gallup consistently asked, "In view of developments since we entered the fighting in Vietnam, do you think the US made a mistake sending troops to fight in Vietnam?" This question is usually used as measuring basic support for the war. Its first poll showed the greatest support for the war, with 61 percent responding "no." This number steadily declined to around half of all respondents by November 1966, when it then plateaued through the first half of 1967. During that period of 1967, the most intense escalation of the war occurred, as well as the rapid growth of public antiwar sentiment, culminating in October 1967 with the March on the Pentagon. By October, the "no" respondents had dropped to 44 percent, and with some slight fluctuations the number continued to shrink for the remaining years of the survey, dropping 10 percent in 1968 and nearly an additional 10 percent by the last time the question was asked in 1971. There was never, therefore, a strong mandate for this war, and for most of its duration, a majority of Americans believed the war to have been a "mistake."

Simultaneous to this steady erosion of basic support, conflicting trends emerged regarding support for the actual policies being implemented by the administrations pursuing the war.[4] According to Gallup polls, during 1966 and especially in 1967, increasing numbers of those polled believed that the war effort should be escalated. In May 1967, support for immediate withdrawal of the troops reached its nadir at 6 percent, with support for "escalation" reaching its all-time high of 80 percent. Measured against the mistake questions, it is therefore important to note that many who believed the war was a mistake believed it should be fought *harder*. But opinions about policy changed slowly over the following year, and more rapidly following the election of President Nixon in late 1968. By the end of 1968, a majority of Americans wanted out, and by September 1970, a majority of Americans wanted *immediate* withdrawal, regardless of the outcome.

Disaggregating the data, William Lunch and Peter Sperlich find that "war supporters tended to be concentrated among the younger, white, male and middle-class respondents." They further observe, "this is one of those instances in which reversing the categories does provide virtually the maximum change in opinion.

A typical war opponent was older, black, female, and of lower-class background."[5] Another "surprising feature" of the polling data, discovered by Philip Converse and Howard Schuman, is that "national surveys did not yield [until the May 1970 explosion of campus protest following the invasion of Cambodia] any distinct relations between age and attitude toward Vietnam. The 'generations gap' that one would have expected, wherein the young oppose the war and the old support it, simply failed to appear," and, as of June 1970, "even now it is not very large." They conclude, "(among whites) college-educated people in their twenties were more likely than older people of grade school education both to justify the war and to favor an intensification of it. The differences are substantial, running to 20 percent or more."[6]

In 1967 a referendum in a white Detroit suburb, Dearborn, Michigan, found 41 percent supporting withdrawal, "with blue collar workers more disapproving of the war than professionals and managers." Orville Hubbard, conservative Republican mayor of Dearborn, opposed the war and noted that it was the residents of West Dearborn, with "a lot of cars and few children," who were against withdrawal, whereas working-class South Dearborn residents, next to the Ford River Rouge plant, "with fewer cars and more children," showed a majority for withdrawal.[7] (In fact, the author of the Dearborn referendum, Johnny Anderson, was a retired autoworker and had served as the president of Fleetwood Local 15 of the United Auto Workers, UAW.[8]) By January 1968, before the Tet offensive soured millions more to the war, the *New York Times* reported that "the solid support given President Johnson and his Vietnam policies demonstrated by the heads of organized labor [at its convention the week before] is not in line with the views of rank-and-file union members" who, like the country as a whole, were evenly split on the "mistake" question about Vietnam. In February, after Tet, George Gallup reported that the public at large was feeling confused, disillusioned, and cynical and "wants desperately to find a way to respond to international problems without going to war." By August, Gallup found that 52 percent of Americans found the war to be "the most important problem facing this country today."[9]

In an article for the *American Sociological Review* in 1968, Richard Hamilton reported that "preferences for 'tough' policy alternatives are most frequent among the following groups: the highly educated; high status occupations; those with high incomes; younger persons; and those paying much attention to newspapers and magazines."[10] Similarly, Harlan Hahn, writing in the *American Political Science Review* about community antiwar referenda (including the one in Dearborn, Michigan), observed that "disapproval of the war appeared to be related to working class rather than high status characteristics. In most communities as the proportion of voters possessing lower status attributes grew, the vote against the war continued to mount" (the exception was Cambridge,

Massachusetts).[11] In May 1970, following the infamous hardhat demonstrations in New York City, 53 percent of unionists disapproved of the hard-hat actions, with 30 percent approving.[12] In December 1970, a Detroit referendum calling for immediate withdrawal passed with its greatest support from blacks and labor.[13] A student survey in 1972 showed virtually no difference along class lines among students holding pacifist views.[14]

James Wright directly addresses the problem of working-class support for the war in his article, "The Working Class, Vietnam, and Authoritarianism." In the article, Wright uses war support as a measure of "authoritarian" values, which sociologist Seymour Martin Lipset had famously attributed to US workers in a famous 1959 article, "Democracy and Working Class Authoritarianism" (see chapter 6). Wright finds, instead, "no support for the theory of authoritarianism" in the survey data. Using the University of Michigan Survey Research Center data from 1964 and 1968, he correlates various background demographic data with policy preferences. Race correlated most significantly with policy preference, with nonwhites half as likely to prefer escalation in both 1964 and 1968, and nearly twice as likely to call for withdrawal in 1964. But class significantly correlated as well, with workers, the less-educated, and those with smaller incomes more likely than those at the higher end in the early years to support withdrawal. By 1968 people in higher-status positions had "come down" to the "enlightened" position held by the lower-status groups all along.[15]

Converse and Schuman argue that over time, as the war progressed, public opinion became increasingly "crystallized," as a result of cumulative "individual experience, information, and motivation."[16] At the beginning of the war, the greatest obstacle to firm opinions was the general lack of knowledge that people had. Lunch and Sperlich examine this and show how public opinion, in those early years, tended to follow what government leaders—in this case, President Johnson—had to say.[17] For example, there were extreme changes of opinion in 1966 (responding to bombing and then the end of bombing), which hinged on a speech by Johnson. Before the speech, the bombings were happening and people supported them; after the speech, which explained the end of the bombings, people supported the end of the bombings. But, Converse and Schuman point out, by 1970 "experience has mounted steeply in terms of deaths, taxes and soldiers not home for Christmas."[18] Opinions became harder, and the antiwar position was the clear majority.

More recently, political scientist Adam Berinsky has returned to the public opinion polls during the Vietnam era, arguing that it is very likely that antiwar sentiment in the early years of the war was undercounted. This was due to the combined power of elites to shape the terrain of public opinion and the special strength of their voice when it is unified, as it was in the years before Tet. "If elites speak in a unified voice on foreign affairs, only those citizens with underlying predispositions in line with that message will be able to give voice to their interests," Berinsky argues. Many respondents in the early data voiced degrees of ignorance or ambivalence, which were not picked up by the polling in the same way that being for or against the war was signaled. He explains, "Individuals who hold predispositions discordant with the dominant message will fall by the wayside. As a result, the creation of a bias in public opinion in line with the dominant discourse is highly likely." He finds that this bias was reduced after 1968 as antiwar voices emerged that were strong enough to create space for dissident opinions.[19]

The statistics discussed here should not be read as presenting a completely upside-down picture of our more common memory of a class polarized opposition to the war. Indeed, some public opinion researchers analyzed the polls leading up to 1970 and discerned precisely some of the patterns otherwise challenged here in a book length study, *Vietnam and the Silent Majority, A Doves Guide*. The goal of the authors is to "'tell it like it is,' or at least what we think it is," to help those engaged in arguments against the war understand their possible audiences. Some trends they note are that people with the greatest level of education—that is, those with degrees beyond college—tended to be more "dovish" than those with regular college degrees and some college, and similar to those with the least education in their dovish sentiments. They also note that in the latter half of the 1960s, graduates from elite schools moved in a dovish direction (in direct opposition to the much larger group of college graduates, who "supplied the very backbone of popular support for the war throughout the whole period.") Both of these trends support the perception that elites are overrepresented among antiwarriors, but they also note that these are a small yet more visible group than others: so the perception outpaces the level of actual participation such elites brought to the movement.[20]

A general picture emerges from all these surveys and studies: working-class people were never more likely than their middle-class counterparts to support the war, and in many instances, they were more likely to oppose it. As far as war policy went, Johnson and Nixon found their most consistent support among more affluent and educated groups. Working-class people formed opinions of the war that showed they were increasingly skeptical of their leaders, even when they were often willing to give them more chances. "Opposition" to the war meant different things to different people, and it took different forms in different contexts. But the myth of the worker-hawk should clearly be laid to rest. And although there were many liberals among the elite, the elite as a whole were far from liberal on the question of war.

Taking Part in the Movement:
Vectors of Working-Class Participation

Sentiment and action are two very different things, however. People do not take social action based on their feelings without a number of other reasons and supports for doing so. Social movement scholars have argued that an individual will take action when (1) social issues seem relevant, somehow wrong or unjust, and can be traced to some kind of source; (2) there is some plan in place for what can be done about it that makes some kind of sense (as Fred Rose argues, "a sense of purpose" is achieved; David Croteau observes the "sense of efficacy" movement activists need); and (3) a connection is made to other people who are engaging in the action through a collective identity or group solidarity.[21] In short, people are more likely to take actions when affirmative answers are given to the following considerations: Am I angered or upset? Is there someone or something to blame? Can I do anything about it that works? And do I relate to other people who are also engaging the problem? According to polling, workers did see the issues of the war as relevant and important, felt divided about who was to blame, and were similarly divided as to what, if anything, could be done about it.[22]

For many working-class people, opposition to or questions about the war did not yield recognizable collective action of the type studied by most scholars or covered as such by most media. But let us remember James Jasper's point: a focus limited to self-identified activists or organizations "renders invisible all the ways that individual acts of protest do or do not feed into more organized movements."[23] In addition, negative (as opposed to positive) resistance was often overlooked as such, as in the case of draft avoidance and desertions. In addition to individual acts of protest, "multi-issue" antiwar action was similarly overlooked. The complex grievances of many working people, which included racism, oppressive treatment in their workplaces (including the military), and limited and unappealing job prospects (for veterans especially), meant that opposition to the war was just one piece—not necessarily the sole aim of their movement work. So antiwar work took place in places where it was just part of the work being done, among people whose collective identities were neither primarily working class nor antiwar.

Did working-class people, by and large, feel connected to the social movement organizations that were created with the sole purpose of opposing the war? Judging from the ease with which they were painted as "middle class" and "elite," as well as the internal debates that took place within these organizations and their core leadership, generally speaking the answer was no. During the early years in particular, but really throughout the period, the action frames, mobilizing vehicles, and perceived political opportunities of many of the dominant antiwar movement organizations reflected the middle-class culture and milieu of its early leadership. And these organizations usually retained their status of "negative reference point" (to use a polling phrase) that that was generated over the course of early formative years of antiwar protest. It is to these early years that I first turn.

• • •

The Early Years of the Movement: Fodder for the Image

In late October 1967, hundreds of thousands of protesters came to Washington, D.C., in what arguably became the most famous of the early antiwar rallies, the National Mobilization to End the War in Vietnam. This action on October 21 capped the end of a burst of national antiwar protest. The previous days, named Stop the Draft Week and spearheaded by the Student Mobilization Committee, included hundreds of protests across the country; spirited direct actions against army inductions in Oakland, California; and students at University of Wisconsin at Madison protesting recruitment efforts by Dow Chemical (the manufacturers of napalm) on campus. The "Mobe," as both the rally and the organization sponsoring it came to be known, featured the Battle for the Pentagon, in which Jerry Rubin, Berkeley-based graduate student activist, claimed that a ring of protesters was going to "levitate" the Pentagon and divest it of its evil spirits. Photographers captured young women placing flowers in the guns of their soldier peers, and a sizable minority of the protesters engaged in a direct action to enter the building.

These protests took place in coordination with another significant antiwar action. In late 1967, a group of over three hundred prominent intellectuals published "A Call to Resist Illegitimate Authority" in the *New York Review of Books* and *The New Republic*. This statement was the most prominent of many written to support draft resistance, attracting over 20,000 signatories by the end of the year. On October 20, the day before the "Mobe," this statement was submitted, along with a briefcase full of draft cards, to the Justice Department by Dr. Benjamin Spock, William Sloane Coffin Jr., Mitchell Goodman, Marcus Raskin, and Michael Ferber. These men, who came to be knows as "the Boston Five," were eventually brought up on criminal charges for their pledge and actions to "lend . . . support" to draft resisters.

The "Call to Resist" calls for men of moral conscience to resist the war. It also asks the government to respect the moral decisions of individuals opposing governmental policy and, further, to recognize such actions as permissible under the First Amendment. Erudite and historically well informed, the "Call to Resist" begins by identifying the kind of protester and reasons for protest with whom such intellectuals stood in solidarity: "An ever growing number of young American men are finding that the American war in Vietnam so outrages their deepest moral and religious sense that they cannot contribute to it in any way. We share their moral outrage." The root of their protest was moral repugnance. It grew in the youth; the barometer of one's resolve was the individual's refusal to cooperate with immoral deeds. The statement does not identify the moral rot as intrinsic to the United States, as later radicals did. Instead, the signatories describe themselves as teachers and patriots who are seeking to *uphold* the values and traditions of a country they "cherish." Thus, in a move that Margit Mayer describes as typical of many US social movements, these protesters locate themselves within the values of the system they protest. It is the inability of this system to live up to its own best ideals that the signatories find so tragic and abhorrent.[24]

It was the estimation of these intellectuals that their stand was the most strategic available: "Many of us believe that open resistance to the war and the draft is the course of action most likely to strengthen the moral resolve with which all of us can oppose the war and most likely to bring an end to the war." Here, a universal moral language is imagined—a communicative action framework within which all can find a home. This liberal universalism presupposes a common set of rationales for opposition to the war and a common set of choices for those seeking to act on their opposition.

But how universal really was this call? To what extent did brave acts of moral righteousness capture—or channel—opposition to the war? Could this movement, as it was developing, make space for all the people who were ambivalent about the US fight in Vietnam? Among the many prominent intellectuals who signed the "Call to Resist" were Norman Mailer and Mary McCarthy, writers who both turned their talents to nonfiction reporting to make sense of the "war at home." Norman Mailer's Pulitzer Prize–winning *The Armies of the Night* offers a close look at both the draft resisters and Pentagon protesters of October 1967. In *Armies*, Mailer is both covetous of the patrician morality of his fellow antiwar intellectuals and mocking of all their high-mindedness; despite his own antiwar stance, he more consistently sympathizes with—some argue romanticizes—the working stiffs he portrays as war supporters.[25] There is no doubt in *Armies* that it is the liberal elites who are running the antiwar show: "It would take a rebirth of Marx for Marxism to explain definitively this middle-class condemnation of an imperialist war in the last Capitalist nation, this working class affirmation." Similarly, in her book *Hanoi*, Mary McCarthy observes, "to be against the Vietnamese war was an economic privilege enjoyed chiefly by the middle and professional classes."[26]

Among those covering the march and Pentagon actions was Jimmy Breslin, *Daily News* columnist. Breslin's account also depicts a class divide in the events in Washington—here between entitled, bad-behaving protesters and upstanding, working-class soldiers. He describes how the "kids" at the march "taunted the soldiers," "went to the bathroom on the side of the Pentagon," "threw a couple of rocks through the first-floor." These "rabble" of "dropouts and drifters" "in raggedy clothes" had "turned a demonstration for peace . . . into a sickening, club-swinging mess." He describes the "kids" as almost a lumpen mob, but it was their entitlement and privilege that made him, and conceivably his readers, so angry. He writes that the demonstration "became an exercise at clawing at soldiers": "At the end of the day, the only concern anybody could have was for the soldiers who were taking the abuse."[27] By October 1967, a new polarization appeared to exist in the movement against the war in Vietnam. It was an entitled, middle-class movement, and those on the other side were the workers, regular Americans, who were written out, ignored, or even taunted by the dissenters.

US Involvement in Vietnam and the Early Peace Movement

Active US involvement in Indochina began during the French colonial war in 1950, when the United States committed itself to military and economic support for France in its effort to maintain colonial rule.[28] The Geneva cease-fire accords of 1954 ended French colonial rule, and the country was partitioned along the seventeenth parallel. The communist Viet Minh government of Ho Chi Minh was granted the north, and the French-supported former Emperor Bao Dai was made "head of state" in the south, with the assurance that national elections were to be held in two years as a step toward unification. But by 1955, Ngo Dinh Diem, then the prime minister, refused to hold elections, which all signs indicated would have given victory to the communists. Diem orchestrated a referendum that produced the Republic of Vietnam, with himself as president. By 1960, the communist-allied National Liberation Front (NLF, also known as the Vietcong) was founded within South Vietnam and began its long guerilla war in the south against the Diem regime.[29]

With the French defeat, the United States had taken over the role of training the military in the south, helping the government there to build its army. As Diem repressed the opposition, US advisers helped fight the insurgents. A "slow, but inexorable" increase in US involvement ensued.[30] The influence of China in Vietnam was perceived as the primary threat to US interests, as was the fear of a "domino effect," a chain reaction of communist victories in the region. Over the course of the decade leading to the Gulf of Tonkin resolution of August 1964, which gave President Johnson the congressional authority for executive expansion of the "police action" in Vietnam, the United States pursued containment through increasingly active support of the anticommunist regimes of the south.

Charles DeBenedetti locates the beginnings of the Vietnam antiwar movement in 1955, following the Geneva Accords, with peace advocates seeking mutual disarmament and an end to the Cold War.[31] Nancy Zaroulis and Gerard Sullivan mark the "teach-ins" that spread from Michigan beginning in March 1965 as the watershed event of the movement; and Tom Wells stresses the decision to hold, and incredible success of, the rally called by SDS in Washington, D.C., in April 1965.[32] Certainly, Vietnam was only just appearing on the radar screen for a very small minority of Americans before summer 1964. Before the Johnson administration manufactured the Gulf of Tonkin incident, and Congress subsequently authorized Johnson's expanded military action, only a few were raising the alarm about the US involvement in the small southeast Asian country.[33]

The first organized response to the war came from US peace movement groups and individuals. DeBenedetti identifies these activists as a loosely coordinated coalition of "liberal internationalists" and "radical pacifists."[34] The former were identified with figures such as I. F. Stone, Norman Thomas, and Norman Cousins; liberal magazines such as *The New Republic, Saturday Review,* and *The Nation;* and organizations such as the Committee for a Sane Nuclear Policy (SANE), United World Federalists, the Federation of American Scientists, and the Women's International League for Peace and Freedom. The last drew their numbers from Quaker-oriented groups such as the American Friends Service Committee, conscientious-objector organizations such as the Fellowship of Reconciliation (FOR), the Catholic Worker Movement, and the anarchist War Resisters League (WRL). A. J. Muste was the initial de facto leader of the "radical pacifist" wing of the peace movement until his death in 1968, with David Dellinger (who founded the journal *Liberation* in 1955) providing continuous guidance throughout the Vietnam years.

During the 1950s, issues such as the arms race, disarmament, and the threat of nuclear war animated these peace groups. The peace movement rallied support for test-ban treaties and criticized civil defense programs. Liberals and radicals agreed on these large issues, but they tended to diverge at the central political fault line of the era, communism. Cold War anticommunism was central to the liberal platform and politics; liberals' critiques of US military and nuclear polices were leveled despite their general enthusiasm for containment strategies. Liberals also accepted the loyalty-oath ethos of the time, often openly refusing to work with communist individuals or communist-tainted groups. For radicals, the policy of communist exclusion and the allegiance to US government positions that such a policy directly or indirectly entailed were becoming increasingly unacceptable.

These divisions heightened at the start of the new decade. When SANE responded to government pressure in 1960 by taking an explicitly anticommunist stance with regard to its own membership, a number of prominent members resigned in protest. A. J. Muste wrote that the actions of SANE indicated that it was unable to undertake "radical criticism of the US political economic regime" that would be necessary for a clear position against militarism: "They do not fully and clearly accept the thesis that 'war is the enemy' and must be resisted in all its forms in every land."[35] This split—between moderate and radical critiques of US foreign policy—shaped the response of the organized domestic movement to Vietnam. But at the time, the points of agreement of the two groups around the irrationalism of nuclear build-up and testing overwhelmed their differences.

Compared to the preceding, more dormant years, the early 1960s saw an impressive growth in the US peace movement. The Student Peace Union attracted thousands of members on campuses by 1960. Turn Towards Peace, a coalition effort launched in 1961, which Michael Harrington called a "politically responsible movement for peace," united figures such as Walter Reuther of the UAW, Martin Luther King, and Eleanor Roosevelt, thereby bringing together various elements of the liberal coalition into one peace tent. Women Strike for Peace (WSP) was founded in 1961, along with Physicians for Social Responsibility. In 1962, Dr. Benjamin Spock, pediatrician, joined SANE, and the famous antinuclear advertisement "Dr. Spock is worried" ran in national newspapers and magazines. Four thousand students demonstrated in 1962 in Washington, D.C., against nuclear proliferation.[36]

Despite this growth and activity, these peace groups were small and relatively isolated as military escalation in Vietnam began under the Kennedy administration, when the number of US military advisors serving Diem's government in South Vietnam increased from a few hundred to over 16,000, their mission considerably expanded. The United States was now committed to "nation-building" in the south, fortifying "strategic hamlets" against the NLF insurgents in support of the "democratic" Diem regime, in what the *New York Times* called in 1962 "a struggle this country cannot shirk."[37] The Johnson administration continued and expanded Kennedy's policies after his assassination.

The broad peace movement began to pay more heed to the growing conflict. WSP, the American Friends Services Committees, and the FOR started to give Vietnam organizational attention, hiring staff to work on the issue and conducting office visits on Capitol Hill to discuss US policies. The New Left became active; the three-year-old SDS, shifting slightly from its primary focus on economic rights, sponsored protests against the visit of Diem's wife, Madame Nhu, to the United States in October 1963. By 1964, intellectually prominent and high-level critics, such as Walter Lippman, journalist and recent Presidential Medal of Freedom recipient; Hans Morgenthau, political theorist; and Senator Ernest Gruening, were publicly voicing their reservations about the war. The influential independent journalist I. F. Stone dedicated multiple issues of his *Weekly* to the problem of Vietnam. Some radical pacifists began anticonscription campaigns. In March 1964, 5,000 people marched in New York to protest the war, calling for a negotiated settlement and attention to domestic reform. Parts of the Old Left joined the response. The Socialist Workers Party began to focus on the war, which over the course of the decade became its primary area of work. Student activists spearheaded demonstrations on May 2, 1964, at Yale University and other schools, creating one of the first student antiwar groups known as the May 2nd Movement (M2M), dominated by the leftist group Progressive Labor.[38]

None of these efforts showed any sign of breaking through the consciousness of the general public, let alone prompting its involvement. (Nor did this dissent register among the powers that be or provoke their response, although Johnson was concerned about defections of liberals who supported his domestic agenda.) Most Americans were not paying close attention to the war, and Johnson's response to the Gulf of Tonkin events of August 1964 had received overwhelming support. Only two senators, Ernest Gruening (D-Alaska) and Wayne Morse (D-Ore.), dissented when Johnson sought Congressional authority to "take all necessary measures to repel any armed attacks against the forces of the United States and to prevent further aggression."[39]

It was not until President Johnson began the bombing campaign against North Vietnam, dubbed Operation Rolling Thunder, in February 1965 that the issue of the war began to catch fire on the campuses and, to a lesser extent, off them. The teach-ins of March and April were the opening salvo of the movement and its first innovation. At over one hundred campuses, beginning with University of Michigan, thousands of students and hundreds of faculty, grappling with the causes and implications of the bombing, vigorously discussed and debated the history of US involvement in Southeast Asia, the Cold War, the draft, and other relevant topics. The teach-ins indicated a concern and thirst for knowledge about the war on the part of students and professors, and their tenor and analysis indicated that an antiwar critique was developing on the campuses.

During its December 1964 meeting in New York City, SDS had voted for a springtime national rally against the war in Washington, D.C., when the motion made by a "liberal" SDS-er to have a national march "squeaked by" against the opposition of the community-oriented Economic Research and Action Project organizers who dominated SDS at the time.[40] Until the bombing and the teach-ins, no one in his or her right (or in this case, left) political mind expected many more than the 5,000 marchers who had come to previous Easter peace rallies to show up on April 17, 1965. Yet 25,000 came, mostly students but also many members of left and peace groups that had unofficially co-sponsored—in places, enthusiastically and, in other instances, reluctantly—the event.[41] This was an unprecedented size for a peace rally in the United States. Groups who had been working on Vietnam and related issues for years were surprised and excited—even shocked—by the turnout. And it was a sign of things to come. In nearly every year of the movement from that point forward, rallies broke records for their sheer size. Soon afterward, A. J. Muste wrote, "I am not at the moment sanguine that *the* 'movement' is about to come into existence. . . . But I am convinced that movement revolt cannot be suppressed."[42]

The Reasoning of the Opposition

Many of the main arguments against the war that were circulated by the movement were largely in place by the time the first substantial protests began—outlined already in the teach-ins of March 1965 and threading through the speeches made at the demonstration called by SDS in April 1965. But others gained currency over time, with the experience of the war. I begin with the arguments that had to do with the conditions in Vietnam itself and nature of the fight there. First, war opponents pointed out that the United States was intervening in a civil war, not a war of aggression from North Vietnam. The United States was, in fact, at war with the nationalist forces in South Vietnam who represented the popular position of unification of the country. Second, the war seemed unwinnable, given the popular support that the NLF received from the Vietnamese peasants and the widespread opposition to the successive governments established in the south in the aftermath of Diem's assassination in late 1963. Third, the South Vietnamese allies of the United States were corrupt, brutal, and antidemocratic. Large-scale population transfers in the "strategic hamlet" program crippled peasant life and culture in (highly unsuccessful) efforts to rout out communists. The Diem and future South Vietnamese regimes engaged in the widespread torture and imprisonment of political dissidents, along with imposing other severe limits on civil rights. As one marine strategist observed, the South Vietnamese government basically served "to loot, collect back taxes, reinstall landlords, and conduct reprisals among the people."[43] Fourth, the war itself was also remarkably brutal and increasingly so over its course; even in the first years its harshness was apparent. The US-adopted strategy of attrition was to conduct search-and-destroy missions aiming to flush out NLF supporters from the countryside that were ranked successful according to the body count of dead Vietnamese. In addition to bombing, the Vietnamese countryside was denuded with Agent Orange, a defoliant; towns and tunnels were bombarded with CS gas (*o*-chlorobenzylidene malononitrile), a tear gas; and fleeing villagers were doused with napalm, a burn agent that was "improved" over the course of the war to include polystyrene to make it stick better to skin and phosphorous to help it work in water. Ultimately between 2 and 3 million Vietnamese were killed and 10 million were displaced.

From its start, some political theorists and politicians disagreed with the "domino theory," pointing out the nationalist (rather than staunchly communist) nature of the resistance. They argued that diplomatic compromises were entertained in the early years that could have contained the communist influence in the region. Others were less than convinced of the immediacy of any threat to the United States, for similar reasons.

Because the war was seen as illegitimate or not worth fighting on all these grounds, the draft emerged as a major flashpoint, and "Hell, no, we won't go!" (and "Girls Say Yes to Boys Who Say No") became the anthem of draft-age protesters. Over time, mounting US casualties, which the news brought home nightly into people's living rooms, underscored the worthlessness of the fight.

The war was also opposed for reasons that had to do with the political and cultural milieu of the period. The civil rights movement had legitimated dissent, encouraging thousands of people to actively challenge the status quo. The antiracist work of that movement created an environment where the war critics could further identify the war in Vietnam as a racist war. Finally, the civil rights movement helped to frame the war as indicative of hypocrisy in the US society, of the system not living up to its best ideals—a major theme for the New Left in general. The United States was called out for defending democracy abroad but not at home. On March 7, 1965, when Alabama Governor George Wallace ordered state troopers to stop the Selma-to-Montgomery civil rights march, which resulted in eighty-six marchers being injured, John Lewis, chairman of the Student Nonviolent Coordinating Committee (SNCC), addressed marchers seeking sanctuary in a church: "I don't see how President Johnson can send troops to Vietnam . . . to the Congo . . . to Africa and can't send troops to Selma, Alabama." The next day, Roy Wilkins, executive director of the National Association for the Advancement of Colored People (NAACP) (who supported the war), said at a press conference when referring to the landing of 3,500 US marines in Vietnam, "Dammit, they can send somebody to Alabama and defend the government right here."[44]

But it was also clear that the United States was, in fact, not defending democracy abroad because the South Vietnamese regimes were authoritarian military governments. That such hypocrisy was publicly recognized was a sign that, for a small but significant number of the population, the time for uncritical acceptance of US foreign policy had passed. So, the antiwar movement was in part a product of a thawing of the strong anticommunism that had characterized US domestic politics and its foreign policy for the preceding two decades.

When looking at these early years of the organized movement—those groups that identified themselves as for peace or as devoted only to the cause of Vietnam—it is clear that the image of elite protesters that has developed in popular culture and textbooks was not created out of whole cloth. In fact, the first years of the organized movement saw participation from typically middle-class constituencies. Specifically, colleges (with the elite colleges being more dominant), the extant peace movement, and sections of the Old Left were the primary tributaries to the growing movement from 1965 to 1967, and each put its stamp on the foci and tenor of the movement.

Student Activism

After World War II, US colleges went from being elite to mass institutions. By contemporary standards, public support was enormous. The GI Bill was the first, and most sweeping, of the funding opportunities and other support offered by the government, which grew to include grants, loans, incentives, and tax breaks. This period also saw a considerably expanded community college system, providing low-cost open admissions coupled with articulation agreements with four-year schools; and school missions that aimed for equal access to higher education for all who desired it.[45]

During the 1960s alone, the college population in the United States more than doubled, from less than 4 million to more than 8 million students, with most of that growth taking place in the public universities, colleges, and particularly public two-year colleges.[46] In 2009–2010 dollars, tuition rates for public schools averaged between approximately $1,700–1,850 per year during the 1960s and early 1970s (with universities topping out at over $2,700 and two-year schools at close to $1,000). At private schools the range was substantially higher—between $7,550 and $9,600 over the course of the decade (with a similar divide between universities and two-year schools). Average dorm and weekly board rates were very similar at all the schools, with private schools being only moderately more expensive—each around $700 more per year. Total average costs, including tuition, room, and board at a public institutions thus came to less than $6,600 a year at the beginning of the war and close to $7,150 by its end; at private schools the range was closer to $13,200–15,350 (again, in 2010 dollars).[47] In other words, compared to today, college was relatively affordable.

The majority of college students during this period were middle-class and higher (although many of these were new middle class, with their fathers having been the first in their families to go to college on the GI Bill). Most working-class families could still not afford to send their children to college, and, perhaps more important, the possibility of finding a decent job without a college education still existed. Yet, according to David Karen, because of affordability and "increases in rates of high school graduation and because top socioeconomic groups reached a ceiling in their rates of college entrance, it appears that class differentials in access to higher education . . . diminished."[48] Overall, in the period of 1960 to 1976, the entrance of working-class students into college increased.

Yet the system remained highly stratified, with access to elite schools limited in terms of class; in fact, it became more stratified as access increased. For example, looking at relatively poor students, "at private universities, students from families with incomes less than half the [national] median were 8 percent of all students in 1966 and 7 percent in 1975," whereas "At the other end of the higher educational spectrum, at public two-year colleges, the students from poorer families increased their representation from 17 to 20 percent in this period."[49] So as the overall number of poor and working-class students increased—some estimate that around one-third of all college students were from working-class backgrounds during this period—the distribution of these students across the college system remained uneven. Overall, the class compositions of the campuses themselves were already tilted, by and large, toward more professional or privileged families. And this skewing increases when the status of the students, the private or public nature of the campuses, and whether the student bodies were commuter- or dorm-based are taken into account.[50]

Significant changes within the youth culture proceeded apace with this vast expansion of higher education. As going to college approached the realm of norm instead of privilege, more young people "found themselves in a new socially determined developmental stage that extended adolescence into the middle twenties or even later."[51] "Youth communities" appeared in college towns, which became the center of lifestyle experimentation even before the counterculture emerged on the scene full force. With the folksingers, jazz musicians, beat poets, and sexual and drug experimentation, these pockets of pre–baby boom youth began to create a generational sensibility that the baby boomers would amplify to new levels in the decade to come.[52] Even more than the emerging peace movement, the civil rights movement indicated that the times were changing, and contemporaneous observers argued that the youth culture as a whole was marked by "identification with outsiders and marginal groups."[53]

Alongside, or even within, the political commitments felt by many of the students who were becoming radicalized at the time, therefore, existed a cultural critique and sense of oppositional identity that set them apart not just from their elders but also from others who did not share in their newly emerging worldview.

Part of this worldview was an insistence on authenticity and moral individualism. Historians attribute this particular valence of radicalism to the experience of SNCC organizing in the South. Becoming political represented a moral transformation, being "real" to oneself and to others. The hallmarks of this model were participatory democracy, deep community organizing, and audacious militancy. Many early SDS leaders were first direct participants in or inspired by SNCC in the early 1960s, for example, Tom and Casey Hayden, Rennie Davis, and Sharon Jeffries.[54] These distinct youth and movement cultures served, on the levels of lifestyle and symbols, to divide parts of the New Left from some of their contemporaries and many of their elders.

Middle-Class Cultures in the Movement

From early on, students gave the antiwar movement its numbers. In certain places such as college towns and at certain national demonstrations, they gave the movement its flavor as well. Some of the antiwar activism of the youth-dominated groups was characterized by disruptive tactics and innovative organizational forms. Most notably, the Vietnam Day Committee in Berkeley and much of the West Coast activism; many of the local campus efforts in Madison, Wisconsin, Harvard, and Columbia; and much of the draft-resistance movement together turned quickly to direct action and the call, identified with SDS, to move from "protest to resistance." These groups also drew on the consensus-seeking, collective models of organizing inspired by the SNCC and SDS early commitment to participatory democracy.[55]

Yet the student organization that helped precipitate this outpouring—SDS—did not play a meaningful *organizational* role in the movement beyond 1965 (I take this up in greater detail in the next chapter). In fact, no purely student or New Left groups exercised significant organizational sway on a mass scale. Overall, to the extent that the early antiwar movement developed infrastructural characteristics typical of organized movements—discrete and organized groups, recognizable leadership, collectively agreed-on tactics, general strategies, literature, grievances, and "frames"—it was more often shaped by existing peace groups, including radical pacifists and liberals, and by various Old Left groups, the Socialist Workers Party (SWP) being prominent among them.[56] For example, because national SDS had rejected the war as its main focus, campus SDS groups frequently turned to pacifist organizations for speakers, materials, and tactics, helping "fill the organizational vacuum for local SDS-ers."[57] On other campuses, the Student Mobilization Committee of the SWP became the prominent vehicle for antiwar expression. The existing peace and left activists had the leadership and organizational experience to give shape to what might otherwise have been more inchoate—and possibly less effective—protest.[58] In other words, the movement was filled with people new to activism, but it frequently took on organizational, strategic, ideological, and tactical forms that predated the movement itself. And as the years progressed, this became increasingly the case, with the organized leftist groups becoming more prominent and liberal efforts within and alongside the Democratic Party increasing in importance.

Parts of the old guard, such as some radical pacifists and nonstudent activists coming out of the civil rights movement, were committed to capturing the youthful energy and encouraged the use of organizational forms and political tactics that corresponded to the participatory democracy and direct action of the New Left. The radicals were also more open to the multi-issue orientation of the New Left and agreed that the problem of Vietnam should be confronted as part of a host of social ills endemic to US society. Others, including the SWP and many liberal and religious groups, tended to insist on the single issue of the war, and they variously encouraged mass protests, lobbying, and education in their youth projects. Over time, brokers emerged, bridging the streams; coalitions formed, uniting divergent groups; and particular organizations moved in and out of different milieus, from campus to street to door-to-door and from electoral work to direct action. Yet the majority of these easily recognized social movement formations had already, from 1965 through 1967, developed middle-class cultures that proved to be quite internally resilient.

What does it mean to say that the movement groups had developed middle-class cultures? In his ethnographic study, *Coalitions across the Class Divide*, Fred Rose argues that movement groups frequently develop their own class character that makes them more or less attractive to possible recruits. He emphasizes the class-specific independent subcultures of movement groups, whose origins he traces to differential experiences rooted in class, most particularly in the workplace. Rose argues that the differences between middle- and working-class forms of work—specifically, the forms of managerial control and organization of the production process experienced by members of each class—create the conditions for the adoption of differing strategies regarding social change within each group.[59]

Following others' work on class-based differences in child rearing, Rose argues that members of the middle class are raised from early on to be self-directed and autonomous, a socialization process that anticipates the internal motivations needed for professional positions. By the time these middle-class people become activists, they have spent their lives learning that authority structures are best understood as internalized value systems governed by initiative and personal responsibility—structures that people carry within themselves more than forces that operate externally or with external coercive power. In turn, they tend to approach social change as a process of personal transformation and education, a result of critical thinking and individual action. (Although Rose does not make this point, a related implication of his theory is that middle-class activists tend toward idealism, the belief that the world is changed through ideas.) Middle-class work is also experienced as "meaningful," involving tasks that are experienced as inherently interesting or worth pursuing. It follows, for Rose, that middle-class politics often reflects universal goals that are noneconomic and worthy of pursuit for their intrinsic or moral value.[60]

Because they are themselves directed from within, middle-class activists assume that others will be similarly self-directed to make change. Furthermore, many observers of (the frequently seen as middle-class) "new social movements" note that, in such movements, activism is defined as a personal value and expression in which the "relation between individual and collective is blurred." One's individual behavior prefigures larger movement goals and is often the goal itself. The slogan "the personal is political" can to some extent be understood in this light. This is related to a common observation of certain middle-class movements that "it often makes little difference whether such movements succeed or fail" because being involved alone is considered sufficient ("the way is the way").[61]

To sum up, middle-class activism will most likely take the following, at times contradictory, forms. It is educational in its internal activities and intellectual (or, at least, idea-oriented) in its outreach. The activists believe that ideas matter, and that they can—perhaps primarily—change social conditions. It tends to emphasize the importance of the activist's personal behavior and level of commitment and to embrace tactics that demonstrate that commitment. In some cases, the righteousness of the cause may eclipse the efficaciousness of the action because symbols and ideas carry such freight.

Looking at the different wings of the early antiwar movement—liberals, students, and radicals—we can trace the extent to which they partook of these middle-class modes of social activism. These modes are echoed in six approaches to social change that some movement analysts have observed to be typical of US peace movements in particular.[62]

- *Transcender* activists conceive of wars as resulting from misunderstanding; therefore, open discussion can relieve the problem.
- *Educator* activists commit themselves to teaching people about the facts regarding war and to continuing to keep people informed of the most up-to-date information, so the group can respond accordingly.
- *Intellectual* activists go beyond facts to provide interpretations of the developments of the war.

- *Politician* activists work through mainstream channels to persuade political elites.
- *Protester activists* disrupt the normal flow of society.
- *Prophet activists* embrace moral action, what the Quakers call "acts of moral witness."

As we will see, transcenders, educators, intellectuals, politicians, protesters, and prophets generally share many of the characteristics of middle-class culture predicted by Rose.

Transcenders and Politicians: Liberal Elites

For liberal antiwarriors in 1965, the existing power structure was understood as generally benign and well intentioned, the sitting administration no exception. The Johnson administration was making extraordinary progress on civil rights and had pledged to make Great Society reforms that the liberals had sought for years. Leading insider critics, as well as many of the peace activists and educated professionals who opposed the war, were culturally close to the warmakers and war supporters among the political and corporate elites. They traveled in similar Washington and New York circles, had attended the same schools, or worked in closely aligned fields. The trust in authority shown by these elite liberals was not the trust shown a superior who may "know best"—it was the trust of peers who would be happiest to stand in solidarity with their efforts, if only those efforts were a little more reasoned or reconsidered.

Early liberals critics were pained by the "mistake" of Vietnam. For those who agreed that Red China was a threat, an independent communist Vietnam could still serve the purpose of containment. Political theorist Hans Morgenthau, among others, saw its potential as an Asian Yugoslavia, a theme he explored in part in a 1965 *New York Times Magazine* article whose title neatly captures the "mistake" mentality: "We Are Deluding Ourselves in Vietnam."[63] Others were not convinced of the geopolitical importance of Vietnam, but they joined *The New Republic* in arguing that, in any event, the war "cannot be won by the United States. It can only be won by the Vietnamese."[64] Early dissenters were appalled by the immorality of the enterprise: killing American boys—Senator Ernest Gruening called it "murder" in 1964—to support a corrupt regime, in a fight better left unfought, was unethical in the extreme.

As these liberals saw it, the battle they were engaging was one of ideas. The "best and the brightest" pursuing the war in Vietnam did not *understand* that the war they were fighting was ill-judged, immoral, and unwinnable. They trusted that their insider statuses and well-reasoned arguments would be able to break through their colleagues' poor analysis and create a policy change. The belief in the power of argument and reason was just as central for those at a greater distance from the corridors of power, such as SANE and other liberal peace groups. The first audience for such lessons were the war-supporting political elites themselves, particularly those within the Democratic Party. Professional groups were appealed to and journalists were courted.

Educators and Intellectuals: Students, One and All

In 1965, the movement also saw itself as educating the public. "We need an American teach-in," exclaimed one early activist; "the people don't know." As some activists remembered, "either the politicians in Washington would understand the error of their ways, or the American people would bring them to their senses."[65]

Movements create social roles for their participants, and teacher-student roles abounded within the early antiwar movement. Primary and secondary school teacher union locals were among the first to oppose the war.[66] The movement enjoyed early and sustained support within academia. Journalists and writers, who perform a kind of public education, were also some early leaders, and many of the alternative presses of the time, such as *Ramparts* and the *Guardian*, as well as more established liberal publications such as the *New York Review of Books*, *The Nation*, and *The New Republic* carried numerous educational pieces about Vietnam. Of course, in addition to teachers, students abounded. Students studied the war, debated it, and learned what they could about US foreign policy, French colonialism, Ho Chi Minh, and Vietnamese nationalism. The teach-ins were the synergy of the knowledge-based orientation of the early antiwar movement and the student unrest that would come to dominate the decade. The format of the teach-ins themselves reflected a faith in the power of ideas. Intellectual dissenters put forward their analyses against the rationales of the warmakers: may the best ideas win.

Getting "the facts straight" was a constant enterprise for the young movement. One SDS organizer, Dena Clamage, who left the national office to organize with the Detroit Committee to End the War in Vietnam, reported that "there was an incredible number of people in middle class neighborhoods who felt vaguely and sometimes concretely very troubled about the war. These people need facts to sharpen their concerns into direct opposition."[67] The movement turned to antiwar intellectuals to learn the history of the region, US foreign policy, and the intricacies of the Cold War so as to teach their middle-class audience about the mistaken nature of the war.

Already by 1965, Marcus Raskin and Bernard Fall had put out *The Viet-Nam Reader: Articles and Documents of American Foreign Policy and the Viet-Nam Crisis*. Another source book on Vietnam of the period was Marvin Gettleman's *Viet Nam: History, Documents and Opinions on a Major World Crisis*.[68] This and a larger 1970 edition sold 600,000 copies during the period. The documents Gettleman and his co-editors collected fit under historical subject headings such as "The Vietnamese Struggle for Independence through WWII," "The War with France," "Geneva—The Peace Subverted," and "The Revolution against Diem." Years later, the editors explained that "most Americans were unaware of this history, and the policy makers in Washington seemed to be oblivious to it." They called the early days of the movement "a spontaneous educational project."[69]

But the education did not seem to be working. As the year 1965 waned, most of the transcenders, educators, politicians, and intellectuals within the movement began to question their capacity for talking their way out of the war. More and more, it seemed like the government was not making a mistake in Vietnam; it was just as aware of the problems as the dissenters were. The antiwarriors were forced to the conclusion that their government was knowingly pursuing an immoral war. Even Clergy and Laymen Concerned About Vietnam (CALCAV), a moderate antiwar coalition of mainline Protestants, Jews, and (few) Catholics, began to change its approach. From 1966, the group increasingly called the war immoral and not just a mistake. In 1967, Richard Fernandez. its executive director, explained, "six months ago most of us would have said that some very good men in Washington had made some very bad mistakes from which they should try to extricate themselves as soon as possible. Today it seems that this kind of judgment is both out-of-date and inaccurate."[70] The analyses and tactics of the radical wing, which had from the beginning argued that the problem of Vietnam was broader than the war, became more dominant in 1966–1967.

Prophets and Protesters: The Radical Wing of the Movement

Alice Herz, Norman Morrison, and Roger Allen Laporte, all pacifists, were three of eight US protesters who publicly immolated themselves in the earliest days of the movement. Prophets, they made the ultimate personal sacrifice to express their horror of war and to show their solidarity with the Vietnamese Buddhist monks who had similarly protested their repression under Diem during 1963. This extreme form of personal sacrifice was atypical, but within the radical and student wings of the movement, individual acts of moral protest were the ideal toward which many worked. In 1962, Dave Dellinger wrote in *Liberation* that there was a choice for peace activists "between being liberals who limit expression of our idealism to activities and goals which minimize personal risk . . . and being radicals who concentrate on historical exigency rather than on personal safety." Writer and activist Paul Goodman, whose work greatly influenced the early New Left, argued that "the Cold War cannot be altered by ordinary political means" and that the movement should break the "narrow confines of symbolic protest to action that will have a real impact on history."[71]

Most of the organizing that took place leading up to and after the April SDS march was based in local committees against the war. Although many of these had been initiated by the Old Left, they were frequently heterogeneous in political content and form, depending on who had joined them. The first attempt at bringing together these local, diverse committees to end the war came with the founding of the National Coordinating Committee to End the War in Vietnam (NCCEWV), founded at the Assembly of Unrecognized People (AUP) that was held in August 1965. The NCCEWV was the closest attempt by the early movement to give mass organizational form to the radicals' insistence on incisive critique, disruptive protest, and the need for personal commitment and action. The NCCEWV helped to sponsor the International Days of Protest in October 1965, the next large-scale student-based radical action following the SDS rally (the organization survived briefly into 1966, collapsing under the weight of Communist Party and SWP battles for influence within the organization). For some, it represented hopes for a New Left form of protest, different from the transcender, educator, and politician models used in other arenas. In extended remarks in the NCCEWV newsletter, *Peace and Freedom News*, Staughton Lynd and Bill Tabb wrote that "a protest organization can survive almost any internal problems if there is a deep-rooted objective need that their organization exist." One of the felt needs for an organization such as the NCCEWV came from the fact that "no existing peace organization was in tune with the style of protest which many of those participating in the AUP had learned in Southern civil rights work." They call this style "collective personal protest": "People acting by personal decision at great personal risk but acting together."[72]

Radical antiwarriors began to use disruptive tactics in the first months of the enlivened movement. The Vietnam Day Committee in Berkeley, founded with the massive Berkeley teach-in during spring 1965, led the West Coast organizing for the International Days of Protest and rediscovered the tactic of the moving picket—what the 1960s generation called "mobile tactics"—to disrupt business as usual in the military. Trains delivering supplies and troops for the war were briefly halted, and protesters were able to meet up and disperse one step ahead of the authorities. In 1966, West Coast protesters stopped buses of troops from leaving the Oakland army base. These actions took a page out of the labor playbook—in a sense, they were seeking to stop the production of the war.

The decision to disrupt, in itself, does not imply a class-specific internal culture to the movement. If anything, the power of disruption is often the best or only point of leverage for otherwise less powerful groups, such as the poor and working class. But in the case of the early movement, it makes some sense to see this disruption in class-specific terms. Irving Howe, Bayard Rustin, Michael Harrington, Lewis Coser, and Penn Kimble singled out disruptive tactics such as those in Berkeley in a 1965 *New York Review of Books* article critical of the radical wing of the movement. Coming from a considerably more moderate political position, they made a number of arguments in their piece that underscored a general abhorrence of radicalism. Civil disobedience, they argued, was a legitimate form of protest, but "we would urge that it be employed only after intense reflection and a full resort to other, more 'normal' methods."[73] Howe et al. developed the case that, unlike civil rights protesters, the antiwar movement had other forms of leverage at its disposal, underscoring the other bases of power—persuasion and electoral—that the mostly middle-class-oriented movement was already using. These liberal critics could be rightly taken to task for overestimating these power bases, but they were not completely wrong to observe the class base of the groups involved in the movement thus far.[74]

Whither the Working Class?

Opposition to the war, as framed by the early movement, carried a great deal of elitism within it. Some of the educational efforts of the antiwar movement created the image that individuals needed to know something to oppose the war—people needed to be schooled in their opposition. That is, some of "us" understand the problems with the war, and we need to convince the rest of "us"—the educated and the political and cultural leaders—that it is a terrible mistake. Many radical protesters created similarly high thresholds for action, upholding personal sacrifice and extraordinary individual commitment as its optimal forms. Almost by definition, protesters in this environment would remain an exclusive group, a reality that some early leaders directly acknowledged. Writing in *Liberation* in early 1966, Muste defended the historical and political analysis of the Vietnam situation that served as a base for radical dissent, as well as the radicals' confrontational politics. "If, as is true, this will at first call for the opposition or skepticism on the part of many Americans, we have to face it and in any case will not be able to evade it."[75]

For liberals, their initial focus on elite or educated groups was in part strategic. Liberal peace advocates believed that the Democratic decision makers with the power to end the war would respond to pressure from respected peers, and if not from them, from their most influential electoral supporters. Of course, trade unions and other working-class groups also worked through electoral politics and were at the center of the Democratic Party base. And an electoral and lobbying strategy is far from class-specific; working-class "machine" politics and trade union political action precisely occupied that arena. But working-class groups were neither considered as possible audiences for the educational process of the movement nor approached as partners in lobbying efforts. The power that workers could bring to the table as voters, in other words, was not sought.

From the standpoint of antiwar movement activists and organizations, the most obvious reason for ignoring organized workers was the intransigent support for the war displayed by the bulk of the US trade union leadership. In September 1965, AFL-CIO President George Meany argued that "For America to surrender, to withdraw, to abandon its solemn commitment to South Vietnam would be the first step toward a world holocaust," and he pledged the "unstinting support" of the AFL for Johnson's war policy at the convention of December 1965.[76] The premier liberal labor leader of the era, UAW President Walter Reuther, called the AFL position "intemperate, hysterical, jingoistic, and unworthy of a policy statement of a free labor movement." But it took two more years, and President Johnson's decision to step down, for Reuther to publicly oppose the war.[77] Despite antiwar organizing efforts within the labor movement (see chapter 4), it was not until October 1967 that any meaningful and high-profile antiwar labor voices challenged the apparent "righteous unanimity" of the pro-Johnson, anticommunist labor leaders.[78] The foreign policy positions of the labor leadership during this period, however, did not reflect the feelings of its members.[79] Polls indicated union-member households were not statistically different from non-union households in their feelings about the war. But the pro-war strength of the mainstream AFL-CIO leadership encouraged even sympathetic observers to hold a jaundiced view. Speaking at a labor conference in St. Louis in 1966, Sidney Lens, long-time labor supporter and current antiwar activist, said that the labor movement in the United States "is no longer dreaming of new vistas. It is imbued with a sense of satisfaction. . . . [S]mugness, arrogance, and the unwillingness to probe new ideas have always been the enemies of the labor movement. Without the right to dissent, the labor movement is nothing. The idea of making a fast buck not only permeates our society, but our unions too, to the point that it is a disease—this veering away from idealism."[80] Given the urgency with which the early movement pursued its goals—which, regardless of the "out now" or "negotiate now" direction of the slogan, always included an immediate end to the bombing—pursuing organized workers would arguably have been time better spent elsewhere.

In short, in the first two years of the antiwar movement, antiwar groups reached for what they perceived as low-hanging fruit. In the case of the most prominent draft-resistance efforts, historian Michael Foley argues that "although Resistance founders in Boston and elsewhere held out some hope of attracting working-class men to their movement, making the mobilization of large numbers of poor and working-class men . . . the main objective of an antiwar movement seemed an unnecessary distraction away from their primary goal of stopping the war."[81] College students and academics, middle-class women, and members of the clergy were the target audiences from early on. SDS, NCCEWV, WSP, SANE, SWP, FOR, WRL, CALCAV—across the political spectrum, in most instances a middle-class audience was explicitly or implicitly sought out by the movement.

Implications of the Early Middle-Class Orientation of the Antiwar Movement

The movement did not grow within middle-class groups because they were more likely to oppose the war than workers were. That the criticisms of the movement did not penetrate working-class communities was not due to their being pro-war. Nevertheless, it *would* be accurate to argue that the movement in its first years organized its opposition to the war in ways that did not, by and large, speak to working-class concerns.

The direct experience of going to war, or sending one's sons there, was borne overwhelmingly by working-class or rural communities, whose reaction to the war was strongly colored by that experience. First and foremost, concern for and pride in those serving in the war were their primary frames of reference. The distant horrors or more abstract threats that were felt or anticipated by middle- and upper-middle-class communities did not translate into the lived, tangible realities of the war as experienced by many working-class people. In many working-class communities, service during wartime was a particular source of pride and was regarded as a duty. Intergenerational service in the military distinguished many working-class families. The military had long served as a site of assimilation for immigrants and as a way for working-class people of all ethnicities and races to advance (despite the racist hurdles faced by nonwhite soldiers, and African Americans in particular, who served in formally segregated forces until 1948).[82] Furthermore, military culture resembled the self-perceptions of working-class culture, with emphases on brotherhood, team work, bravery, and ruggedness. Criticisms of military culture could therefore be construed as criticisms of working-class culture as well.[83] As I detail in later chapters, organizers who did try to encourage draft resistance in working-class communities discovered it was hard to overcome the pro-military legacy. Similarly, support for the Democratic Party and the federal government among workers made criticism difficult. Sharon Jeffrey, an SDS Economic Research and Action Project (ERAP) organizer in Cleveland, explained that the war became a "volatile element" in the relationship between the ERAP organizers and poor communities. During summer 1965, Jeffrey found that community views of local government were frequently quite critical but that this was not so at the national level: "The government (federal government) somehow is honest, moral, and good. . . . If the US was involved in a war, then it must be for good reasons. . . . Given that the government fought only just wars and war was to prevent the spread of Communism . . . it was wrong . . . to question the role of the United States in war."[84] Working class anticommunism, particularly high among many Catholics and Eastern European ethnics, was another steep hill for those who might challenge the Vietnam war in such communities. Especially in its early years, when the anticommunist rationales for war were particularly loud, war opposition ran counter to fundamental US values for many workers.

The main movement critiques—that the war was unjust, unnecessary, and brutal—therefore had high thresholds to overcome in communities whose sons' lives were at stake and who were predisposed to identify with the military, the federal government, or both. Movement critiques could be seen as abstract in this context, if not offensive. The messengers delivering the critique—hippies, college students, those associated with the counter-culture—were themselves highly suspect for workers, a factor which, perhaps more than any, helped create distance between the groups (see chapter 7). As early as 1967 one activist noted, somewhat romantically, "I have said we are less popular than the war. . . . I am not altogether unsympathetic with the popular judgment of us, manipulated and outrageously unfair as it is. The media would not be able to achieve such results if we had not handed them a culturally-prescribed handout for doing so; we march, we debate, we talk, we write, we burn draft cards, we work for peace as if we were living in a world carved out by John Stuart Mill while real men, women and children are making and unmaking history in the hell of organized warfare."[85] Any conversation about the problems of the war that would resonate among less affluent communities needed to be deeply respectful of the mortal risk undertaken by young US soldiers and the proud service of their veteran fathers, uncles, and friends; attentive to the burdens on families whose children served or were more likely to be drafted; and cognizant of the pride and fear that could live alongside skepticism and questioning of the war and its aims. None of these factors put workers irretrievably beyond the reach of the antiwar movement, but all bespoke the cultural distance between the two groups and obstacle-strewn nature of the path to be traveled for such a connection to take place, given the initial sources and orientation of the organized movement.

The movement thus began in such a way that there were class-based limita-tions in the breadth of its audience. To some extent, these constitutive limitations were reproduced over time. Because it had started where it did and how it did, the later forms and public presentation of the antiwar movement were constrained by its roots. Yet, even in its core organizations, there existed more class diversity and attention to class cultures than my sketch thus far reveals, as the next chapter takes up.

COUNTERCURRENTS IN THE MOVEMENT

Complicating the Class Base

> I had tended up to that point to take peace activists to be . . . kind of academic lefties who were not very practical and so forth. But when I really began to get a look at people like that I saw that [the antiwar movement] was quite a different thing from what I had imagined . . . by getting out and getting into those campaigns . . . I began to get a look at the actual composition of the peace movement, and saw that is was a very, very broad spectrum of the public, even by 1966.
>
> —Tom Wicker, reporting on the 1966 Congressional elections and antiwar movement

Elite and idealistic, radical and naïve, the most privileged youth leading the charge and opposed by hard-working Americans—when asked about the movement to end the war in Vietnam, this is the image commonly evoked. But a close examination of the extent to which working-class people opposed the war in Vietnam, acted on that opposition, or joined the movement to end the war reveals a significantly more complex class dynamic, which at certain points is starkly different from the received wisdom concerning the class dynamics of antiwar sentiment and action. In fact, if we ask a different set of questions, a nearly opposing set of answers emerges. Who opposed the war? Who took part in actions either directly or indirectly against the war? Who caused the greatest disruption to the US capacity to fight in Vietnam? In the answers to these questions, working-class people are at the forefront.

In chapters 3 through 5, I present a countermemory to the image of an elite antiwar movement that has become preserved in our historical memory, supported, in part, by the early years of the movement. Yet even in the formative years of the movement, the class dynamics of the antiwar movement, in terms of its members and orientation, were more complex than the dominant memory allows. Numerous efforts were made from the outset of the movement to evolve it from its middle-class nature. As one activist put it, "We need to talk to people who work for a living because this is where it's at. Middle class [people] won't end the war."[1]

The antiwar movement is known for its mass marches and rallies. Beginning in 1965, nearly every fall and spring of the duration of the war saw major marches in Washington, New York, or San Francisco (and often on both coasts simultaneously), and every year saw hundreds or thousands of smaller demonstrations at many places in between. Figures for the major marches range from the breakthrough SDS-sponsored rally of 25,000 in April 1965 to the million-plus who came to Washington in April 1971 as hundreds of thousands gathered on the West Coast as well. Local events included the largest demonstrations that US cities had ever seen, including repeated rallies of hundreds of thousands of marchers in New York City and San Francisco, a hundred thousand in Boston, tens of thousands in Los Angeles, and similar numbers at sites in Minneapolis, Denver, Chicago, and Detroit. And these were not the university protests—college rallies of thousands, and smaller local vigils, rallies, marches, and other gatherings took place in every state in the country. It is estimated that nationwide over 2 million, and possibly as many as 3 million, participated in the October 15, 1969, Moratorium events alone. Overall, it is estimated that tens of millions of people in the United States at some point participated in the antiwar movement, making it among the largest social uprisings the country has ever experienced.[2]

To offer a banal observation, by definition a mass march or rally is not an elite phenomenon. These protests, whose size peaked in April 1971, should not be confused with the marches of the unemployed or the union rallies of the 1930s. Rather, reports from participants, media coverage, and historical accounts point to a broad spectrum of involvement that tipped toward white, middle-class, and young but that was not exclusively any of these. As sections of the movement radicalized, activists contrasted the mass march to forms of nonviolent civil disobedience against the war; in later days, the question of violence itself was debated. The tactic of the legal mass march was often defended by its supporters as the best form in which regular working-class people could participate in the movement—they did not have to risk arrest or take a position that might make them stick out.[3] And the legal mass march was disdained for some of the same reasons, as being too dilute in its critique (and ultimately ineffective, when the vast public antipathy to war did not appear to affect the policies of the warmakers). But both sides agreed that the marches indicated the breadth of opposition to the war.

It was clearly the case that thousands of workers took part in the marches, rallies, and other peaceful gatherings. Beginning with the SANE Washington, D.C., march in 1965, union delegations attended every mass mobilization in the US capital, growing each year until the April 1971 march that brought "tens of thousands" of unionists to Washington, D.C., in addition to the thousands of veterans, working-class African Americans, Latinos, and others.[4] But a working-class presence was probably felt more in the events outside of Washington, D.C. In the New York City Spring Mobilization to End the War in April 1967, when trying to estimate the crowd (the conservative police estimate was 100,000 to 125,000), the *New York Times* (April 16, 1967) noted the difficulty in doing so, saying, "it was also almost impossible to distinguish the demonstrators from the passersby and spectators."

The mass movement did not, in any straightforward way, catalyze or coordinate the majority antiwar sentiment that existed for much of its duration. Charles Chatfield's reflections, which conclude DeBenedetti's history, *An America Ordeal*, argues that the antiwar movement never succeeded in becoming a "positive reference point" for the sentiment against the war, a feeling whose parameters he estimates exceeded the organized movement by a ratio of 60 to 1. "Organized opposition to the war came mainly from middle-class, college educated whites, materially comfortable and motivated by largely moral considerations." These middle-class whites, who largely approved of the domestic liberal reforms of the era, are contrasted to the "great majority" of Vietnam dissenters, who were a "people apart." From the "lower economic class, often women and black, with grade school educations and low-prestige jobs," this majoritarian group was tangential to the political institutions of the era. Chatfield describes them as "isolationist," "politically inarticulate," and "disaffected"; their opposition to the war resting on pragmatic grounds—"a waste of men and money."[5]

Here, I both qualify and challenge these conclusions. The much larger group that opposed the war did not always directly participate in the active movement created by a minority of the opponents of the war, but the mass movement did influence sectors beyond its initial base. It did so in part by creating a pole of attraction for many individuals and groups, even as it alienated others, and by polarizing the political discourse about the war. It also interacted with other social movements. Civil rights, black power, and ethnicity-based movements were not simply parallel to the antiwar struggle. Each movement developed its own form of antiwar critique and mobilized against the war on its own terms. In doing so, over time a broader antiwar struggle emerged that encompassed a broad diversity of participants and reasons for opposing the war that more directly spoke to working-class experiences.

Student Activism's Changing Social Base

The teach-ins of March 1965 began with an all-night, 3,000-student, faculty, and staff event at University of Michigan, Ann Arbor. The Michigan example

inspired other schools across the country to hold similar events, including Columbia, Harvard, and, most famously, Berkeley (the University of California)—
all moderately to highly selective campuses associated with the campus-based
ferment of the decade. But Ann Arbor had more local effects as well, with both
Michigan State and Flint Junior College hosting teach-ins in the weeks that followed. Other land-grant institutions that held teach-ins included University of
Illinois, Rutgers, and University of Oregon. In fact, a look at the early days of
antiwar protest indicates that it was precisely the issue of the war that brought
the burgeoning student movement to the lower-ranked, and relatively more
working-class, campuses.[6]

The teach-ins, combined with the April SDS march, convinced antiwar forces
that there was a base to draw from, people who could be mobilized to act. Yet
throughout this period following its incredible April success, SDS, for one, was
tentative about giving its official endorsement to many Vietnam-related actions
because it was ambivalent about its new position as the magnet for student antiwar activity. SDS was resolutely multi-issue in that it saw the war as only one part
of the system it was fighting against. In the next few months, the national office
continued to use its extensive contacts to build for the major antiwar events
of 1965, such as the August Assembly of Unrepresented People in Washington,
D.C., and the October International Days of Protest. In much of the correspondence from the SDS National Office during the period were admonishments like
this one, written to the Swarthmore chapter urging it to "publicize [the AUP]
to local groups and encourage them to send small contingencies to attend. We
really think this is an important idea in terms of beginning to set up lines of
communication for building a mass, broad-based social movement. We hope
that you will be able to send a few members from various constituencies from
the Philadelphia area."[7] In this way, SDS probably helped to bring hundreds of
the 2,000 people to the AUP (and many more to the 5,000-person march on
August 9), where the first national antiwar coalition, the National Coordinating
Committee to End the War in Vietnam, was founded.[8] Yet, at the same time, in
its June meeting at Kewadin, Michigan, SDS officially decided not to focus on
antiwar work.

Despite this official decision to remain multi-issue, the opposition to the
war among students swelled the membership of SDS and helped transform
the nature of the organization. Before the April rally, SDS had just over 1,000
dues-paying members in over 40 chapters. Early SDS members were "young
intelligentsia," "bright," "aggressive," and "elite," who saw themselves, in Todd
Gitlin's words, as the "voice, conscience, and goad of its generation."[9] These
members were concentrated on the East Coast in elite liberal arts schools.[10] But
judging from the copious SDS correspondence in the weeks following the April

rally, schools with few of the cultural and economic resources of the early SDS strongholds were reaching out to SDS and forming chapters. These included State University of New York (SUNY) Buffalo, University of Iowa, Wayne State, Indiana University, Central Missouri State, and the University of Florida at Gainesville. They were joined by Adelphi, Arizona State, Brooklyn College, City College of New York, Kansas, Long Island University, North Texas State, SUNY Plattsburgh, Queensboro Community College, and San Diego State (schools with relatively economically diverse student bodies) as well as new recruits from more elite schools, such as Amherst, Bard, Columbia, Oberlin, Princeton, and Stanford. By the end of the year, after playing a large role in the First International Day of Protest against the war in October, the number of SDS chapters had grown to 124. Of the fifty-nine college-based chapters that were either new or renewed in the months after the April rally, one-third were based at lower-ranked "state" schools or community colleges, one-third at more competitive and expensive public university systems, and one-third at private colleges with varying degrees of prestige (ranging from the middle-class commuter campus of New York University to Yale).[11]

Although it is rarely described in this way, the first break within SDS leadership that arose as a result of this changing base can be understood in part through the lens of class cultures. The new students who were to dominate the organization in the coming years came to be known as the "prairie power" generation as SDS, and much of the movement, grew beyond the coasts and big cities and turned "from protest to resistance." These new SDS-ers were quite different from the old guard members of SDS described above—from the East Coast; attending liberal arts and elite private schools; from generally liberal, solidly middle- and upper-middle-class families; and disproportionately Jewish.[12] The first generation of SDS leadership, which remained the generation that wrote the books and taught the classes, fit the relatively privileged, intellectually precocious, and academically proficient profile; Paul Booth, Richard Flacks, Todd Gitlin, Paul Potter, and Lee Webb are some of the prominent figures from that time, all of whom were either in the media spotlight or writing influential pieces about the movement. Tom Hayden, principal author of the ur-document of the New Left, the "Port Huron Statement" of 1962, was a partial exception, having grown up middle class in a predominantly working-class Midwest milieu.[13]

The new group came from the Midwest and West, were as likely to attend state schools as private universities, and more often hailed from Catholic and Protestant families who were also less likely to be supportive of their current political work. In addition, they often came from lower-middle-class backgrounds, including most of the new national leaders such as Carl Davidson,

Greg Calvert, Jeff Shero, and Carl Oglesby. Jeff Shero, who came from a military family and was elected as vice president at the first convention after the April march, argued:

> We were by instinct much more radical, much more willing to take risks, in a way because to become a part of something like SDS meant a tremendous number of breaks. If you were a New York student and became a member of SDS, it was essentially joining a political organization, which was a common experience. In Texas, to join SDS meant breaking with your family, it meant being cut off . . . and the break was so much more total. . . . you had to be much more highly committed, and you were in a sense freed, 'cause you'd get written off.[14]

Kirkpatrick Sale, SDS historian, describes this new generation as more "alienated" than the first SDS leaders; Ken Heineman, student movement scholar, stresses its more working-class roots. The emergence of the new generation clearly indicated that the heartland was affected by the war and that the culture and concerns of the movement were being experienced outside the original corridors of the student movement—the civil rights struggle in the South and the culturally liberal and more elite Northeast.[15]

Some of the strife in the new SDS leadership around "intellectualism" and "speechifying" in the 1965 summer national committee meeting at Kewadin was a reaction to this change. Heineman makes the observation, "In New Left circles, these [working- and lower-middle-class] activists often found themselves condescended to and ridiculed because they were unfamiliar with the jargon employed, and authorities cited, by middle- and upper-middle-class students." Sale documents many of these kinds of fights in 1965–1966, before the old guard was finally routed.[16]

Undoubtedly, the combined influence of the teach-ins at leading universities, the overachieving first generation of SDS, and the intellectual reach of the Port Huron Statement helped create an image of student protesters as an elite group. Richard Flacks's 1967 essay, "The Liberated Generation: Roots of Student Protest, a Revolt of the Advantaged" argued explicitly that "the current group of student activists is predominantly upper-middle-class, and frequently these students are of elite origins." This article has been cited in hundreds of books and articles, and it is cited close to six times more than a later article co-written by Flacks that observes a different social base for the student movement.[17] "The Liberated Generation" is an impressionistic account that captures the flavor of early SDS (Flacks himself joined in 1963) and its argument fits—and helped create—the stereotype of the "elite New Left." The problem is that by 1965 it was no longer true.

Flacks's later 1970 article, "The Changing Social Base of the Student Movement," written with Milton Mankoff, counters the arguments he had made in "The Liberated Generation," showing that the student base was actually much more diverse than he had originally described, even at the time that he wrote his first essay. Mankoff and Flacks describe this as a change that takes place over time in the movement itself—that as the movement changed, different students became involved.[18]

Little empirical research backs up the stereotype of elite student protesters for the period of the antiwar movement, 1965–1973. Multiple studies of college students from the period indicate that, at least by 1966, the socioeconomic background of student protesters was not different from the student bodies as a whole, when the quality of the school was controlled for.[19] It was more likely for elite schools to be engaged in protest as a whole, but no particular economic group of students was more likely to engage in protest. As one such study concludes, "since about the middle 1960s, socioeconomic family status does not predict student leftist political action."[20]

Elite Institutions and Changes to Campus-Based Revolt

In *Campus Wars*, Ken Heineman profiles the antiwar movement at four nonelite schools: Kent State, Penn State, Michigan State, and SUNY Buffalo. Based on his survey data, he concludes that "activists from the less prestigious universities drew upon a diverse membership of red diaper babies, upper-middle-class secularized Protestants, and working- and lower-middle-class Catholics and Protestants."[21] Elite schools, however, were more likely to host protest action. Why was this the case? Interestingly, studies do not directly explain why the elite nature of the schools fostered activism in the early years. The authoritative studies of the movement tend to look at *who* the activists were, as opposed to *where* they learned their activism. Only one contemporary study observes that the elite schools "somehow encourage activism among their most able and intellectually oriented students," speculating that perhaps these schools provide "a stimulus to intellectualism and critical social thought" as well as being "symbolic and strategic targets" in light of their standing in national and international affairs.[22]

These are hypotheses that warrant further study. The university did emerge as a target unto itself as the decade progressed as students objected to the multiple connections their "multiversities" had to the military, major corporations, and the government. We could also complicate the first hypothesis, in further support of the second, and observe that, although some of the curricula at the elite universities might encourage critical thought, elite universities also encourage conformity and socialize their students to join the power elite of the country. In that way, these schools might provoke a reaction among students, confronting the workings of hegemony, who might be moved by the contradiction of seemingly open inquiry within college and what appeared to be constrained and limited social careers beyond. Certainly, many of the students opposed to the new "technocratic" regime were objecting to precisely this contradiction. Another angle to consider, unexplored in the literature, is the more quotidian aspects of university life: Do students live on campus? Do the students hold jobs? What are the town-gown relationships like? And how enclosed or porous is the campus community within its larger town or city? All these factors could help encourage or constrain activism on a given set of campuses. The dorm-based, campus-centered nature of many elite schools may have enabled political involvement.

By the end of the decade, however, even the singularity of elite, or level 1, schools, had faded. College culture as a whole had changed. The great student strike of 1970 that followed the invasion of Cambodia, in which 50 percent of US colleges played some part, was a sign that the movement had spread to every corner of the US higher education system.[23] A more recent study of "the political development of sixties' activists" that looks at the longitudinal data of a cohort of high school students and their parents in 1965 and then 1972 finds that having gone to college was the most significant factor in whether or not a young person became an activist but that the class background of the student had only indirect effects that subside when considered alongside college attendance: "The effect of income falls to non-significance once college attendance is controlled."[24] So, although it is true that the first student activists to get the ball rolling in an antiwar direction were generally from elite backgrounds, that changed as the momentum of the movement grew. And as the decade progressed, antiwar students' class diversity increased.

Poor Man's Fight?

The decision by antiwar groups to bypass workers, to the extent that most groups in the movement consciously made it, received attention at the time; in certain places, it was questioned or reconsidered. Many movement organizers recognized the relationship between the frames they were using to reach constituencies, the social institutions and communities they worked in, and the resulting middle-class demographic of the movement they were building. Some of the first major debates within the antiwar movement concerned questions that directly related to the class composition of the group and audience: What is it about the war that we oppose? How do we build the biggest movement possible? What are we asking others to do? And who are we seeking to recruit and ally ourselves with?

In an early meeting of the NCCEWV Standing Committee, a representative from the Lower East Side Milwaukee Project, whose members were working-class and poor whites, Italians and Poles, noted the "lack of discussion about reaching the working class." According to notes from the meeting, he argued that "it isn't a question of discussion in terms of right versus wrong but there are other issues" that would arise for his members. He described them as people who were critical of the war but who were "veterans, Democrats, conformist" and would therefore be concerned with "troop welfare" in Vietnam as a primary issue. The movement needed to address the issue of the troops if it was going to "establish legitimacy" with the people he worked with.[25]

Of all the organizations active in the antiwar movement, the Socialist Workers Party was the most consistently and explicitly concerned with working-class participation in the movement. The SWP was one of the earliest groups to focus on organizing within the military. Rather than resist the draft, SWP members were encouraged to join up so as to agitate within the military, and the SWP repeatedly gave solidarity support to GI resisters (such as the Fort Hood Three) in the early years of the war. The SWP, largely through the Student Mobilization Committee and its involvement in the "Mobe," was also the dominant force behind the mass-march tactic of the antiwar movement, which it explicitly embraced for its openness to working-class participation. In a typical "Antiwar Report" from early 1968, Lew Jones, a member, wrote, "the Gallup poll showing over 40% opposition to the war in the union movement, in contrast to Meany's prowar position, cries out for propaganda initiatives by the antiwar movement."[26]

The SWP efforts notwithstanding, the attention given to workers by the movement was often brief, symbolic, and at times insulting. In January 1966, members of the Detroit Committee to End the War in Vietnam (DCEWV) who worked at the Ford River Rouge plant distributed thousands of fliers, "and the response on an individual level is very positive," reported one activist. River Rouge was the site of some of the most pitched battles of the 1930s, and Local 600 remained one of the most active UAW locals in the country, exercising extreme political independence and a penchant for wildcat strikes.[27] But the movement flier did not reach out to the Rouge workers based on their own self-interest. It read, "The Union movement generally and the Ford workers particularly have in the past always had the courage to struggle for the common people." "For the common people" was an interesting projection on the part of the DCEWV—workers at the River Rouge were having their history of militant self-activity recast as work done *for* others. The flyer also made use of the same kinds of knowledge-based appeals used in middle-class organizing. "Armed with the truth of what is really happening in Vietnam, the organized workers can be a decisive force for peace in our country."[28] The following year, the DCEWV helped organize the "Vietnam

Work In: A Revolutionary Step for Radicals with a Cause but Without A Base," in which activists took summer jobs to "bring" their ideas to the workers.[29] Others were more tone-deaf. In Redwood City, California, anti-napalm activists distributed fliers asking workers to quit their defense industry jobs.[30]

The Vietnam Summer project of 1967 was another early case of trying to straddle both working- and middle-class constituencies. In March 1967, Gar Alperovitz wrote an article that served as the basis for the project, titled "What Can be Done about the War?" Rather than mobilizing for one-off events such as demonstrations or advertisements, Alperovitz urged a community-based approach that could *"reach personally every household"* in a given area, *"initially to educate, secondly to commit the members of the household . . . to opposition to the war."* This committed action would ultimately be electoral: "it must be viewed as a continuous and calculated strategy aimed at preparing the foundations for the 1968 election in such a way that the opposition candidate will be forced, by the depth of public sentiment, to campaign on a platform to end the war."[31]

Alperovitz explicitly identified the communities in question as middle class. Speaking of Boston, but extending his observations to other cities, he writes "there are four groups of potential organizers who . . . could be mobilized to reach deeply into the middle-class community . . . 1) the intellectual community, 2) the student community, 3) the clergy, and 4) the growing number of middle-class community conscious women."[32]

Yet as Alperovitz's proposal was turned into program it changed. Vietnam Summer was announced on April 23, 1967, by Dr. Martin Luther King, Benjamin Spock, Carl Oglesby of SDS, and Robert Sheer, former *Ramparts* editor and Congressional candidate. Its publicity materials suggested that it was "an attempt to expand and diversify the anti-war movement, building a base outside the existing constituency."[33] Rather than pursue one centralized kind of work, as Alperovitz recommended, Vietnam Summer took the "many hats" approach more typical of SDS and reflecting the heterogeneous coalition of groups that eventually coalesced to endorse the effort. As the publicity materials for students said, "there is not a preconceived mold that students must fit into." They offered to "train organizers, develop educational materials, and provided funds for many types of activities." These included "community teach-outs," "draft resistance," and "university projects" but also "selected projects in poor and working class communities."

Those projects that did focus on "poor and working class communities" were, by and large, a bust. Lee Webb reflected at the end of the summer that despite reaching into many localities where the peace movement had little presence (over 700 projects in all), "we did not reach out enough to . . . labor unions [among others], . . . a serious omission [that] meant our program was not as comprehensive as it should have been."[34] Many of the young staffers who went into working class communities had little knowledge of the people and perspectives of those they were canvassing, beyond a few pages of orientation from the Vietnam Summer organizing manual. One summer's work was unlikely to bridge the political and cultural gulf between these staffers and communities. The experience caused activists to critically reflect on how to frame the issue of the war depending on the organizing circumstance. For instance, a Chicago community organizer reported to the *Vietnam Summer News* that "there is tremendous anti-war feeling" in poor and working class communities, but war was not an issue they used to mobilize people.

> The poor know all too well that they are powerless. What the organizer must do is to give them confidence and show them that if they organize they can get some changes, even though they are slight. . . . letter writing campaigns and marches against the war produce no visible results. We must find actions which yield some small reward to keep the poor working together for social change.[35]

These kinds of reflections helped individuals and groups in the movement expand its base in the coming year. Vietnam Summer hired Corky Gonzalez, an emerging leader in the Chicano movement, as a staffer in Denver, and across the West Vietnam Summer projects in Mexican American neighborhoods helped lay the groundwork for the Chicano Moratorium efforts of a couple years later.[36] Another Vietnam Summer project which had some success was the Boston Draft Resistance Group. Lasting for years beyond Vietnam Summer, it made solid efforts to adopt to the goal of working-class mobilization. But draft resistance was also an area in which the cultural gap between middle-class antiwar activists and workers proved daunting.

Public draft-card burnings were one of the earliest tactics of the radical wing of the movement. There were also refusals to accept receipt of draft cards. The group known as the Resistance coordinated the October 1967 return of draft cards to the Selective Service, and it was this action that the "Call to Resist" (see chapter 2) was designed to support. The card burnings, reflecting a combination of New Left and religious values, were often explained in terms of moral witness and were carried out predominantly by white upper- and middle-class college students. As draft-resistance historian Michael Foley notes, the burnings were an "act of resistance [that] took on an air of condescension for some working-class observers."[37]

By 1967, before the National Mobilization in Washington, D.C., some of the debates about the strategy of draft resistance and the particular tactics used by draft resisters revolved around the question of class participation within the movement itself. SDS had decided to participate in draft resistance, but internal questions were raised about the class base of that movement. SDS member Steve Hamilton argued that the tactic of individual imprisonment would be an unlikely vehicle through which to organize working people: "I don't think moral witness on our part can have any concrete effect on those who cannot afford to make a moral witness. . . . No revolution is built on bad consciences but on the organizations of those who are exploited. Middle-class tears and money mean very little." Hamilton urged an organizing approach over a focus on "public effect" and criticized the Resistance for "building a movement that hoped to stir one more wave of middle-class liberal sentiment against the war and American militarism" rather than organize more people to be involved.[38]

The question of who should be doing the resisting was at the core of the strategy of resistance to the draft. Refusing the draft should have meant jail time for the resisters. Locking up the Ivy League sons of the relatively affluent could help to create a public relations crisis in the war effort, so the organizers hoped. Yet, on the other hand, focusing on the numbers involved, the resistance would have to be operating at a much more massive scale to actually disrupt the war efforts, as millions of men reached draft age during this period, and the vast majority had neither a reason for deferment nor a significant-enough social status to raise a public relations fracas. Other measures needed to be taken to enlist working-class young men into the fight.

Inspired by these kinds of analyses, the Boston Draft Resistance Group (BDRG) began organizing on the heels of the Resistance, in an attempt to use a mostly middle-class base of students to reach out to working-class communities. The core of the BDRG, a mix of college-educated and local working-class organizers, criticized the way that the Resistance, and efforts such as the "Call to Resist," required a moral commitment to partake in the actions. Harold Hector, an African American organizer from Roxbury, was one of three main organizers of the group, and he cautioned that the approach taken by the BDRG must disassociate itself from "affluent draft dodgers whose political dissent was a function of class privilege." Some BDRG organizers, after working in working-class communities for months, came to be critical of the tactic of burning draft cards: "Card burnings are seen as a gesture of contempt directed at the guys who are already fighting, and people do not believe that card burners are exposing themselves to punishment: they assume that card burners are simply destroying evidence." Without the time spent organizing in working-class communities, these organizers would not have seen how their tactics were seen through the eyes of others.[39]

Nick Egleson, former president of SDS and then head of BDRG, spoke at a rally a few days before the October National Mobilization, criticizing the ideas behind draft resistance: "Equipped only with a standard of individual conduct and a calculus of right and courage, we lose sight not only of the many kinds of change needed but also of the motivation for change. So equipped, we easily confine our organizing to the campus. . . . But all the while the men of Charleston and South Boston and Riverside, of Roxbury and Dorchester and of the working-class parts of cities all over the country are threatened by the draft."[40] Egleson laid out a vision for how the movement might begin to meet and enlist these men:

> Our solution must be to begin to organize those most threatened by the US armed forces. How many people gave out information about the October 16 rally in Boston in poor and working-class neighborhoods? Who put up posters speaking the language of those communities? Who tried to counter, thereby, the image the press promotes of us as hippies, cowards, and peace finks? Who suggested in those places that we—not the US Army—speak to people's immediate and long-range interests?[41]

The BRDG took a number of steps in this direction. Rather than emphasizing the political content of the "We Won't Go" statement circulated by the Resistance, the BRDG made the statement: "a symbol of commitment to work actively against the war through other activities of the Group."[42] Foley quotes a member of the BRDG explaining that the group strived "to reach those who were anti-war out of self-interest as well as those who had firm moral and political conviction." Their goal was to broaden the base of resisters through wider, community-based organizing. Those in the Resistance tended to believe that their personal sacrifice was a necessary moral act, but that it could also inspire others to do the same while disrupting the Selective Service's ability to smoothly recruit. Many from SDS, and the Boston Draft Resistance Group, saw imprisonment as a zero sum game, however, with each arrest meaning another organizer taken out of the real action of community organizing. The BRDG called it a form of "useless martyrdom."[43]

BRDG used a tactic described as the "Early Morning Show" to reach people showing up for their pre-induction physicals. By "early February 1968 a pool of more than 100 volunteers helped to pull off Early Morning Shows at more than twenty draft boards each month." They did this for two years. In these actions, organizers talked to the potential draftees at the induction centers about the war and the draft. Tim Wright, one of the main organizers, said, "Mostly we were not successful," with about half of the people there hostile to the movement, another third passive, and the remaining minority sympathetic. But "the basic rationale for the 'early morning show' is to broaden the antiwar movement. Unless you get a man's name and phone number we can't see if he knows other men who need counseling or whether he or his friends will help us with anti-draft and anti-war work."[44] The draft counselors from the BRDG specialized in finding loopholes for deferments, but they always included political discussion in their counseling.

They also used a community-organizing model, going door to door in working-class neighborhoods discussing the draft as a community issue. In a profile in *The Harvard Crimson*, this approach is summarized as follows: "The idea is that people in the neighborhood should watch out for each other and make each other more secure about the draft."[45] Although they were not always successful in convincing the young men to get involved, "some counselees went on to organize in their own neighborhoods, become counselors themselves, or even volunteer for Early Morning Shows."[46]

Until 1968, however, even the efforts of the BRDG to reach working-class young men met with mixed success. Looking back, the organizers estimated that in the first year, 80 percent of the young men they saw were college students (presumably largely middle class), despite having explicitly targeted working-class draftees. Given the many factors at work—the middle-class base of the local antiwar movement, the basic support for the military (and in these years, the war) in most working-class communities, and the lack of many meaningful or possible alternatives for young working-class men who were not drafted—a change in tactics and orientation was not enough to mobilize the young working-class men en masse against the war. Tet, the cumulative experience of the war, and the normalization of dissent did eventually combine to change the face and class base of the antiwar movement. But in its early years, the middle-class focus, politics, and milieu of the draft resistance efforts were difficult to overcome.

In the early years of the movement, organized antiwar efforts within working-class communities that appeared to gain the most traction were not spearheaded by antiwar activists per se but, rather, by civil rights and eventually other activists within what can loosely be called the third-world people's movements of the era. These antiracist, often nationalist, sometimes anti-imperialist rights and identity-based groups identified the struggle against the war as part of their struggle.

Race and Class: Antiwar Action in the Antiracist Rights Movements

As we have seen, in the immediate post-war decades, *working class* and *white working class* were often synonymous terms. This was not a new phenomenon. Class formation in the US context has depended to a large degree on racial differentiation. As Herbert Hill, among others, has argued, in the United States "the historical development of working class identity [has been a] racial identity."[47] To the extent that the working class was even seen as a distinct economic group—which was not very often during the heyday of the post-war boom—it was a white and often a white ethnic group: a racial and cultural construct (see chapter 7). This racially distinct understanding in US society of a white working class has ob-scured recognition of working-class antiwar action among people of color.

In fact, working class people of color overwhelmingly opposed the war and often came to actively fight against it—but these responses were largely a result of interactions with the civil rights and social justice movements, less than the antiwar movement per se. The class identity of these movement activists was not their primary social bond or the public face of their social action. The civil rights movement enabled a forging of a black identity for all African Ameri-cans—poor, working-class, middle-class, and elite.[48] And similarly, the struggles of Puerto Ricans, Chicanos, and American Indians—as well as women and gays and lesbians—helped to forge collective identities among groups that frequently cut across class lines. It was in the name of these identities, and within fights against oppression and for equality, that the war, too, came under attack among working-class people of color.

Just as our limited understanding of class elides the extent to which class ex-perience played a role in antiwar opposition among people of color, our limited understanding of the antiwar movement has elided the powerful contribution made by the various domestic-rights fights to the antiwar cause. Taken together, although the organized antiwar movement remained largely white, workers of color and organizations that offered leadership in their milieu were overwhelm-ingly opposed to the war. With the notable exception of Chicano organizing, the war did not become a primary focus for antiracist struggles. But the hegemony of antiwar sentiment within the movement communities of color contributed to active and passive opposition to the war.

Civil Rights and Black Power at Home and Abroad

African American opposition to the war was during all periods of the war ahead of that of other groups, and Vietnam continually ranked at or near the top of black concerns for the duration of the war. Blacks were more in favor of with-drawal than whites and considerably—by ratios of 2 and 3 to 1—more opposed to escalation. Like other groups, African Americans opposed the war because they did not want to see US soldiers killed, because it deflected resources from problems at home, and because the overall rationales for the war did not seem convincing. In the early years of the war, African American soldiers suffered a disproportionate number of casualties as well, a fact widely publicized in African American communities by the antiwar and civil rights movements, especially Martin Luther King.[49] But the breadth of African American opposition to the war is also understandable in light of the movement activism in black communities that encompassed the issue of the war and how the issues surrounding Vietnam were directly related to African American life in the United States.

The civil rights movement made much of the hypocrisy of US society, and the example provided by Vietnam was an early rhetorical riposte for its leaders. Many in the civil rights movement made use of the hypocrisy of the stated freedoms and standards of justice of the United States compared to its practices of de jure and de facto discrimination and segregation. The logic followed these lines: "You say this is a free country, but are we free to sit where we want to sit, to go to school where we want to go to school, to live where we want to live? You call this a democracy, but can we vote?" War policy underscored these domestic contradictions.

A petition circulated by the McComb branch of the Mississippi Freedom Democratic Party (MFDP) in July 1965 was the first—and a highly controversial—civil rights statement that took the hypocrisy frame a step farther. This petition was written after a young civil rights worker was killed in Vietnam. Elucidating "five reasons why Negroes should not be in any war fighting for America," the petition called for draft resistance, explaining that "no Mississippi Negroes should be fighting in Vietnam for the White man's freedom, until all the Negro people are free in Mississippi" and that "we don't know anything about Communism, Socialism, and all that, but we do know that Negroes have caught hell right here under this American Democracy."[50] This petition precipitated a major fight over the question of Vietnam within the MFDP and SNCC as a whole, one that was resolved six months later when, in January 1966, SNCC became the first civil rights organization officially to oppose the war. Calling the United States "deceptive" rather than hypocritical, the SNCC position paper asserts that "the United States government has never guaranteed the freedom of oppressed citizens and is not yet truly determined to end the rule of terror and oppression within its own borders." It accused the United States of "pursuing an aggressive policy in violation of international law," and said forthrightly, "The US is not a respecter of persons or laws when such persons or laws run counter to its needs and desires." "Freedom" and "democracy" are used in scare quotes when discussed in relation to the United States. Six months later, the Congress for Racial Equality also came forward in opposition to the war, calling for immediate withdrawal.[51]

Other arguments resonated among those in the sphere of the civil rights and new Black Power movements in 1966–1967. The civil rights movement had preached nonviolence while blacks in the South had been subject to terrible violence and terror. As the African American movement increasingly called the violence in Southeast Asia racist violence, and pointed out its indiscriminate and brutal nature, it found sympathetic ears among blacks at home: The United States appeared willing to commit racist terrorism across the globe. This strain of solidarity with the Vietnamese was greatly amplified in the nationalist wings of the African American and other movements of ethnic minorities. Furthermore, the civil rights movement drew inspiration from the anticolonial movements of self-determination and extended solidarity with people of color throughout the world. A minority in the United States, movement activists hailed a worldwide network of brothers and sisters—they were not a "minority" in the global sense. Thus international solidarity helped to pave the way for the early and strong criticism of Vietnam policy voiced by radical and nationalist African American groups, as both a war against people fighting for self-determination and a war against people of color.

Class within the Civil Rights Movement

The personnel overlap between the civil rights and antiwar movements was extensive. Many of the activists in the existing peace movement, as well as Old and New Left, who were to later play a role in antiwar organizing, were participants in the early days of civil rights. And as civil rights turned to Black Power, both black radicals and disaffiliated whites turned to the issue of Vietnam with increased vigor. Martin Luther King, Staughton Lynd, Bob Moses, James Farmer, A. J. Muste, Julian Bond, Bob Zellner, and Ray Robinson were just some of the leaders who embraced both movements—dozens more straddled leading roles, and many more participants spanned the two.[52]

Many early movement leaders were considered middle class in the black community, particularly those who gained national recognition: Rosa Parks and the women and men who ran the Montgomery Bus Boycott; all of the early leaders of the Southern Christian Leadership Council, including Martin Luther King; the students who initiated the sit-downs at Woolworth's; the bulk of the leadership of the NAACP; and most of the eventual leaders of SNCC, including Bob Moses. (There were, of course, numerous and notable exceptions, such as James Farmer and Fannie Lou Hamer.)

This middle-class leadership helped forge alliances among educated and elite political networks around the country. The In Friendship program, a network of northern financial and political supporters established by King, Ella Baker, Bayard Rustin, and Stanley Levison, was the first effort to spread the movement beyond the boycott in Montgomery. By 1963, the SNCC summer projects were reaching Northern students. Elites were not the only supporters, however; other liberal groups also lent their support. The UAW was central to providing funding and mobilization for the 1963 March on Washington, and numerous other unions pledged their support.[53]

The class base of much of the civil rights leadership did not mean that the early movement in the South was a middle-class movement, however. By the standards of white America, very few blacks were middle class, and nearly none were elite. Postal employees, sales clerks, and factory workers were often the best paid and educated members of African American communities and held status positions within their communities that were higher than their counterparts in white communities. In fact, precisely these "middle-class workers" made up some of the leadership and much of the membership of organizations such as the NAACP and the Southern Christian Leadership Conference. Furthermore, poor, working-class, and middle-class African Americans shared caste status, and the central experience of racial oppression transcended class as much as it was marked by it. Racial segregation ensured that, for the most part, African Americans lived in racially homogenous and economically heterogeneous communities in the Southern cities that were the birthplace of the movement. Geographical connections were coupled with strong religious networks that further united African Americans across possible class divisions. And because industry was still concentrated in the North, black industrial workers were uncommon outside Northern cities (Los Angeles, New Orleans, Birmingham, and Memphis were notable exceptions). So even though a majority of African Americans self-identified as working class throughout the era, the collective experience of caste oppression frequently contributed to cross-class community cohesion.[54] In the early years of the movement, the black community in the urban South could thus be organized and mobilized as such.

The sociological categories familiar to US culture at the time, in which the category "working class" was subsumed by "middle class" or "poor," were confirmed by the black mobilization, which, until the later part of the 1960s and the move North did not have strong roots in an industrialized working-class base. And activists observed additional concrete actions that further shaped attitudes about class in the early days of the movement. The decision by SNCC to organize in the rural South in 1962–1965 created a model for middle class–poor alliance that was celebrated and imitated by Northern student radicals in the SDS Economic Rights Action Project, which was intended to do in the North what SNCC was achieving in the South. White Northern liberals, in the meantime, were generally sympathetic to the demands of the Southern movement. Activists who came out of, or learned about, Southern civil rights organizing were thus part of a cross-class coalition effecting social change; and they observed liberal elites who were responsive to a progressive politics. These experiences and observations undoubtedly helped set the tone for the early years of antiwar organizing.

Divisions Sown by Vietnam

In these early years, Vietnam proved to be a fault-line along which moderate and radical civil rights organizations eventually split. When the McComb Mississippi petition first circulated, the MFDP was also in the process of trying to seat its Democratic convention delegation. It came under criticism from groups ranging from the American Legion to Congress to the NAACP for advocating draft evasion. Like labor leaders, many civil rights leaders were close to the Johnson administration and were reluctant to take a position that would put them at odds with the president or his party. (For example, the NAACP did not take a position against the war until the 1969 Vietnam Moratorium.)[55] With the passage of the Civil Rights (1964) and Voting Rights (1965) Acts, leaders such as James Bevel and Martin Luther King initially envisioned the reinvigoration of their movement in the possibility of a strong coalition between peace and civil rights groups.[56] But fears of alienating their liberal base (and funders), provoking (greater) red-baiting and repression, and losing their domestic focus forestalled active participation in the peace movement among the more moderate groups. After a failed educational mission to the US ambassador to the United Nations in September 1965, King told his advisers, "I really don't have the strength to fight this issue and keep my civil rights fight going."[57]

By the time King publicly joined the antiwar fight in 1967 the African American movement was divided over the question of Vietnam, with no group holding it as a priority. The Nation of Islam (NOI) made military nonparticipation a norm, and in 1967 Muhammad Ali, NOI member, was stripped of his world heavyweight boxing champion title and fined for refusing induction. The Black Panthers had formed and joined SNCC in its condemnation of the war; both groups were regularly participating in antiwar marches and demonstrations. But the focus of the radical organizations of the movement remained the problems of racism at home, with Vietnam as yet another example of US racism and exploitation but not one that was the focus of their energies. The liberal groups, on the other hand, were still a part of Johnson's coalition.

On April 4, 1967, at Riverside Church in New York, Dr. King made his break with Johnson's war public when he famously declared he would "study war no more." In doing so, he articulated elements of an antiwar frame that were sensitive to the concerns of the poor and working class, white and black alike.

> I am as deeply concerned about our own troops there as anything else. For it occurs to me that what we are submitting them to in Vietnam is not simply the brutalizing process that goes on in any war where armies face each other and seek to destroy. We are adding cynicism to

the process of death, for they must know after a short period there that none of the things we claim to be fighting for are really involved. Before long they must know that their government has sent them into a struggle among Vietnamese, and the more sophisticated surely realize that we are on the side of the wealthy and the secure while we create a hell for the poor.[58]

In this speech, and similar ones made in the year before his death, King forged a path for soldiers' supporters to partake in a criticism of the war that did not forsake solidarity with the Vietnamese. He also insisted that the brutalization and cynical use to which US soldiers were being put be part of the consciousness of the antiwar movement.

The establishment came down hard on King after his speech at Riverside Church. Ralph Bunche, Nobel laureate and United Nations diplomat; Roy Wilkins, NAACP director; the New York Freedom House; the *New York Times;* and Vice President Hubert Humphrey were among those who criticized his embrace of the peace movement, a move that the critics claimed "confused" his message about civil rights. King persisted and helped launch Vietnam Summer that year. Even without the active support of most civil rights organizations, King's stand had a large impact on sentiment against the war, legitimizing dissent for many who looked to him as a leader.[59]

Despite the growing connection between the movements, "arguments about emphasis and multi-issuism, the cultural and 'intellectual' barriers between white student antiwar activists and black civil rights workers, and interracial tensions, would, throughout the decade, plague efforts to build a broad, radical, multiracial, multi-issue antiwar coalition."[60] In practice, this meant that the movements intersected but remained distinct. One small incident seems to capture this sometimes united, sometimes fractured relationship. In May 1970, on the same day as the hardhat attacks in lower Manhattan, just across the Hudson River in Newark 2,000 black and white high school students who were striking their schools marched from the Rutgers University campus to the US Federal Building. Some college students from the Rutgers Black Organization of Students addressed the marchers, arguing that antiwar protest was a "white thing." According to the newspaper report, some black high students were persuaded, whereas "others debated the question and then went on to march."[61]

Many African Americans criticized the movement for not taking antiracist work seriously enough, and this criticism did help to move the antiwar movement toward a more consistent antiracist politics in its later days. But, for the most part, a racial divide persisted between the movements; antiwar work was being done on both sides but in different organizational and identity-based contexts. That is, in the civilian movements. In contrast, in the military Black Power, nationalism, and the fight for equality combined with antiwar critique to give rise to extraordinary antiwar action (see chapter 4).

Chicano Organizing

There were other parts of the movement in which antiracism, ethnic nationalism, and antiwar protest directly combined. Chicano organizing in the late 1960s made antiwar protest a focus at the grassroots (much more so than was the case among the African American groups at the time), suggesting another route through which antiwar activism compelled a working-class base. Beginning in 1969, inspired by the young Brown Berets, who had begun working with West Coast antiwar organizers, as well as the experience of working with peace organizations in programs like Vietnam Summer, Chicano/a activists joined together to create the National Chicano Moratorium Committee, taking the National Moratorium as their model. The Chicano Moratorium was reacting to death rate of Chicano GIs (double that of whites) and connecting this to the poor living conditions facing Chicano youth, wherein "poor schools . . . scarcity of jobs, police harassment, poverty—all conspire to push Chicano youth into the military." Probationary policies ("enlist and get off the hook") and welfare incentives (families with enlisted men were still eligible for benefits) further encouraged Chicano enlistment, which was also buttressed by "a tradition of taking pride in military service." The Chicano Moratorium highlighted shortcomings of the draft-resistance movement similar to those detailed by the BRDG, arguing that the "antiwar movement to this time has been a racist movement, not dealing with stopping inductions of people of color."[62]

"Once introduced to center stage, the previously untapped power of the war issue became an extraordinary organizational catalyst," observes historian Lorena Oropeza.[63] At the twenty or so demonstrations across the Southwest called by the Chicano Moratorium coalition from late 1969 through 1970, they protested the war while honoring the war dead, acknowledging the respect Mexican Americans accorded those having served in the military. Appealing to Atlzán nationalism, organizers then went to the community to argue that it was better to fight for your own people than to fight for Uncle Sam. Making use of the grievances of the community, demonstrators "offered a twist on tradition by pointing out that dying in Viet Nam and previous conflicts had not ensured Mexican Americans equal treatment."[64] Courted by the organized antiwar movement and widely admired by the left, the Chicano Moratorium was touted as the "most dramatic and successful movement of Third World people against the war."[65]

The Chicano Moratorium movement climaxed on August 29, 1970, in a mass march in East Los Angeles. Flyers for this march explained, "We are of the opinion that the millions of dollars spent and destroyed in a war that brings no benefits to anyone, that they should be spent in solving the unemployment problems, smog, drugs, housing, hospitalization, etc., etc." By this time, the Chicano Moratorium coalition had expanded to include hundreds of small and large Mexican American and other Latino organizations, including groups such as the Congress of Mexican American Unity, the Mexican American Political Association, the American GI Forum, and the Movimiento Estudiantil Chicano de Atlzán (MEChA). The 25,000 participants made it the biggest Chicano demonstration of the period. Severe police repression at the march resulted in the deaths of three participants, including Ruben Salazar, a popular journalist. Although this repression demobilized the movement, it also "shook many nonactive residents of the area into a new concern for their community." One Chicano Moratorium organizer reflected a year later, "A new solidarity emerged here. This is an atmosphere in which many things can be built. Hopefully, the community can use it as a base to move forward."[66] On a smaller scale than before, the Chicano Moratorium continued to raise awareness of the connections between the war abroad and conditions at home, sponsoring events such as a three-month march to the California capital of Sacramento to "expose and morally destroy the policies of 'punish the poor' pushed by [then-governor Ronald] Reagan."[67]

The movements of oppressed people in the United States brought greater depth to the domestic opposition against the war, highlighting the connections between repression at home and war abroad, racism and imperialism, and poverty and military spending. At the August 1965 peace rally called by the Assembly of Unrepresented Peoples, Bob (Parris) Moses, former SNCC leader, made a speech, his third public statement against the war: "Negroes better than anyone else are in a position to question the war. Not because they understand the war better, but because they understand the United States."[68] By identifying the problems faced at home as the same problems represented and exacerbated by war, the civil rights and nationalist movements of the 1960s solidified and radicalized antiwar sentiment, and brought thousands of working-class people of color to actively oppose the war.

COUNTERMEMORY I

"A Rich Man's War and a Poor Man's Fight"

Hawk or dove, we are all clay pigeons.

—Labor Peace Committee advertisement, *Washington Post,* 1970

In August 1965, Jesse Olsen, a vice president of Local 1199 of the Drug and Hospital Employees Union, testified before Congress during hearings on Vietnam about the antiwar activity of his union: "On April 17, 100 members went to the march on Washington to end the war in Vietnam. On June 8, 500 members participated in the largest peace rally in the history of the City of New York."[1] A few months later, another Local 1199 official, Moe Foner, was preparing an advertisement that 1199 took out in the *New York Times,* the first of such antiwar ads that became common in the years to come. Over 1,000 members lent their names to a statement that read, "Negotiate—Don't Escalate the War in Vietnam." The ad predicted, "there can be no military solution to this war," and called on the government to "stop the bombings, seek an immediate cease-fire, negotiate an international settlement."[2]

The first unions and labor groups to take public stands against the war were the Drug and Hospital Employees Union Local 1199; the United Electrical, Radio, and Machine Workers (UE); the International Fur and Leather Workers; the Mine, Mill and Smelter Workers; the International Longshoremen and Warehouse Union (ILWU); and the Negro American Labor Council (NALC).[3] These organizations, most of which were "independent" (outside of the AFL-CIO), fit a pattern specific to antiwar unions in the first years of the war. Broadly speaking, they were influenced by their continued ties to the Old Left or invigorated by the actions of the New Left, including the civil rights movement and the upsurge of college-educated youth.[4] In other words, these unions were exceptional, representing a small fraction of the organized working class. They joined two other, more dominant modes of the labor response to the war.

The more liberal and progressive wing of mainstream labor, exemplified by the behemoth United Auto Workers, initially supported the anticommunist militarism of the post-war era, lending first active, then fading to lukewarm, support for US military endeavors. They sought to balance the fight for freedom abroad with international and domestic commitments to core liberal values and economic measures—guns *and* butter. During the war in Korea, Walter Reuther addressed the 1951 UAW convention with the argument that "the struggle between tyranny and freedom, between Communism and Democracy, is a struggle for men's minds, their hearts and their loyalties, and you cannot win that struggle if you fight only on the battlefield. If we are going to make freedom secure in the world and really stop the forces of Communist tyranny, then we have to fight against poverty and hunger and insecurity in the world with the same devotion with which we fight against Communist aggression on the battleground."[5] Over time, this position was elaborated, with greater emphasis placed on the responsibilities on the home front matching responsibilities abroad.

Beyond their ideological reasons for supporting militarism, material and political considerations obtained as well. Unions such as the Steelworkers; the Oil, Chemical and Atomic Workers; and the UAW represented workers in or associated with the defense industry. Some labor leaders openly viewed the war as good for the economy more generally **and** advocated pro-war positions as pro-employment positions. Wars tended to bring jobs, job security, and economic growth. As the *Wall Street Journal* reported, "Full employment, with the unemployment rate under 4 percent, for this country at least has been a phenomenon of war periods. . . . These are the only times we've had it." Although some unionists were beginning to doubt the long-term sustainability linking defense spending to job security (the Machinists, for example, questioned the reliability of Pentagon contracts over civilian work in Congress as early as 1962), for many leaders, and possibly members, it made good sense that war spending meant prolonged employment.[6]

Politically, pressure to support the war policy of the Democratic administration was extreme and the rewards for doing so not incidental. President Johnson was known for retaliating against those who broke with him. Already in 1965, fractures within the UAW leadership had appeared, with Executive Board members such as Emil Mazey, Paul Schrade, and even Walter Reuther's brother Victor raising questions about the tactics, purpose, and cost of the war. Yet as another board member remembered, "You antagonize Johnson you're really in the soup with him; he had that reputation"—and it was that cautionary principle that prevailed for the rest of Johnson's tenure.[7] Beyond pragmatically avoiding what seemed like unnecessary fissures, labor liberals such as Reuther saw Johnson as an ally for many of their most pressing Great Society visions. Among other advances for working people won during this period was Medicare, signed into law in 1966, which, together with other policy gains, probably helped to neutralize public labor defections to the antiwar camp. From the earliest days of the US escalation, the labor liberals were set for a response to Vietnam that neatly paralleled Johnson's own belief in the possibility of simultaneous victories in the domestic Great Society and Vietnam.

At the conservative end of the spectrum, labor leaders put forward a form of jingoistic anticommunism that profoundly colored the labor response to Vietnam as well as the public perceptions of that response. George Meany, president of the AFL-CIO, and most of the leaders of international unions affiliated with the AFL-CIO were aggressively pro-government policy, when not outright supportive of war: their allegiance to the Johnson administration was strong, and their anticommunism was stronger. The *Wall Street Journal* wryly noted in late 1967 that even the labor peaceniks recognized that "it would be easier . . . to convince Mr. Johnson to change his mind on Vietnam than it would be to convince Mr. Meany to change his."[8]

When we examine the foreign policy of the AFL-CIO in the years following its merged formation in 1955, evidence of a profoundly anticommunist and generally hawkish foreign policy abounds. At the core of AFL-CIO foreign policy was its embrace of Free Trade Unionism, in opposition to the state-sponsored unions common to the Eastern Bloc. US unions operated through the International Confederation of Free Trade Unions, the rival international federation to the World Federation of Trade Unions that was supported by Communist Bloc and socialist-oriented unions. The AFL-CIO supported efforts to tamp down movements for socialism or social democracy across the world, particularly in Latin America, and helped to destabilize or overthrow democratic regimes abroad, such as Guatemala in 1954, Brazil in 1964, and the Dominican Republic in 1965.[9] As it later came to be branded by radicals, the "AFL-CIA" both employed US intelligence agents within its ranks and acted directly on behalf of the Central Intelligence Agency (CIA) and other government agencies. This official anticommunism and conservatism at the top had intimidating effects, delimiting antiwar expression—or even open questioning or skepticism of the war—at all levels.

In 1965, Harry Bridges, president of the International Longshore and Warehouse Union, explained the contradictory support of his union for antiwar protesters and nonparticipation in antiwar protest: "With few exceptions, the trade union movement in the US, if not wholeheartedly in support of the war, is not raising any strenuous objections to it. The ILWU is an exception. But effective action—such as trying to stop shipments—not only requires real understanding and unity of our own members, but a national movement willing to stand by and help out if we get ourselves into trouble. Our union—tough as it always has been, and is today—must face the facts of life: must act and work as part of the trade union movement of the US."[10]

These were the constraints faced by antiwar forces trying to maneuver in the anticommunist and conservative institutional setting of the AFL-CIO. Overall, big labor worked against the antiwar movement, tending to retard or discourage involvement. This role of labor had a profound effect on the public apprehension of working-class sentiment.

In the post-war era, then, anticommunist political orthodoxy helped guarantee that "the range of public debate concerning US foreign policy . . . narrowed considerably."[11] But the experience of the Vietnam War also marked the beginning of an open debate on the merits of staunch anticommunism. Ultimately, labor politics as a whole underwent important transformations during this period. Beginning with the actions of Local 1199 in 1965 and culminating in Meany's own renunciation of his pro-war stance in 1974, the period of the antiwar movement marked the time in which US labor largely shed its Cold War conservatism and began to flex more militant muscles in directions both economic and political. Although the involvement of labor in the antiwar movement as such was uneven, it grew consistently over the course of the decade. And although union members, like workers and the country as whole, were moving in heterogeneous (and sometimes opposing) directions, significant numbers joined the struggle to end the war.

Labor Peace Initiatives during Vietnam

The earliest efforts to bring labor into the peace camp took place within the networks of Labor for Peace, also called Trade Unionists for Peace, in the early 1960s. These networks typically organized educational speakers and, eventually, passed mild peace resolutions in their locals. Peace did not yet mean antiwar— few people had recognized the potential scope of the US involvement in Vietnam. Peace meant an end to the Cold War, nuclear disarmament, and a critical eye on the ever-expanding military-industrial complex. Taking such a peace position meant challenging the anticommunist orthodoxy of the labor movement, which had direct implications in those days for one's livelihood and reputation.[12] At the time, progressive labor activists recognized that, without some official sanction from unions themselves, rank-and-file union members would not, and in many cases perceived they could not, join efforts for peace.

Progressive leaders inside and alongside labor began to organize publicly against the war. The NALC, under A. Philip Randolph's leadership, unanimously passed a resolution for "World Peace" in May 1965, which called for an end to the war in Vietnam and condemned military action as "no remedy for the settlement of the problem in Southeast Asia." Martin Luther King, Bayard Rustin, and Cleveland Robinson, from Local 65 of the Retail, Wholesale, and Department Store Union (RWDSU), leant their voices in support of the motion. The networks created by the early Trade Unionists for Peace became the same groups that started the Trade Union Division (TUD) of SANE. The Trade Union Division of SANE was formed on May 3, 1966, with 173 union officers and staff members present from 30 local unions in the New York metropolitan area. TUD-SANE was precisely a formation that leant some institutional cover for peace—which now meant antiwar—organizing. *The Nation* observed at the New York meeting, "No high union officials were among them, but many represented not only themselves but the officers and rank and file of their unions."[13] That December, Chicago followed suit, and in the following January, California unionists created their own chapter. This effort dovetailed with small signs of unrest at union conventions, including those of the Amalgamated Clothing Workers, the Packinghouse workers, the RWDSU, and the UAW, all of which passed resolutions critical of the war at their 1966 conventions. Each resolution called on the Johnson administration to take up negotiations; beyond that, they represented a range of positions, with the Packinghouse workers most explicitly calling for an end to the war and the UAW being the most sympathetic to Johnson while opposing the escalation of the war.[14]

Unions participating in the TUD-SANE activities proceeded gingerly with their dissent to avoid provoking the labor anticommunist forces. The Chicago chapter sent a letter to union locals across the city offering to meet with the leadership or provide speakers or other materials for membership meetings, and they couched their appeal in this conciliatory manner: "Organized labor has always thought of itself as the conscience of America. We must not be silent onlookers to policies and programs we believe to be wrong. Much as we respect our leaders, we are concerned with the war in Vietnam and its impact on our lives here at home. The labor movement has a necessary interest and responsibility to aid in the search for peace."[15] Contrasting their work to the anticommunist materials from the AFL-CIO summer schools, a letter from a Rubber Workers local to TUD organizers recommended that "[our] education should not be propaganda and we should insist that education means free discussion."[16]

By early 1967, TUD-SANE was co-sponsoring marches and rallies around the country. For the antiwar movement, the official presence of labor on the masthead and the dais had positive effects, encouraging the coalitions to cast a wider net in their outreach efforts. For example, an educational flyer for the Chicago Area Peace Parade and Rally of March 25, 1967, asked the uninitiated, "Isn't it time you joined a peace march?"[17] The flyer was directed at people who supported the president, believed in the justice of the war, or felt resigned because there appeared to be no good way out. In other words, the flyer was directed precisely at the profile of union members, most of whom continued to support Johnson while beginning to question the war. Gently and sympathetically rebutting these positions, the coalition demanded an end to the bombing, a cease-fire, and full negotiations. Their reasons for marching combined morality and practicality, the latter being fairly new to this wing of the movement and undoubtedly a reflection of the involvement of TUD-SANE:

It is in this spirit that we march—
To end an immoral and senseless war
To spare the lives of American and Vietnamese alike
To urge an end to the draft in 1967
To use the $24 billion a year wasted
To end poverty, to rebuild our cities and to improve the quality of life for all Americans.[18]

A month later, Cleveland Robinson of the RWDSU and NALC made a direct appeal to workers' sensibilities and interests when he spoke to the mass rally of the Spring Mobilization to End the War in Vietnam in New York City. He framed opposition to the war as "our right and duty as citizens," citing Abraham Lincoln and John Kennedy as leaders who embraced dissent and arguing against anyone who might find such criticism "disloyal." He distinguished himself from the "top labor leaders who have found it convenient and expedient to support the administration policy, because we know that here today there are tens of thousands of working men and women and they are against the war, so we don't see how George Meany could speak for them." His speech laid out the cost of the war—in lives and taxes—to workers and their families, and the gains being made by those who "are raking in unconscionable profits from this war."[19]

Encouraged by the local TUD-SANE chapters, a group of antiwar labor leaders convened a Labor Leadership Assembly for Peace (LLAP) in Chicago on Veterans Day in 1967. Its four main sponsors came from AFL-CIO unions, including the UAW secretary-treasurer, Emil Mazey.[20] There, 523 trade union leaders from 50 international unions signed a statement of policy that condemned the war on moral and pragmatic grounds, and called for negotiations and an end to the bombing. Norman Thomas (in his last public appearance), Martin Luther King, John Kenneth Galbraith, and Retired Rear Admiral Arnold True were among those who addressed the meeting, as well as soon-to-be presidential hopeful Eugene McCarthy. Solidarity greetings were sent from Abraham Heschel, co-chair of CALCAV, and from Senators Mark Hatfield (R-Ore.), Ernest Gruening (D-Alaska), and George McGovern (D-S.D.).[21] The Labor Leadership Assembly for Peace was, in this way, aligning itself with the liberal end of an increasingly radical antiwar movement.

For all its relative mildness, the LLAP represented a significant break with the house of labor, one that mainstream and other observers noted at the time: "Wobble in Labor's Pro-Vietnam Stance," wrote the *Wall Street Journal* (November 9, 1967), "Labor's 'Doves' on a Warpath," declared the *Christian Science Monitor* (November 4, 1967). Stanley Aronowitz, writing for the influential progressive weekly *Guardian* (December 23, 1967), called it "the most important anti-war expression by sections of the trade union movement" thus far and a "legitimate vehicle from which to depart from labor officialdom," noting that it was a "little bigger and a little broader than past efforts," and not "a hopeless exercise in liberal futility" as some radicals might conclude.[22] The *New York Post* wrote it was "the ultimate triumph of the new generation's rebels: they have created an ordeal of conscience for many elders tempted to sit things out, elude controversial issues and deplore 'excesses' of protest."[23]

For all of their breakthrough character, the leadership-heavy, often more staid positions of the early antiwar efforts within labor were usually limited incursions against the pro-war direction of the rest of labor officialdom. The participants signed statements, made speeches, posted advertisements, and held conferences. Nevertheless, they represented a growing trend in labor as a whole as the war wore on, one that is usually ignored or forgotten.[24]

The intention behind much of the early trade union organizing against the war was to put a stake in the ground in the war of opinions within the halls of power and to add unionist voices to those of concerned liberals who sought negotiations and an end to the bombing. For most unions, such political expression was seen as appropriately flowing from the leadership. This orientation was clear in a 1965 letter from Moe Foner to Robert Gilmore of Turn Toward Peace: "We at 1199 have been deeply concerned at the labor movement's passivity and downright hostility on the Vietnam issue. We have therefore initiated a rank-and-file statement to be inserted as an ad in the NYT [*New York Times*]." He went on to argue, "We do not believe that our ad will attract nationwide significance, but we do feel that it will encourage others in the labor movement to speak out on this issue. And it will at least demonstrate to the public that there are trade unionists in our city who do feel strongly about a peaceful settlement."[25] The early involvement of the Local 1199 rank and file was, however, exceptional. Although these leadership initiatives reflected rank-and-file disaffection from the war, very few antiwar unions appeared to have actively mobilized their own members during this period to support the movement. Given the growing ambivalence about the war among union members, why did these leadership initiatives not reach into the ranks to gain support for a cause that so many felt so keenly?

The leadership orientation of the labor peace forces reflected certain realities of the 1960s trade union movement: the concentrated power of the bureaucracy, the intimidating presence of anticommunist leadership, and the limited involvement of the rank and file. The political scope of most unions' activity had narrowed considerably during the previous decades, channeled through Committee on Political Education (COPE) funds to political departments and electoral lobbying. Few unions had a regular practice of working with union members in nonelectoral political arenas. The business union culture of the unions (see chapter 6) certainly played a role. Stan Weir, a rank-and-file activist, argues that "officials of business unions find it necessary to believe that their members are meek at heart and incapable of thinking though anything other than simple problems," a belief that he argues justified patterns of unaccountable action by leaders.[26] More generously, perhaps, leaders downplayed the skills of their members to justify their own leadership as necessary and their own decisions as best. Usually, they were interested in responsible, respectful calls for peace, ones that could reasonably withstand the inevitable red-baiting critiques from their pro-war counterparts in labor while convincing their allies in the liberal establishment that the labor movement was not a monolith. Judging from the voluminous correspondence between the organizers of the 1967 Labor Leadership Assembly for Peace, antiwar unionists were implicitly arguing, "We are not all uncivilized barbarians like Meany."

An example of this orientation was the first petition circulated by TUD-SANE, under the auspices of Negotiations Now!, an early liberal antiwar coalition. Of the notable signatories who set their name at the bottom of the mass-produced petition, only UAW Vice President Victor Reuther signed on from labor—even on the version of the literature whose heading read "Trade Unionists Say Negotiations Now in Vietnam!" The other official signatories included six members of the clergy, five intellectuals, and three heads of major corporations. The petition began, "We trade unionists are confronted almost daily with the choice of one of two courses of action: either constant, senseless strife—or negotiations." This responsible corporatism of the Negotiations Now statement reflected the reality of the leaders who sat in negotiations and whose role in post-war labor relations was in part to tamp down strife. We could contrast this to the experience of rank-and-file unionists, perhaps especially in the wildcat-strike-prone UAW, who also knew from experience that negotiations did not signify an end to strife and did not necessarily see strife as senseless, if it was aimed toward a better contract, against unsafe conditions, or against a production speedup. So while the headline of the petition invoked trade unionists, the audience it might have resonated with best was other labor leaders and the liberal antiwar establishment.

This is not to say that the labor antiwar organizers were unconcerned about the rank and file. Art Gundersheim, acting as the executive secretary for the LLAP, explained to an American Federation of Teachers (AFT) local president in a letter: "Do not be disturbed by our use of the word 'leadership.' Certainly our major interest is in educating and changing the attitudes of rank and file unionists. We only use that elitist word because in some of our major cities, it is necessary to further our group's prestige and respectability. In operating within the national political arena such as it presently exists, you must make some minor compromises with the status quo."[27] At a strategic level, these leadership groups gave cover to rank-and-file members, who could then participate in the antiwar movement without fear of reprisal from their unions. To counter Meany and company, they reasoned, comparable leaders must be mobilized. Trade union political activity in the vast majority of unions originated from and was controlled by the bureaucracy; without a push from the top, the peace forces would go nowhere. Having a union take a position against the war could allow workers who might individually oppose the war connect it to their collective identity as union members. Analyzing the importance of a socially conscious bureaucracy within the unions, Fred Halstead compared the antiwar involvement of two New York unions, Local 65 of RWDSU and the International Ladies Garment Workers Union. These unions had similar memberships who shared similar cultures, and yet Local 65 and its membership opposed the war nearly from the start, while the ILGWU toed the AFL-CIO line and saw little participation of its members in the antiwar movement.[28]

With a few exceptions, the small rank-and-file efforts that did exist seem to have attracted the already political, often isolated members of various unions rather than growing roots within particular locals. Individuals in unions whose climate was hostile to independent politics often faced intimidation and harassment. For example, Tony Mazzocchi of the Oil, Chemical and Atomic Workers Union (OCAW), a later leader of antiwar union groups and the fight for occupational safety and health in the United States, was derided within his union for having hired Stanley Aronowitz, veteran organizer and antiwar activist (and later journalist and sociologist), as a rep in 1963. Mazzocchi, a war opponent, had been bringing antiwar speakers to educational forums hosted by the OCAW for years. But Aronowitz "didn't use other public figures to address controversial war issues"—he spoke out himself. Aronowitz was publicly red-baited, and by 1967, Aronowitz had been transferred to Puerto Rico.[29] Even the most forthright radicals in the movement proceeded with caution, as Harry Bridges's discussion (cited previously) makes clear.

For some leaders, member involvement meant the possibility that their members would *oppose* their peace efforts—in these cases, the leaders thought of themselves as being ahead of the membership, which, in some cases, they no doubt were. Mazzocchi organized an informal poll of his members on the question of war in summer 1967. Many OCAW members were among the most highly paid, often most highly skilled workers in the labor movement, and their work was directly tied to war production, including the manufacture of jungle defoliants. Mazzocchi hoped that the poll would indicate that support for war was wavering, yet the unscientific poll indicated more hawkishness than not. (It should be noted, however, that by 1969 the OCAW had joined the Alliance for Labor Action and officially called for an end to the war in Vietnam.)

Even in the most progressive locals, some internal resistance was stirred by antiwar efforts. The Executive Committee of Local 1199, a union known at the time for its empowered rank and file, received petitions from close to one hundred members who "hereby protest the undemocratic procedure used by the executive committee to support the Oct 16 'March to Stop the War in Vietnam Now.' We should like to point out that on political issues, foreign and domestic, the union should not be allowed to take a stand as a union without the following safeguards" of rank-and-file discussion and vote.[30]

For antiwar labor leaders, their belief in being ahead of the members might have been a convenient fiction that allowed them to evade some of the tougher issues of union democracy in general during the period. Opening up a public discussion might mean that members would feel emboldened to push their leadership on other questions as well, ones that the leadership was happy to leave alone. And, most important for some of these unions, opening up the question to the membership would mean opening themselves up to the radicals, communist and other, who remained in the locals and whose voices might jeopardize the carefully orchestrated leadership initiatives. The UAW was a good case of this last. In 1967, the leadership conducted a poll that indicated the rates of dovishness were higher in the UAW than in the public at large. As historian Frank Koscielski shows, in at least some of the locals, such as the 32,000-member River Rouge 600, sentiment was even more radical, with the leadership of the local as a whole having taken antiwar positions years before the UAW leadership did. Yet in an interview conducted close to thirty years later, Doug Fraser, then Executive Board member and later UAW president, recounted, "Even in Local 600 workers were generally more supportive of Vietnam until late in the day, very late in the day." Reflecting on Fraser's false memory, Koscielski concludes, "Geographically, Solidarity House, UAW headquarters in Detroit, was only a few miles apart from Local 600's headquarters in Dearborn. But in other ways they were worlds apart."[31]

But some of the early antiwar efforts of labor went beyond leadership assemblies. San Francisco TUD-SANE made use of a November 1967 local referendum to reach out to union members. The referendum stated, "It is the policy of the people of the City and County of San Francisco that there be an immediate ceasefire and withdrawal of US troops from Vietnam so that the Vietnamese people can settle their own problems." (The referendum failed, but it was close.) The San Francisco chapter of TUD-SANE wrote a pamphlet asking, "Why do trade unionists have a stake in peace?" They answered this question by articulating what would become elements of the dominant frame through which movement organizations sought to include working people over the coming years. The list of "stakes" indicates a consideration of a rank-and-file audience:

- Working people pay for war
- Their sons do the fighting and dying
- Their paychecks are being cut by higher taxes and prices
- Their children are being brutalized by the horrors of war
- They are being asked to be the world's policemen . . . spending billions abroad and pennies at home
- The war economy endangers the trade union movement by proposals of compulsory arbitration and laws denying the right to strike.[32]

In Detroit in 1968, a group called Concerned Unionists was formed to address problems of "The Vietnam War, inflation, ever-increasing taxes, and the problems of the Ghettoes, the poor, and the Negroes." It met regularly till 1971, eventually joining forces with a rank-and-file dissident movement within the UAW called the National United Caucus. Concerned Unionists conducted educational meetings, linking the problems of war and the stagnating economy and failed Great Society programs while working in coalition with groups such as the Detroit Committee to End the War in Vietnam.[33] In the same period, Chicago TUD instigated a citywide educational campaign.

Few of such attempts were made to directly involve rank-and-file workers before 1968. Yet as the war dragged on, the rationale for active working-class opposition to the war spelled out by these efforts proved compelling. In the weeks following the LLAP in late 1967 and the weeks before Tet, the Gallup organization polled union members and reported that they were "closely divided on the President's handling of the Vietnam situation." The poll found that 43 percent thought that Vietnam was a mistake, which was just under the national average of 45 percent. In the period after Tet, union members' disapproval of the war outpaced the national average.[34]

The increasingly apparent senselessness and horror of the war helped spur greater participation in the movement. By the end of Johnson's administration, over 35,000 US soldiers and at least half a million Vietnamese had been killed, with hundreds of thousands of more wounded.[35] The United States still had half a million troops in Southeast Asia and had not made any progress in its explicit goal of "defending South Vietnam" from communism. The Tet offensive of January 1968 gave the lie to the assertions made by President Johnson, General William Westmoreland, and others that the North Vietnamese were in retreat and the South Vietnamese army in ascendance. The mainstream media increasingly acknowledged the antidemocratic, intolerant, and vicious nature of the various South Vietnamese regimes propped up by the United States.

By the end of the decade, labor antiwar activity had outgrown the leadership assemblies, with much greater direct rank-and-file participation in and collaboration with the movement. And the domestic urgency of the antiwar effort was becoming more apparent. In Jesse Olsen's initial testimony before Congress in 1965, his reasons for opposing the war were almost entirely based on a geopolitical critique of the war effort. But five years later, the situation was more desperate at home. Organizers working on a flyer written in March 1970 enunciated the reasons for a Labor Assembly for Peace being planned in the San Francisco Bay Area that would target rank-and-file workers, drafting various points:

> We have worked hard all our lives, trying to make a home for our families, assure our children the chance for a better future, and provide security for our old age. Now we see these dreams being shattered by the war. Working People are hit hardest by the war.
>
> The Working Person must pay for the war
>
> • Last five years $150 billion—10% surtax and withholding doubled
> • Profits of the largest 500 corporations up 50%
>
> *Who profits, who pays?*
>
> • Inflation threatens our future
> • Our sons die needlessly—we never voted to get involved in the first place, nor did we vote to send our boys there to die protecting some corrupt dictator[36]

This flier reflects a clearly worsening economy, one in which the impossibility of sustaining the war at the same time as funding important social goods—let alone social gains—seemed increasingly clear. But it also taps into and expresses a greater degree of restiveness and class anger that was emerging throughout the US working class at the end of the 1960s and in the first years of the 1970s.

In 1970, unemployment began to rise, from 3.5 percent in 1969, to 4.9 percent in 1970, and to 5.9 percent in 1971. These average unemployment rates do not capture the intermittent work of many blue-collar workers, whose cyclical patterns of unemployment became more extended. In 1970, for instance, nearly one-quarter of machine operatives were unemployed for an average of three months, and nearly 20 percent of craftsmen, 25 percent of laborers, and 30 percent of construction workers had similar stretches of no work.[37] At the same time, inflation was on the rise and profits on the decline. The research director for the AFL-CIO told *Fortune*, "The non-supervisory employee has been getting the short end of the stick all through the 1960s, and now the pressure from the membership is on."[38] A former SDS comrade wrote Paul Booth in 1970 correcting his theory that "corporate profits have been standing still along with real wages ... [for in fact] in terms of real money, they are down, not just standing still." He went on to ask, "who would recover lost ground first?"[39] This question set the framework for the labor-management showdowns of the decade, a period of labor upsurge that has only recently gained scholarly attention.[40]

The Vietnam War and the antiwar movement both contributed to the conditions for this uptick in workers struggles. War spending was widely recognized as contributing to inflation and generally destabilizing the economic prospects of the country; as *Time* magazine argued in July 1970, "the myth that capitalism thrives on war has never been more fallacious."[41] As far as the audacity of the workers themselves was concerned, contemporary and historical observers connected both experiences within the social movements of the day and the examples set by them to the anti-authoritarian strains of rank-and-file discontent of the period.[42]

During the 1960s, challenges to sitting labor leaders spread from union to union. These started with mid-level challenges that were more like "palace coups" but that nevertheless reflected widespread disaffection among memberships: I. W. Abel replaced David McDonald in the Steelworkers in 1965; the International Union of Electrical Workers got rid of their long-time leader James Carey in 1964; and OCAW came under new leadership in 1964, as did the Rubber Workers in 1966—together the first meaningful set of leadership changes of international unions in the AFL-CIO era. Soon rank-and-file challenges to all sorts of leadership prerogatives were widespread, with black nationalists, radicals, Vietnam veterans, and young workers influenced by the social movements of the period taking the lead. Beginning in 1968, African American autoworkers created rank-and-file caucuses within the UAW that challenged both the car companies and the racism within the UAW itself. These Revolutionary Union Movement groups—DRUM (Dodge), FRUM (Ford River Rouge), and ELRUM (Eldon Avenue)—eventually came together in 1969 as the core of the League of

Revolutionary Black Workers. As the 1970s dawned, so did other rank-and-file rebellions, with Miners for Democracy, Teamsters for a Democratic Union, and Steelworkers Fight Back waging substantial battles against their leaders.

Workers were making efforts to recover lost ground by rejecting contracts at record levels and engaging in both official and wildcat strikes that paralleled the upsurge of 1945–1946. *Fortune* magazine reported in October 1969 that labor was "aggressive, active, and acquisitive." In 1970 alone, there were 5,600 work stoppages, with about 6.2 million lost worker-days. Postal workers and teamsters carried off some of the largest wildcat strikes of the era, and Standard Oil, Ford, General Motors, AT&T, and General Electric were among the major companies that were successfully struck by their unions by the end of the war. Yet worker militancy continued to keep corporations on their toes; as a GM executive complained, "you can sign a decent contract with the international and still have half your operation closed down by strikes."[43]

Starting with the General Electric strike of 1969–1970, which the *Guardian* (December 12, 1969) called the "opening round in one of the most intense periods of labor struggle in recent history," concerted efforts were made by movement activists to bring together the struggle against the war with the labor struggle against employers. General Electric (GE) was the fourth largest corporation in the United States and the second biggest defense contractor. GE was also renowned for its anti-union bargaining strategy, known as Boulwarism (after the GE official Lemuel Boulware, who perfected the approach), which exploited the balkanized workforce—thirteen unions in the company—by encouraging intra-union competition and eschewing the partnership rhetoric (and limited reality) of postwar labor relations for open hostility to the presence of any unions in its plants. In 1969, however, all thirteen unions created a coalition to bargain against this behemoth and commenced what was to become a 122-day strike with 133,000 workers off the job.[44] The *Guardian* urged radicals to seize the GE strike as an opportunity to "redirect the antiwar movement toward reaching new constituencies and making its protest more germane to social reality."[45] Protesters, the paper argued, were not connecting the demands that they made against the war with the lived reality that most people in the United States were facing, a reality that included direct conflict with the "masters of industry" who profited mightily from the war.

Activists began to follow the advice. Movement papers detailed the military contracts held by GE and other companies and raised the problem of "conversion" (to peacetime manufacturing) facing US workers. Student support for GE workers was unusually strong, with nationwide solidarity efforts launched by a number of organizations, including former SDS members, other unions, and antiwar groups. "They're doing a hell of a job for us," reported one striker.

"They give us food, money, help out in the boycott. They're the leaders of the future."[46] The antiwar movement was directly responsible for some of this solidarity. In early 1970, the group Movement to Support the GE Strikers was formed out of the New Mobilization Committee "Who Pays, Who Profits" subcommittee, composed of veteran SDS-ers such as Paul Booth, Prue Posner, Carl Ogelsby, and Nick Egelson. Support committees had been formed in Syracuse, Newark, Boston, Los Angeles, Elmira (New York), Louisville, and Bridgeport (Connecticut).[47] The group pledged material support to the strikers and the coordination of the solidarity efforts around the country.

Students had come out to support OCAW workers in early 1969 in California and had seen their own struggles at San Francisco State backed in turn by the local. GE strikers rallied with students repeatedly in Boston and Philadelphia. One UE flyer read, "'Welcome to the struggle.' We are glad to have you as brothers, sisters, and allies."[48] The strike wave of the time was clearly transformative for the many thousands of workers who participated in it. One UE union representative from eastern Massachusetts commented, "There are a lot of fears of opposing capitalism in the United States. I think it will ease off the large part of the population the same way the fear of being opposed to the Vietnam War eased off. There is an element in the United States which is not afraid; that's the students and the black people. As these people carry on the fight they're doing, it makes it a lot easier for other sections of the population to do the same. The students had to show us the way."[49] Contrary to the image created by the May 1970 attacks on students by construction workers in New York, this period saw greater student-labor solidarity than any previous part of the decade.[50]

Within these churning unions, antiwar sentiment grew. The Alliance for Labor Action, a breakaway federation created in 1968 and led by the massive United Auto Workers and Teamsters, came out against the war. In Washington, D.C., and Madison, Wisconsin, regular antiwar labor groups met, and in New York City the first peace rally called by the official labor movement convened in May 1970 in the weeks following the Kent State shootings and the hardhat attacks downtown. Central labor councils nationwide adopted resolutions against the war. UAW President Walter Reuther's last official communication before his death in 1970 was an antiwar statement sent to President Nixon.[51]

In 1971, the Washington, D.C., Labor for Peace distributed thousands of copies of a book it had compiled, *A Rich Man's War and a Poor Man's Fight: A Handbook for Trade Unionists on the Vietnam War*, which both echoed and altered prevailing reasons for opposition to the war. Its authors wrote, "We're a little behind schedule. But that union train's a-coming."[52] Close to one hundred pages in length, *Rich Man's War* included a summary of the history of US involvement in Vietnam and took up issues such as the war and the economy, the tax burdens

of the war, the class-discriminatory nature of the draft, the hardships facing returning veterans, the profits of the military industrial complex, and the (mis)
allocation of public funds. After addressing these issues in down-to-earth language, the authors turned to the "hard questions" that workers might raise. These
included: "Don't we have an obligation to help Vietnam? Doesn't the president
have more facts than we do? Isn't 'Vietnamization' and the 'Phased Withdrawal'
of American troops really ending our involvement? Why should the United States
lose a war for the first time?" And, finally, "Isn't the peace movement just a bunch
of freaks and subversives? Why should I care if a bunch of 'crazies' gets busted?"[53]
The handbook offered answers to these questions and then turned to an anno-
tated list of thirty strategies and tactics for antiwar union members to consider
pursuing.

Labor for Peace, the final large-scale antiwar initiative of the labor movement,
brought over 1,200 labor leaders to St. Louis in 1972. Its endorsers included the
leadership of nineteen international unions, representing 4 million unionized
workers. This effort was similar to the Trade Union Division of SANE and to
the LLAP in that it was leadership-heavy. But, reflecting the intervening years
of internal membership education, mobilization, and successful antiwar resolutions, the leaders of Labor for Peace spoke openly for their members, not only for
themselves as dissidents, signifying their comfort in marking a break on behalf of
nearly a quarter of organized unionists from the AFL-CIO pro-war line. Reflecting the changing tenor of the times, the Labor For Peace gathering was also the
first to experience a serious challenge of its leadership strategy, including a prolonged debate over the possibility of calling for a work stoppage against the war.[54]

In November 1974, in an interview on the *Dick Cavett Show*, George Meany
expressed some regret about his hard-line approach. He said, "If I knew then,
what I know now, I would not have backed [Nixon and Johnson].... When you're
wrong, you're wrong and I've lived a long time and I've made a lot of mistakes."[55]
For many, this was clearly too little and too late. The intransigence of the Meany
group haunted the labor antiwar efforts throughout the period. In 1970, Frank
Rosenblum, a long-time leader of the Amalgamated Clothing Workers, observed,
"The labor movement has lost its image. Labor is now thought of as part of the
Establishment. Once the defender of economic and social justice, in the vanguard of progressive movement, we now find the AFL-CIO endorsing the war
in Vietnam. It has totally alienated our youth, and antagonized others as well."[56]
Millions of working-class people encountered either full-throated support or
qualified criticisms of the war within their primary political reference groups,
the unions and the Democratic Party.

The antiwar activities of labor groups are not beyond criticism. In large
part, the early antiwar response of labor was tiny, tepid, and tailored toward

nonconfrontation. In particular, the leadership orientation of much of the early antiwar efforts directly reproduced some of the problematic modes of internal organization of the US labor movement in the postwar period and, therefore, did not represent a meaningful break from the way labor leaders were engaging their own membership or seeing themselves as working on behalf of a greater set of class interests. So in this way, the antiwar response was a step forward but not a break in the kind of political activity undertaken by labor groups in the United States.

But, contrary to popular representations of labor during the period, labor was never a monolith. All polls indicate that Meany and the anticommunist leaders of labor were more conservative than their members. Efforts made by antiwar labor leaders helped break the Cold War consensus of the movement as a whole. More tellingly, in some places antiwar organizing represented a pole of the labor movement that was not hostile to the movements of the day but, rather, sought to revitalize labor through its connections to the progressive movements for change. New York, San Francisco, Chicago, Washington, D.C., Cleveland, and Detroit were among the most active hubs of the labor antiwar organizing; in these cities local coalitions went beyond the leadership assemblies to engage in rank-and-file antiwar activity and connect antiwar unionists and the organized antiwar movement. Things might have been worse for the labor movement itself, and for the antiwar movement as a whole, had these breaks with Cold War anticommunism not taken place. Given the strength of Cold War anticommunism in the US labor movement, the breaks made by significant minorities of the unions were impressive, and they paved the way for the more progressive foreign and domestic policy positions that the US labor movement increasingly embraced in the post-Vietnam era.

COUNTERMEMORY II

GIs and Veterans Join the Movement

> . . . General, your tank is a mighty vehicle.
> It smashes down forests.
> And crushes a hundred men.
> But it has one defect:
> It needs a driver.
>
> General, your bomber is powerful—
> It flies faster than a storm
> And carries more than an elephant.
> But it has one defect:
> It needs a mechanic.
>
> General, a man is very useful.
> He can fly and he can kill.
> But he has one defect:
> **HE CAN THINK!**
>
> —Bertolt Brecht, excerpt from "From a German War Primer," quoted in Movement for a Democratic Military pamphlet, 1970

The military is, by design, an antidemocratic institution. The authority of leaders is absolute; decision making is top down. The culture of the military encourages a contradictory mix of intense group solidarity with absolute obedience. When functioning smoothly, groups engage in horizontally solidaristic offensive and defensive actions subordinate to commanding authorities.[1]

"Smoothly functioning" was perhaps the last way we would describe the Vietnam-era military. Over the course of the war, increasing numbers of young men (and some women) did not agree with the mission they were ordered to undertake, and more important, they resisted the efforts made to force them. The disagreement took the form of outspoken dissent or more private doubts; the resistance took multiple forms. The breakdown in the armed forces occurred at all levels—draft and recruitment, basic training, deployment, and combat. In fact, along with the college campus, the military itself must be seen as the other great mobilizing vehicle through which antiwar sentiment was stoked and action un-leashed. According to military historians, close to a quarter of all service personnel participated in the military antiwar movement as soldiers or veterans.[2] One signif-icant aspect of these numbers is that they equaled the peak proportion of student activists and exceeded the percentage of all activism among youth. And another significant aspect of these numbers was the working-class character of the revolt.

Unlike the vast majority of their civilian counterparts, the draftees and sol-diers who resisted the war often did so at serious risk to themselves. The conse-quences of insubordination in the military or disobedience to the laws governing the armed forces were extreme. One small example used by the GI movement un-derscores the differences between participating in the GI and the civilian move-ments: the penalty faced by students for disruptively sitting-in at Sproul Hall on the Berkeley campus was $100, whereas the original sentence of the Presidio 27 soldiers for protesting inhumane treatment in the stockade was 14–16 years hard labor.[3] Challenging military prerogatives as a drafted civilian could lead to an upgrading of one's draft status, arrest, or imprisonment; as a soldier, it could lead to a less-than-honorable discharge or undesirable transfers; and as a mem-ber of a combat unit, it led to retaliatory measures that could end in death or in charges of mutiny that could end likewise. Given the high risks faced by soldiers in revolt, their tactics often resembled the "weapons of the weak" described by James Scott, including "foot dragging, dissimulation, desertion, false compli-ance, pilfering, feigned ignorance, slander, arson, sabotage," an arsenal used in response to conditions in which direct confrontation carries sufficient risks for the protester to militate against it. Scott describes the common aspects of these forms of struggle: "They require little to no coordination or planning; they often represent a form of individual self-help; and they typically avoid any direct sym-bolic confrontation with authority or with elite norms."[4]

But, despite the harsh levels of possible retaliation, the dissent and resistance in and against the military went further than using the "weapons of the weak" to also directly confronting "authority and elite norms." Scott, reflecting on the efficacy of these tactics in peasant communities, concludes that "they are unlikely to do more than marginally affect the forms of exploitation" experienced.[5] Soldiers, however, have access to a completely higher order of leverage. What is remarkable about the "soldiers revolt" is how effective such measures were in achieving both their goals of self-help and their antiwar goals—their rebellion was so successful that the military changed its internal organization as well as its war strategy in response. At the end of the war and in the following years, the US military was substantially reorganized to forestall the occurrence of another such breakdown. And military commanders advised civilian leaders to avoid committing US forces to any en-gagements whose mission might incur large-scale resistance among the troops.

Statistics compiled by David Cortright in the immediate aftermath of the Paris Peace Accords, together with those collected later by other scholars and the army itself, present an incredible picture of the breakdown of the armed forces in the last years of the war. Yet this history may be the least-told story about the Vietnam War. With only one exception, none of the history textbooks I surveyed (see chapter 1) even alludes to this breakdown; the one that does, Alan Brinkley's *The Unfinished Nation,* very briefly mentions it in a paragraph whose main focus is the "deterioration" of "morale and discipline" typified by the My Lai massacre and subsequent conviction of William Calley, the officer in charge at My Lai. Brinkley concludes this paragraph by saying, "Less publicized were other, more widespread problems among American troops in Vietnam: desertion, drug addiction, racial bias, refusal to obey orders, even the killing of unpopular officers by enlisted men." In highlighting My Lai, Brinkley accurately touches on the most famous instance of the perceived problems with the US military, but by pairing the indiscriminate killing of Vietnamese civilians with soldiers' refusal to kill Vietnamese or obey military commands—forms of disobedience linking all the "problems" he lists, except "racial bias"—he obscures the story of the soldiers' resistance.[6]

David Cortright's *Soldiers in Revolt* (1975) places the problems listed by Brinkley in a context appreciated by the military leadership itself during the war—the breakdown of the armed forces. Marine Colonel Robert Heinl argued in 1971 in the *Armed Forces Journal* that "the morale, discipline and battle-worthiness of the US armed forces are, with a few salient exceptions, lower and worse than at any time in this century and possibly in the history of the United States."[7] Over the course of the war 27 million men came of draft age, and 40 percent of them served in the military. Of that group, one-quarter—2.5 million—served in Vietnam; they were joined by another half million older soldiers, for a total of nearly 3 million men serving in Southeast Asia during hostilities. Active-duty military strength peaked at close to 4 million in 1969 and had fallen to 2.2 million by the end of the war, whereas the largest number of soldiers deployed to Vietnam reached close to half a million in 1968. Alongside these large numbers are extraordinary rates of resistance to service, creating what Cortright describes as a "manpower crisis" whose roots were "unprecedented opposition to military service among young people."[8]

College, draft-exempt occupations, and graduate school were the first line of defense for more affluent young men, along with service in the National Guard. After receiving draft notices, millions of US men were successfully exempted or deferred, or successfully sought methods of disqualification—think of the famous stories of drastic weight loss, feigned psychiatric illnesses, "phantom disabilities," and other means of escaping the eligible classification. Others legally refused. Conscientious objection began as a rare and difficult-to-obtain status; but after prolonged movement pressure, the Supreme Court considerably expanded the conscientious objector guidelines. During the last three years of the military draft, almost 145,000 people successfully obtained conscientious objector status, with a one-year record in 1971 of 61,000. In 1972, amid full "Vietnamization" and with the war in its final stages, there were more conscientious objectors than draftees. In addition, tens of thousands overtly refused induction, facing (although, as a result of pressure by the moment, infrequently serving) jail time for their resistance. Many early draft resisters had asked the question, "What if you called a war and no one came?" By the end of the US war in Southeast Asia, that question was becoming more than a coy slogan.[9]

Working-class men did not participate in self-proclaimed draft avoidance and refusal at nearly the same rate as their middle-class peers. The most important reason for this was the class bias of the Selective Service System itself, which made draft avoidance for those enrolled in higher education and those in high-skill occupations relatively easy for the first and heaviest years of the draft. Graduate school exemptions were sharply restricted in 1967, college deferments became more rigorous as draft calls increased, and a lottery system was introduced at the end of 1969 that was more democratic (although college deferments did not end until 1971). Regardless, altogether "millions of men used college deferments to postpone their confrontations with the draft."[10] When the laws changed, deferments expired, or low lottery numbers were unluckily assigned, middle-class draft-age men were still significantly more likely to get and accept the kind of counseling, medical, and legal representation that nearly assured them a way out of the draft. Similarly, applications for conscientious objector status were lengthy and difficult, which made it easier for teenagers with access to educated parents or lawyers to obtain but nearly beyond the reach of working-class and poor draftees. The strategies and tactical decisions of the movement itself sometimes counteracted this middle-class bias, but in other cases they reinforced it.

Another reason for a lesser degree of draft avoidance among working-class youth, particularly through 1968 when the draft calls were running 30,000–40,000 a month, was the particular social context of the call. Historian Christian Appy observes, "[Middle-class men] wrestled with the moral dilemma of whether or not to avoid the draft, but most working-class draftees did not see the matter as open to debate. For them, the draft notice represented an order, not a dilemma."[11] Then, like today, the armed forces offered opportunities for advancement and security, an economic "pull" for poor and working-class youth that helps account for both their voluntary enlistment and straightforward acceptance of the draft.[12] The inferior deployment options of draftees served as a "push" for many young men to enlist, as did not infrequent bartering with law enforcement officials:

picked up for minor infractions of the law, many were offered jail time or enlistment, and opted for the latter.[13] For many, seeking a way to avoid the draft would betray their family and friends who had served or were serving. As a medical professional who assisted draft evaders explained, "The people we saw were all middle class. It wasn't that the others didn't have the money. They just never thought of going for professional help." In their book on the draft, *Chance and Circumstance*, Lawrence Baskir and William Strauss point out that "even at the draft-counseling medical clinic of predominantly black Fisk University, walk-ins were overwhelmingly well-educated, middle-class whites."[14] Political resistance, however, had greater ideological traction in working-class communities of color than in white communities. As previously noted, draft resistance was advocated by the Mississippi Freedom Democratic Party as early as 1965, and SNCC, the Panthers, and Afrocentric nationalist organizations were united in the slogan, "Hell No, We Won't Go." In 1970, Mexican American mothers embraced their own slogan, "I'd rather have my sons die for La Raza than in Vietnam."[15]

Early efforts to increase draft avoidance and overt resistance among working-class youth were only marginally successful. The Boston Draft Resistance Group made some headway in 1967–1969, as did groups such as the Wisconsin Draft Resistance Union.[16] These groups made efforts to coach draftees in avoidance tactics or in pursuing conscientious objector status in addition to, or in lieu of, overtly taking the political (and illegal) stand of resistance. But, even though they participated less frequently in official resistance and avoidance strategies, working-class youth explicitly embraced other forms of resistance and delinquency for the duration of the war. From the beginning, nonregistrants and deserters were "disproportionately black, poorly educated youth from low-income families," whereas draft delinquents were from varied class backgrounds.[17] By the end of the war, over 200,000 men were no-shows—reported as "delinquent" by the Selective Service to the Justice Department. The government, in addition, estimates that 360,000 men were never formally accused. In Oakland, California, "50 per cent of those called failed to report, and 11 per cent of those that did show refused induction" during the six months of October 1969 to March 1970.[18] Another way to get out of the draft was to fail to register for it. In small towns, draft boards used high school yearbooks to ensure compliance, making noncompliance quite difficult for many rural youth. White middle-class children were likely to be informed of and intimidated by the risks involved in noncompliance with the Selective Service, which included prison and risks affecting future employment. The same was not true for those who were more anonymous or invisible to their draft boards or whose future careers did not predictably hinge on compliance with the Selective Service laws. According to Baskir and Strauss's survey, "almost half the non-registrants were black, and most had low incomes and little education." Furthermore, nonregistrants were clearly influenced by the mood against the war; the survey also found "that almost all black non-registration offences occurred during the latter half of the war." They conclude, "Apparently, rising black consciousness and the plight of black veterans made many inner-city youths reluctant to join the military." Of the over 1,800 convicted draft resisters whose cases were reviewed by the Clemency Board in 1975, "an unexpectedly large percentage came from economically disadvantaged backgrounds."[19]

Yet millions of men were successfully drafted, and the majority of them were from poor and working-class backgrounds. Surveys of volunteers reported that nearly one-half were "draft motivated," and of the soldiers who served in Vietnam over the course of the war, one-third were true volunteers, one-third were draft-motivated volunteers, and the last third were simply drafted. Over the course of the war, draftees were increasingly sent to Vietnam over those who enlisted and were increasingly used in combat.[20]

Unsurprisingly, it was only after becoming part of the military that many young men desired to escape it, either out of antipathy for the military itself, for the war, or both. Over a million and a half incidences of absenteeism (being AWOL) were recorded over the course of the war, a half million of which became official desertions. According to all studies done, deserters were significantly more likely to be from working- or lower-class backgrounds and were also more likely to come from rural backgrounds. This was the case in the larger deserter communities in Sweden and Canada as well.[21] The rate of desertion in Vietnam was higher than that during World War II and three times the rate during the Korean War—and World War II desertions generally took place under fire, whereas the opposite was true in Vietnam; the desertions mostly occurred before soldiers were shipped overseas. Stateside AWOL cases were an early inspiration for the GI movement. For example, in 1968 a guard in the Presidio stockade in San Francisco killed a prisoner who was being held for having gone AWOL. The other prisoners "tore it apart," and charges of mutiny were brought against this group, which came to be known as the Presidio 27. These soldiers found mass support from the local antiwar movement, including solidarity demonstrations of thousands at the gates of the army base, marking a major development in the growing alliance between antiwar GIs and civilians.

These record levels of avoidance and desertion convey part of the instability created by an unwilling populace and army during Vietnam. But, ultimately, much of the fight against the war in the military took place by those actually fighting the war or getting ready to do so. The army contracted two reports in 1970 and 1971 to study this unrest, finding that 37 percent of the soldiers surveyed had engaged in either "dissent" or "disobedience," with a third having done so repeatedly—figures that do not include drug use.[22] Dissent was understood as being typical movement-style participation: attending a demonstration, working on the GI press, or spending time at a GI coffeehouse. Disobedience included the more physically resistant acts of sabotage, refusing orders, and general insubordination. The surveys indicated that there was generally a class division between these two kinds of rebellion. The more educated and middle-class soldiers engaged in dissent; the more working-class and less educated soldiers engaged in disobedience. Reviewing similar data, John Helmer argues that "defiance of the military system was predominantly the working-class soldier's protest, and that it is at least as high in numerical terms as the level of resistance to the war expressed as draft resistance by middle-class youth at home."[23]

The *GI Movement* usually refers to the organized, dissenting types of actions and organizations that proliferated in the latter half of the war on and near military bases in the United States and abroad. The constraints on such efforts were vast, of course; leaders were constantly being transferred, papers confiscated, meetings busted up, and activists harassed. Some of the relative stability and continuity within the GI movement can be traced to its connections to the civilian movement, most notably in the form of GI coffeehouses, which started with the openings of the UFO in late 1967 near Fort Jackson, South Carolina, and the Oleo Strut near Fort Hood, Texas. GI coffeehouses were founded and staffed by civilian antiwar activists, and they became places where soldiers could read the GI antiwar press and talk politics—but also just hang out, listen to music, and escape army life. Coffeehouses were also places where returning soldiers could talk to departing soldiers, giving them the "real story" of the war that they were not going to hear from the brass; Dave Cline, Veterans for Peace activist, described the roles played by these veteran soldiers as "subversive."[24] A pamphlet distributed in 1970, "Free the Fort Ord 40,000," described the multilayered functions of the coffeehouses:

> It was crucial to find a way of countering the attempt of the military to isolate GI's from the "real" civilian world—a world which was and still is a serious threat to maintaining a "disciplined" army. At the coffeehouse a GI could talk to people about their experiences in Nam and their lives in the military, they could eat good food, and essentially reinstate their identity as human beings after a day of mowing lawns with razorblades for punishment, or of practicing on the rifle range where a 40 foot billboard taunts them with the orders to "kill, kill, kill."[25]

By 1969 the coffeehouses were themselves the target of government repression and other attacks, with arrests, closures, and raids becoming more common, and, in one case, a firebombing.[26]

GIs created dozens of their own organizations, such as the American Serviceman's Union (started 1967), the United States Serviceman's Fund (1969),

GIs United Against the War in Vietnam (1969), the Movement for a Democratic Military (1968), and the Black Brothers Union (1971). These organizations were directly linked to the civilian movement (through the coffeehouses, movement organizations, or organized leftist groups) and served a variety of functions, ranging from fund-raising to political mobilization and agitation and from providing legal advice to organizing entertainment and cultural events for soldiers on bases around the country. The most successful and well known of these events were the Free the Army tours with luminaries such as Jane Fonda, Dick Gregory, and Donald Sutherland, who helped to lead what amounted to an anti–Bob Hope, anti-USO act that played at bases around the country and the world ("Fun, Travel and Adventure" was the army recruitment slogan that Free the Army played off of; "F*#% the Army" was another frequently used slogan). As reported in a GI paper *Camp News*, in one sketch performed in Fayetteville, North Carolina in 1970, "Mrs. Nixon, in flowered hat, tells the-President that dissidents are storming the White House demanding an end to the war. 'You'd better call the 82d Airborne,' he replies. 'But you don't understand, Richard. This IS the 82d Airborne.'"[27]

There were also officers who organized against the war, such as the Concerned Officers Movement, and as the years went on, navy and air force chapters of antiwar organizations were started as well.[28] Two thousand overseas GIs joined Vietnam Veterans Against the War (VVAW) before their return (and VVAW office workers remember their sadness at getting their correspondence returned, unopened, stamped "person deceased"), and thousands of others stayed active through the GI movement after their return.[29] The GI press was run from the bases and the nearby coffeehouses, and represented GI organizations or just particular locales, including many from bases abroad. It totaled at least three hundred individual papers, some of which—such as *Vietnam GI*, *The Bond*, *Veteran Stars and Stripes for Peace*, *Bragg Briefs*, and *FTA*—had nationwide readerships and circulations that went from the thousands to the tens of thousands.

The draft resistance movement itself had "strong relations with servicemen and veterans" years before many of these organizations came to be.[30] By fall 1968, the New England Resistance was focusing on GI outreach and creating sanctuaries for men who had gone AWOL. Deserters were aided by official and unofficial underground railroads of sorts, which helped bring men to Canada, establish them in new identities, or facilitate their own underground existence in the United States.

Resistance Overseas

Cortright argues that "for soldiers already in the combat zone, there was little point in anti-war protest action. Opposition to the war was not a matter of politics but of survival; signing petitions or attending rallies was less important than simply avoiding personal injury."[31] Many men took the perspective that they would get through the fighting and fight against the war when they got home. A few typical protest actions did occur overseas over the course of the war, including demonstrations, picketing, and one known rally; petitions that were circulated and publicized; and leafleting. But survival and resistance were the foci of antiwar GIs in Vietnam.

Direct disobedience started early in the war, but it grew much more slowly than the stateside GI movement. Some early cases, such as Howard Levy (a doctor who refused orders to continue training others in Vietnam) and the Fort Hood Three (who refused to depart for war), garnered a lot of attention, but these were seen as isolated events. Similarly, in the front lines of Vietnam itself, combat refusals began quietly and sporadically. In 1969, when platoon Sergeant Bill Short refused to continue providing "the body count" to his superiors, he did so ignorant of the extent of the opposition that had already begun in the armed forces, and he was shocked to find out he was not alone. But from 1969 onward, through the GI press and the infusion of movement-aware servicemen into the ranks, an increasing number of soldiers were aware of the resistance of others.[32]

"Ghosting," or "half-stepping," involved fabricating an illness, a death in the family, or another appropriate excuse to leave the front lines. Christian Appy explains that the problem with this form of combat avoidance was that it left fellow soldiers facing the battle, and it was therefore condemned or discouraged by peers. But other, more collective forms of avoidance caught on. Early on, in 1968, "sandbagging" was common, in which soldiers would "search and evade," rather than "search and destroy," or otherwise duck the (often suicidal) missions on which they were ordered.[33] One veteran, recalling such orders and the officers who made them, remembers, "we really were lower than whale shit at the bottom of the ocean to those people."[34] Soldiers and officers commonly "worked out" the orders that came in to minimize confrontation and casualties. An infantry officer in Vietnam told Marine Colonel Heinl, "You can't give them an order and expect them to obey immediately. . . . [T]hey ask why, and you have to tell them."[35] In a sense, the military chain of command was replaced by a consensus process; the most authoritarian of institutions made a bit democratic. This practice was common enough—Heinl called it "virtually a principle"—that it was widely reported and was even broadcast as part of a news segment on *ABC* in 1970.[36] A necessary correlate of this practice, therefore, was that there was no guarantee the men would fight. Large-scale mutinies did occur, with only some reported, when "working it out" failed or was not an option. Cortright details a dozen cases of mass mutiny in the army and describes them as "the tip of the iceberg."[37] For example, several troops and companies refused to invade Cambodia and Laos, and their reluctance in the latter case in particular may have cut short operations. The mutinies that were reported in 1969, 1970, and 1971 received almost no retribution, even though such actions were technically punishable by death.[38]

Another similarly high-stakes form of disobedience was "fragging," in which enlisted men attempted to kill, or did kill, their officers. (The term is derived from the use of fragmentation grenades in many such incidents.)[39] Heinl, again, reports: "Word of the deaths of officers will bring cheers at troop movies or in bivouacs of certain units. In one such division—the morale plagued Americal— fraggings during 1971 have been authoritatively estimated to be running about one a week."[40] Given the widespread availability of guns and the chaos of combat conditions, it is likely that thousands of officers were attacked by their own men over the course of the war, with at least hundreds of resulting deaths. In a radio interview in 2000, Terry Anderson, historian and Vietnam veteran, explained, "During the years of 1969 down to 1973, we have the rise of fragging—that is, shooting or hand-grenading your NCO or your officer who orders you out into the field. The US Army itself does not know exactly how many . . . officers were murdered. But they know at least 600 were murdered, and then they have another 1400 that died mysteriously."[41] It was not uncommon for companies to place bounties on the heads of particularly hated officers, which were awarded to the soldier who did the deed. In the last years of the ground war, the "lifers"—a derisive term used by the troops for career military officers—were locking up the guns to make sure that the regular soldiers could not kill them. That is, they were taking guns away from men who were supposed to be fighting a war.[42]

Although men of all races and backgrounds participated in the soldier's revolt, the disruption caused by African American soldiers stands out. In 1969–1970, Wallace Terry surveyed and interviewed hundreds of African American and white soldiers about their attitudes toward the war and the movements at home, comparing the results to earlier interviews he had conducted in 1967. The soldiers, he found, had dramatically radicalized in the intervening years. "A large majority of enlisted men agreed that black people should not fight in Vietnam because they have problems of discrimination at home." More than half, again, believed the war to be a "race war." He found that 45 percent of the black soldiers, compared to 15 percent of the whites, thought that the war should end immediately and that 40 percent of blacks believed that Vietnam was a civil war in which the United States had no place. In other words, among enlisted African Americans fighting in Vietnam, support for immediate withdrawal exceeded the sentiment at home, and some of the main arguments of the movement found an audience with nearly half of the group. It is not surprising, therefore, that Terry

also found that a majority of enlisted African Americans supported antiwar protest at home, either through the more moderate "they have a right to protest" line
or more outright positive support.[43]

This relatively greater degree of disagreement with the war and overt resistance among African American soldiers was understandable. These soldiers came
to Vietnam having witnessed (or even participated in) the civil rights movement
and the ghetto uprisings of 1965–1968, having seen most of the leaders of the
black movement embrace antiwar positions, and having heard about the early
high casualty rates among their brothers on the home front only to then find
themselves fighting within an oppressive military system. Growing antiwar feeling meant that African American reenlistment rates—as high as two-thirds in
1966—dropped to half that in 1968.[44] Evasion and desertion rates went through
the roof. African American protest over unequal treatment in the armed forces
escalated in tandem with antiwar sentiment. For example, on July 4, 1970, in
Heidelberg Germany, a meeting of (mostly) black soldiers drew 1,000 participants. The demands of the group included equal promotions and family housing for all black GIs, a committee of enlisted men which could veto sending any
GI to the stockade, college preparatory classes for all GIs, and the immediate
withdrawal of all US forces from Southeast Asia and all US forces from Africa.[45]

In Vietnam, their nationalism and militancy made many African American
soldiers the least trustworthy group on the front lines from the perspective of the
brass. The unreliability of these soldiers meant they were pulled out of the fighting (i.e., blacks received fewer front-line duties), and, subsequently, the casualty
rate fell from 25 percent black soldiers in 1965, to 13 percent in 1968, and to
7.6 percent in 1972.[46] Black soldiers' fighting against racist treatment and refusing to obey orders meant that there was often open warfare between the troops
in Vietnam, destabilizing the war effort. Black resistance in the armed forces
had direct repercussions on the home front as well. In August 1968, African
American National Guard units at Ft. Hood refused to go to Chicago to police
the Democratic Convention, and their rebellion sparked a greater protest, such
that the cherry-picked troops who were eventually sent from Texas to Chicago
were not actually deployed at the protests because it was not clear which side
they would fight on.[47]

Heinl wrote, "Nowhere, however, in the history of the Armed Forces have
comparable past troubles presented themselves in such general magnitude,
acuteness, or concentrated focus as today." Historians and participants in the
GI movement conclude that the mutinous conditions of the army as a whole
made it impossible for the brass to fight the kind of war they wanted to fight.
Antiwar veterans frequently refer to the "genocidal" plans of the United States,
an assessment they reached through their participation and observation of the

"bloodbath" in Vietnam. Their refusal to continue such participation helped to end the draft and arguably expedited the withdrawal of ground troops while the brass intensified the air war in the final years of the war.

During the worst year of decline of the army (1971), Cortright summarizes, "we find seven acts of desertion, seventeen incidents of unauthorized absence, two disciplinary discharges, twelve complaints to congressmen, and eighteen non-judicial punishments for every one hundred soldiers; at the same time, 20 percent of the men smoked marijuana frequently, while 10 percent used narcotics on a regular basis." He concludes, "In an organizational environment requiring intense interpersonal loyalty and a high degree of cooperation, defiance of this magnitude necessarily exerted a profound influence on operational effectiveness. No armed force can function properly when faced with such internal disruption and resistance."[48]

To what extent were these actions of the movement? I argue that we should not separate the actions of the two resistance groups, stateside and front line. The problem with morale in the Vietnam-era military was directly related to the doubts and criticisms that soldiers had concerning their mission, and the problems with the mission were highlighted among the public largely by the actions taken by and educational practices of the antiwar movement. Men in any war receive orders that seem wrong, unclear, or unjust; killing other people is itself exceedingly difficult, with much of military training tailored toward enabling soldiers to overcome their repugnance of such violence.[49] Yet in most wars, most soldiers soldier on, obey orders, and (in modern times) kill the enemy. The sustained attention of the antiwar movement to the overall problems with the war in Vietnam helped soldiers, who were in Vietnam on one-year rotations, connect their own experiences with broader criticisms of the fight. This in turn enabled them to interpret their own disagreements with the war in a less isolating way. As the war progressed and more soldiers rotated in and out of service, the new enlistees and drafted men came from a domestic milieu that was by then saturated with antiwar opinion and unrest. Even when the specific critiques made by the movement were not embraced by the soldiers, the highly visible public debate spearheaded by movement activists opened questions that silence could have helped conceal.

Nevertheless, these antiwar soldiers had an uneasy and sometimes hostile reaction to the antiwar movement itself. The movement back home protested the war "at a safe and privileged distance." Here, the class identity of the typical soldier clashed with what the soldiers understood as the class identity of the typical antiwarrior—elite students who risked little or nothing in their fight. Christian Appy paraphrases this sentiment: "Our protests against the war are the truly important ones; we are the real hippies; if anyone is going to bring the war to an end it will be grunts like us."[50]

Role of Veterans in the Movement

If there was one section of the official movement that was prototypically work-ing class in composition, culture, and orientation, it was the veteran's movement. John Helmer cites a 1969 Nielson study of veterans that found that only 10 per-cent supported the purpose and tactics of the war they had just left. The plural-ity, 44 percent, said it was a mistake, with another 40 percent saying it had been fought the wrong way.[51] The extent that these antiwar sentiments were translated into action was exemplified in the organization Vietnam Veterans Against the War. This group, which grew to 30,000 active members by the end of the war, pro-vides a template for what to do right if you want an active working-class base for a social movement organization and for how to make working-class audiences take you seriously. VVAW, although never completely comfortable inside the main-stream movement, served as a critical bridge linking veterans, active GIs, and the organized protests of the mass movement. Perhaps more important, their protests reached the hearts of the general public in a way that no civilian protest ever succeeded in doing. In 1971, the day before the largest antiwar demonstra-tion of the war, hundreds of VVAW members spent hours lining up by the steps of the US Capitol building in Washington, D.C., and one by one (and then later in groups) throwing their medals back at the government that had issued them. This scene, broadcast on the major networks, is one of the most remembered of the era, and it came to define the tragedy and waste of the war for a generation.

As Christian Appy has documented, Vietnam was a working-class war. Close to 80 percent of the soldiers who fought in the war were from working- or lower-class families. The antiwar veterans did not have to go to the working class to recruit—they were already there. VVAW members came to their political and moral stances against the war through the experience of going through it, and having gone through that hell, veterans had an authority in the movement un-matched by any other group. Turning on a war in which they had lost friends, health, and peace of mind involved higher stakes, greater courage, and more commitment than other movement participants had. In 1971, as the organized movement elsewhere faltered, VVAW emerged as the most influential—as one of its historians writes, "venerated"—organization against the war. It "filled a leadership vacuum."[52]

VVAW got its first start at the April 1967 Spring Mobilization to End the War in New York City, in which six veterans marched behind a ready-made banner, Vietnam Veterans Against the War. (Apocryphally, the banner had been prepared by the Communist Party, ready for anyone to pick up at the parade offices.) Members trickled in to the nascent organization through word of mouth, put out through the hard work of veterans such as Jan Barry, who helped to lead and sustain VVAW in its early years.[53] The initial base of the organization was veterans who had entered colleges on the GI Bill. Although reports of protester hostility were wildly (and widely) exaggerated, some early movement activists did call the veterans "baby killers" and insult them. For this reason and others, the antiwar veterans in VVAW were distrustful of the radical end of the antiwar movement and did not want their outreach to be associated with it. They dressed in a conservative fashion to distinguish themselves from the counterculture, and they undertook milder educational antiwar work. When VVAW first began, its then mostly middle-class members organized themselves as a speakers' bureau for veterans to talk to groups in schools, hospitals, and other gatherings about why they opposed the war. Like many in the movement, the election of 1968 became the main VVAW focus in that year, and presidential politics split the veterans' movement. Some of the newer members, such as Jeff Sharlet, editor of *Vietnam GI* and close to SDS in politics, advocated more radical anti-electoral actions. Most antiwar veterans supported Eugene McCarthy, and a number left VVAW to work on his campaign. VVAW organized antiwar veterans in every state to lobby Chicago-convention delegates to adopt an antiwar plank in the Democratic Party platform. Their failure to achieve this, combined with the other events in Chicago (see chapter 7) and the election of President Nixon, was demoralizing for the veterans along with many other factions of the movement, which together entered a period of relative quiet the following year.

This was VVAW, phase one. Its more moderate politics reflected the educational aspirations of its college-based demographic as well as the anticounterculture suspicions of the group as a whole. But the organization changed dramatically after its growth spurts following the Moratorium of 1969 and the Kent State killings of 1970. In its later incarnation, the majority of VVAW members were from working-class backgrounds both inside and outside college. Yale graduate and future United States Senator John Kerry emerged for a few months in 1971 as the nationwide spokesperson of the group, but his patrician background was exceptional (and cause for much internal consternation). VVAW members who participated in the events of the Dewey Canyon III action—which included Kerry's renowned testimony before Congress, extensive antiwar lobbying, an encampment on the Washington Mall, and the televised return of medals to the Capitol—were surveyed during their week-long stay in Washington. In the results, published in the VVAW book *The New Soldier*, over three-quarters of the men described their families (indexed by the father's occupation) as working class.[54]

The VVAW shifted its orientation from education to addressing problems immediately pertinent to their members' and other veterans' lives. The members protested conditions at veterans' hospitals (which became a major recruiting ground for the group). They exposed atrocities they had witnessed and participated in during the war (in events such as the Winter Soldier Investigation of December 1970), and they helped each other with their memories and the experience of post-traumatic stress disorder (PTSD). VVAW pioneered the first "rap groups," peer counseling sessions that were reproduced across the country by psychologists such as Robert Jay Lifton for the rest of the decade because of their effectiveness. They turned their public statements, organizing, and protest pressure to the problems of joblessness among returning soldiers. Decisions made about where to locate VVAW actions reflected the base the members hoped to reach. For example, the Winter Soldier Investigation, at which over 100 veterans testified about war crimes, was held in Detroit instead of the more obvious choice of Washington, D.C., to reach the working-class Detroit audience; the major New York event in June 1971 in was in Prospect Park, Brooklyn, instead of Central Park in Manhattan, the movement center; and the first New York–based store-fronts for "rap sessions" and draft counseling were set up along working-class Fifth Avenue in Brooklyn.

Whereas other groups engaged in "pig-baiting" police officers, before their major protests VVAW members wrote letters to the police (many of whom were veterans like themselves because veterans were given incentives to join the force). Before Dewey Canyon III, they wrote to the Washington, D.C., police department:

> The violence of Vietnam is something we vets understand because we were the ones who performed that violence. And, having that experience, we are totally committed to non-violence in our actions. We have been through one war and we don't want another one. So, we are writing this letter to you, the "pig", the "cop", the "bull", because we understand what it is like to wear a uniform. We understand what it is like to wear a gun and be placed in situation where there is paranoia and fear. We understand these things and we want to reassure you that we do not want to place you in that position.[55]

VVAW had almost no trouble with the police in Washington, D.C., despite the fact that they were camping on the mall without a permit for doing so; the threatened mass arrests never occurred, with police from top to bottom refusing or evading orders to clear the encampment. In a similar letter to National Guardsmen before the 1972 Republican National Convention, VVAW members wrote, "if they call you down to Miami, don't worry, we won't consider you the pigs. We know who the pigs are—lifers, politicians, and big business men."[56] Unfortunately, the veterans did not fare as well with the military and civil security dispatched at the convention—they were gassed and arrested by the dozens.

One story, related in a history of VVAW, indicates the counterintuitive alliances made possible in a movement organization working close to the ground in working class communities. Among the many government infiltrators dispatched during the war years to gather information about and to derail the movement was a former air force medic named John O'Connor, who had joined the Washington, D.C., police department on his return from the war and who was immediately assigned to infiltrate the newly formed National Peace Action Coalition in spring 1970. He told Andrew Hunt, VVAW historian, that he generally disliked the activists he met and that he "cheered the hardhats when they smacked them around" that May. Working in the office, he met VVAW organizers, who asked him to help out with their work. O'Connor's attitude shifted: "These guys were different. They had paid their dues. They earned the right to say what they were saying. And they were good guys. It was interesting to hear their story. I started to have different outlook on the war." O'Connor moved in with some of the VVAW guys and later reported that "we were the core of the [D.C. VVAW]." O'Connor continued to report to the police, but he also provided "invaluable" support for the organizing of Dewey Canyon III. One of his housemates, a VVAW organizer named Tim Butz, later told Hunt, "Contrary to the image of a police officer as an agent provocateur, John. . . . really helped lessen the tension, and did whatever was asked of him. He could've fucked us up good on several occasions, and he didn't do it."[57]

VVAW, according to Mary Treadwell, former activist, was "[o]ne of the few white antiwar groups that backed up its words with actions" and that gave "active support" to "black peoples struggles against repression."[58] Treadwell is referring here, in part, to the Cairo Campaign that VVAW embarked on in 1971 in the immediate aftermath of Dewey Canyon III. VVAW gave direct support to the besieged African American community of Cairo, Illinois, whose boycott of white-owned businesses had provoked a murderous response from the white townspeople. The VVAW Lifeline to Cairo collected food and supplies from all over the country and delivered them to the town. Echoing the black and Chicano organizers of the period, one VVAW leader said, "The government of this country has . . . [said] that we are fighting for freedom and equality and self-determination for the Vietnamese, and yet here in our own country people are denied that right and are involved in a struggle to obtain that right." Many in VVAW were "making the connection" among the war, racism, sexism, and the economy, following the same general radicalization that was occurring in the movement as a whole. VVAW publications, such as *First Casualty*, had articles that went beyond strictly military concerns. Women's rights, housing, education, and health care were some of the topics broached in their writings.[59]

In an interview with historian Richard Moser, Ben Chitty, VVAW organizer (and former petty officer aboard the *USS Richmond K. Turner*[60]) provides this analysis of the impact of the veteran's movement:

The most common charge leveled against the antiwar movement is that it was composed of cowards and draft dodgers. To have in it people who had served in the military . . . who were in fact patriots by the pro-war folks' own definition, was a tremendous thing. VVAW in 1970 and 1971 was unlike almost anything I'd seen in terms of its impact on the public. . . . We took away more and more of the symbolic and rhetorical tools available to the pro-war folks—just gradually squeezed them into the corner. . . . We took away little by little the response people had not to listen to the antiwar movement.[61]

VVAW was also not immune to the fractures that plagued the movement as a whole, although its real dissolution occurred after the Paris Peace Accords of 1973. But during its three years at the center of the antiwar movement, VVAW, like the Chicano moratoriums, showed the possibility for reaching and retaining a committed mass of working-class Americans in the antiwar movement. The primary identity of these activists was not working class, but neither was their class identity subsumed or negated by their identities of Chicana, veteran, soldier, and so on. Rather, their experiences as working-class people directly contributed to their opposition to the war, and their opposition to the war was in turn understood through their particular class-based experiences. These groups provide a model for what an antiwar movement based in working-class issues can, and did, look like.

• • •

The October 1969 Moratorium against the war was the largest coordinated nationwide protest in the history of the United States. An estimated 3 million people took part in local actions against the war in hundreds of places around the country. *Life* magazine reported, "It was a display without historical parallel, the largest expression of public dissent ever seen in this country." One organizer convincingly likened it to a "general strike," in that schools, businesses, and even some government offices observed the Moratorium dictate that "business as usual" be suspended so that "students, faculty members and concerned citizens can devote time and energy to the important work of taking the issue of peace in Vietnam to the larger community."[62]

Dozens of cities hosted rallies of tens of thousands of antiwar protesters, nearly all breaking previous records for any kind of demonstrating. Church bells tolled regularly throughout the day; religious organizations across the country passed resolutions in support of the peace efforts, such as the 2 million–member United Church of Christ, which found the war to be "destroying the spiritual, moral, physical and economic health" of the United States; and the National Cathedral in Washington, D.C., offered prayers for peace at every hour. All over the country, schools emptied and colleges were shut down. In New York City, the Board of Education estimated that 90 percent of high school students and 75 percent of junior high and elementary school students were absent that day. The Moratorium was endorsed by the UAW and the United Farmworkers, as well as the Steelworkers, Teamsters, Chemical Workers, and hundreds more union locals around the nation. United Electrical members in Paterson, New Jersey, called for an end to the war even though their company made bulletproof vests and body bags for the US military. Endorsers ranged from dozens of US senators and representatives to the Americans for Democratic Action, National Welfare Rights Organization, NAACP, and National Urban League. In the case of these last two, both of which had been very close to the Johnson administration, this was the first public antiwar stance they had taken. It took place during the fourth game of the World Series, and Tom Seaver, New York Mets starting pitcher, told Jimmy Breslin, "If the Mets can get to the World Series, the US can get out of Vietnam." The Moratorium exercise in quiet, peaceful, and local antiwar protest demonstrated to the nation how widespread and normal opposition to the war had become, as well as the potential for regular people to be at the forefront of the movement.[63]

One month later, on November 15, the largest single demonstration in the history of the country to that time took place in Washington, D.C., under the auspices of the New Mobilization Committee to End the War in Vietnam (the "New Mobe"). Crowd estimates ranged from one half to 1 million participants, with another quarter or half million assembling in San Francisco. In Washington, D.C., 40,000 individuals participated in a March of Death, which for 40 hours, through often inclement weather, marched single file from Arlington Cemetery to the front of the White House, where one by one the marchers spoke the name of a US soldier who had been killed in Vietnam. The demonstration included speakers such as Dick Gregory, who told the crowd, "The President says nothing you kids do will have any effect on him. Well, I suggest that he make one long distance call to the LBJ ranch and ask that boy how much effect you can have on him."[64]

The movement had spread considerably from the campuses. GI coffeehouses had been set up near dozens of bases. In the days prior to the Mobilization, 1,365 active GIs, including nearly 200 who were stationed in Vietnam, had signed a public letter published in the *New York Times* urging that soldiers support the demonstration. In Oceanside, California, 1,000 marines marched in their own military moratorium on December 14, 1969, and similar actions took place around the country.[65] Vietnam Veterans Against the War was being sought out by returning soldiers. Since the Tet offensive in January 1968, support for the war had entered terminal decline. The potential for mass mobilization appeared great.

Beginning of the End?

Yet the 1969 Moratorium and Mobilization are often seen, in retrospect, as the last great events of the antiwar movement. As David Dellinger told historian Tom Wells, "That's when things did begin to fall apart. . . . That was the beginning of the end." Melvin Small writes, "The antiwar movement peaked in the fall of 1969." As Small and others explain, many more significant protest events were still to come, including the nationwide college strikes of May 1970 and the second largest demonstration in US history in April 1971 (featuring the VVAW Dewey Canyon III exercises). But to the extent that the antiwar movement had been able to attain some degree of *organizational* cohesiveness and focus, that level of organization and identity deteriorated in the years following 1969.[66]

Within the organized movement, internal disagreements among the various factions, which had haunted the direction of the movement from its outset, were boiling over. Under the auspices of the "Mobes," the tactical directions, political content, and organization of the large events had represented an uneasy alliance among liberals, radicals, and leftist groups, all of which felt continually compromised in their visions of the best way forward for the movement. This fractious coalition came together and came apart, and it would only be partially in jest to say that they spent as much time arguing with each other as they spent recruiting others to the movement. The other leading group that emerged that year, the Vietnam Moratorium Committee, represented a liberal wing of the movement, which at the organizer level consisted, for the most part, of former staffers and supporters of Eugene McCarthy and Robert Kennedy.

In April 1970, two weeks before the invasion of Cambodia, the Moratorium closed shop. The "New Mobe" called its final rally the week of May 8, 1970. The various groups of the "Mobe" then split to form the National Peace Action Coalition and the National Coalition Against War, Racism, and Repression, which later reconstituted itself as the People's Coalition for Peace and Justice. Although these groups collaborated on future events, the organized movement had effectively splintered.[67]

The troubling recurring questions for organizers and their organizations were: What would the movement do? What power did it have? And was it actually stopping the war? By the end of 1969, many of the leading activists and some of the newer organizers were discouraged and felt they were not making a difference. Burnout became a real problem. Old arguments about tactics were refreshed. Big demonstrations were seen by the newly constituted radical caucus of the Mobilization as "gathering[s] in the park" or by liberals as "a political fad that has worn off," as a Morartorium leader told the *New York Times* on April 20, 1970. Electoral work continued to make sense to many liberals, whereas radicals argued that direct action was the best way forward. Direct action was, in turn, seen by others, such as members of the SWP, as alienating the larger audience that the movement was seemingly beginning to reach. Still others countered that an exclusive focus on the war was tamping the capacity of the movement to extend its reach to the black movement and the other movements of oppressed peoples. But, countered the SWP and others, losing the focus on the war would confuse and demobilize the growing numbers of people who were against it. The radicals argued, you are failing to seize the momentum of the movement, or to see the generalized radicalism in US culture. In response, those more inclined to maintaining a war focus fumed, but you are raising the threshold to action so high that you will get too far ahead of the people turning against the war. The radicals countered, compromising your political vision means failure; "They think that numbers will be enough," Angela Davis remarked, disbelievingly.[68] In short, antiwar work was increasingly viewed by many in the movement as insufficient by itself to either address the problems of US society or end the war, whereas for others a single-issue focus on the war was the only possible way for the movement to grow and make a difference. Along these real fault lines, the movement came closer and closer to fracture.[69] Ultimately, fall 1969 marked the end of the period in which the groups representing all these different positions worked together with any real degree of productivity for a sustained period.

The break-up of SDS was emblematic of this period of radical fragmentation, and it bore directly on the perceptions that the media and general public developed about the class nature of the movement during this period. The SDS central leadership had long before abandoned antiwar organizing as a main focus, having relinquished its lead role as early as 1965 and disbanded most of its antidraft work by early 1968. Its early leaders had moved on. In March 1968, Carl Ogelesby successfully argued that SDS had done all it could to end the war and that black liberation should be its first priority.[70] In an unironic description of the winter 1968 national SDS meeting, Carl Davidson, former SDS national secretary, then of the *Guardian*, wrote in the January 11, 1969, issue, "The meeting, characterized by intense factionalism and infighting, was considered the best national gathering SDS ever held in its seven year history, according to many experienced participants." He further noted that "among the major motions defeated at the hectic five-day meeting was one calling for support of the antiwar mobilization during the inauguration," which was deemed "too reformist" by the majority of participants.

Yet, for the general public, SDS remained the most visible student organization and, alongside the Student Mobilization Committee (the student wing of the "Mobe," largely led by the SWP), the most prominent student antiwar organization. Fractious infighting in SDS gave rise to the final split in the organization that took place in summer 1969. Emerging from the group was a very small but prominent group that became known as Weatherman. Weatherman included some young people from wealthy families, whose rhetoric was particularly inciting and whose violent tactics (such as bombings) were particularly despised by the mainstream, movement and nonmovement alike. Although they oriented their activities around working-class youth, members of Weatherman appeared to many to be adventurist, ultra-radical, and culturally foreign to the people they believed themselves to be organizing. In March 1970, three members of Weatherman were killed when a bomb they were building exploded in a townhouse in Greenwich Village that was the family home of a member of the group. The radical elitism of this fragment of the movement was widely publicized and tarred the movement as a whole.[71]

In parallel fashion, the press predilection for elite antiwarriors was so entrenched that even the most working-class organization of the later period of the war, VVAW, had as its most nationally prominent figure Lieutenant John Kerry. VVAW faced a bind that many movement groups faced: without celebrity or connections, how could it get the resources or media attention it needed to spread its message? But the media focus on figures such as the Yale-educated and articulate Kerry and Jane Fonda, the main sponsor of the Winter Soldier Investigation, meant that the real base of the group was obscured. In the aftermath of the Dewey Canyon events of April 1971, at which Kerry had testified before Congress, the organization made a conscious decision to work toward its own base of working-class veterans. With "numerous veterans engaged in behind-the-scenes work . . . often aimed at improving conditions for soldiers and other veterans," VVAW lost some of its high public profile.[72]

The Long Arc of the Movement

Despite the organizational fragmentation of the movement, what SDS had discovered at the beginning of the movement still held true: the movement was there whether anyone organized it or not. Hundreds of thousands of people joined the movement in its fractured, varied forms during its final years. The final years of the war saw the rise of the Chicano Moratorium, the unanimous embrace of the antiwar cause by African American groups across the political spectrum, and the rise of the GI and veterans movements. A sizable minority of labor unions, eventually representing a quarter of organized workers, turned against the war and began to actively protest in greater numbers. The actual number of people active in antiwar protest, counting both movement protest in the United States and troop protest abroad, did not peak until 1971. The April 1971 protests against the war in Washington, D.C., and San Francisco were the largest of the era and had wide-ranging sponsorship and participation. The National Welfare Rights Organization, SNCC (now the Student National Coordinating Committee), the Teamsters (which served as marshals) and other unions, the Gay Liberation Front, and dozens of other movement organizations and liberal and community groups joined the march, making it the most politically, racially, and economically diverse of the era.[73]

In chapter 1, we examined the problems with locating the peak of the movement in 1968, as most textbooks do. Locating the end of the movement with the collapse of its leading organizations has similarly limiting effects on the way we remember it. In sheer numbers, more people understood themselves as being part of the antiwar movement in 1971 than in 1969, and more people in 1969 than in 1967, and so on. Much of this antiwar work took place in the context of other movement work, and participants' identities as part of the movement were not crystallized, attached to particular organizations or groups. This was true for black and Chicano antiwar activists, whose organizations had conflicted with the single-issue orientation of the predominantly white organized antiwar movement, instead consistently arguing that racism should be at the center of the antiwar fight. This was true for GIs and veterans, whose opposition to the war was tied up with survival, the problems of the military, and their deeply problematic return to civilian life.

There are advantages to the organization-centered approach. Certainly, it tells us something about the challenges of sustaining political organization. For our purposes, it draws our attention to the fragmentation that contributed to the conditions in which erroneous claims about the nature of antiwar sentiment and movement could take hold. Just as the prototypical representatives of the working class, labor leaders, were unable to capture the multiple political directions in which workers were moving, the "movement," as such, did not exist to counter false claims made about it at the level of political discourse. Its own splintered nature was used as evidence of destructive and antisocial tendencies by its critics (see chapter 7).

Yet the countermemory sketched in previous chapters—the great diversification of the antiwar movement—is eclipsed when only the movement organizations are looked at. Understanding the arc of the movement, its rise and fall, is essential for answering such questions as: Why do movements grow? How do movements sustain themselves? And what are the limits to particular organizational forms or political frames? In the case of the Vietnam antiwar movement, however, the decline of its leading organizations predated the decline of its actual membership and appeal, a fact overlooked in an organization-centered approach. Instead, the last years of the war were marked by a period in which actively opposing the war had become an acceptable part of countless communities in the United States.

Part II

HARDHAT HAWKS?

Working-Class Conservatism

ANTICIPATION OF THE CLASS DIVIDE

**Identities are the names we give to the different ways we are
positioned by, and position ourselves in, the narratives of the past.**

—Stuart Hall, *Identity: Community, Culture, Difference,* 1990

**They call my people the White Lower Middle Class these days. It is
an ugly, ice-cold phrase, the result, I suppose, of the missionary zeal
of those sociologists who still think you can place human beings on
charts.**

—Pete Hamill, "The Revolt of the White Lower Middle Class,"
New York Magazine, 1969

If antiwar sentiment and the class base of the movement were together more
multivalenced than our memory generally allows, where do we get the image of
working-class war supporters? White male production workers and their families
are the historical figures assigned a conservative and, at times, reactionary role
in the face of Vietnam antiwar protest and the other social movements of the
period. This was not a new characterization but, rather, one that developed in the
decades before the Vietnam War.

This chapter marks a break from our historical narrative in that it looks back
to the period before the war for the roots of the image of working-class conservatism. These years marked a substantial transformation in the experience of
workers, as well as in public discussion concerning their political leanings and
behavior. As we will see, that discussion outpaced the experience; the "boom"
years improved the lives of millions of workers, but they neither erased class
differences nor inoculated workers against liberalism or progressivism, as many
observers would have it.

No doubt, the post-war working class appeared very far from satisfying
the search for a "revolutionary agent" by the US left. It is to this problem that
C. Wright Mills in part addressed in his "Letter to the New Left" in 1960. In it, he
famously wrote, "I do not quite understand about some New-Left writers why
they cling so mightily to 'the working class' of the advanced capitalist societies as
the historic agency, or even as the most important agency, in the face of the really
historical evidence that now stands against this expectation. Such a labor metaphysic, I think, is a legacy from Victorian Marxism that is now quite unrealistic.

It is an historically specific idea that has been turned into an a-historical and un-specific hope." Mills predicted that, for the time being, the Western working class would not act as the transformative class that Marxist theory had predicted. He was clear that he could not speak to the future but also that he thought it unlikely that the "social and historical conditions under which industrial workers tend to become a class-for-themselves" were unlikely to be created any time soon.[1]

For generations previously, workers had been at the forefront of fights for social change. Trade union organizing, syndicalism, socialism, anarchism, and communism—all were movements that explicitly addressed exploitation and engaged in class-based struggle. Although middle-class leaders and support-ers played roles in some sectors of these old movements, working-class leaders, constituencies, and concerns were dominant. Yet the new social movements that emerged in the 1960s were a far cry from the specifically working-class-based politics that had dominated Western social movements for the preceding hun-dred years. The fact that US workers did not rise up as a revolutionary class certainly challenged the "Victorian" Marxist expectation that they might. But did the political behavior of workers conform to the image of those analysts who observed the exceptionally conservative nature of the US working class?

A great deal of research and writing has been devoted to the problem of the class consciousness—or lack thereof—of the US worker.[2] To the extent that such a debate had existed in public in prior years, the participants were largely union-ists or organizers themselves, with some academic support from labor relations experts in various universities, on the one side, and radical agitators, on the other.[3] The period following World War II was the historical moment when theories that supported an exceptional, peculiarly conservative working class not only circu-lated widely but appeared by most to be true in their present moment. Popular and academic discourses held that class differences no longer existed in any mean-ingful way in the United States. The major institutions of the working class were an important part of the ruling liberal coalition, and workers were understood as being, more likely than not, conservative or complacent, if not reactionary.

Many future leaders of the antiwar movement, along with the politicians and journalists of the Vietnam era, grew up or came of age during these years. It is these narratives of class experience that directly informed the perceptions of workers held by the activists, media, and mass culture during Vietnam.

The Affluent White Working Class?

The post-war boom is by now a cliché, rosily invoked or recalled with some bit-terness in light of the volatile, insecure, and more ruthless economic climate of recent decades. During the period of 1945–1973, the years that are conventionally used to demarcate the boundaries of the boom, the United States experienced unprecedented economic growth, including mostly proportional income gains up and down the income ladder—a rising tide did lift nearly all boats.[4] A new middle class grew rapidly, with service-sector and office jobs outpacing growth in other sectors and salaried employees increasing as a share of the workforce. Postwar government support for housing and immense outlays for highways encouraged suburbanization, and the GI Bill swelled the colleges. Income distribution became more equal; real living standards rose. Even counting the recessions of the period, the relative security achieved by industrial workers during these years was unprecedented in the industrial age. Economic growth was a necessary factor determining this new situation for workers, as were the New Deal era reforms that had been bitterly fought for in the 1930s. But it is unlikely that this security and improvement for workers would have been achieved or sustained were it not for the strength of the labor movement.

For much of this period, unionized workers made up over 30 percent of the private-sector workforce (and well over 50 percent in many core industries), and the terms and conditions of their employment set standards for workers in similar non-unionized jobs. Among other gains, which varied across industries, unions won health care, pensions, cost-of-living adjustments (known as COLA, or "escalator clauses"), and earlier retirement. More consistently, industrywide agreements raised the floor for wages and simplified salary increments, thereby decreasing wage stratification and drastically reducing the labor ranks of the "working poor."

As Jack Metzgar, the son of a skilled steelworker, remembers it, there were real grounds for optimism during the period: "There were choices. There were prospects. There were possibilities. Few of these had been there before. Now they were."[5] With the post-war boom, it increasingly appeared to many that workers were no longer a class apart but, rather, incorporated into the fabric of the American dream. In the eyes of mainstream culture, economic growth and its attendant optimism transformed workers from oppositional to mostly integrated figures. The New Deal orientation of the Democratic Party spoke to working-class concerns, and labor had gained political influence. From a liberal perspective, the problem of the working class had been largely solved through strong unions and Keynesian economic policies.

Limits to the Boom

A problem with this story is that it does not correspond to the full reality of working-class lives. The true security and something close to affluence that was achieved during the boom existed among the growing middle class of upper- and lower-level professionals in the expanding salaried economy. Workers were not excluded from the boom, but their gains were more circumscribed.

The gains that were made among workers went overwhelmingly to the white, male, and unionized; thus many workers were excluded from these arrangements. In the wake of their post-war migrations from the South to the industrialized North and West, African American workers had joined unionized industries in significant numbers, but they tended to be hired in the lowest rungs of job classifications, whose levels were often "safeguarded" along ethnic and racial lines. White "hillbillies" or "hayseeds" from the South often shared a similar experience.[6] More frequently, African Americans held jobs in non-unionized shops or non-union sectors, including government, service, agriculture, and domestic work.[7] They were joined in these capacities by Chicano and Puerto Rican workers, and together they faced direct discrimination from employers and few legal protections. Women fared little better. Although their workplace participation increased by one-third during the post-war era, women were confined to sex-segregated occupations (domestic help, teachers, clerical and secretarial support, and health care) with lower pay. On the other hand, women's class status was usually linked to that of their families, and during the post-war boom the wives and daughters of workers who had won a family wage were assured lifestyle changes.

Inequalities persisted among organized workers as well. Although less so than before, the unionized working class was itself stratified, with a minority of skilled workers doing significantly better than the majority. Unions were actively complicit in the classification schemes that encouraged racial, ethnic, and gender stratification and that served to benefit management with their divisiveness and, in the narrow sense, the skilled craftsmen and white workers with their exclusiveness. Progressive policies such as seniority lists, which derailed management favoritism and improved the chances of both job security and opportunity in the workplace, simultaneously contributed to this stratification, favoring white and male workers who had held their jobs longer than the more recently hired African Americans and women. Overall job security was good, and much better than it had been during the Depression. But seasonal shutdowns and recessions were hard for workers without seniority—unemployment benefits had to be extended a number of times throughout this period, including for as long as a year in the middle of the 1950s.

Part of what made the post-war boom feel so expansive was the contrast from the extreme deprivation that had characterized much of working-class life in the previous period. The Bureau of Labor Statistics suggested a "minimum budget" in the late 1940s that Metzgar recalls "almost perfectly described my immediate family's situation in 1959":

> This budget envisioned a family of four, living in a rented apartment, consisting of a kitchen, bath, and three other rooms. The family had hot running water and owned a washing machine [a wringer-washer, not an automatic]. On the budget "it should be possible to serve meat for dinner several times a week, if the cheaper cuts are served." Each child could have a bottle of pop every other day, and one beer a week could be consumed. Three shirts and two pairs of pants could be purchased each year for the growing boy. The family did not own a car and there was not money in the budget for any vacation ever, but every three weeks the family could afford a movie, if they bought no food at the theater.[8]

As a son of a skilled and unionized steelworker, Metzgar's experience was close to the top of the heap. In 1959, the "modest but adequate" budget for a family of four was $5,180 according to the Bureau of Labor Statistics, an income level at which people could be said to have achieved "health and decency," or what labor leaders called "shabby, but respectable" living.[9] Not, it is important to emphasize, affluence nor anything approaching it. Census income statistics indicate that this modest budget was just below the median budget for all white families in that year.[10] Later studies show that, in the 1960s, at least 60 percent of the working class lived at or below the "shabby, but respectable" living sketched by the minimum budget for a family of four, whereas nearly one-third lived at or below the "poor" level of minimum income. According to those same later studies, by 1970 only 15 percent of workers were, by income, within the levels considered "affluent" according to the Bureau of Labor Statistics understanding of family budgets.[11] Given the steady rise in real income that attended the boom, the number of workers who actually achieved affluence during the post-war era appears to have topped out at that 15 percent; in the earlier years, when affluence studies, discussed later in the chapter, were all the rage, it was probably closer to one-tenth of all workers. Life was significantly better than it had been during the Depression and before, but it was still a tenuous experience, often only a paycheck ahead of the bills.

Some visible forms of class struggle had subsided in the post-war United States, but they did not disappear. The 1950s marked a period in which the more militant and democratic rank-and-file upsurges of the 1930s and, to a lesser extent, 1940s were largely put down through a combination of factors, including state regulation of labor and government repression, attacks on the political left, business unionist practices on the part of labor leadership, and sufficient wealth in the system to provide economic gains made by workers, as already described.

In negotiations, labor leaders and business focused almost exclusively on promoting wage and benefit gains during this period. More and more, unions explicitly linked their fortunes to the success of US business. This connection between contract success and corporate growth helps explain the union positions on many pro-business policy initiatives, including those in the realm of foreign policy. Yet increased wages were not the sole, or in many cases, most important demands of workers, and the emphasis on monetary compensation came at the expense of working-class demands to basic rights and control over the terms and conditions of work. For management, worker control was *the* central target for post-war business; anti-union laws such as Taft-Hartley and major contract demands were directed at its limitation and erosion. "Give the union the money, the least possible, but give them what it takes," advised one General Motors executive. "But don't let them take the business away from us."[12] Even within the unionized context, the work itself frequently remained tedious, onerous, dangerous, and filthy; the stretch out (the imposing of additional tasks) and speedup (the insistence on faster work) remained central points of contention for workers; and automation was often making work faster and workers redundant.

Economic gains were thus made, but working conditions were hard and shop-floor power was under attack. Tensions, therefore, existed throughout the 1950s and into the 1960s over what constituted labor power—monetary gains or power over work rules—and whether the expanding labor bureaucracies were representing their members' best interests.

The restiveness of workers with regard to conditions at work and power on the job caused a great deal of consternation among labor leaders. Longer contracts were one strategy for forestalling struggle, as were the escalator clauses, both of which became norms or goals for most unions in the 1950s. But the Treaty of Detroit, the five-year UAW contract signed in 1950, precipitated fights over conditions; although the contract stipulated no strikes during the five years of the contract, thousands of workers repeatedly walked out in its later years when the line sped up. As a result, the UAW brought the contract length down to three years in the next round and permitted local bargaining.[13] Strikes did not disappear—in fact, there were more strikes per year in the 1950s than in any other decade of the century, with the early 1950s seeing the most.[14] Many of these strikes in the early 1950s were wildcats, including over four hundred at Ford Motor alone. With economic gains increasing over the decade, fights over work rules intensified. The 116-day strike in the steel industry in 1959 was primarily concerned with protecting the "local practices" clause—Section 2-B in the contract—that impeded the ability of management to reorganize the labor process. Longshoremen, rubber workers, miners, and meat-cutters resisted similar incursions in 1959, with varying degrees of success. At the dawn of the 1960s, conflict between the bureaucratization of bargaining and the erosion of shop-floor power were the preconditions for rank-and-file political revolts in nearly every CIO union, as well as a few old AFL standards such as the Teamsters and Miners that played out over the next decade.[15]

Overall, the pre-Vietnam period saw material improvements for workers, but there was little indication that rank-and-file workers had achieved contentment at work or standards of living solid enough to assure their quiescence or assimilation. Stability, satisfaction, and quiet were not at the center of working-class life, and by the end of the 1960s, the continued fragility and brittleness of the lived reality of many workers lives became clearer.

The discourses of the affluent worker that circulated in the era that I take up next are best viewed, therefore, in terms of performing ideological work rather than reflecting objective reality. The imaginary picture of an American idyll kept the turbulence of the pre-war era at bay and fed on the promises of the post-war boom. The images of contented workers that proliferated during this period could stand not only because of the obvious benefits such images lent politicians and corporations but also because they benefitted labor leaders as well. Labor leaders were proud of the economic gains won by US workers, as well as their own newfound political influence; maintaining focus on the economic security they helped achieve was expedient for their own careers. It was not in their interests to voice too much unsettledness outside of the normal fighting words voiced at contract time.

Beyond their leaders, the working class did not have institutional or cultural modes of self-representation that could highlight the problems in the otherwise smooth story of their "up and coming" ascent into the middle class. In fact, such independent representation was arguably less available in the McCarthy-ist and business union climate of the 1950s than it would be in later years. That meant that the much more unsettled, more politically and economically indeterminate direction of US workers did not register in the mainstream culture of the period. What people read about in the newspapers or saw on TV or in movies seemed to confirm the idea that industrial conflict had been overcome and that workers were increasingly middle class.

The Disappearance of the Working Class

Television was a primary vehicle through which this new ideological representation was performed for the public at large. During the 1950s, a number of shows focused on the lives of blue-collar ethnic workers adjusting to or living in the new prosperity. George Lipsitz argues that on shows like *The Goldbergs* (1949–1956),

Life of Riley (1949–1950, 1953–1958), and *Mama* (1949–1957) working-class families were schooled in the arts of consumerism and, increasingly, life in the suburbs—some, like the Rileys, started there, whereas others, like the Goldbergs, moved there. The shows, Lipsitz points out, "made new economic and social relations credible and legitimate to audiences haunted by ghosts of the past."[16] They also brought to prime time a depiction of working-class life that, over the course of the decade, became increasingly indistinguishable from the lives of the generic middle-class families that dominated TV shows in the late 1950s and 1960s. The migration of the Goldbergs from the Bronx to "Haverville"[17] sums up the trajectory of many of these families, whose children lead lives buying on the installment plan and worrying about dates and schoolwork. On these shows, bosses and the rich were still pilloried, the work ethic subverted, and representations of class solidarity remained, but many characters were just as much "everyman" as they were "workingmen." By the late 1950s, these families (with the exception of the going-nowhere-fast *Honeymooners*, and some others in syndication) had disappeared from the air, symbolizing what for many was becoming "obvious"— that class no longer existed as a salient economic category in the United States.[18]

By the late 1950s, many were convinced that the class society was a fading vestige of the past. Of course, there still existed pockets of poor people scattered across the country, and the new civil rights movement raised the issue of racial inequalities. Still, by and large, economic inequality appeared to be behind us. Certainly, as an example, the approbation with which Michael Harrington's exposé of the scale and depth of US poverty, *The Other America* (1962), was greeted—the *New York Times* called it "alarming," the *Los Angeles Times* called it "deeply disturbing"—was an indication that, for many in the growing middle and upper-middle classes, economic inequality had become largely invisible.[19]

For many academic observers, the growth of economic security gave rise to contradictory but related theories of the contemporary class scene in the United States. One popular theory was the "embourgeoisement" of the "affluent worker"; another, related set of theories argued for a purely culturalist (as opposed to structural or power-related) approach to class differences. The first tended to deny that there was any real difference among better-off workers and the middle class, whereas the latter took affluence for granted but posited real cultural differences between workers and middle-class citizens. Although their conclusions were opposite, their foundations were common.

According to the embourgeoisement thesis popular in both Great Britain and the United States, the recent material gains made by workers had effected a change in their political and cultural proclivities. Income gains led to changes in attitude and behavior, so that better-off workers acted like their middle-class income-equivalents. Among other predictions, this theory anticipated that workers would begin to vote for middle-class parties, supporting the Tory or Republican parties over the Labor or Democratic. This theory was more explicitly raised—and refuted—in Great Britain than in the United States.[20] Later empirical studies critical of the embourgeoisement thesis showed that, beyond real limits to workers' monetary gains, the type of job performed and the relative freedom exercised by the person doing the job—in short, the degree of individual power exercised on the job—continued to have a greater effect on class consciousness and political behavior than did income. Thus, the most affluent (unionized, higher-income, skilled) workers continued to act like their brothers and sisters "beneath" them in socioeconomic status and did not act like the middle-class people who were closer to them in income or living standards.[21]

In the United States, working-class affluence was rarely directly studied; in fact, a 1971 review essay surveying the field of such "affluent worker" studies pointed out the "neglect" shown by sociologists in the post-war era in actually studying "class consciousness, industrial unrest, and nascent forms of labor organization" in light of the perception that all was quiet on those fronts.[22] Another book-length study, Arthur Shostak's *Blue-Collar Life*, notes that "data will not sustain" studies of the "heterogeneous amalgam" of workers beyond erroneously treating them as a "single construct," and it laments the "crude state of development" of conceptual frameworks accounting for their political behavior.[23] But until such theories were challenged in 1970s, the assumption of embourgeoisement was taken for granted across the political spectrum, as a priori rather than proven. Workers, for many observers, had disappeared as a distinct economic group.

At the conservative end of the spectrum, Robert Nisbet was one influential sociologist whose work pursued this reasoning to its logical end. He asks, "may American society at the present time reasonably and objectively be called a class society?" Nisbet relegates the very existence of the category of class to the "conceptual memory" of sociology as a stubborn relic whose obdurate nature distorted scholarly investigation. In fact, "the term social class is . . . nearly valueless for the clarification of the data of wealth, power and social status in contemporary United States"—"we are," rather, "living in a society governed by status."[24]

Status, in fact, was the new by-word for much of the literature devoted to studying *social stratification*, which became the dominant sociological way of speaking about class. Sociologists in the United States attribute their attention to status to the work of Max Weber, whose writings were being translated into English during this period. During the 1930s and early 1940s, the relational nature of class was observed in the public discourses surrounding the subject—that is, class was viewed as a form of power, as in who had it and who did not, who was vying for it, and who was losing it. Elements of this discourse included ideas such as workers and owners being structurally prone to conflict and that "the working class" was identifiable through its independent organizations, and in many places in the industrialized world, political parties. In other words, economic, political, and interactive understandings of class were at the forefront of the popular imagination.[25] Yet the US sociological perspectives that were to blossom in the post-war era instead described class differences in terms of stratification, a largely distributional model developed most cogently in the influential work of W. Lloyd Warner, Kenneth Eells, and Marchia Meeker, *Social Class in America* (1949).[26] Stratification theory à la Warner and colleagues marked a decisive rejection of (most obviously) Marxist versions of class, but it was also an oversimplification of Weber's own more nuanced understanding of "class, status, and party."[27] Warner's taxonomy—upper, middle, and lower classes, subdivided therein—eradicated historical and structural determinations of class and radically deemphasized power, substituting instead a prestige and income scale through which modulations in class location could be numerically recorded. As workers gained in "respectability" and wages, up the scale they moved.[28]

These years saw an explosion in the study of stratification, thus conceived.[29] The community study was the most popular method for its study, in which prestige, status behavior, and affiliation (social relationships) were described, with stratification patterns identified from the survey and observation data collected.[30] This was also the period in which significant sections of sociology renewed an on-again, off-again quest for scientific respectability through quantitative methodology—if it could not be counted, it did not count. Needless to say, an empirical focus on income scales was eminently suited for such a project, whereas a theoretical model examining sites of leverage within the means of production was not.

With such a culturalist, quantifiable definition of *class* in place, wherein class is defined by a person's prestige and paycheck—a kind of "you know it when you see it" model—what happens when it seems the researcher cannot see it all so clearly? What happens when so many people are eating meat, buying kitchen appliances, watching television, and listening to the new rock and roll? The differences between classes, seemingly erased or toned down at the level of materiality, were then to be found in educational attainment and cultural background. For many observers, class therefore became a category of culture and behavior; considerations of structure, work conditions, and power receded from analytic view. As a sociologist argued at the time, social stratification "plays the largest immediate role in producing these social divisions . . . of American communities which center around intimate friendships, clique life, association membership and participation and intermarriage." Lifestyle, leisure activities, and personal relations were thence the proper province for studies of what-was-once-thought-of-as "class."[31]

Here, analysts were divided. Did lifestyle considerations warrant attention to economic class distinctions or not? Without taking it to the extreme of Nisbet, some theorists posited that the increasingly similar lifestyles and life chances of the expanded "middle class" meant that differences based on economic experience were less important than similarities based on these other factors. This too meant the end of any meaningful stratification in the United States within this expanded middle class—arguing for a "middle-mass" over a "middle class." Influential books such as *The Lonely Crowd* (1950) and *The End of Ideology* (1962) focused on the middle class to the exclusion of a separate working class, usually because the latter was understood as being significantly incorporated into the former. Another best seller of the period, John Kenneth Galbraith's *The Affluent Society* (1958) took for granted that the vast majority of the United States had achieved stable, post-scarcity conditions, and his warning of the need for public investment for the poorest assumed income and cultural experience scales like Warner's.[32]

From the left, Paul Goodman also made use of a cultural stratification scale to explain classes in the contemporary United States, eclipsing economic boundaries that might be drawn between middle- and working-class groups and, instead, accepting a cultural framework to distinguish them. Goodman was an influential intellectual for the New Left of the 1960s. He had early and sustained contact with SDS; was a supporter of the Free Speech Movement at Berkeley; and spent some years working from the Institute for Policy Studies, which served as home to many of the leading leftist intellectuals of the period. His work of social criticism, *Growing Up Absurd* (1960) was a best seller and was widely invoked by movement activists, the movement press, and mainstream commentators in the years that followed its publication.

In *Growing Up Absurd*, Goodman does not deny the existence of class differences in the United States, but he deemphasizes their import. Following William H. Whyte's *The Organization Man*, Goodman divides the United States into three classes, "the Poor, the Organization, and the Independents," with "three statuses within the dominant class, the Organization": Workers, Organization Men, and Managers.[33] Workers therefore exist, but their distinct identity is analytically subordinate to their position within the Organization. To be working class, for Goodman, is to inhabit a status and cultural position, not one with distinct economic or power consequences.

Like much of the social commentary with which Goodman is in dialogue, Goodman views conformity and mass consumption as the salient characteristics of organized society, with problems of inequity persisting, for example, between the large majority of the Organization and "our poor black and brown brothers" but not *within* the Organization itself.[34] The metaphor Goodman creates for contemporary society (also following Whyte) is that of "an apparently closed room in which there is a large rat race as the dominant center of attention."[35] Echoing the sociological consensus, he argues that workers and the middle class, inside the "closed room," are distinguished by their value systems, although he insists in seeing these values as mutually oppositional:

> A persistent error of the sociologist has been to regard middle-class values and working-class values as *co-ordinate* rival systems. Rather, they are related vertically: each is a defense against some threat of the other. Primary values are *human* values. . . . [T]he working-class "values" are nothing but ignorance, resignation, and resentment of classless human values of enterprise and culture, at present available only to the middle class; and many a poor boy escapes petty class attitudes and achieves something.[36]

Ignorance, resignation, and resentment of classless human values? Ascribing this reactive recoiling to workers was fairly typical, and it exemplifies the last characteristic feature of some academic treatments of the working class during the period. Workers, when singled out for consideration, tended to be portrayed as politically inert or apathetic, or as bigoted, small-minded, and even proto-fascist. These theses strongly colored movement and popular apprehensions of working-class behavior during the turbulent 1960s.

Authoritarian Workers in the Mainstream

With the exception of prominent labor leaders such as Walter Reuther and George Meany, individual workers were largely absent from mainstream political and intellectual culture. An exception, whose views were therefore taken as exemplary, was Eric Hoffer, the "longshoreman philosopher." Hoffer was an autodidact from a struggling background who worked on the docks for much of his adult life, reading voraciously and writing copiously on breaks and during off-hours. Like many other intellectuals of the era, Hoffer sought to understand the rise of Nazism in Germany and—making the connection that most others made during the Cold War—"communist totalitarianism" in Russia. His analysis of the genesis of these and other "mass movements," *The True Believer* (1951), sold over half a million copies and made him a household name. He followed this book with many others (which also sold well), made memorable appearances on TV, contributed pieces to the *New York Times* and other publications, and remained a public figure until the early 1970s.

Like others at the time, Hoffer argued that mass movements arose out of the frustrations of individuals whose own lives lacked meaning and inner confidence. This social-psychological view saw particular ideologies as largely interchangeable for the righteous "true believers," whose own emptiness caused them to identify externally with the social whole. Hoffer embraced an individualist, and frankly self-centered, life of stability and comfort as the pinnacle of personal and social achievement, and although he was skeptical, like many of his contemporaries, of the conformism he found in the contemporary United States, he initially held up US culture against others as one that was less conducive to the growth of the mass movements that he found so problematic. Hoffer distrusted abrupt social change and believed that a society undergoing rapid change was regressing, in the throes of juvenilia.

In his work during the 1950s, Hoffer can be read as the perfect ideologue for the complacent corporate capitalism and submerged political tensions of the period. And in the 1960s, as tensions rose and the economic ship began to sway, Hoffer was a voice of conservatism—and increasingly, reaction—in the face of change. In the face of 1964 civil rights demands and movement, Hoffer advocated a bootstrapping model of self-help for African Americans, and in the aftermath of the Columbia University building takeovers in 1968 (but before Kent State), he suggested that Columbia University President Grayson Kirk might have been better off shooting the protesters who took over his office.[37] Although Hoffer did not make attempts to speak "for" his class, he frequently invoked his own experiences to make observations about the nature of the social world, thereby making it easy for commentators and audiences alike to link him to the attitudes of workers—whom they did not otherwise see—as a whole. By 1969, Arthur Shostak named him as the "best single short introduction to the general political philosophy of American's blue-collarites."[38]

Arthur Shostak's own *Blue-Collar Life* (1969) is typical of mainstream sociological treatments of the working class during the period. Despite his own caveats about the lack of empirical data to support his arguments, Shostak nevertheless makes an effort to discern "the essence of the blue collar political stance." Eric Hoffer is his first and primary example, strangely enough, given the fact that Hoffer's own story was nothing if not exceptional. (It is also troublesome because Shostak seems to quote primarily from other people's reviews of Hoffer's work rather than Hoffer's own words.) Workers, according to Shostak's Hoffer, are "staunch defender[s] of the country." They can be counted on further to "defen[d] the status quo." "Social conventions must be vigorously defended against the intellectuals" as well as youth. Shostak summarizes his understanding of working-class political philosophy as gleaned through Hoffer: "a 'them-versus-us' feeling and [a] nostalgia for times past when common sense and the common man were allegedly in the saddle. . . . intolerance of dissent and distrust of patriotic and moralistic nonconformity. Above all, Eric Hoffer's variations on blue-collar political philosophy are consistent with the tight-laced, backward glancing, and phobic character of blue-collar politics."[39]

Shostak's work drew in part on that of Seymour Martin Lipset, whose 1959 article "Democracy and Working Class Authoritarianism" served as a reference point for nearly all sociological—as well as many popular—discussions of working-class politics during the Vietnam era. Many social scientists of the period had sought to understand the rise of fascism in Germany, Italy, and Japan in the previous decades. Whereas some traced the structural and institutional bases for authoritarianism, social psychologists sought to understand what they termed the "authoritarian personality," individual attributes that might help to explain the personal appeal of fascism. Stanley Milgram's electrocution experiments of the early 1960s were ultimately most famous in this regard, and they indicated the situational basis for obedience.[40] But in the years prior to Milgram's studies, other studies sought to measure the extent to which people in general, or particular groups, were susceptible to authoritarian behavior—a kind of methodological individualism that fit the "end of ideology" age. In the US context, it was the working class that bore the brunt of "proto-fascist" social-psychological scaremongering.

Seymour Martin Lipset collected evidence from these and other sources to support his discovery of "working class authoritarianism." First published in the *American Sociological Review*, his essay argues, "many studies suggest that the lower-class way of life produces individuals with rigid and intolerant approaches to politics. These findings . . . imply that one may anticipate wide-spread support by lower-class individuals and groups for extremist movements." The authoritarian tendency of the "lower-classes," a concept used interchangeably by Lipset with the working class, is a "tragic dilemma" for "those intellectuals of the democratic left who once believed the proletariat necessarily to be a force for liberty, racial equality, and social progress."[41] Rather, lower-class individuals personally espouse authoritarian attitudes and, all things being equal, will tend to support extremist over democratic movements.

Lipset's work attracted criticism at the time, and it has been repeatedly and effectively challenged on the bases of both theory and evidence.[42] Yet putting to one side the question of its accuracy, what is important to note is that Lipset's thesis played a major role in shaping the public conversation about working-class politics and that it did so in a particular way. The critical move he makes is to locate the authoritarianism of workers in variables such as family structure and social isolation—factors that are themselves influenced by political and economic realities but that are not specifically political or economic. Lipset argues that workers often act against type, supporting democratic or liberal policies because of their institutional affiliation with democratic or liberal institutions. But their natural tendency, their emotive core, is authoritarian. Their political orientation is thus posited as organic and essential rather than contextual or historical.

Political Man: The Social Bases of Politics,[43] the book in which Lipset's essay eventually appeared, became one of the most widely assigned works in political sociology during the decade, selling over 400,000 copies. The original *New York Times* review, otherwise positive, singled out his discussion of working-class authoritarianism—the "rigid, intolerant approach to politics" that Lipset finds—as particularly unconvincing. Yet by 1964, the paperback edition was called "a brilliant, searching inquiry" in the same paper.[44]

Working-Class Political Behavior as Seen from the Left

These interpretations of the class dynamics of the period—disappeared, irrelevant, or turned upside down from decades before—shaped the common sense about class in the years before Vietnam. Yet members of the future antiwar movement did not move only inside the mainstream. For movement activists-to-be, the dominant discourses of "bourgeois social science" probably held less appeal than those of the radical critics of that tradition. Todd Gitlin of the SDS recalls the first time he met Tom Hayden: "He seemed to have read everything. Hayden's every word seems chosen: he never hesitated, never stumbled, as he crisply assaulted the social science establishment, especially the idea of 'the end of ideology' then in circulation from the influential sociologists Daniel Bell and Seymour Martin Lipset."[45] Like Hayden, activists at the time looked elsewhere for critical interpretations of the political moment and its possibilities.

But the prediction by the Old Left of the central role to be played by the working class in progressive movements for social change was also largely rejected by the progressive intellectuals of the post-war period. The obvious reason for this was the near-unanimous embrace of Cold War anticommunism in the ranks of labor and the collapse of Communist Party influence within the class. For those leftists who shunned communism, there was no indication that any other progressive political tendency was developing in the house of labor either. But the hegemonic apprehension of widespread affluence was the other main contributor to the emerging New Left skepticism concerning worker radicalism. For most, workers and their unions were variously seen as economically or politically incorporated. And for some leftists or progressives, the authoritarian label stuck, especially from people who were opposed to the conformity of the era and who saw workers as emblematic of it. A kind of middle-class exceptionalism was often present among these radical thinkers, who held for themselves, as radical individualists, the possibilities of escaping mass society but saw for workers no incentive or capacity to do so. When it came to considerations of class politics, their arguments were not very dissimilar from those of Lipset and others.

Paul Goodman's discussion of labor leaders and organized workers is a case in point. As far as leaders went, "their attitude toward poverty is no longer part of their fighting economic theory. As labor economists, they do not have solidarity with [the] poor." This is because "now the rate of interest does not fall, the system cushions its crises; there is high employment . . . or insurance." Although inequality persists, "workers on a fairly high standard don't much bother who has millions."[46] Implicit in these comments is an understanding that class solidarity among organized workers was a deterministic product of material adversity and that, lacking adversity, workers lack concern for those beneath them or anger at those above. That Goodman attributes a sectional, rather than class-based, solidarity among labor leaders is in keeping with long traditions of "labor aristocracy" arguments made on the left, although it ignored the great extent to which such labor leaders supported the expansion of the welfare state during the period and the Great Society programs that were to develop. But his reservation of a mechanistically materialistic sense of class solidarity for workers in general reduces working-class attitudes to a thin stereotype.

In the years after the war, C. Wright Mills viewed the unorganized working class as a potentially progressive force and the labor organizations of the class as the potential vehicles for the unfolding of this force. His *New Men of Power* (1948) set great hope in the capacity of labor leaders and their unions to steer workers in a progressive direction. Although the "underdogs," who were not so much at the bottom as "largely outside" US society, had acquired "habits of submission" and were "underprivileged socially and psychologically" as well as economically, workers might nevertheless be reached by unions in such a way that "politics would become so much a part of the life of the worker, so connected with his daily work and his social routine, that political alertness would be part of his human alertness as a social being." Ideally, it would be "through the union as a community that the political consciousness of the US worker [could] be aroused."[47]

Yet by 1960, Mills had changed his tune. As previously noted, in his "Letter to the New Left" Mills makes it clear that the new generation should abandon the "unrealistic" "labor metaphysic" of previous generations. In this essay, he asserts that historical conditions may indeed rise in which workers might play such a role and allows that "where labor exists as an agency, of course we must work with it" but that the attention of the New Left should be elsewhere. Mills was eventually the subject of Tom Hayden's master's thesis, and the Port Huron Statement was deeply influenced by his theories and style, as well as those of Goodman.

Herbert Marcuse was another influential theorist for the new generation of activists coming of age in the 1960s—Douglas Kellner called him the "Guru of the New Left."[48] Although his influence was most obvious among the white college-educated left, black radicals were also in his intellectual orbit; Angela Davis had been his teaching assistant while he was at the University of California at San Diego. A Frankfurt school Marxist, Marcuse recognized the limitations of "actually existing socialism," as well as the "scientific socialist" and economic determinist theories frequently invoked by its supporters. Like Theodor Adorno, Max Horkheimer, Walter Benjamin, and others, Marcuse emphasized cultural production, ideology, and sociopsychological experience as the central sites for making sense of the endurance, strength, and possible schisms of capitalism. Unlike stratification theorists, Frankfurt school theorists maintained structural analyses of capitalism and class relations; like stratification theorists, nonmaterial phenomena were foregrounded in their studies of industrial society.

Marcuse's *One-Dimensional Man* (1964) was the Marxist analog to *The Lonely Crowd* and *The End of Ideology*. In it, Marcuse wrote of the problem of "society without opposition," in which "capitalist development has altered the structure and function of [the bourgeoisie and the proletariat] in such a way that they no longer appear to be agents of historical transformation. An overriding interest in the preservation and improvement of the institutional status quo unites the former antagonists in the most advanced areas of contemporary society." Although "there are still the basic classes," he observes, "the people recognize themselves in their commodities. They find their souls in their automobile, hi-fi set, split level home, kitchen equipment." Elsewhere, he stresses the resilience of the system, describing its success "in channeling antagonisms in such a way that it can manipulate them. Materially as well as ideologically, the very classes which were once the absolute negation of the capitalist system are now more and more integrated into it."[49]

For Marcuse, then, by the mid-1960s, the inherent class contradiction of capitalism had been largely overcome. Marcuse's work was very influential in the New Left search for other "agents of social change," which came to include themselves as alienated youth and future technical workers, third-world peoples, and the poor—people who were still, unlike "traditional" workers, materially or culturally alienated from the system.

What many of the analysts of the time (and the culture at large) failed to see were the limits to the gains made by the working class and the continuing existence of a restive rank and file. They failed to see that workers were not only "in it for the money," bought off by a few cents an hour, and that "the persistence of nonmaterial values at the point of production, the symbolic nature of many struggles over wages, and the willingness of workers to actually lose money rather than surrender dignity or happiness continuously threatened to undermine the foundation of labor peace in capitalist society."[50] In short, they lost sight of the more complex material and existential realities lived by most working-class people in the United States and of the extent to which the same terms of exploitation that had prompted workers into action in the 1930s and 1940s had not mysteriously disappeared, even if workers were not then engaged in political struggle over these questions. Instead, analysts too often fell into a psychological reductionism that accepted with insufficient criticism culturally based assertions and observations about the nature of class consciousness. Such an over-correction against crude materialism meant that even writers sympathetic to struggles for equality and justice tended to see the organized working class as essentially integrated, inside the system, and outside social dynamics of change.

Politicians, journalists, professors, students, and activists thus entered the Vietnam War period in a milieu saturated with anticipations of a peculiarly conservative orientation among that fraction of the lower middle class formerly known as workers. This was fertile ground for the explosion of attention suddenly given to the "blue-collar backlash" from 1968 through the defeat of George McGovern in 1972. These critical years cemented the image of the war-supporting hardhat, furious at the antiwar movement and estranged from progressive forces.

HARDHATS VERSUS ELITE DOVES
Consolidation of the Image

> "I'm scared. If this is what the class struggle is all about there's something wrong somewhere."
>
> Cliff Sloane of Brooklyn, a freshman at the University of Michigan, watching the May 20, 1970, march in New York City, *New York Times*

> [A]lthough opinion polls demonstrate that workers' views on major issues actually span a wide range from left to right, many college-educated Americans still hold stereotypes of blue-collar workers as conservative "hard hats." . . . The Archie Bunker stereotype survives not because it is accurate but because those who live outside working-class America have no other image with which to replace it.
>
> Andrew Levison, "Who Lost the Working Class?" *The Nation*, 2001

The invasion of Cambodia, announced by President Nixon on April 30, 1970, precipitated a mass outpouring of antiwar actions across the country, particularly on college campuses. Nixon had promised the war would be winding down, yet Cambodia marked an expansion. When four students at Kent State University were killed by National Guardsmen on May 4, 1970, college protests gave way to shutdowns, with 1.5 million students closing 20 percent of campuses nationwide. Over half of all campuses reported that some protest took place in those weeks, and some colleges remained closed for the rest of the semester.

On the morning of May 8 in New York City, a small group of antiwar protesters had gathered on Wall Street to protest the expansion of the war and once again demand immediate US withdrawal. At lunchtime, an even smaller crowd of around two hundred construction workers arrived at the antiwar rally chanting, "Love it or Leave It" and "Impeach Lindsay," the liberal Republican mayor of New York City. In the next few hours, backed by hundreds of Wall Street employees and more construction workers from the World Trade Center site, hundreds of workers "rampaged" through lower Manhattan, storming City Hall and Pace University, injuring seventy antiwar protesters and bystanders. This protest was followed by daily lunchtime marches of hundreds of workers and supporters, culminating in an Honor America, Honor the Flag rally on May 20, organized by the Building Trades Council and its president, Peter Brennan. Describing this final rally, for which the crowd estimates went as high as 100,000, one reporter wrote, "There was a swagger to the crowd, built of a kind of joy at being what participants saw as the first counter-response from a long-suffering middle America." The *New York Times* reported that many "described themselves as ordinary people, mainly family men and veterans, who had become fed up with various facets of the peace movement."[1]

In the later period of the war described here, public attention given to the "blue-collar backlash" and the actions and attitudes of blue-collar workers themselves contributed to the image of the worker-hawk that served, with the elite protester, to create the polarized expression of the "class war" of the period. As a representation, the hardhat hawk served to pull out the white working class from the larger group of white Americans as being particularly reactionary and pro-war, when in fact the opposite was true—non-working-class whites tended to be more supportive of the war than were workers.

This is not the first study to point out that we have misremembered the working class as particularly hawkish during Vietnam. Many historians and cultural critics have written about the hawkish image of the blue-collar worker promulgated during this period. Peter Levy's study of the New Left and labor seeks to understand the more complex political affiliations of organized workers and movement activists during the period. Jefferson Cowie observes that the enduring image of the 1970s working class is not, for example, the militant workplace insurgency of labor (a 1969–1971 strike wave that rivaled that of 1946 in depth and duration, with wildcat strikes and other rank-and-file rebellions lasting to the mid-1970s). It was, rather, the "beer slugging bigot of the blue collar backlash," an image he refutes with his evidence that the 1970s working class should best be understood as participating in political activity across the left-right spectrum. Barbara Ehrenreich, writing about the media coverage and political discourses around blue-collar workers at the time, similarly notes, "they did not discover the working class that was—in the late sixties and early seventies—caught up in the greatest wave of labor militancy since World War II." Ehrenreich argues that the "blue collar backlash was a highly biased and selective interpretation of the mood of working class Americans at a certain time."[2] Christian Appy writes,

> During the war, the mass media . . . reduced workers to a grossly misleading stereotype. Rather than documenting the class inequalities of military service and the complex feeling soldiers and their families had about their society and the war in Vietnam, the media more commonly contributed to the construction of an image of workers as the

war's strongest supporters. . . . These "hard-hats" or "rednecks" were
frequently portrayed as "Joe six-pack," a flag-waving blue-collar anti-
intellectual who, on top of everything else, was assumed to be a bigot.[3]

These authors supplement an argument that had already been outlined in the
1970s by writers such as Andrew Levison, Patricia Cayo Sexton, and Brendan
Sexton. These earlier authors confronted the larger myth of the blue-collar
reactionary and countered it with book-length studies detailing the working
conditions, community relations, and diverging political attitudes of blue-collar
workers in the 1960s and 1970s.[4]

In observing and refuting the myth of the blue-collar reactionary in this chapter,
then, I walk on well-traveled ground. In doing so, however, I draw attention to the
ways in which this image has functioned to curtail our appreciation of the actual
political currents and possibilities of the period, and by extension, today. First, the
point I have made throughout this book is that the image of the reactionary working class was tied to the image of the elitism of the protest movement, a specific
polarization that even many of those authors just cited accept as given. Why does it
matter that the reaction to Vietnam has been characterized as a two-sided coin? One
reason is that, at the time, such class-war rhetoric helped deflect attention away from
the criticisms of the war abroad to the problems raised by the "war at home," thereby
disabling antiwar criticism. A second reason is that the two sides of the image have
functioned together over the years to create the impression of an unbreachable gulf
between these two groups, an opposition that delimited the possibility of shared
political attitudes or actions. The success of the images of callous Harvard students
abandoning Southie (south Boston) proles and of the hardhats rampaging against
elite antiwarriors—their seeming salience and consistent invocation in the period
that followed—assured that a discursive wedge was driven between the majority
who agreed with the basic criticisms of the movement and the movement activists
themselves. Such images helped divide an increasingly restive organized US working
class from allies it might find in the movements, and vice versa.

The success of the image of the blue-collar conservative is also symptomatic
of what I find to have been a crisis in the public representation of US workers,
one that worsened during this period and that extends to the present day. This
crisis operated on two levels. At the level of popular discourse, self perception,
and the perception of others, working-class identities were in flux. The class itself had grown more diverse in terms of people and jobs, as growing numbers
of people of color and women joined the labor market, particularly in the expanding public and service sectors. This "new working class," as Dorothy Sue
Cobble and others have described it, co-existed with the "old" working class, but
often without significant institutional or cultural interpenetration.[5] Movements

representing women and people of color had helped create collective identities for, as well as foreground the collective claims of, some parts of the new working class. Economic conditions had worsened since the peak of the boom, increasing the insecurity of all workers. Where white, male goods-producing workers fit into this changing society became a popular question, and a source of some anxiety internal to those workers and their communities.

This popular and cultural crisis of representation developed within a structural crisis, wherein the political institutions that might otherwise organize workers as a coherent (political, cultural) group were spectacularly failing to do so. Unions and, more anemically, the Democratic Party had traditionally represented workers in the public sphere, but the power of each to do so was eroding, in large part because the liberal consensus they represented was collapsing. No coherent institutions existed that captured the left, right and center political directions that workers were moving in.

It turns out that society, too, abhors a vacuum. And into that vacuum stepped two powerful institutions: the media and the Republican Party. The media were fascinated by what they saw as blue-collar backlash against the politics and policies of liberal elites, obvious examples of which included the hardhats, and the at times violent resistance from white working-class communities to civil rights gains. Story after story was written about the angry ethnics who found no place among the New Politics of the Democrats and the socially liberal society they represented. As dramatically, the polarized struggle of the disgruntled blue-collar worker reacting to the liberal elite played a prominent role in President Nixon's attempt to consolidate the "emerging Republican majority" that he and his party sought. The Republican Party generally, and the Nixon administration specifically, fanned the flames of polarization and reaped its rewards. Although it has received less attention in the historical record than Nixon's racially divisive "law and order" strategy, the antiwar movement also served as a primary rhetorical foil during the first Nixon administration. In Vice President Spiro Agnew's and President Nixon's discourse, antiwar protesters played prominent roles in the chorus of contemporary ills.

It was against the antiwar movement that the "silent majority," the group that became central to the conservative realignment in US politics in the era, was most notably and repeatedly invoked. The hardhat demonstrations of 1970 were pivotal. New York construction workers and, by discursive extension, blue-collar workers around the country became a site of condensation for the discourse circulating at the time about the "troubled Americans," of white middle-class and working-class people who were by and large not involved in the movements of the period. As political scientists Paul Frymer and John David Skrentny argue, the hardhat demonstrations indicated to Nixon that the white working class was a Democratic constituency that might be peeled away from the Democratic Party.[6]

Focusing his amorphous appeal to the "silent majority" as a more specific appeal to workers, while using the image of the antiwar protester as a more specific incarnation of the lawlessness of the movement culture, was, in 1970, a key tactic in Nixon's mid-cycle electoral strategy.[7] In other words, we should read Nixon's invocation of a "silent majority" as being as much directive as description. The myriad voices of working people were not being captured or set forth in the public discussion, and it was essential that such silence be maintained for Nixon and his party to effectively speak for them.

The apparent success of the Republicans in winning a working-class base—where Nixon did not clinch the deal, Reagan did a few years later—has been a central theme in US politics for the past forty years. By drawing attention to the multilayered crisis in representation that preceded it, I underscore the shakiness of this electoral realignment and the unreliability of any narrative that too neatly links social conservatism to the electoral migration of working-class whites. The failure of the contemporary social movements, the Democrats, and the labor movement to effectively represent the diverse streams of political opinion and action among these workers played—and continues to play—a major role in their electoral shifts and variability.

The Discovery of Middle America

With upheavals that many compared to the Civil War, 1968 was a year unlike any the country had seen in memory. President Johnson did not run for reelection as a result of the Vietnam War; Dr. Martin Luther King and Robert Kennedy were assassinated; and hundreds of cities erupted in either rebellions or riots, depending on who was describing them. By this time, another turning point had also been reached that had a profound effect on the popular perceptions of the antiwar movement, the shape of mainstream politics, and—most central for present purposes—the perception of the class dynamics of antiwar sentiment and protest. This was the discovery of the "Middle American."

In August 1968, antiwar Democrats came to Chicago to protest the nomination of Vice President Hubert Humphrey, who seemed clear to win against the antiwar Senator Eugene McCarthy (D-Minn.). Initial plans for a large peaceful week of protests and rallies shrank considerably in the weeks before the convention. Chicago Mayor Richard Daley's violent antipathy to protesters promised confrontation with the 12,000 Chicago police officers, as did the refusal of the city to issue any permits for protest. McCarthy asked that his supporters not attend en masse, and his sure defeat discouraged many more moderates from coming at all.

In excess of even the most pessimistic predictions, Daley's police beat and gassed the protesters in Chicago, sweeping up participants and bystanders alike in mass arrests and hospitalizing hundreds. The media, later joined by the Walker report of the National Commission on the Causes and Prevention of Violence, reached consensus that the events of Chicago consisted of a "police riot." As the report read, "the nature of the response [to protester provocation] was unrestrained and indiscriminate police violence on many occasions."[8]

But, as the country was to find out in the following weeks, a majority of Americans apparently did not agree. In later polls, "less than 20% said the police had used too much force," and interviews indicated that many white Americans were outraged by the protesters. Polls began to bear witness to the fact that protesters were disliked as much, if not more, than the Vietnam War itself. Rather than restrain the police, a majority of Americans seemed in favor of letting them off the leash. In the direct aftermath of the Democratic National Convention, a poll found that even those who opposed the war opposed the protesters. In one survey, 75 percent of respondents placed "Vietnam War protesters" on the negative end of a feeling scale, with 33 percent placing them at the far end. Of those respondents who viewed the war negatively, 63 percent placed the protesters there as well, and even 53 percent of those who called for complete withdrawal rated the protesters negatively.[9]

Who were these disgruntled masses, wondered the press. How could they condone such terrible police violence, and so despise the movement? A professor surveying the press identified a pattern of reportage prior to Chicago: "the young, the disenchanted, the revolutionary, the pacifistic and idealistic, the draft resisting, the McCarthy-supporting and those concerned with the desperate plight of the blacks and of a nation in a horrendous war [were contrasted to] the complacent, the contented, the Nixonites and Humphreyites, the ones who have it made."[10] The press, he seemed to say, sympathized with the young idealists and paid little attention (beyond sneering) to what they saw as the self-satisfied masses. Following the Chicago Democratic National Convention, Joseph Kraft, the syndicated columnist who coined the term "Middle America," wrote:

> Most of us in what is called the communications field are not rooted in the great mass of ordinary Americans—in Middle America. And the results show up not merely in occasional episodes such as the Chicago violence but more importantly in the systematic bias toward young people, minority groups, and the presidential candidates who appeal to them.
>
> To get a feel of this bias it is first necessary to understand the antagonism that divides the middle class of this country. On the one hand

> there are highly educated upper-income whites sure of and brimming
> with ideas for doing things differently. On the other hand, there is Mid-
> dle America, the large majority of low-income whites, traditional in
> their values and on the defensive against innovation.[11]

Kraft lays out the basic outline that the public discussion of class, race, and values
took in the years to come. There is an elite of upper-income whites (including
the media) who are systematically biased in support of youth and blacks pointing
toward change, and there is a lower-income white group suspicious of change
and defensive concerning the traditional values for which they stand. We, the
media—and by extension, other elites in the country—have not paid sufficient
attention to these ordinary people. In a kind of self-correction to redress this
unbalance (detailed in Barbara Ehrenreich's *Fear of Falling*), Chicago proved to
be the moment of soul-searching for this "liberal media."[12]

In bursts from 1968 through 1970 and beyond, the focus of the US media
became these "forgotten" people. *Time* magazine awarded the Man and Woman
of the Year slot to "The Middle Americans" in January 1970, following a long
year in which attention to these "little guys," or "average citizens" mushroomed.
The precise definition of these ordinary Joes remained somewhat vague, defined
more by who they were not—not black, not radical youth, not "pointy headed
professors"; a burgeoning social force distinguished by its lack of force, notable
for its normality. The social class of this group was unclear. In the book-length
version of the *Newsweek* October 1969 coverage of "The Troubled American,"
the author posits that "middle Americans" made up 55 percent of the population and defines them as "white Americans whose income ranged from $5,000
to $15,000," a range that collapsed affluent families with working-class people
living much closer to the bone. Pete Hamill's April 1969 "The Revolt of the White
Lower Middle Class" in *New York Magazine* looked only at those he called "working class," who made $5,000 to $10,000, and made up nearly 40 percent of the
total population.[13] The conceptual fuzziness concerning class was important because this group merged with Nixon's appeals to the "silent majority." On the one
hand, a totality of white Americans was envisioned as having similar interests in
common—and in opposition to blacks and social movement forces. In this way,
"Middle American" was a political term that adamantly eschewed class clarity.
On the other, increasingly, the "blue-collar workers" and "white ethnics" making up the less-privileged section of this white group were being singled out for
greater attention and approbation.

What were the political attitudes of these blue collar "Middle American" workers? The dominant stereotype, echoing the sociological consensus
of the previous decade, predicted that the white working class was moving to

the right—and recent indications of a possible rightward drift were plentiful. Hamill reported, "George Wallace received 10 million votes last year, not all of them from rednecked racists. That should have been a warning, strong and clear. If the stereotyped black man is becoming the working-class white man's enemy, the eventual enemy might be the democratic process itself."[14] He raised the specter of anti-democratic demagoguery in white working-class anger. These workers' concerns about crime and civil disorder; their hostility to student demonstrations; and most important, their negative, racist, and at times violent reactions to civil rights gains were taken as positive evidence that Republicans seeking an expanded conservative base could find in workers fertile soil.

On the other hand, some of the early media discussions of this group observed the indeterminacy of the political direction that these "lower-middle-class" white workers might take. Hamill again: "the working-class white man is actually in revolt against taxes, joyless work, the double standards and short memories of professional politicians, hypocrisy and what he considers the debasement of the American dream."[15] Alienation, defensive feelings about traditional values, anger at economic instability, an aggrieved sense that the system was not treating them fairly, and a growing distrust of government—these sentiments, culled from polls and interviews, could go in many directions. White workers remained economically liberal. The fear in 1968 that the Northern white working class would go over to Wallace proved unfounded when he ultimately received only a small fraction of their vote. Bobby Kennedy's brief candidacy indicated that blacks and white workers could still exuberantly support a shared candidate, and Humphrey ultimately received a number of votes from white workers similar to John Kennedy in 1960. Democrats continued to do well among this group at the local level in the elections of 1968, 1970, and even 1972, when Nixon's landslide came without coattails for his party.[16] Polling data indicates that on most questions this large, varied group was not more intolerant or illiberal than whites with higher incomes or prestige.[17] As we have explored in chapter 4, rank-and-file workers were already showing signs of the restiveness that came to characterize the early 1970s, which saw the greatest strike wave the country had seen since the 1940s.

The activist Left was also speculating about the political directions that white working-class people were moving in. Weeks before the 1968 election, Carl Davidson, former SDS-er and the editor of the *Guardian* declared, "In the past few months, most of the new left has accepted the idea that the working class is the central force for revolutionary change in the advanced capitalist countries." The events of May in France indicated one direction. But for the United States, George Wallace's campaign provided the lesson: "In the coming period, the white American working class is going to be militant, radical and activist. The problem for us is whether that insurgency will move to the right or to the left." Davidson noted the fears with which radicals apprehended the Wallace development, fears certainly stoked by mainstream press coverage of the "white ethnics." White workers were caricatured in the press and entertainment media, he argued, whereas radicals were in the grips of "class prejudice," which "is often as dehumanizing to us and white industrial workers as racism is to both whites and blacks. In many ways, the fears many radical students have of white workers are similar to the fears white workers have of black people."[18]

For a period, a number of left streams sought to "relate" to the working class, black and white.[19] The *Guardian* had hired former union organizer Stanley Aronowitz to write a column on the labor movement, and the paper editorialized that there was "No More Life of Riley" for the working class—restive, alienated workers were themselves possible allies in the struggle. Having left the antiwar and student movements, many former SDS-ers were working as labor staffers and were creating networks of progressive labor organizers, researchers, and the like.[20] Each side of the 1969 SDS split put forward orientations toward the working class but disagreed about what that meant. The Progressive Labor "worker-student alliance" hoped to unite factory workers and students into a revolutionary vanguard; the SDS Revolutionary Youth Movement leadership groups, much of which eventually became Maoists or Weatherman, for the most part rejected the possibility of older workers joining the struggle but urged "working class youth" to follow a revolutionary vanguard (best represented by the Black Panthers and third-world revolutionaries). A small leftist group, the International Socialists, developed its own orientation toward the rank-and-file rebellion within labor, laying the groundwork for future decades of organizing in unions and campuses with a "class perspective."

Republican Courtship

For Republicans, the opportunities for and challenges to attracting the working-class vote were clear. But their strategy for consolidating a new majority was, at first, less so. During his 1968 campaign, Nixon's appeals to "Middle Americans" were a central plank of his "southern strategy," the organization of a racial and regional realignment for the Republican grassroots. With the help of advisers such as Kevin Philips (who wrote *The Emerging Republican Majority* in 1969), Nixon recognized the growing influence in US politics of the Sunbelt—the long Southern swath of the United States ranging from Florida; through the growing Southern cities and suburbs of Atlanta, Charlotte, Richmond; over to Arizona and the desert Southwest; and across to southern California.[21] Many of the key issues that came to define the conservative agenda of the coming decades—tax cuts, law and order, defense spending, and "family values"—found their roots in this region. Barry Goldwater's 1964 Republican campaign, which indicated the salience of many of these issues for formerly Democratic voters in the South, and Wallace's successful racist and populist challenges within the Democratic Party and as an independent candidate together gave "clear signs that a conservative Republican realignment might be imminent." But Nixon did not stop with the Sunbelt: he and his supporters saw the possibility that "sunbelt attitudes . . . might eventually spread into the suburbs and working class neighborhoods of the old North."[22]

Nixon's campaign and first years in office witnessed a scattershot approach to attracting Democrats and creating a new Republican Majority, a story that has been detailed elsewhere.[23] Polarizing a "silent majority" from antiwar protesters was an early rhetorical tactic. From 1968 to 1970, the youthful protester joined blacks as the "other" to the working-class majority.

Within days of the Chicago Democratic National Convention, Nixon chose that Democratic Party stronghold to launch his campaign and was greeted by hundreds of thousands of supporters: "Veteran observers said they never had seen a Republican candidate for any office get such a welcome here in 30 years."[24] It was in Chicago that he began to hammer home the theme of law and order, which became a central plank of his campaign, and addressed himself to the "forgotten Americans" who had supported the police against the protesters during the August days.

In his speeches leading up to election day, Nixon frequently invoked a theme of "unity" that quite obviously played into a politics of division. Recognizing this, Vice President Humphrey argued from the stump that "you can't vote your anger" and positioned the Democrats as the party of "hope." When Johnson halted the bombing campaign in September, Humphrey's support jumped, and a Democratic victory appeared viable for the first time since Robert Kennedy's death. Northern and urban white working-class support for George Wallace largely evaporated. Nixon did, however, win the day, with Humphrey trailing by half a million votes and Wallace doing well in the deep South. Nixon's "southern strategy" persisted after the election: Having won a plurality of 43 percent in the 1968 election wither fewer actual voters than he had attracted in 1960, Nixon still had a majority to pursue.

Nixon and the Antiwar Movement

Within a year of taking office, President Nixon began to draw down troops in Vietnam (as part of the policy of Vietnamization) and reinstated the draft lottery. These policy changes served to create the impression that the war was winding down while removing a major grievance concerning the fairness of the draft system, thereby taking wind out of an already-fragmenting antiwar movement. But abetting the internal troubles of the movement was an external campaign waged by the Nixon administration to discredit the movement and isolate the protesters, which began immediately after Nixon came into office. In the first months of the Nixon administration, surveillance of all protest movements was dramatically increased. The universities, where possible, were assigned numerous military agents; CIA domestic counterintelligence expanded, along with wiretap rights; and the FBI increased its number of agents on the ground. Fred Halstead, antiwar leader and Socialist Worker Party presidential candidate in 1968, told an interviewer, "The Nixon administration was different in that sense. I mean, suddenly you were covered like a blanket. You could feel it," and the superintendent of the Illinois State police reported, "I've never seen anything like the intensity of current investigations in all my years in law enforcement." The antiwar movement, like the Black Power and civil rights movements before it, was under ongoing surveillance; infiltrated; red-baited; and subjected to varying degrees of repression, including arrests, *agents provocateur*, break-ins, intimidation, and physical violence.[25]

In addition to intensifying its repressive tactics, the Nixon administration launched a special campaign in anticipation of movement plans for protests in fall 1969. The October Moratorium and November Mobilization represented the first large-scale protests during Nixon's tenure, and the White House spent months formulating plans to defuse and disrupt the demonstrations and instigate countermobilization efforts. Memos drawing up the plans circulated within the White House for weeks; as one aide recalled, "We all felt threatened, put on the defensive, by the imminence of these two well-organized, well-publicized demonstrations, and the President was taking the initiative in suggesting how we might counter our critics."[26] Nixon said he was "not going to be pushed around by the demonstrators and the rabble in the streets."[27] The plans that were later executed included active manipulation of the media, pressure on antiwar members of Congress, and the creation and facilitation of pro-Nixon groups and actions during the fall. Together, these actions were meant to fulfill the central objectives of the White House counteroffensive: ensure that "those people who are loyal to the country and who have been disillusioned by the war . . . [are] pulled back into the fold of national consciousness" while making sure to "isolate the leaders" of the protests.[28] Attracting the "people who are loyal" was the work of Nixon; attacking the protesters was the job of Spiro Agnew, Nixon's vice president.

Nixon's "Silent Majority" speech of November 3, 1969, was his most successful gambit in this direction. Like in the days following the Chicago Democratic National Convention, Nixon positioned himself, and the silent or forgotten

Americans he claimed to represent, against the antiwar protesters. In that speech, he famously declared, "The more support that I can have from the American people the sooner that pledge [to end the war and "win the peace"] can be redeemed. For the more divided we are at home, the less likely the enemy is to negotiate in Paris. Let us be united for peace. Let us also be united against defeat. Because let us understand North Vietnam cannot defeat or humiliate the United States. Only Americans can do that. . . . You, the great silent majority of my fellow Americans, I ask for your support."

Nixon's approval ratings soared in the aftermath of the speech. Afterward, the Harris poll asked, "In general, just as far as their objectives are concerned, do you sympathize with the goals of the people who are demonstrating, marching, and protesting against the war in Vietnam or do you disagree?" Indicating that Nixon's polarization was moderately successful, 45 percent of the people surveyed disagreed with the goals of antiwar protesters, 39 percent sympathized, and 16 percent were not sure—this after the very popular October Moratorium, at a time when large majorities opposed the war.[29]

The potential unpopularity of the protesters created an opportunity; in the weeks of the Moratorium and Mobilization the Nixon administration unleashed Spiro Agnew to lead the charge. Young Nixon staffers who were unhappy about the vitriol from the Administration reported that senior aides such as H. R. Haldeman felt "there is . . . political mileage in attacking student radicals."[30] The administration questioned the patriotism of the protesters, who were accused of "taking orders from Hanoi."[31] Vice President Spiro Agnew, who initially made a name for himself facing down black activists in Baltimore, expended his greatest invectives during his first years in national office on the antiwar movement—which he characterized as being led by "effete corps of impudent snobs," consisting of "ideological eunuchs," "merchants of hate," and "parasites of passion." Agnew called the Moratorium demonstrations a "carnival in the streets" led by a "strident minority" filled with "intolerant clamor and cacophony." Playing the bad cop (or as Eugene McCarthy observed, "Nixon's Nixon," referring to Nixon's pugnacious anticommunist turn as vice president under Dwight Eisenhower), Agnew referred to the president's inaugural plea that the country "lower our voices" by saying, "I, for one, will not lower my voice until the restoration of sanity and civil order allow a quiet voice to be heard once again. The Mobe, the Mobilization, the Moratorium have become somewhat fashionable forms of citizen expression," which are "negative in content, disruptive in effect."[32]

Agnew consistently painted a picture of an elite protester. As *Time* magazine reported in 1969, he ridiculed "campus protesters who 'take their tactics from Castro and their money from Daddy.'"[33] But Agnew's charge of elitism was not original. This image, combined with the image of civil disorder that such privileged elite recklessly produced, can be found in the rhetoric of George Wallace's campaign in 1968. Wallace proved to be popular when he rhetorically went after hippies and antiwar protesters, and the "briefcase totin' bureaucrats, ivory-tower guideline writers, bearded anarchists, smart-aleck editorial writers and pointy-headed professors."[34]

With this kind of rhetoric, the amorphous status of the Middle American became more class-specific. In Wallace's and Agnew's right-wing populist language, an "us," white workers, was posited against a "them," liberal bureaucrats and protesters. Wallace's economic populism and flamboyant language of class resentment helped him to achieve a popular following among Northern urban workers for a period during his presidential campaign. Wallace reached out to "the average man on the street, this man in the textile mill, this man in the steel mill, this barber, this beautician, the policemen on the beat," and he described how "a select group have written guidelines in bureaus and court decisions, have spoken from some pulpits, some college campuses, some newspaper offices, looking down their noses" at them. These elites say "that you do not know how to get up in the morning or go to bed at night unless we write you a guideline."[35] Agnew, in words more rousing than the president's, called on the "silent young majority who go to school and to work and war, if necessary," to "make itself heard, to come to its own defense."[36] Theirs was the most vivid, most consistent, loud and publicized class-specific rhetoric of the period.

The tone of these angry invectives undoubtedly connected with many whites in a cathartic manner.[37] *Time* magazine quoted Paul M. Deac, executive vice president of the National Confederation of American Ethnic Groups, who "expressed the especially virulent outrage of the poorer Middle Americans. . . . 'The Moratorium was a stab in the back to our boys on the firing lines. Our families don't have long-haired brats—they'd tear the hair off them. Our boys don't smoke pot or raise hell or seek deferments. Our people are too busy making a living and trying to be good Americans.'"[38] Writing forty years later, political scientist Adolph Reed observes, "Wallace and Nixon took postwar liberalism's stereotypes of an element of the white working class and revalorized them, offering them as the basis of a coherent, affirmative political identity."[39]

Coming from powerful politicians and the media, such rhetoric also lent discursive organization to sentiments where such organization was otherwise lacking. Specifically, the other reference groups that might have competed for that discursive space—the antiwar movement, the Democratic Party, and the labor movement—were unable, unsuccessful, or uninterested in doing so. The outcome of this angry virulence and successful Republican organization were the hardhat demonstrations of 1970.

In the aftermath of Nixon's "Silent Majority" speech, the *New York Times* (November 23, 1969) reported that "many American were convinced by Mr Nixon's speech that he was striving hard to end the war. Their comments also indicate that he left with them an expectation that we will remove US troops from Vietnam within a reasonable time." His approval ratings peaked, and Henry Kissinger claimed that the speech "turned the public around completely."[40] But progress on the war proved elusive, and the high approval of his handling of the war proved short-lived, dropping from 65 percent in November to 46 percent in April. In February, an aide to Haldeman reported, "the President noted that it seems that our silent majority group has lost its steam."[41] At the same time, Nixon sought to make a decisive turn in the war because peace talks had stalled. The invasion and bombing of North Vietnamese strongholds in Cambodia was the strategy chosen by Nixon, and supported by the military, to deliver the blow.

Making Sense of the Hardhat Rallies

During the weeks in May when the country surged against the invasion of Cambodia and construction workers and allies took to the streets of New York, local and some national media outlets dispatched dozens of reporters to get a sense of the attitudes of workers in New York and around the country. In the context of the period described here, the quotations selected by local papers need to be taken critically because the selection process by the media—as well as the words spoken by the workers they interviewed—were already framed by the stereotypes of the angry worker and within the discourses of the workers' resentment.[42] Unsurprisingly, among the themes that prominently emerged in the reporting were anger and reaction: "These hippies are getting what they deserve." A "double standard" argument was frequently cited. In a long magazine piece, Joe Kelly, an electrician who participated in the hardhat demonstrations, explained that he didn't support the war. What got him angry, however, among other things, was that "These kids . . . they can do as they feel like. I mean, burn, loot, steal, do anything they feel like in the name of social reform. But can the average Joe Blow citizen go out and do this?"[43]

The media depicted a conservative, authority-leaning group. As one worker who was interviewed stated, "I think it's about time something like this has being done [*sic*]. Everybody grows up and everybody has somebody over them, and when the parents don't take over, things go wrong." Another worker, also invoking the need for greater parental discipline, explained that, if your kids disagreed with you, "Well let me tell you the old-fashioned way: Use your hand. My father didn't stop to hit me. If I said I didn't like something, he hit me. I larned [sic] to like it. That's the way it has to be." Another reporter quoted a rally participant as saying about the dead students at Kent, "I have no sympathy for them. I'm not a college man, I'm not smart. But I know one thing: when a guy's got a gun, I don't throw rocks at him. I go the other way. . . . If I attacked that cop over there, I'd expect him to shoot me." The *New York Times* editors opined about the "antidemocratic currents, from opposite political extremes" that were harming the country.[44]

Vice President Agnew observed that it was "understandable" that construction workers attacked antiwar demonstrators. He argued there was a "fundamental difference" between campus protest and the hardhats: "campus disruptions were not spontaneous. They were not the result of a rage that swept a person who worked with his hands to build America [and saw] people advocating that it be torn down. This [the hardhat attack] was a wave in defense of a country, not a wave to destroy a country."[45] Subsequent investigations by scholars indicate that the hardhat rallies that followed the first were themselves far from spontaneous. Labor leaders authorized them, and workers were told they would lose no pay if they left work to join them. As the month of May progressed, Building Trade Council leaders in New York played increasingly active roles organizing their members to support the cause, culminating in the May 20 Honor the Flag, Honor America rally.

What the hardhat protesters were defending was much less clear than Agnew or the mainstream coverage indicated. There was a consistent focus in the national press on the "pro-war" nature of the rallies. But it is clear from most of the local coverage, even given its biases, that the working-class people rallying did not share a common response to the war. (It is also clear that working-class people were not the only ones rallying and that Wall Street workers contributed mightily in numbers to all the events that were described as "hardhat" events.) One thirty-seven-year-old worker said, "personally I think this war has lasted too long: anyone who's simply for war is crazy." Playing on the banner heading for the Honor the Flag, Honor America, a twenty-three-year-old "long-haired" worker said, "I don't think you honor America by beating someone over the head with the flag." A dock worker argued, "'Listen, all of us have a breaking point. My son asks me, Why is there war, why are there troops over there. Sometimes I really can't give him an answer. All I know is we have one leader and one country and must back them to the limit." He thought for a minute and added, "If my son were over there I'd want the country to back him."[46]

The frustration expressed by many workers who were interviewed, as many later analysts and further studies have noted, seemed to be less about the war and more about class and power.[47] Socially liberal and aristocratic Republican Mayor John Lindsay, for example, was the primary political target of the protesters; signs opposing Lindsay overwhelmed other expressions of negativity in the May 20 rally. For some, the gulf between their experience and those of the college protesters loomed large. An unnamed wife of a worker who witnessed the demonstration from her office told the paper, "We were watching and wanted to go get down there with them. We wanted to tell off those kids. They have too much." Another argued, "I feel they [college demonstrators] have been with the silver spoon in their mouth too long and somebody has to take a hand in this to stop them, because if not, the country itself will come to ruins." Repeatedly, a class resentment of privileged youth was echoed. Echoing Nixon, another man said, "The students who throw bottles, close colleges and use foul language are bums."[48]

But this class resentment was complicated, for some, not by a gulf between themselves and the protesters but by a disturbing proximity. These workers had dedicated their lives to getting a leg up for their children, and the college campuses where they sent their children appeared to be closing and coming apart at the seams. The secretary-treasurer of the Electrical, Radio and Machine Workers Union explained of his members, "I would say that the majority were opposed to the decision to go into Cambodia. They feel that the students should have a right to dissent. They can't understand how the students can tear up their own facilities. They are paying high tuition and see the schools closed down. Their kids missing class. This isn't right." The president of the Carpenters said, "These guys have worked hard to send kids to college. Kid [sic] have a right to protest but not to burn down buildings. Our men see them throwing away a great opportunity that they wish they could have had." One young man who had recently worked on a construction crew wrote of his former foreman: "He says that he has worked hard all these years for his kids to go to college and now he see college as a place 'where kids run wild, doing whatever the hell they please.'"[49]

Similar sentiments were expressed by workers from Boston interviewed by Richard Sennett and Jonathan Cobb in the course of ethnographic research conducted from July 1969 to July 1970. They tease out an even deeper level of anxiety in their subjects on the topic of having sent their children to college. "Education" is a "cover term," they argue, that "stands in for a whole range of experiences and feelings that may in fact have little to do with formal schooling." From their interviews, they conclude that *education* is interpreted by the workers they spoke to as giving people the chance not only to have better jobs, more money, and respect but also greater "personal, rational control," which Sennett and Cobb call "the weapons of self." But this feeling is combined with a sense of "revulsion" about the actual life of middle-class people and the less honest work that they do.

> Capturing respect in the larger America, then, meant to [one man they spoke with] getting into an educated position; but capturing that respect means that he no longer respects himself. This contradiction ran through every discussion we held, as an image either of what people felt compelled to do with their own lives or of what they sought for their sons. If the boys could get educated, anybody in America would respect them; and yet . . . the fathers felt education would lead the young into work not as "real" as their own.[50]

Lurking, therefore, close enough to the surface for the media to pick it up was a class resentment and unease among workers that was in part expressed around the issues of war and protest.

To return to themes raised in chapter 2, the cultural gulf between the protesters and white workers was exacerbated by the actions of the movement, which frequently presented itself and framed its arguments in a manner that was likely to alienate workers who might sympathize with their opposition to the war. The countercultural expression of many parts of the movement challenged core values of many workers (and non-workers). Just as the movements were unpopular with the country at large, they were unpopular with many workers for their seeming disrespect for norms of behavior, dress, and speech. "Radicalism" itself was something to distance oneself from, rather than embrace. Sociologist and priest, Father Andrew Greeley, argued at the time, "If the white ethnic is told in effect that to support peace he must also support the Black Panthers, women's liberation, widespread use of drugs, free love, campus radicals, Dr. Spock, long hair, and picketing clergyman, he may find it very difficult to put himself on the side of peace."[51]

The movement was indisputably *moralistic*, in that it carried a judging attitude in its expression of opposition. This moralism of many of the war opponents, and their perception of a morally righteous movement—"Hey, hey, LBJ, how many kids did you kill today?"—contributed to the difficulty and resistance that many people felt in identifying their own disagreements with the war with those of the movement. Moralistic opposition to the war carried with it the potential for the perception that the moralists were judging the soldiers, their families, people who supported the president or who believed in the country. It was that sense of judgment, this other group sitting on high and telling everyone else how to live their lives that Wallace and Agnew fed on with their accusations of "impudent snobbery." One of the interviews described by Sennett and Cobb was with a young man who had returned from Vietnam hating the war but also hating the protesters. As he explained, "Their advantages, you know, wealth, education, the suburbs, all that, make them think they can be more moral. They can understand *you*, with all their fancy words, but you can't understand them, 'cause you're just part of the scenery."[52] Another interviewee, Victor Belloti, who went to Vietnam in 1965 and returned for much of the movement, told Appy, "To me most of them were the arch-liberals from suburban communities, having never really worked in their lives. They were kids who had never had anything go wrong with them and they went on 'marches' and they protested the Vietnam War. They didn't have the slightest idea what was going on over there. Politically they were right, I'm not saying they weren't."[53]

Furthermore, the abstraction with which many antiwar activists made their cases was part of the problem, as we have previously seen. This abstraction was coupled with highly ideological and political criticisms of US imperialism, which cast the North Vietnamese as sympathetic freedom fighters. Chants such as "Ho ho ho Chi Minh, the NLF is gonna win" and displays of North Vietnamese flags at demonstrations, although always representative of only a small minority of the movement as a whole, garnered significant media attention and contributed to the distance that many felt from the message of the movement. It was the NLF, after all, that sons, brothers, and fathers were fighting against.

Although the abstract, moral, or political reasons for opposing the war were often suspect, for workers experiential reasons were more likely to be seen as legitimate. But the most vocal opponents of the war *appeared* to be the people least affected by it. In this way, the problem went beyond the fact that working-class people felt that they were being judged by upper-middle-class people. It was the very idea that these upper-middle-class people felt they could judge anything at all from where they sat that also fueled a class-based anger, particularly among veterans. The young veteran who spoke with Sennett and Cobb explained, "I had to fight over there. . . . I mean, I grew up with all the patriotism, the VFW [Veterans of Foreign Wars] crap, and like, it *hurt* to change, I went through hell."[54] Antiwar opposition from the protected sons and daughters of the elite was facile, shallow, even offensive.

And in some, if not many, situations, there was not only the appearance of the potential of moral judgment; antiwar activists also held workers in contempt. "It was clear," wrote a working-class antiwar activist, "that ordinary students who were against the war thought that workers were all crypto-Nazis. Many students and active leftists really did believe that 'working people are the enemy.'" Although this activist goes on to say that this was not true of the movement as a whole, Sennett and Cobb argue that elite liberals were both assigned and themselves took up "badges of ability" conferred on them for their morally righteous opposition to the war. "Badges of ability," according to Sennett and Cobb, are ways in which individuals come to be seen as standing out from the group. The traction of the image of the hardhat, they suggest, lay in the fact that it confirmed the "social ideal" that there existed a few, a moral minority, who understood the true, socially just path—being against the war—who stood against the mass of people "whose sensitivity they believe inferior to their own."[55] Classical conservatives (in the mode of José Ortega y Gasset) and contemporary liberals (along the lines of Seymour Martin Lipset) could together agree on this kind of demarcation of the few from the mass.

It was not for nothing that the movement had an elitist image—there were people, such as James Fallows's friends, who looked down on workers and bought the stereotypes. The appearance of moral superiority and denigrating attitudes from some protesters were among the more explicit manifestations of a conflicted relationship, largely based in class dynamics, between parts of the antiwar movement and workers. This climate of friction was, occasionally, punctuated by physical acts of violence, including fights at protests and, obviously, the hardhat demonstrations themselves. And the image of the belligerent hardhat who was infuriated with elite protesters and whose significance was to take on mythic proportions was not conjured out of thin air either. Real class anger and real frustrations with the antiwar movement provided cultural space for the image to be amplified, despite its narrow empirical basis.

The Crisis of Representation

Within weeks of the riotous demonstrations, that cultural space was filled with another rapacious image of a right-wing worker in the popular and critically acclaimed film *Joe* (1970). Joe Curran, the antihero of this instant cult classic, is a white "working stiff" who spends his days "burning his balls" in front of a furnace. The audience first meets Joe at a bar, where we watch him in a rant about the social problems of the day. "Niggers are getting all the money," he complains in a long racist soliloquy about welfare; "they're not doing nothing"; "burn a few buildings you get paid for it"; "I ain't even been inside of Macy's and they want a charge account." Affirmative action is skewered: "If you can't read you have a better chance of getting hired"; Joe's own "kids couldn't get into a regular college." But the "white kids are worse than the niggers. . . . money don't mean nothing to them." "White kids, rich white kids, the worst hippies," "they used to be idealistic, now they go on those peace marches, wacked out on drugs." They have "no respect for the president." They go to "Ivy leagues colleges," the "best colleges," and they're just into "sex, drugs, pissing on America." Worst of all, "poor kids and middle-class kids are copying the rich kids." Joe concludes, "I'd like to kill one of them." And by the end of the film, he has killed quite a few in a shootout at a rural "commune," a scene that was, according to the lead actor, inspired by the My Lai massacre.[56] Joe's unlikely ally and inspiration is an advertising executive who begins the film accidentally killing his daughter's drug-dealing, hippie artist boyfriend—arguably the least sympathetic character in the film, Joe included—and ends it by "accidentally" killing his daughter.

"The message" of the movie, as explained by Peter Boyle, the actor who plays Joe, "is very plain. It says that we'd just better stop that war in Vietnam now; that we'd just better stop killing our children there or we're going to be killing our children in the streets here."[57] What seems plainer is the depiction in the movie of a US social fabric strained to the point of rupture. According to *Joe*, the catalytic elements in this rupture are the hedonistic, narcissistic, drug-addled youth on the one side and the bitter, resentful, hyperpatriotic white workers on the other. The two sides are seen as hating one another—Joe, quite obviously, shows this in nearly everything he says; and the hippies consistently mock Joe ("he looks like a truck driver") when they see him. Joe is also envious of the life that these young people lead and their freedoms while at the same time he is unsettled by what he sees as the meaninglessness of their lives. "How do they fall in love?" he plaintively asks, watching the beginning of a free-love "orgy."

Yet the fulcrum of the film is the advertising executive father, who is much less sure about his own place in this new world. He takes action, but it is unconscious, without clear intent. He does not mean to kill his daughter's boyfriend, and he consistently argues with Joe to be more restrained. He is concerned about his hippie daughter but is not clear what to do about her, and his passive acquiescence to Joe's actions results in the worst possible catastrophe. The "culture" is getting away from him, just like it is getting away from Joe, but whereas Joe is ready to "go to war," the executive seems like a man who is caught in the wrong place at the wrong time. He finds a strange ally in the murderous Joe—scenes where the two families come together or where each man enters the other's cultural sphere are strained and deeply uncomfortable. Joe's bowling buddies joke that his new friend "better stick to golf," and the executive's wife, in turn, is clearly horrified by Joe. The apparent argument of the movie is that the soul of the establishment, roiled by the changing culture, is vulnerable to the worst instincts of reaction, with Joe embodying those very passions.

Such a caricature leaned for its support on the post-war reformulations of the working class sketched in chapter 6, what Adolph Reed describes as "a notion of the working class and its political characteristics that . . . is fundamentally a folk theory, more allegory than social science."[58] But the eagerness with which culture makers and elite politicians seized on the figure of the reactionary worker raises the possibility that a great deal of projection was at work as well. Establishment

figures were recoiling from the social unrest of the period, appalled by the behavior of their own sons and daughters but constrained by their own propriety
(including the "badges of ability" they had conferred on themselves) from actually engaging in a reactionary fight. Who better than the macho, authoritarian
white working class to step in and "right" the situation? Joe, Archie Bunker, and
the hardhats themselves became figures that could be held responsible for forcing
a corrective course, one that was in fact desired by many of their elite brethren.

Released in the aftermath of the hardhat demonstrations, the movie showed an
alignment of white workers with the forces of reaction that seemed "prophetic,"
and the rift between the "hippies" and "workers" was at its zenith. Boyle reported,
"I hear that kids are standing up at the end of the movie and yelling, 'I'm going
to shoot back, Joe.'"[59] Within months, *All in the Family* aired for the first time,
and Archie Bunker was piped into millions of US homes. The cultural icon of the
reactionary worker had been firmly established.

Who could better represent workers? A week after the hardhat demonstrations, one construction worker on a site near City College in New York explained
to students there, "most construction guys don't go looking for trouble. . . . But
they feel they're getting stepped on. We built this country and I don't think we
have a say now."[60] This feeling of "not having a say" was prevalent in the reporting of working-class attitudes of the period. The media, as we have seen, were in
the throes of a correction on that front, in their largely one-sided remembrance
of the forgotten Americans. But substantial representation proved more elusive.

Labor parties and trade unions are the institutionalized forms typically
available to working-class self-representation in the public sphere. Lacking a
labor party, for substantial representation most US workers and unions have
turned to the Democratic Party since the early part of the twentieth century,
not always with enthusiasm. At the level of local elections, this affinity stayed
true throughout the post–World War II period, through the elections of 1980.
In presidential elections, this base had not been not as reliable or consistent
in the post-war period as the story of its more recent decline might indicate.
The Democratic Party continued to be the de facto party of the working class,
but during the 1950s its leadership did not inspire the confidence of unionized
workers to the same degree that Franklin Roosevelt and Harry Truman had.
President Truman won almost 80 percent of the union vote in 1948 campaign-
ing against the Taft-Hartley Act; but in 1952, Democratic candidate Adlai Stevenson's labor record was considerably weaker than Truman's, who had himself
used Taft-Hartley injunctions thirty-seven times during his second term. The
New York Times noted that Stevenson "managed to retain the admiration of the
Northern liberals without alienating the Southern Conservatives," but he had
alienated labor for actions such as criticizing Truman for not using Taft-Hartley

to further discipline striking steel workers earlier that year.[61] Stevenson won a little more than half of union voters in 1952 and even fewer in 1956. Johnson, promising a Great Society and running against Barry "in your guts you know he's nuts" Goldwater in 1964 again secured 80 percent of the union vote, but Humphrey's support in 1968 paralleled Stevenson's. The real falling off for Democrats, however, was among white working-class voters more generally—a majority of whom began to vote Republican starting with Nixon, a voting pattern that has continued to this day.[62]

Over the course of the 1960s, the big Democratic tent seemed to be covering less ground. Democrats were losing the South, an inevitability following their embrace of civil and voting rights. Labor and the social movements appeared miles apart on foreign policy and, to some extent, domestic policy. In an editorial written the day after the hardhat rally, the New York Times opined, "Looking toward 1972 and later, the Democrats will have to reform their own warring ranks—sectional, racial, traditional and liberal—if they are to recover their position as the party of progress and the bearer of the occasional politics of happiness."[63] But reform their own warring ranks they did not, and it is questionable whether they could have. The Democrats, always fractured, responded to the pressures from their myriad supporters unevenly and in contradictory fashions, playing to, while also challenging, the politics of division, depending on the leader, context, and issue.

Among its mainstream leaders, the more general liberal party line on the social issues of the day was blamed for its decline. The solution of the mainstream party leaders to the challenges facing them from their white working-class base was to move closer to the Republicans on social issues. In August 1970, Humphrey told a crowd that the Democrats needed to "let the hardhats know we understand what is bugging them—that we, too, condemn criminality and riots and violence and extreme social turbulence." The "conservative" Humphrey wing of the Democratic Party moved away from the movement-sympathetic New Politics supporters, and for much of the 1970 election cycle, Democrats were fairly successful at "cutting right" to undercut the law-and-order campaign of their Republican rivals. For example, polling indicated that most of the electorate could see no difference between the positions of the two parties on crime.[64]

On the left flank were party activists still angered by the antidemocratic exclusion of McCarthy's antiwar candidacy in 1968 and the hardball tactics pursued by the traditional Democratic machine in keeping the more liberal delegates and positions at bay during the Chicago convention. Teddy Kennedy, following his brother, was one bridge between the wings of the party, and he argued that "the umbrella of the Democratic Party is broad enough to cover every type of young American—the young hardhat as well as the young Dove, the worker as well as the student."[65] But for many left Democrats, seeking to maintain a connection with a revanchist labor bureaucracy and what appeared to be a reactionary white working class did not seem worth the effort. For them, "all the myths of authoritarianism and relative well-being were simply updated to include an explanation of why 'backlash' or 'conservatism' were now inevitable."[66]

As Jefferson Cowie demonstrates, the George McGovern candidacy and his ultimate defeat in 1972 marked the culmination of these factional trends that had been developing in the party and confirmed the declining significance of the role of the Democratic Party as a reliable reference group for white workers in the United States.[67] The AFL-CIO, having been effectively cut out of the party nomination process, in large part due to its own intransigence regarding rule changes put in effect two years before, for the first (and only) time in its history decided to remain neutral in the 1972 presidential elections. (Forty national unions nevertheless campaigned vigorously for McGovern.) Labor, when looked at through the votes of unionized white voters, did not completely abandon the Democrats—McGovern got 40 percent of the white unionist vote. But the New Politics wing of the party did alienate many working-class Democrats.

This alienation was complex, and it stemmed from a number of sources that included intolerance and bigotry among workers, the conservatism of big labor, and deep-seated cultural mores held by workers that were upset by the rapidly changing culture. Sociologist Jonathan Rieder argues that the racist attitudes attributed to many white ethnic workers during this period "were often displaced conflicts of class." White ethnics associated the ghetto with incivility and moral decline and associated welfare with handouts.[68] The segregated distance marking white working-class neighborhoods and working-class suburbs from working-class people of color exaggerated these distorted perceptions all the more.

And the roots of the divide were fostered by policy as well. Structurally, as Frances Fox Piven, Nelson Lichtenstein, and others point out, the US welfare state was both too fragmented and too meager to buttress class solidarity. During the post-war era, labor and progressive Democrats had failed to significantly expand national social democratic policy, with private benefit arrangements providing weak and sectional alternatives to European-style universal programs covering health care, education, and family support. Because these economic supports remained private, and such public programs were not created, the Democrats were neither looked to for such remedies nor held to the standards of their vision. The expansion of the welfare state under Johnson and Nixon came as a response to African American mobilization and resulted in greater support for some programs that benefited the disproportionately minority poor. These urban-renewal projects, cash benefits, and health programs were paid for through regressive taxes, whose burden therefore fell disproportionately on lower-income people.

Another kind of welfare state was also growing during the post-war period—but here the beneficiaries were overwhelmingly white suburbanites, mostly affluent and middle class. The GI Bill, Federal Housing Administration, and Interstate Highway Act all provided the necessary infrastructural support for suburban enclaves, whose political power and residential and economic isolation protected their residents from the political projects of housing and school desegregation efforts. Historian Matthew Lassiter argues, "In the intersection of electoral politics and metropolitan space, the protection of the class privileges of affluent suburbs consistently displaced the burdens of racial integration onto working-class white neighborhoods, a volatile process that severely undermined the moral authority of liberalism and simultaneously disproved the populist solidarity proclaimed by the champions of the Silent Majority."[69]

To align social democratic welfare-state policies solely with the interests of people of color itself reflects a conservative framing. Many of the advances of the era—civil rights legislation, Medicare, and educational investments—directly benefited white workers, women, and working-class communities more broadly. But the conservative revolts against these social initiatives, taking the forms of tax revolts by property holders and revolts by parents against "interference" in the schools, sometimes explicitly and often implicitly racist, offered a competing frame for white workers to make sense of the changes. On the one hand, affluent whites demanded "freedom" from government programs and interference (while benefiting from select policies and tax cuts); on the other, social movements for the poor demanded government income and infrastructural support. White workers perceived themselves as being squeezed between the two. The answer to the question of whether the government was working to support their interests became more muddled. This became increasingly the case as the economic prospects for workers worsened at the end of the decade, sowing the ground for scarcity-fueled, self-protective insularity. For many white workers, the basic meaning of liberalism was transmuted, a change in perception facilitated by the campaigns of the conservative Republicans. Liberalism came to be seen as a "force inimical to the working and lower middle classes."[70] The racial "populist solidarity" of whites that the Republicans sought exerted (a tenuous) hold on white working-class collective identity, and the politics of resentment against liberal social changes had greater traction.

Missing from the dominant visions offered by either party were economic and social policies that explicitly acknowledged the concerns and desires of many white workers. Andrew Levison's *The Working Class Majority*, published in 1974, goes so far as to make the argument that "none of the social programs of the great society period were aimed at championing the new and growing social and economic grievances of all working people."[71] Levison lists a number of issues on which the Democrats could have better served a working-class base while continuing to practice antiracist and other social justice politics. Desegregation efforts in schools and housing were disproportionately enacted in working-class neighborhoods, and the first affirmative action programs took place in union workplaces. Targeting such efforts at middle-class and affluent communities as well might have buttressed working-class support for these programs. As it went, while racism contributed to the resistance that many white workers showed toward these programs, their reactions were often predicated on a sense of having to bear an undue burden. "Why us?" was the question most frequently asked. Writing in 1971, Sexton and Sexton quote pollster Lou Harris arguing, "The privileged have become the progenitors of change, while the underprivileged whites have become the steadfast defenders of the status quo." Sexton and Sexton then argue, "He misunderstands. Workers simply oppose change that always benefits others and hurts them. In this, they resemble many who serve on college faculties. That is, they resist change that threatens them personally, and can afford to take grandstand postures on issues that do not." And Levison argues, "To be sure, there is substantial racism of the most overt and mindless type. But clearly, the hostility to busing, quotas, and public housing was made far worse, and many additional workers were alienated because, instead of seeking to meet black needs as part of a general assault on the social and economic problems of all workers, these programs put black improvement directly in conflict with the objective interest of white workers."[72] I think Levison exaggerates the extent of the objective conflict in his argument, but it is certainly true that at the level of perception, many white workers saw themselves as losing ground *because* others—African Americans, the poor—were gaining. Other public policy efforts at the time facilitated division as well. The Democratic Party failed to fight for "economic conversion" as it fought for peace, leaving factories whose production were tied to the military industry with layoffs and limited prospects; and it failed to fight for jobs as it fought for a cleaner environment, making it more likely that constituencies who might have joined hands could be divided by competing interests. He concludes,

> The worker who had voted for George Wallace in 1968 had seen nothing since then to make him changes his mind. Wallace's potent message, "Send them a message!" was precisely geared to the rising anger of

blue-collar workers. One does not need elegant sociopolitical theories or the incomprehensible musing about "consciousness" of a Marcuse or Reich to understand the "drift to the right," or the "emerging Republican majority." The only way progressives have won a majority of the American people is by offering genuine programs that meet the needs of ordinary people. There is nothing strange in the fact that workers began deserting liberalism once liberalism so decisively deserted them.[73]

The question became whether such "genuine programs" were too much to expect from the Democratic Party. It was not, nor had it ever been, a labor party or source of social democracy in the United States, and its steps in those directions had been as reactions to economic cataclysm (the Depression), organized electoral pressure groups, and militant forces from below. The post-war privatized welfare state did not represent universal class issues, and no group of progressives, including labor, had successfully campaigned for such an expansive class vision in that period (or, arguably, ever). But to the extent that workers did find their interests represented by the Democrats, that support was weaker at the dawn of the 1970s than it had been before. On the other side was the recent history of sectional, narrow-minded labor politics. As we have seen, the intolerant and conservative leadership of George Meany and others narrowed the political reach of the AFL-CIO and alienated labor from its progressive allies.

The Consolidation of the Image

By the beginning of the 1970s, the lines of the "class war" had been drawn. "Liberal elites" faced off against "blue-collar bigots," and every major institution in the country—political party, media, labor, and social movement—accepted or articulated, or at the very least did not challenge, this common sense. Such a realignment had been anticipated for years, but it was not until 1968 that its true crystallization seemed to begin. Perversely, the popular response to the Vietnam War was held up as the prototype, the divide. The hardhats, Joes, and Archie Bunkers stood in for the workers. To the extent that white working-class people were radical or militant, such sentiment and behavior was eclipsed by their apparent electoral conservatism and pro-war, racist reactions. The Republican Party under Nixon did what it could to amplify this picture, the official labor movement (against whom workers were themselves rebelling) contributed to it, and the Democratic Party was a fractured and already anemic "voice of working people." The media magnified these aspects of the institutions, trumpeting the "upside-down" political alignments that the United States was suddenly experiencing.

On the other side, the antiwar movement appeared to exemplify the excesses of the elite. Despite the inaccuracy of this picture, that the movement could be seen as such was in no small part related to its own middle-class and elite character in its early years. The eventual diversification of the antiwar movement and sentiment went largely unacknowledged and, in any event, did not bridge the real gaps that existed between the white working class and the "typical" movement types as seen on TV, reported in the news, and described by the politicians. Over time, most people who opposed the war in this country did so for similar reasons—the unnecessary death and destruction, and its fundamental immorality. The movement never united all the people who felt this way—nor did any social institution. But when all parts of the active opposition to the war are taken into account, together they do point to a kind of unity—in a distrust of the government, a dislike of war, and a determination to fight against those policies that contributed to the degradation or destruction of their own lives and the lives of others.

Conclusion

The useful research heuristic is to understand that as opportunities for new wars . . . arise, the elites of the day and their homefront adversaries will strive to shape public interpretation and reinterpretation. As a more general matter, the capacity to make war, even as wars now change in their nature, will turn on just how those involved in the discourse succeed, at any given point, to give meaning to wars gone by and to those who opposed them.

—Thomas Beamish, Harvey Molotch, and Richard Flacks,
"Who Supports the Troops?" 1995

We need to dispense with essentialist conceptions of working-class identity and recognize that there is no single route decreed by history, God, or any other force; that political identity within the working class is and will be various, and that the challenge of politics is to struggle in concert with others to cultivate those forms of class conscientiousness we believe to be most true and humane.

—Adolph Reed, "Reinventing the Working Class," 2004

It is lunchtime on Wall Street. Long-haired, slightly grungy youth are chanting within yards of the stock exchange, carrying protest signs, and shouting for the passersby to join them. A group of slightly older white men wearing work clothes approach from the west.

How does this story end?

Until recently, most people familiar with the outlines of the historical period addressed in this book would most certainly answer, "Those kids get a serious beating." Seared into our collective memory, the image of hardhats assaulting antiwar protesters in May 1970 crystallized long-standing popular narratives about class, race, and protest in this country. The hardhats are invoked as evidence of the conservatism of the white working class, as opposed to the protest-prone liberal elite; their confrontation on Wall Street epitomizes difficulties in creating coalitions across the class divide.

But when the Occupy Wall Street protests began in fall 2011, it all played out a bit differently. "God bless you," said a white trackworker standing among an

interracial group of his fellow Transport Workers Union (TWU) members taking a break by the Wall Street subway station as I passed out flyers critical of
baking giant JP Morgan Chase a few weeks after the protests began. "Where is
Zuccotti Park?" asked another group of white middle-age men and women—
from Dayton, Ohio, I was to discover, autoworkers and at least one nurse. Over
the first months, polling indicated that the Occupy movement had struck a
nerve among the country's non-affluent groups, with support for the movement outpacing opposition.[1] The largest and most influential US labor unions
endorsed the protests from their international headquarters. On the ground in
New York, union delegations from health care, transit, laborers, city workers and
teachers, building services, and more enthusiastically marched to Occupy Wall
Street; and Occupy Wall Street enthusiastically marched to join postal workers, communication workers, and even Teamsters, whose flirtation with Tur-
tles in Seattle during the 1999 World Trade Organization meetings had told a
similar tale.

Regardless of the direction this fledgling movement takes, the early outpouring
of blue-collar support for something so radical and so culturally dissimilar from
"typical" working-class political action seems to contradict the long-standing
narratives of working-class conservatism embedded in our memory of Vietnam
protest. And it is easy to simply say that "things are different" today. The 1960s
and 1970s were an incredibly different moment from the 2010s, with protest
movements, the labor movement, and the overall political and economic climate
in very different places today than they were forty years ago. Most important, the
recent protests have economic grievances at their center. But it would be wrong to
see the present as entirely dissimilar from our past. The story of class polarization
that we tell about the past is not the whole story, and our partial, distorted images
of that time has obscured the possibilities of the present as well.

In this book I have traced a countermemory that complicates the popular narrative that insistently polarizes the reactions to the Vietnam War along the lines of
class. As we have seen, elites were always more likely to support the war, workers
were more likely to oppose it, and the mass, multifaceted movement that actively
fought against the war eventually comprised Americans across the class spectrum.
The student and mass movements were more economically diverse than are remembered, and even labor began to break from its Cold War foreign policy as a
result of Vietnam. Working-class resistance to the war in the armed forces was a
necessary ingredient in the eventual end of the war, and working-class organizations such as the Vietnam Veterans Against the War and the Chicano Moratorium
Committee indicate the salience of antiwar action to the lives of working people.

It is true, and significant, that the early shape taken by the dominant antiwar movement organizations, growing as they did among liberal and radical

peace groups and on the college campuses, largely precluded an early inclusion of workers and created a middle-class movement, culture, an orientation that proved difficult to shake in later years. Elitist attitudes within the organized movement, as well as strategies to reach what appeared to be the easiest audiences—that is, people like themselves—further steered most of the early groups away from a working-class audience and working-class audiences away from these groups. Despite widespread antiwar sentiment among African American workers—who, due to the racialized definitions and identities of working class in the United States, were not usually included as part of it within popular and scholarly conceptions—the African American and mainstream antiwar movements did not successfully conjoin. The seeming intransigence of mainstream labor on the question of war further discouraged working-class outreach among many antiwar activists, although this did not mean that many groups and individuals within both the labor and antiwar movements did not make efforts in that direction.

By the time antiwar sentiment and the movement had broadened, and workers were joining new or existing movement organizations or otherwise resisting the war, other social tensions that had been building had been exposed and encouraged by the media and political elites. The working-class segment of "Middle Americans," those who had not participated in the social movements of the era, were discovered by the press to be angry about social unrest, uncertain about their future, and resentful of the social changes that were taking place, which appeared to benefit others while often hurting them. Republicans fixated on the popular anger at protesters following the 1968 Chicago Democratic National Convention and sought to polarize the "impudent" antiwar "snobs" from the "silent majority" of middle- and working-class white Americans.

The image of hardhats, followed by other right-wing icons in film and television, cemented a picture of white working-class pro-war conservatism. But, in fact, workers were in movement across the political spectrum during this period. This same few years saw an abrupt rise in labor struggles, a rekindling of a labor left, and ongoing support for Democratic Party politicians at the local level among white workers. But there was a problem in all this back then—a problem that has persisted in various forms to this day. The bulk of the labor movement, embodied in figures such as George Meany, remained to the right of its members on issues of war and peace, and remained sclerotic and unyielding on the issue of rank-and-file democracy. The Democrats, internally riven, accelerated their long journey away from their New Deal heritage of economic populism and meaningful representation of working-class needs. Sectional governmental policy increased divisions within the class and factionalized special interests that were engaged political struggles along narrow lines. Racism, fear, and anger existed among the white working class—along with confusion and disillusionment; along with progressivism, militancy, and hope for change. But the primary institutions whose role it had been to represent workers were not capturing the "left, right, and center" (to once again use Jefferson Cowie's phrase) directions that workers as a whole were headed in. And as the "one-sided class war" of increasing corporate power arrayed against unions and workers' rights accelerated in the 1970s, workers' institutions grew even more fractured and weak.[2]

We know who ended up benefiting the most from this dissolution. In an article published in 1981 following President Reagan's election, Johanna Brenner and Robert Brenner explained the "increasing support" that white workers lent "right-wing political alternatives" against both the "absence of any significant working class mobilization" as well as "material forces" that pushed workers towards more reactionary positions. They argued that the failure of workers to win advances, let alone stave off defeats in the latter part of the 1970s meant that many workers turned from the possibility of collective action toward more individualist, "me" or "us" first strategies. Racist ideologies, anti-tax, anti-affirmative action positions, they argue, make more sense to workers competing against each other for a bit of the shrinking economic pie. The ideas of the right, as espoused by the Reagan Republicans, could hold some more appeal.[3] But although Nixon, Reagan, and the Republican Party attracted new supporters in many white workers, more of them either stopped voting or continued to vote Democratic. Judging by party identification, white workers are today nearly evenly split between Democrats and Republicans, a significant change from the New Deal; white workers have also supported Republican presidential candidates by wide margins in most elections since the 1970s. Yet the "selective demobilization" of these voters, caused by their perception that the differences between the Democratic and Republican parties have narrowed on questions of the economy and social welfare, combined with the reduced outreach made by the Democratic Party, implies that the real story of the working-class vote is not *who* they vote for but *why* they do not vote at all most of the time.[4] Frances Piven and Richard Cloward suggest that political representation has a recursive effect whereby a more robust political representation of the economically disadvantaged gives them courage for more social action whereas less representation delimits the political space for such engagement. The combination of Democratic abandonment and Republican wooing together partially explains the vanishing working-class voter and the conservative voting patterns of those who continue to participate.[5]

Measures of actual political persuasion are not easily come by, with voting records being a poor stand-in. This leads me back to the problem encountered throughout the period studied here. Without adequate or comprehensive representative forms through which to express the heterogeneity of working-class demands, beliefs, and desires, the field was open for other groups—elites, organizations, and institutions—to present their own versions of working-class political consciousness. These versions have some accuracy but many limits. Their partial and contradictory qualities help explain why election experts see the white working class as "volatile," that is, as a demobilized, disorganized group whose direction remains indeterminate.[6]

In recent years, questions such as "What's the matter with Kansas?" have become a shorthand route for scholars and pundits to grapple with the apparent contradiction of white workers whose support for socially conservative Republicans means that they vote "against" their material interests. Thomas Frank's book of that title places its analytic focus on the strength of "backlash" politics among these worker, and their successful recruitment by the Republican Party. The problem, as he sees it, is that in the last few decades "culture outweighs economics as a matter of public concern—that Values Matter Most, as one backlash title has it." Thus the primary contradiction of the backlash: it is "a working class movement that has done incalculable, historic harm to working class people." From the perspective of the first years of the millennium, "The trick [that culture outweighs economics] never ages; the illusion never wears off."[7]

But this emphasis is in the wrong place. First, it rests on the assumption that voting Democratic *would* reflect working-class economic interests, which is precisely what workers were calling into question during that era and a question that remains open today. Certainly some sections of the working class calculated that Republican economic policies would in fact bolster their economic positions against the reality of decline faced by all workers—I can at least get mine, might be their motto. But those who did not go so far as to embrace the economic platform of the Republican party but who did become "values voters" likely did not see the Democrats as a viable party for their economic advancement, either. Democrats, like Republicans, appear dominated by business interests; Democrats support free trade, deregulation—more or less as aggressively as Republicans— and have wasted little political capital in the direction of workers' rights. Second, the larger problem with this line of thought is that it is predicated on a stable vision of working-class social conservatism. The idea that workers have been "tricked" into this position ascribes to them a false consciousness, as if conservative workers were not making rational choices about what their vote means and how politics works for them. White working-class voters have certainly voted in more socially conservative directions over the past forty years. But, as Frank himself observes but does not develop, the relative significance of such conservatism shrinks or grows among workers in the context of their attitudes about the government and its representation of their core material interests, and in the context of what they think they can do to change their circumstances. People do not vote on social issues because social issues are of transcendental importance. People vote on social issues when other meaningful things that people care about—such as policies that address economic opportunity, insecurity, and inequality—are effectively off the table. Frank acknowledges this in his conclusion, writing that "by dropping the class language that once distinguished them sharply from Republicans [Democrats] have left themselves vulnerable to cultural wedge issues like guns and abortion and the rest whose hallucinatory appeal would ordinarily be far overshadowed by material concerns."[8] Yet his criticisms of the Democrats and labor are themselves overshadowed by his emphasis on working-class social conservatism.

In the late 1960s and early 1970s, a time of increasing economic insecurity, material and cultural factors coalesced for many white workers in a conservative direction. Since that time, working-class demands on the state—regarding labor law reform, investment in manufacturing, adequate support for education, and fair taxation—have failed, whereas other economic policies—such as deregulation and neo-liberal free-trade agreements—have done direct harm. Still other ideas, such as universal health-care coverage, find popular support but lie outside the realm of normal discourse. Overall, feelings of betrayal and distrust characterize many workers' attitudes toward the state.[9] The width, depth, and importance of working-class social conservatism therefore rest on shifting sands; its expression can be better understood by assessing its context rather than the thing itself. By emphasizing the conservatism rather than the context against which it emerges, progressive authors such as Frank help to reinforce an image of its stability and solidity in the left and liberal audiences they address.

The bigger contextual problem has been the failure of many social movements, the Democrats, labor, and other possible social formations to represent at levels of actual practice and social discourse broader working-class politics in effective and compelling ways. I am not saying this would have been easy to do so, just that this failure is the bigger story. Had material concerns been successfully foregrounded by any social institution or political movement in the 1970s, it is likely that the image of the hardhat would never have gained the traction it did because the existing contradictory political currents on the ground would have found sustained public expression.

There is a circularity to this logic, of course—had things been different, they would have been different. But a counterfactual imagination is part of the work of historical sociology. Delineating "alternative scenarios made plausible" gives us space to consider parts of our history that may not have had particular conjunctural punch at the moment when they occurred but that can shape social outcomes in the longer term. William Sewell's questions about the "complex temporal conundrums" of historical processes framed my introduction, and this last question is of particular importance here at my conclusion: "How do long-term trends reassert themselves in situations where they seem to have been eclipsed by more pressing political processes?" I have argued that our categorization of liberalism as the province of elites and conservatism the province of the underprivileged has more the character of current pressing political processes than of long-term trends. By highlighting the antiwar actions of a diverse spectrum of working-class actors whose collective identities were more forged by their military, student, racial, or ethnic identities, I invoke a broader working class than the more immediate conjunctural narratives of conservatism and decline allow. The story of conservatism and decline is really linked to the white goods-producing working class that was the majority of organized and unorganized labor for much of the twentieth century. And even among these workers, more complicated dynamics obtained.[10]

At the level of countermemory, in the more subterranean, or at least subhegemonic, narratives available are the actions of the black, white, and brown working classes that did "surprising" things by opposing the war, with knowledge of one another, at times in interaction with one another and at times parallel to one another. From the vantage point of today, focusing on how this more diverse spectrum of workers actually acted is all the more important because their actions are closer to the political expression of the working class we see now, unionized and non-union. In fact, the spaciousness inherent to the collective identity of working class has been borne out, just as it was in the periods before Vietnam. Today the dominant working-class institutions—AFL-CIO, Change to Win, workers centers, and labor-community coalitions—represent multiracial and multiethnic male and female workers. Socially liberal policies—immigration reform, gay rights, and antipoverty initiatives—are regularly supported by these workers' organizations. Underneath the story of the political class polarization of the Vietnam era exist the political currents that help explain these more progressive working-class social forces of today. A "values" orientation and the appeal of anti-government rhetoric remain characteristics of the US working class, which continues to lack meaningful political and institutional representation. But, like before, that's not all there is.

Such framing allows us to revisit assumptions about who supports wars and why. Although less explicitly in the recent wars in Iraq and Afghanistan, war supporters continued to draw a connection between opposition to the wars and opposition to the soldiers fighting them, pointing to the economic and cultural gulf between the elite antiwarriors and the hardworking troops. In his 2004 presidential race, Senator John Kerry (D-Mass.) distanced himself from his brave and principled antiwar activity as a young veteran and instead campaigned from what was essentially a pro-war position on Iraq War: he had voted for it, he had criticized it, and he made no promise to end it. The ability of the Republicans to "swift boat" this war hero was in part a result of their success in framing his service and dissent as a product of his elite background. It was, of course, easy to make "latte" jokes about the Kerry the Boston Brahmin; the Republicans had practiced first with Howard Dean, the popular antiwar Democratic primary candidate. With echoes of George Wallace, Dean was portrayed as being part of a "tax-hiking, government-expanding, latte-drinking, sushi-eating, Volvo-driving, New York Times-reading . . . body-piercing, Hollywood-loving, left-wing freak show" in an attack ad that ran during the primaries. This "elitist" candidate (actually, a physician originally from a middle-class family) could never represent the ordinary people he purported to respect.

Which brings me to the implications for antiwar work in our era. In February 2003, during the build-up to the Iraq War, a mass demonstration against that war—the largest single-day demonstration in history—took place in cities around the world and included millions of people demonstrating in the United States alone. The antiwar movement was quickly supported by the US labor movement and organizations of military families, constituencies whose antiwar participation had taken years to develop during Vietnam. For almost its entire duration, a majority of Americans opposed the war in Iraq and, for most of that time, supported calls for either an immediate or specified end to the occupation. Given the fictitious and farcical case made for the Iraq War by the George W. Bush administration, the disastrous chaos that resulted from the US invasion, and the corruption and stagnation in the efforts to "rebuild" Iraq, the case could be made that the Iraq War was more widely discredited and unsupported in its first two years than the Vietnam War was in its first ten.

Yet the antiwar movement that emerged at the start of the war was almost nowhere to be seen a year later. When the Abu Ghraib scandal broke in April 2004, not a single major protest was called. Similar silences followed repeated revelations of corruption among US contractors and the large-scale protests in Iraq against the occupation in 2005. Beginning with numbers provided in a classified State Department report described by the *Washington Post* in June 2006, a majority of Iraqis consistently wanted the immediate or close to immediate withdrawal of US troops, believing that the situation would get better faster without the United States there. But these polls—in 2006, 2007, and 2008—were not responded to.

A full analysis of the early collapse and ongoing struggle to rebuild the more recent antiwar movement is beyond my current project. But one striking motif was an early reluctance on the part of some antiwar groups, such as MoveOn.org, to take positions—such as "immediate withdrawal"—that might alienate "ordinary Americans." And nearly all parts of the antiwar movement, eager to see John Kerry elected in the presidential election of 2004, did not challenge the continued support by the Democratic Party for the occupation. The movement never recovered from its election-year demobilization. In their own way, both the moderate and more radical antiwar groups such as United For Peace and Justice (UFPJ) compromised their political independence and moderated their own antiwar positions in deference to the "NASCAR dads and soccer moms" being courted by Democrats.

My research does not indicate that working class "Middle America" would have embraced "immediate withdrawal" in 2004 any more than it did during the Vietnam War in 1968. But "ordinary people" did come to oppose that war, and they did so in a climate created by an independent and politically diverse antiwar movement. Working people did not necessarily agree with the Vietnam antiwar movement, and they were often alienated by its more militant actions. But the presence of the massive movement helped normalize all kinds of dissent, from liberal to moral to pragmatic to experiential to radical. The presence of a mass, visible antiwar movement helped create the cultural space in which millions of people came to criticize the war, and the relative porousness and sheer size of the movement enabled a smaller but substantial number to take action on their concerns as well. The movement became its own pole of attraction, forcing the Democratic Party to turn against the war it had initiated, forcing all candidates to become "peace candidates." And it gave rise to the GI movement, which in turn supported the soldier's revolt.

Cindy Sheehan's occupation in Crawford, Texas, in August 2005 was one type of action that did tap into the otherwise unexpressed feelings felt by many. While she was camped in Crawford, I was reminded of a campaign I had read about that was launched by Clergy and Laymen Concerned About Vietnam in 1971, which included the Minnesota CALCAV peace walk through fifty-three towns (440 miles) in thirty days. Local newspapers gave the march advance press, and most editorials were supportive of the marchers' action. The marchers "faced only minimal opposition during the journey," and "for the most part" they found "receptive audiences who walked with them, offered them food along the road, and seemed surprised that so many were not students. What they also found was a great deal of discouragement and frustration growing out of the deception of politicians and their own [personal] inability to end the war." According to the special report issued by the Minnesota group, "The arrival of visible support from CALCAV brought together people who discovered, often for the first time, that there were others in their own town who felt as they did."[11]

The recent antiwar movement does not seem to have consistently, or with enough focus, seen the strong inroads it could make with "ordinary Americans" by focusing on the goal it embraces first—ending the war and bringing the soldiers home. If the antiwar movement had responded to Abu Ghraib, it could have focused on the use of the lower-level "grunts" who were prosecuted for crimes there as scapegoats, thus protecting the architects of Bush's war and torture strategy, at the same time that it condemned the inhumanity of the war. As it was, the recent movement missed an opportunity to reach out to soldiers and veterans living under immoral orders and following destructive strategies with insufficient supplies in a racist climate, all for a war of occupation. Most soldiers and veterans, perhaps, did not share these feelings, but if the Iraq Veterans Against the War (IVAW) and the memoirs of returning soldiers are to be believed, many did. The lack of a military draft has been cited to explain the lack of a mass antiwar movement today, but the economic draft has also not become a consistent focus of the movement. Antirecruitment drives—such as those among the outstanding IVAW—have been excellent, but they could have been linked to groups working for greater economic opportunity for the young people who still see the military as their best way forward.

Since the beginning of the economic crisis, antiwar groups have slowly shifted their focus to the relationship between the economy and military spending. US Labor Against War and Military Families Speak Out have always shared this focus, but they are now joined by UFPJ, American Friends Services Committee, and others. These groups, now focused on the war in Afghanistan, have come together in the New Priorities Project, which calls for reassigning the vast sums allocated to military spending to jobs and infrastructural development. These are promising developments, and I hope this history is encouraging to those who are moving in these directions.

• • •

Jeffrey Olick and Joyce Robbins describe the persistence of collective memories as being traceable to the cultural resonance they strike; instrumental uses to which they are put; and inertia, the lack of adequate force to shake their hold.[12] The cultural resonance of the polarizing images of the hardhat hawk and liberal elite is rooted in part in experiential divides that exist between people and groups from different classes. But their particular political valence continues to resonate because they fit with our *current* story of the political class divide in this country. The distorted images we carry of the popular responses to Vietnam have served all war-supporting political elites, whether they directly propagate such remembrances or not. A memory of a fractured, class-divided populace at war with itself distracts us from the meaningful connections that were forged in the broad antiwar movement, and the widespread abhorrence of the war that existed across classes in this country.

Is there a force that might shake the inertia that upholds our incomplete and distorted memory? This depends on the capacity of new and existing social movement formations to hold and build links between workers, youth, and students, and their broader communities in common coalition. Such formations could mirror the actual and potential common causes of the Vietnam era, a link that might add resonance to the countermemories I've detailed in this book. There are significant challenges of scale, organization, and power facing such efforts at change. Whether or not movements beyond Occupy take root in the United States will have much to do with how well the groups energized by the demonstrations and actions of 2011 and 2012—labor pre-eminent among them—continue to embrace the solidaristic impulses of the 99 percent, deepening connections across race, culture, and education, in rooted and strategic campaigns.

Class and cultural divides did exist in the antiwar movement of the Vietnam era, but the specter of that divide was always larger than its reality. The possibilities for a united, cross-class movement were apparent to some organizers at the time. In the mid-1970s, optimistic activists trumpeted what they saw as the "new reformers" and argued, "A movement for social reform in America exists today without a leader and without a party." Others described "a crazy-quilt alliance of 'longhairs' and 'hardhats,' black and white, young and old" who were seeking social change.[13] Whether such a "crazy quilt" will be achieved in a contemporary movement against war, and the devastation and waste created in its wake, remains to be seen. But the movements of today appear poised to build on these deeper currents of solidarity that existed despite the divisions of yesterday and, perhaps, shake off the legacy of the real and imagined polarization that has characterized our politics since Vietnam.

Notes

INTRODUCTION

1. See, for example, Hermann Graham III, *The Brother's Vietnam War: Black Power, Manhood and the Military Experience* (Gainesville: University Press of Florida, 2003).

2. Betsy Leondar-Wright, *Class Matters: Cross-Class Alliance Building for Middle-Class Activists* (Gabriola, Canada: New Society Publishers, 2005), 10.

3. Works that have either implicitly or explicitly touched on the more complex class dynamics of antiwar sentiment and movement include Christian Appy, *Working Class War* (Chapel Hill: University of North Carolina Press, 1993); Keith Heineman, *Campus Wars: The Peace Movement at American State Universities in the Vietnam Era* (New York: New York University Press, 1993); Peter Levy, *The New Left and Labor in the 1960s* (Urbana: University of Illinois Press, 1994); Richard Moser, *The New Winter Soldiers: GI and Veteran Dissent during the Vietnam Era* (New Brunswick, N.J.: Rutgers University Press, 1996); Andrew Hunt, *The Turning: A History of Vietnam Veterans Against the War* (New York: New York University Press, 1999); H. Bruce Franklin, *Vietnam and Other American Fantasies* (Amherst: University of Massachusetts Press, 2000); Jonathan Neale, *The American War* (London: Bookmarks, 2001); Michael Foley, *Confronting the War Machine: Draft Resistance during the Vietnam War* (Chapel Hill: University of North Carolina Press, 2003); James Lewes, *Protest and Survive* (Westport, Conn.: Praeger, 2003). Works providing contemporaneous criticism of the middle-class biases common to most analysis of the era include Patricia Cayo Sexton and Brendan Sexton, *Blue Collars and Hard Hats* (New York: Vintage, 1971); Clyde Taylor, ed., *Vietnam and Black America* (Garden City, N.Y.: Anchor Books, 1973); Andrew Levison, *The Working Class Majority* (New York: Coward, McCann, and Geoghagen, 1974); David Cortright, *Soldiers in Revolt: the American Military Today* (New York: Anchor Press, 1975).

4. Robert Alford, *The Craft of Inquiry* (New York: Oxford University Press, 1998), 46.

5. "Organic" here refers to situations, or social conditions that are relatively permanent, which he opposed to more fleeting—"occasional, immediate" conjunctural phenomena. Gramsci cautions against misting the relationship between the two, which could lead the analyst toward structural determinism or voluntarism in her attributions of historical causality. It is my sense that most apprehensions of how class interacted with the political behaviors of the period made errors on both sides. Class, defined narrowly, is at times seen as an overwhelming determinant to the action of particular groups, while in other instances, conjunctural behaviors of particular groups are taken as sufficiently representative of the whole of class behaviors. Antonio Gramsci, *Selections from the Prison Notebooks* (New York: International Publishers, 1971), 177–78.

6. William H. Sewell Jr., *The Logics Of History* (Chicago: University of Chicago Press, 2005), 9.

7. See the Bibliography.

8. The distinction between class "in itself" and "for itself" that I'm taking up here is Marx's famous distinction in *The Poverty of Philosophy*, in Karl Marx and Frederick Engels, *Collected Works of Karl Marx and Friedrich Engels, 1845–48*, Vol. 6, *The Poverty of Philosophy, the Communist Manifesto, the Polish Question* (New York: International Publishers, 1976); 211: "Economic conditions had first transformed the mass of the people of the

country into workers. The combination of capital has created for this mass a common situation, common interests. This mass is thus already a class as against capital, but not yet for itself. In the struggle, of which we have noted only a few phases, this mass becomes united, and constitutes itself as a class for itself. The interests it defends becomes class interests. But the struggle of class against class is a political struggle." For a concise discussion of this more structural definition of *class* and of class as a conscious relationship of power, see Michael Zweig, *The Working-Class Majority: America's Best Kept Secret* (Ithaca: Cornell University Press, 2012), Chapter 1. Erick Olin Wright would use *class location* for class category here and similarly situate these locations within the structural relations listed. Eric Olin Wright, *Classes* (London: Verso, 1985); Eric Olin Wright, ed., *Approaches to Class Analysis* (London: Verso, 2005).

9. See Robert and Johanna Brenner, "Reagan, The Right and the Working Class," *Against the Current* 2 (1981), 29–35), discussed in more detail in the conclusion.

10. Gramsci, *Selections from the Prison Notebooks*; Nicos Poulantzas, *Classes in Contemporary Capitalism* (London: New Left Books, 1975). See also Pierre Bourdieu: "the movement from probability to reality, from theoretical class to practical class, is never given." "What Makes a Social Class? On the Theoretical and Practical Existence of Groups," *Berkeley Journal of Sociology* 32 (1987), 7.

11. Rick Fantasia's work on cultures of solidarity underscores this point. These cultures, which he describes as emergent in periods of labor unrest and strife, indicate that class consciousness does not necessarily precede collective action but, rather, that radicalism and collective identity emerge out of struggle. Thus action itself can be understood as what gives rise to consciousness. Rick Fantasia, *Cultures of Solidarity* (Berkeley: University of California Press, 1988). Similarly, Adam Przeworski situates classes as "effects of struggle" inherent to this combative, interactive process: classes arise from frictional relationships. Adam Przeworski, "Proletariat into a Class: The Process of Class Formation from Karl Kautsky's *The Class Struggle* to Recent Controversies" *Politics & Society* 7 (1977): 343–401. Here, Przeworski is elaborating Marx's distinction in *The Poverty of Philosophy*, discussed above. Stanley Aronowitz elaborates on this emergent, action-based understanding of class in *How Class Works* (New Haven: Yale University Press, 2003). For a broader exploration of this process of social movement identity formation, see Francesca Polletta and James Jasper, "Collective Identity and Social Movements," *Annual Review of Sociology* 27 (2001): 283–305.

12. For a discussion of the interactive impacts of segregation, racism, and white identities in the postwar era, see Thomas Sugrue, *The Origins of the Urban Crisis: Race and Inequality in Postwar Detroit* (Princeton: Princeton University Press, 1996); Arnold Hirsch *Making the Second Ghetto: Race and Housing in Chicago 1940–1960* (Chicago: University of Chicago Press, 1998).

13. James Max Fendrich, "The Forgotten Movement," *Sociological Inquiry* 73 (2003), 338. Fendrich finds "From 1951 to 1979, there were 1575 articles in the American Sociological Review . . . [and] there was not a single article analyzing the Vietnam War, and only one research note (Hamilton 1968). Only one article on the Vietnam antiwar protest movement (McAdam and Su 2002) has appeared in the American Sociological Review since 1979. Two search engines—JSTOR and the ISI Web of Science—were checked for articles on the Vietnam antiwar protest movement. JSTOR has three articles that mention the Vietnam antiwar movement in passing while focusing on other theories and data. In contrast, it contains 322 sources on the civil-rights movement and 252 on the labor movement. . . . [The Web of Science contained no articles at all on the movement. Major social movement books, anthologies, review articles, and research monographs said little about the movement]. It is clear that the Vietnam antiwar protest movement has been understudied" (338–39). As of this writing, a JSTOR search yields one more sociological article

written specifically about Vietnam, Val Burris, "From Vietnam to Iraq: Continuity and Change in Between-Group Differences in Support for Military Action," *Social Problems* 55, no. 4 (November 2008): 443–79.

14. For a synopsis of the movement, see Mel Small, *Antiwarriors: The Vietnam War and the Battle for America's Hearts and Minds* (Lanham, Md.: Rowman & Littlefield, 2002), 3–4.

15. I qualify this statement because at different moments the movement took on different demands, such as, "End the Bombing" or "Negotiate Now."

16. Maurice Isserman and Michael Kazin, "The Failure and Success of the New Radicalism," in *The Rise and Fall of the New Deal Order, 1930–1980*, edited by Steve Fraser and Gary Gerstle (Princeton: Princeton University Press, 1989), 223.

17. Charles DeBenedetti, *An American Ordeal* (Syracuse, N.Y.: Syracuse University Press, 1990); Tom Wells, *The War Within* (Berkeley: University of California Press, 1994).

18. Charles Tilly, "Social Movements and National Politics," in *Statemaking and Social Movement: Essays in History and Theory, edited by* Charles Bright and Susan Harding (Ann Arbor: University of Michigan Press, 1984), 313, quoted in DeBenedetti, *American Ordeal*, 1.

19. James Jasper, *The Art of Moral Protest* (Chicago: University of Chicago Press, 1997), 5; Margit Mayer, "Social Movement Research in the United States: A European Perspective," *International Journal of Politics, Culture and Society* 4, no. 4 (1991): 459–78; Margit Mayer, "Theoretical Assumptions of American Social Movement Research and Their Implications," paper presented at International Sociological Association World Congress Madrid, July 1990, 8. The strengths of the political process or "American" model of social movement analysis, and of academic theorizing more generally, are that they allow for broad conceptual framings of many social movement processes—what theorist John Lofland also terms "generic propositions." *Social Movement Organizations: Guide to Research on Insurgent Realities* (New Brunswick: Transaction Publishers, 1996). (For a discussion of Lofland's work, see Laurence Cox and Colin Barker, "What Would a Marxist Theory of Social Movements Look Like?" in *Alternative Futures and Popular Protest, Conference Papers II*, edited by Colin Barker and Mike Tyldesley (Manchester, UK: Manchester Metropolitan University, 2005).) Such generic propositions allow for consistent descriptions of social change processes. Some of the helpful propositions developed within the political process model include concepts that help to explain the genesis, growth, and operations of social movements, such as frames and political opportunity structures; more recently, movement mechanisms have been explicated, such as "brokerage," "category formation," and others. The later mechanisms introduced by Doug McAdam, Charles Tilly, and Sidney Tarrow (e.g., "brokerage") were developed in part to correct the problems implicit in some of their earlier concepts (such as "political opportunity structure"). See Robert Benford and David A. Snow, "Framing Processes and Social Movements: An Overview and Assessment," *Annual Review of Sociology* 26 (August 2000): 611–39; Doug McAdam, *Political Process and the Development of the Black Insurgency, 1930–1970* (Chicago: University of Chicago Press, 1982); Doug McAdam, Sidney Tarrow, and Charles Tilly, *Dynamics of Contention* (Cambridge, UK: Cambridge University Press, 2001); Sidney Tarrow, *Power in Movement,* 2nd ed. (Cambridge, UK: Cambridge University Press, 1998). But these propositions frequently suffer from what Jeff Goodwin and James Jasper call "over-extension," or being so widely applied as to lose their specific meaning, and from a related illusion of universality, an inflated sense that what happened in one or a few places at one time is true for all places at all times. It seems impossible not to agree that, as Goodwin and Jasper argue, "the search for universally valid propositions and models at least for anything so complex as social movements

is bound to fail." "Caught in a Winding Snarling Vine: The Structural Bias of Political Process," *Sociological Forum* 14, no. 1 (March 1999), 51. Yet the field is filled with claims that raise the modest observations of particular movements to the status of general theory. Contrast this to the work of movement-based intellectuals, who, as Cox and Barker argue, are primarily interested in "case propositions" that "take the form, in essence, of practical proposals, i.e. propositions that 'This is what we should do.'" "What Would a Marxist Theory," 2.

20. See especially, Neale, *American War*.

21. The interaction of social movement forces with "powerful others" is the focus of Tom Wells's outstanding opus, *The War Within*. Yet Wells is similarly quiet on these three groups. See, however, the discussion in chapter 1 and its notes for good alternative histories that better raise the complexities of the era.

22. See chapters 3, 4, and 6. For GI resistance, see Neale, *American War*; David Zieger, *Sir! No Sir!* Displaced Films and BBC documentary, 2005. For the differences between morality and pragmatism, see Howard Schuman, "Two Sources of Antiwar Sentiment in America," *American Journal of Sociology* 78, no. 3 (November 1972): 513–36.

23. Richard Flacks, "Knowledge for What? Thoughts on the State of Social Movement Studies," in *Rethinking Social Movements: Structure, Culture, and Emotion*, edited by J. Goodwin and J. Jasper (Lanham, Md.: Rowman & Littlefield, 2004), quoted in Douglas Bevington and Chris Dixon, "Movement-Relevant Theory: Rethinking Social Movement Scholarship and Activism," *Social Movement Studies* 4, no. 3 (2005), 189.

24. Bevington and Dixon, 198.

25. John Burdick, *Blessed Anastacia: Women, Race and Popular Christianity in Brazil* (New York: Routledge, 1998), 191. Commenting on this method, Marc Edelman notes, "In order to accomplish this, though, it is not the movement itself that becomes the object of study, but rather the broader social field within which it operates." "Social Movements: Changing Paradigms and Forms of Politics," *Annual Review of Anthropology* 30 (2001), 311.

26. Michel Foucault, *Language, Counter-Memory, Practice: Selected Essays and Interviews* (Ithaca: Cornell University Press, 1977).

27. Maurice Halbwachs, *On Collective Memory* (Chicago: University of Chicago Press. 1982).

28. Mike Davis, *Prisoners of the American Dream* (London: Verso, 1986), 8; Jefferson Cowie, "Vigorously Left, Right and Center: The Crosscurrents of Working Class Life in the 1970s," in *America in the Seventies* edited by Beth Bailey and David Farber, 75–106 (Lawrence: University Press of Kansas, 2004).

29. Pierre Bourdieu, *Language and Symbolic Power* (Cambridge, Mass.: Polity, 1991), 251; see also, 173–74. Bourdieu is writing in the context of Europe, where class cultures are more rigidly demarcated; in contrast, in the United States they are tempered by ideologies of individualism, egalitarianism, and meritocracy that create a more fluid cultural space for workers. Also, in Europe class-based parties are the norm. But such class-based parties have rarely exerted influence in the United States and certainly did not so during the 1960s.

30. Eliot Weininger, "Foundations of Pierre Bourdieu's Class Analysis," in *Approaches to Class Analysis* edited by Erik Olin Wright (Cambridge, UK: Cambridge University Press, 2005), 104.

31. Precursors include William Appleman Williams, *Contours of American History* (Chicago: Quadrangle, 1961); C. Wright Mills, *The Marxists* (New York: Delta Books, 1963); Herbert Marcuse, *One-Dimensional Man* (Boston: Beacon Press, 1964). See also, Pat Walker, ed., *Between Labor and Capital* (Boston: South End Press, 1979); Todd Gitlin, *The Sixties: Years of Hope, Days of Rage* (Toronto: Bantam Books, 1987); and more recent

social movement theory, including Enrique Larana, Hank Johnston, and Joseph Gusfield, eds., *New Social Movements, From Ideology to Identity* (Philadelphia: Temple University Press, 1994); David Croteau, *Politics And the Class Divide: Working People and the Middle Class Left* (Philadelphia: Temple University Press, 1995); Marcy Darnovsky, Barbara Epstein, and Richard Flacks, eds., *Cultural Politics and Social Movements* (Philadelphia: Temple University Press, 1995); Jasper, *Art of Moral Protest*; Nancy Whittier, Belinda Robnett, and David S. Meyer, *Social Movements: Identity, Culture, and the State* (Oxford: Oxford University Press, 2002).

CHAPTER 1

1. James Loewen, *Lies My Teacher Told Me: Everything Your American History Textbook Got Wrong* (New York: New Press, 1995).

2. Ibid., 303. I first came across Loewen's exercise in James Loewen, "Introductory Sociology: Four Classroom Exercises," in *Teaching Sociology* 6 (1979): 221–44, and then again in H. Bruce Franklin, "Vietnam: The Antiwar Movement We Are Supposed to Forget," *International Socialist Review*, no. 22 (January–February 2002), http://www.isreview.org/issues/22/feat-franklin.shtml. The themes I raise here echo ones briefly raised there, as well as similar issues raised in the introductory articles in the reader by Marvin E. Gettleman et al., eds., *Vietnam and America* (New York: Grove Press, 1995). These essays encouraged me to dig deeper into the problem.

3. Loewen, *Lies My Teacher Told Me*, 303–7.

4. "Veteran's Day," *Law and Order* (television series), NBC, February 18, 2004.

5. Larry Heinemann, interview in the *Chicago Tribune*, 1988, quoted in Milton J. Bates, *The Wars We Took to Vietnam: Cultural Conflict and Storytelling* (Berkeley: University of California Press, 1996), 120.

6. John Micklethwait and Adrian Wooldridge, *The Right Nation: Conservative Power in America* (New York: Penguin, 2004), 66.

7. Philip Foner, *US Labor and the Vietnam War* (New York: International Publishers, 1989); Levy, *New Left and Labor*.

8. Fred Halstead, *Out Now!* (New York: Monad Press, 1978); Nancy Zaroulis and Gerard Sullivan, *Who Spoke Up?* (Garden City, N.Y.: Doubleday, 1984); Melvin Small and William D. Hoover, eds., *Give Peace a Chance: Exploring the Vietnam Antiwar Movement.* (Syracuse, N.Y.: Syracuse University Press, 1992); Small, *Antiwarriors*; DeBenedetti, *American Ordeal*; Bates, *The Wars We Took to Vietnam*; Keith Beattie, *The Scar That Binds: American Culture and the Vietnam War* (New York: New York University Press, 1998); Wells, *War Within*.

9. Halbwachs, *On Collective Memory*, 38.

10. See, among many others, John Bodnar, *Blue-Collar Hollywood: Liberalism, Democracy, and Working People in American Film* (Baltimore: Johns Hopkins University Press, 2003); Yael Zerubavel, *Recovered Roots: Collective Memory and the Making of Israeli National Tradition* (Chicago: University of Chicago Press, 1997).

11. Barry Schwartz, "Memory as Cultural System: Abraham Lincoln in World War II," *American Sociological Review* 61 (October 1995): 908–27.

12. For more on memory as a site of contestation, see, for example, George Lipsitz, *The Possessive Investment in Whiteness* (Philadelphia: Temple University Press, 1998).

13. George H. W. Bush, "Inaugural Address," January 20, 1989, http://bushlibrary.tamu.edu/research/public_papers.php?id=1&year=1989&month=01 (accessed on May 10, 2012).

14. Podhoretz quoted in Cynthia Peters, *Collateral Damage: The New World Order at Home and Abroad* (Boston: South End Press, 1992), 56.

15. Noam Chomsky, *Towards a New Cold War: Essays on the Current Crisis and How We Got There* (New York: Pantheon Books, 1982), 4. It was not only the left that argued

this. Nathan Glazer, wrote in *Commentary* in May 1971, "the experience of Vietnam has turned Americans into haters of war." "Vietnam, The Case for Immediate Withdrawal," *Commentary* 51, no. 5 (May 1971), 35.

16. Among many other articles connecting the two eras, see William Schneider, "The Vietnam Syndrome Mutates," *Atlantic D.C. Dispatch,* April 25, 2006. There are exceptions to this, of course, given the revisionist and distorted interpretations the Vietnam War has been subjected to; for those who would argue that Vietnam was a "noble cause," comparisons with contemporary debacles are welcome.

17. Fallows, "What Did You Do In the Class War, Daddy?" *Washington Monthly,* October 1975, 5–19.

18. Arnold Isaacs, *Vietnam Shadows The War, Its Ghosts, and Its Legacy* (Baltimore: Johns Hopkins University Press, 2000), 36.

19. Chris Buckley, "Viet Guilt," *Esquire,* September 1983.

20. Fallows collapses the proponents of draft evasion and resistance by mistakenly attributing to Michael Ferber, a leader of the Resistance, a speech espousing evasion. Fallows writes that Ferber said "as committed opponents of the war, we had a responsibility to save ourselves from the war machine." Ferber rebuts this description in a later article, explaining that the Resistance's clear position at the time was "our place was up against the war machine, and in prison." Ferber, "Why I Joined the Resistance," in *Against the War: Writings By Activists,* edited by Mary Susannah Robbins (Syracuse, N.Y.: Syracuse University Press, 1999), 115.

21. Fallows describes draft counseling sessions, writing "the boys of Chelsea were not often mentioned during these sessions; when they were, regret was expressed that they had not yet understood the correct approach to the draft. We resolved to launch political-education programs, some under the auspices of the Worker-Student Alliance, to help straighten them out. In the meantime, there was the physical to prepare for." The WSA was a project of the left group Progressive Labor Party, which had relatively strong roots in the Cambridge chapter of SDS. But, PL was a negligible force in the anti-draft movement. They were among the most dogmatic and doctrinaire of the groups, hardly a stand-in for the antiwar movement or draft counseling.

22. See discussion of the BDRG in chapter 3.

23. Draft resistance historian Michael Foley explains "the New England Resistance had steadily established good relations with Vietnam veterans who returned to the United States and began working, individually and collectively, against the war." This alliance brought veterans into working class high schools in Lowell, Lynn, Lawrence, New Bedford, Fall River, and Mission Hill. Contrast this with Fallows' anecdotal, "among any highbrow audience, it is scarcely possible to attract a minute's attention on the subject of Vietnam veterans." Fallows wants to draw a connection between the movement and his "highbrow" friends, but the movement did not behave in such a contemptuous manner, even though his friends might have. Foley, *Confronting the War Machine,* 307, 340; Fallows, "Which Side," 18.

24. Nearly twenty years later, before making his own similar turn, Christopher Hitchens wrote of Fallows, "anyone who believes that the objection of antiwar activists was to personal danger rather than to complicity in atrocity and aggression just wasn't there at the time." He lambastes Fallows for raising the question of "who served," rather than "how people thought about the war, or what they did to stop it." Regarding his point that the war was fought by the poor and Black, Hitchens writes, "I distinctly remember making this point about the draft, as did the whole of the antiwar movement and in particular the much-forgotten GI Coffeehouse and GI counseling groups," and remarks that he doesn't remember any other time that a "neo-liberal like Fallows has felt compelled to stress that America is a class society." Hitchens, *For the Sake of Argument,* 69.

25. Fallows, "Which Side," 8-9.

NOTES TO PAGES 28–31

26. See chapter 3.

27. For an analysis that agrees with Fallows main argument regarding the negative impact of the movement, see Adam Garfinkle, *Telltale Hearts The Origins and Impact of the Vietnam Antiwar Movement* (New York: St. Martins, 1995); for a summary case of the movement's overall positive effect on the war's outcome, see Small, *Antiwarriors*.

28. Because I am concerned with memory, I turn to the representations of the period made after the fact. But the reader should note—as I do explicitly in future chapters, most extensively in chapter 7—that these representations found their substance in much of the contemporaneous news reporting of the movement. Todd Gitlin's *The Whole World Is Watching*, which focuses on the ways in which the *New York Times* and CBS reported about Students for a Democratic Society, makes valuable theoretical contributions to the study of how the media shape the story of protest in the moment and why the story takes the shapes it does; *The Whole World Is Watching; Mass Media in the Making and Unmaking of the New Left* (Berkeley: University of California Press., 1980). For my purposes, his attention to micro considerations, such as the media's role in the amplification and containing of movement messages, creating celebrity leaders, and inflating rhetoric, are particularly important. But I also echo his overall argument about the reproduction of hegemony created through the media in my conclusion.

29. See Samuel G. Freedman's interesting article on this, "The War and the Arts," *New York Times*, March 31, 1985.

30. Guenter Lewy, *America in Vietnam* (New York: Oxford University Press, 1978); Norman Podhoretz, *Why We Were in Vietnam* (New York: Simon and Schuster, 1982); Harry Summers Jr., *On Strategy: A Critical Analysis of the Vietnam War* (New York: Bantam, 1984).

31. DeBenedetti *American Ordeal*; Marilyn Blatt Young, *The Vietnam Wars, 1945–1990* (New York: HarperCollins, 1991). Others are cited throughout the chapter.

32. *M*A*S*H* technically took place in Korea, but it was a film and series about Vietnam, as I discuss later in this chapter.

33. Hundreds of documentaries and films were made about Vietnam. In this section, I consider a selection of the best known and most widely seen. *Law and Order* and *M*A*S*H* are two of the longest-running and most popular TV shows in history. The movie *Rambo* became a massive cultural phenomenon, and *Apocalypse Now* (discussed in footnote 37) was a critical and popular hit. *The Deer Hunter, Platoon,* and *Forrest Gump* all won Best Picture in the years they were released and received multiple other awards and nominations; *Born on the Fourth of July* was nominated for eight Academy Awards and received the award for Best Director, among other awards; *The Big Chill* was nominated for three Oscars and did well at the box office. *Hair* (the movie) reached fewer people, but I include it because of the centrality of the original Broadway musical to the antiwar period. *Hair* (the musical) has also experienced recent popular revivals in New York. See the Box Office Mojo website, http://www.boxofficemojo.com/ for historical box office data (accessed December 8, 2008).

34. See especially, Linda Dittmar and Gene Marchaud, *From Hanoi to Hollywood: The Vietnam War in American Film* (New Brunswick, N.J.: Rutgers University Press, 1991). Milton Bates, *The Wars We Took to Vietnam* (Berkeley: University of California Press, 1996), includes incisive discussion of Platoon in particular.

35. For expanded commentary along this vein, see Michael Klein, "Historical Memory, Film and the Vietnam Era." In *From Hanoi to Hollywood: The Vietnam War in American Film*, edited by Linda Dittmar and Gene Marchaud. New Brunswick, N.J.: Rutgers University Press, 1991.

36. In limiting the dramatic story line to conflict between individual warriors, Stone makes use of a common device in military films. Leo Cawley, cultural critic, wryly notes

that in watching Vietnam films like this, or more notably the *Rambo* and *Missing in Action* series, "we should not underestimate the extreme effort of imagination and will that is necessary to come up with plots that allow military men to undertake these solitary missions in total opposition to the doctrine and practice of the United States military." "War about the War: Vietnam Films and American Myth." In *From Hanoi to Hollywood: The Vietnam War in American Film*, edited by Linda Dittmar and Gene Marchaud. New Brunswick, N.J.: Rutgers University Press, 1991, 71.

37. The phantasmagoric *Apocalypse Now* (1979) similarly confines its antiwar critique to a singular witness. The wanton destruction of Vietnam and its people is stunningly depicted in the film, as is the casual violence of the US military leadership. But the central story, of Captain Willard's trip upriver into the "heart of darkness," is a more ambivalent one. Again, the problems of the war are largely confined to a struggle between individuals, although the symbolic nature of every individual—of nearly every action in the film—is relentlessly underscored. Willard (Martin Sheen) is trying to solve the mystery of Colonel Kurtz (Marlon Brando), an outstanding soldier and leader who joined the Green Berets at the age of thirty-eight after returning from an advisory trip to Vietnam and making a classified report that Willard does not see. Colonel Kurtz thereby took himself off his military career ladder so that he might get on the ground to fight and lead. Kurtz, it seems, thought that the United States was fighting the war the wrong way—and it appears he had a better one. He scored consistent victories but did so outside the chain of command. His "methods were questionable." From Willard's point of view, we discover a war in which insanity rules when there is leadership, and chaos rules when there is not. People are fighting desperately, and for no good reason; one company destroys a town to surf at its beach, although, for good measure, the town contains "Charlie" (the Vietcong) and even the women villagers are National Liberation Front (NLF). Colonel Kurtz has followed the logic of war to its irrational end—"the horror." "Destroy them all" is his final scrawled command, but he clearly wants himself killed before he can do that; "his soul is sick" with where the inexorable logic of war has taken him. The antiwar critique is delivered, as usual, through elites, though in the form of antiheroes; the grunts are victims of a bad war and bad circumstances.

38. Ron Kovic, *Born on the Fourth of July* (New York: Pocket Books, 1976), 73.

39. In fact, more like Oliver Stone himself, whose own service in Vietnam paralleled that of Taylor, the protagonist of *Platoon*. Stone grew up in an affluent family and attended elite private schools, including Yale, before enlisting for combat duty in Vietnam in 1967. See Leslie Bennetts, "Oliver Stone Easing Out of Violence," *New York Times*, April 13, 1987.

40. Kovic, *Born on the Fourth of July*, 182–83.

41. Quoted in Beattie, *Scar That Binds*, 51.

42. For a full discussion of working-class victimization in film, see Bodnar, *Blue-Collar Hollywood*.

43. Dittmar and Marchaud, *From Hanoi to Hollywood*.

44. H. Bruce Franklin, *M.I.A, or Mythmaking in America* (New Brunswick, N.J.: Rutgers University Press, 1993).

45. Despite the distance it takes from the antiwar movement, *Coming Home* (1978) is otherwise sympathetic to movement critiques of the war.

46. Jerry Lembcke, *The Spitting Image: Myth, Memory and the Legacy of Vietnam* (New York: New York University Press, 1998). During the 2004 presidential campaign, a prolonged exchange took place on the blog "Talking Points Memo" between some Vietnam veterans and other readers/writers about the reception that vets received upon returning to the United States. One wrote about a relative who had been spat on, and a number of other writers then added other secondhand tales of abuse at the hands of antiwar activists. Many posts in, someone wrote about Lembcke's finding that he was unable to find one instance of spitting in the contemporary news reporting or a single reliable case and

his conclusion that the spitting story was an urban myth. The discussion thread then exploded with debate, with dozens of writers lining up on opposing sides of the fact or fiction debate over the spitting incidents. (From author's printed record, TPM, October 7–11, 2004, http://talkingpointsmemo.com/)

47. Appy, *Working Class War*, 242.

48. Ibid, 243.

49. Moser, *New Winter Soldiers*.

50. Neale, *American War*, 135.

51. Melvin Small, *Covering Dissent: The Media and the Anti-Vietnam War Movement* (New Brunswick, N.J.: Rutgers University Press, 1994), 161.

52. See, among others, Margaret Braungart and Richard G. Braungart, "The Effects of the 1960s Political Generation on Former Left- and Right-Wing Youth Activist Leaders," *Social Problems* 38, no. 3 (August 1991): 297–315; M. Kent Jennings, "Generation Units and the Student Protest Movement in the United States: An Intra- and Intergenerational Analysis," *Political Psychology* 23, no. 2 (June 2002): 303–24; Gerald Marwell, Michael T. Aiken, and Nicholas J. Demerath III, "Persistence of Political Attitudes among 1960s Civil Rights Activists," *Public Opinion Quarterly* 51, no. 3 (August 1987): 359–75.

53. Cawley, "War about the War," 72

54. I chose a selection of the most commonly used multiple-author textbooks based on a recent study of college syllabi, Daniel J. Cohen, "By the Book: Assessing the Place of Text-books in U.S. Survey Courses," *Journal of American History* 91 (2005): 1405–15. Some of the editions I used were more recent than the ones cited in the survey. The textbooks discussed here are Alan Brinkley, *The Unfinished Nation: A Concise History of the American People* (Boston: McGraw Hill, 2004); James West Davidson et al., *Nation of Nations: A Concise Narrative of the American Republic* (Boston: McGraw-Hill, 2002); Robert A. Divine et al., *American Story* (New York: Longman, 2006); John Mack Faragher et al., *Out of Many: A History of the American People* (Upper Saddle River: Pearson, 2003); John A. Garraty and Mark C. Carnes, *American Nation* (New York: Longman, 2000); James A. Henretta, David Brody, and Lynn Dumenil, *America: A Concise History* (Boston: Bedford, 2006); James Henretta, David Brody, and Lynn Dumenil, *America's History* (Boston: Bedford, 2004); Mary Beth Norton et al., *People and a Nation: A History of the United States,* 6th ed. (Boston: Houghton Mifflin, 2001); George Brown Tindall and David Shi, *America: A Narrative History* (New York: W. W. Norton, 2004). I also chose three college-level narrative histories written by a single author or a pair of authors: Paul Johnson, *A History of the American People* (New York: Harper, 1997); Allen Weinstein and David Rubel, *The Story of America: Freedom and Crisis from Settlement to Superpower* (London: DK Publishing, 2002); Esmond Wright, *The American Dream* (London: Blackwell, 1996). Finally, I chose one textbook that went through four editions from 1977 to 1992 but that appears to have fallen out of use, Bernard Bailyn et al., *The Great Republic: A History of the American People* (Boston: Little, Brown, 1992).

55. Textbooks on the more conservative end of the spectrum are not the only ones that do this. The textbook whose sympathies most clearly lie with the antiwar movement, *Out Of Many*, is similarly myopic in what it relates about the early years of the US war in Vietnam. Its initial story of the war itself (highlighting its brutality and futility) is told very much from the perspective of what everyone came to know in later days, and its foreshadowing of massive antiwar sentiment in the 1965–1967 period distracts attention from the fact that the country was largely supportive of the war until 1968 Tet offensive. Faragher et. al., *Out Of Many*.

56. Henretta, Brody, and Dumenil, *America's History*.

57. Weinstein and Rubel, *Story of America*, 615.

58. Wright, *American Dream*, 379. The hysteria in this particular coverage is heightened in the next sentences: "Some of the members of this (so-called) family were devil-worshipers,

and some were murderers. Much of their language was incoherent." (Read against his argumentative logic, an ironic observation indeed). The next paragraph gets even stranger: "Some saw the 'high' priest of this cult as Charles Manson. . . . But the society in which he caused so much alarm was torn not only by the fear of a race war, but the reality of the war in Vietnam . . . [and that] drugs were easily available" (379).

59. Bailyn et al., *Great Republic*, 1235.

60. Divine et al., *American Story*, 803.

61. Ibid., 804.

62. Davidson et al., *Nation of Nations*.

63. Anita Louise McCormick, *The Vietnam Antiwar Movement in American History* (Berkeley Heights, N.J.: Enslow Publishers, 2000), 35; Henretta, Brody, and Dumenil, *America*, 891.

64. Bailyn et al., *Great Republic*, 1239.

65. Garraty and Carnes, *American Nation*, 852.

66. Norton, Henretta, and Tindall do not take up the issue of class, an ellipsis that both avoids distortion but misses part of the story of the social dynamics of the period. Two other books are generally accurate. Faragher's *Out of Many* does not discuss blue-collar conservatism and finds the roots of "the Conservative Ascendance" in white middle-class Sunbelt communities such as Orange County, California, and the rise of evangelical Christianity. Of the group, Davidson et al. is by far the most nuanced accounting of the class politics of the time. George Wallace's political appeal, for example, is described not just in terms of his pro-war racist overtures but also his economic populism. The return of white workers to the Democratic fold by the 1968 election is attributed to Hubert Humphrey's late antiwar tack, in September 1968. And the frustrations felt by the white working class are summed up in this way: they were antiwar but infuriated by the protesters, suspicious of the "establishment" that held power, worried about their own children, and by and large abandoned by the New Left. Norton et al., *People and a Nation*; Henretta, Brody, and Dumenil, *America's History*; Tindall and Shi, *America*; Faragher et al., *Out of Many*; and Davidson et al., *Nation of Nations*.

67. Divine et al., *American Story*, 809.

68. Weinstein and Rubel, *Story of America*, 614.

69. Johnson, *History of the American People*, 894.

70. Fredric Jameson, "Periodizing the 60s," in *The 60s without Apology*, edited by Sohnya Sayres et al. (Minneapolis: University of Minnesota Press, 1984).

71. See, for example, Tariq Ali and Susan Watkins, *1968, Marching in the Streets* (New York: Free Press, 1998); Alaine Touraine, *The May Movement: Revolt and Reform*, translated by Leonard Mayhew (New York: Irvington Publishers, 1979); Mark Kurlansky, *1968: The Year That Rocked the World* (London: Jonathan Cape, 2004); Carole Fink et. al, eds., *1968: The World Transformed* (Cambridge, UK: Cambridge University Press, 1998); Wilber W. Caldwell, *1968: Dreams of Revolution* (New York: Algora Publishing, 2008).

72. Gitlin, *Sixties*, 4.

73. Judith Clavir Albert and Stewart Edward Albert, eds., *The Sixties Papers: Documents of a Rebellious Decade* (New York: Praeger, 1984); Sohnya Sayres et al, eds. *The 60s without Apology* (Minneapolis: University of Minnesota Press, 1984); James Miller, *Democracy Is in the Streets: From Port Huron to the Siege of Chicago* (New York: Simon and Schuster, 1987).

74. Wini Breines makes a similar point about the preponderance of SDS-based histories; *Community and Organization in the New Left: The Great Refusal* (New Brunswick, N.J.: Rutgers University Press, 1989). For self-criticism in this regard, responding to Breines, see also Maurice Isserman. "You Don't Need a Weatherman, but a Postman Can be Helpful: Thoughts on the History of SDS and the Antiwar Movement," in *Give*

Peace a Chance, edited by Mel Small and William Hoover, 22–34 (Syracuse, N.Y.: Syracuse University Press, 1992). A similar question is raised by Richard Flacks, who points to the importance of the students who joined SDS in later years in particular; "What Happened to the New Left?" *Socialist Review* 19 (January–February 1988): 91–110. Terry Anderson explicitly limits his book to the revolt of the youth and breaks out of the early-peak norm (and the SDS focus) of many of the other books. He sees the movement itself as comprising two waves. The first went to college in the early 1960s and were "intellectual, idealistic, and ideological." SDS is the prototype here, and the Student Nonviolent Coordinating Committee (SNCC) as well. The second wave was their younger siblings, who graduated after 1968 and who agreed with the first wave about the corrupt nature of the system, but who were then a part of a movement so broad, Anderson argues, that you did not have to join an organization to be a part of it. *The Movement and the Sixties* (New York: Oxford University Press, 1995).

75. For example, DeBenedetti, *American Ordeal*; Small, *Antiwarriors*; Zaroulis and Sullivan, *Who Spoke Up?*.

76. For example, Cortright, *Soldiers in Revolt*; Foley, *Confronting the War Machine*; Foner, *US Labor and the Vietnam War*; Gitlin, *Sixties*; Halstead, *Out Now!*; Hunt, *Turning*; Heineman, *Campus Wars*; Frank Koscielski, *Divided Loyalties: American Unions and the Vietnam War* (New York: Garland Publications, 1999); Moser, *New Winter Soldiers*.

77. For example, Melvin Small, *Johnson, Nixon, and the Doves* (New Brunswick, N.J.: Rutgers University Press, 1988); Wells, *War Within*.

78. For example, Anderson, *Movement and the Sixties*; Breines, *Community and Organization*; Kirkpatrick Sale, *SDS* (New York: Random House, 1973); Nigel Young, *An Infantile Disorder?: The Crisis and Decline of the New Left* (New York: Routledge, 1977).

79. For example, Simon Hall, *Peace and Freedom: The Civil Rights and Antiwar Movements in the 1960s* (Philadelphia: University of Pennsylvania Press, 2006); Levy, *New Left and Labor*.

80. For example, Gettleman et al., *Vietnam and America*; George Katsiaficas, *Vietnam Documents: American and Vietnamese Views of the War* (New York: M. E. Sharpe, 1992); Sayres et al., *60s without Apology*; Small and Hoover, *Give Peace a Chance*. The first and last of these anthologies also provide two of the most complete renderings of the breadth of the movement; *Give Peace a Chance* is particularly comprehensive, considering within its pages soldiers, veterans, civil rights, religious groups, and women, in addition to students, pacifists, the official organized movement, and the like. Mitchell Hall's more recent textbook *The Vietnam War,* 2nd rev. ed. (Upper Saddle River: Pearson Longman, 2008), and the companion book of social history essays he edited, *Vietnam War Era: People and Perspectives* (Santa Barbara, Calif.: ABC-CLIO, 2009), also take up some of the more nuanced problems of class and representation during Vietnam.

81. For example, Bates, *The Wars We Took to Vietnam*; Beattie, *Scar That Binds*; Franklin, *Vietnam and Other American Fantasies*; Adam Garfinkle, *Telltale Hearts: The Origins and Impact of the Vietnam Antiwar Movement* (New York: St. Martins, 1995).

82. Nelson Lichtenstein et al. *Who Built America?: Working People and the Nation's Economy, Politics, Culture, and Society,* Vol. 2, *Since 1877,* 2nd ed. (New York: Bedford/St. Martin's, 2000), 576, 578, 605.

CHAPTER 2

1. Foucault, *Language, Counter-Memory, Practice*; Jeffrey Olick and Joyce Robbins, "Social Memory Studies: From 'Collective Memory' to the Historical Sociology of Mnemonic Practices," *Annual Review of Sociology* 24 (1998): 105–40.

2. Howard Zinn, *The Twentieth Century: A People's History* (New York: HarperCollins, 2003), 241.

3. The information from Gallup Polls is drawn from numerous articles cited through-out this chapter, but see especially Philip Converse and Howard Schuman, "Silent Majori-ties and the Vietnam War," *Scientific American* 222 (1970): 17–25; William Lunch and Peter Sperlich, "American Public Opinion and the War in Vietnam," *Western Political Quarterly* 32 (1979): 21–44; and contemporaneous *New York Times* reporting cited in this chapter.

4. It is important to point this out because President Johnson's disapproval rating might be misconstrued as opposition to the war at all times, a mistake that some histori-ans fall into. For example, Peter Levy uses the disapproval of Johnson's policies to rebut George Meany's claims that peaceniks were "communist dupes" and represented only a fraction of labor. To make this point, Levy refers to a figure that shows national, manual-worker, and youth discontent ratings of Johnson's handling of the war in near lock-step from 1965 to 1968. Levy, *New Left and Labor*, 57. Although Meany's paranoid red-baiting is certainly misleading and contrary to the facts, the public disapproval of Johnson does not prove this; many disapproved of Johnson for doing too little rather than too much. See also "Poll Finds Labor Split on Vietnam," *New York Times*, January 3, 1968.

5. Lunch and Sperlich, "American Public Opinion," 34.

6. Converse and Schuman, "Silent Majorities and the Vietnam War," 22.

7. Koscielski, *Divided Loyalties*, 93.

8. Wells, *War Within*, 112. For a discussion of Johnny Anderson, see Halstead, *Out Now!* 203–4.

9. *New York Times* January 3, 1968; February 10, 1968; August 4, 1968.

10. Hamilton, "Research Note," 439.

11. Harlan Hahn, "Correlates of Public Sentiments about War: Local Referenda on the Vietnam Issue," *American Political Science Review* 64, no. 4 (December 1970), 1190.

12. Levy, *New Left and Labor*, 61.

13. Harlan Hahn, "Dove Sentiments among Blue Collar Workers," *Dissent* 17 (May–June 1970), 204.

14. Roger Handberg, "The Vietnam Analogy: Student Attitudes on War," *Public Opinion Quarterly* 36, no. 4 (winter 1972–1973): 612–61.

15. James Wright, "The Working Class, Authoritarianism, and the War in Vietnam," *Social Problems* 20, no. 2 (autumn 1972), 148, 138, 141. By choosing to compare these two years, however, he leaves out the "years of the hawk," 1966 and 1967, when an increasing number of Americans supported escalation after Johnson's steep escalation in 1965 and while the troop levels were high.

16. Converse and Schuman, "Silent Majorities and the Vietnam War, " 24.

17. Lunch and Sperlich, "American Public Opinion."

18. Converse and Schuman, "Silent Majorities and the Vietnam War," 21.

19. Adam Berinsky, *Silent Voices: Public Opinion and Political Participation in America* (Princeton: Princeton University Press, 2004), 139; see also chapter 6.

20. Milton J. Rosenberg, Sidney Verba, and Philip Converse, *Vietnam and the Silent Majority, A Doves Guide* (New York: Harpers and Row, 1970), 2–3, 58; see also Chapter III, Group Differences in Vietnam Opinion. They note that supporters of the war from elite colleges or with post-college degrees (frequently the same group) didn't appear to be as vocal in their support as those who opposed, so that the perception of elite opposition was greater than the reality warranted: "Since activity creates visibility and a sense of large numbers, such differences mean that both the size and the homogeneity of antiwar feeling in these [elite professional] categories have been further overestimated" (61). The authors also argue that young, white, blue collar men "make up the hawkish middle ground of Americans" (68), but they are on shakier ground in this extrapolation from the data. Writ-ing during the height of the debates about white ethnics and the silent majorities, they lament the fact that there is no real poll data to clarify the war views of this group, and

they therefore rest their interpretations on the writings of Father Andrew Greeley, who worked closely with Eastern European whites in Chicago during the period. They themselves recognize that extrapolating from this one group to young, white workers as a whole is problematic. But Greeley's points are most directed to the large cultural difference that the workers he works with feel between themselves and the "radicals," themselves and the "Establishment," as well as their sense that the "rules have changed" in the United States, and that the rules they grew up by no longer seem to work, while the affluent seem to break them with impunity (see 68–71). These are themes I take up in chapter 7.

21. Frances Fox Piven and Richard Cloward, *Poor People's Movements: How They Succeed, How They Fail* (New York: Pantheon, 1977); Fred Rose, *Coalitions across the Class Divide: Lessons from the Labor, Peace and Environmental Movements* (Ithaca: Cornell University Press, 2000), 31; David Croteau, *Politics Across the Class Divide: Working People and the Middle Class Left* (Philadelphia: Temple University Press, 1994), 98.

22. Arguably, middle-class and young people tended to have greater senses of "efficacy"; that is, they felt their actions to be relevant.

23. Jasper, *Art of Moral Protest*, 5.

24. Mayer, "Theoretical Assumptions," 21. In tone, the "Call to Resist" is therefore also similar to the SDS Port Huron statement of 1962.

25. Bates, *Wars We Took*, 104.

26. Norman Mailer, *The Armies of the Night: History as a Novel, the Novel as History* (London: Weidenfeld and Nicolson, 1968), 257. Mary McCarthy, *Hanoi* (New York: Harcourt, Brace & World, 1968), 112. Discussed in ibid., 102–6.

27. *New York Daily News*, October 21, 1967.

28. The United States initially began its diplomatic involvement with Vietnam in 1945. For a full history of US involvement, see Young, *Vietnam Wars 1945–1990*.

29. Ibid., 52–54, 70–74.

30. Carl Mydans and Shelley Mydans, *The Violent Peace* (New York: Atheneum, 1968), 407.

31. DeBenedetti's definition of *social movements* (taken from Tilly), discussed in the introduction, helps to explain the marked difference between his timing of the beginning of the movement and those of the other historians. He focuses on the organizational continuity between existent peace organizations and latter-day antiwar organizations.

32. Zaroulis and Sullivan, *Who Spoke Up?*; Wells, *War Within*, 13–26.

33. As revealed in the Pentagon Papers, the Gulf of Tonkin incident was a false premise for the war (see also note 40). For an excellent discussion, see Young, *Vietnam Wars*, 117–21. Chandler Davidson, a sociology graduate student at Princeton, wrote the SDS national office in July 1964, a month before the Gulf of Tonkin resolution, urging SDS to get involved in the growing problem of Vietnam. He set forward exactly what he thought might happen in the future—escalation and a possible no-win situation. Paul Booth, later to lead SDS Vietnam work, as well as its retreat from such work, wrote back, "I agree with you almost completely. I, however, don't believe that we will affect our policy makers on the Vietnam issue." Booth Papers, Box 33, series 2C projects, related groups, and Peace Education Project, SHSW.

34. DeBenedetti, *American Ordeal*, 13.

35. Quoted in ibid., 48.

36. Ibid., 54, 57.

37. Quoted in Stanley Karnow, *Vietnam: A History* (New York: Viking Press, 1983), 255.

38. DeBenedetti, *American Ordeal*, 87–102; Sale, *SDS*, 119–20.

39. Wells, *War Within*, 10–11. On August 2, 1964, the US destroyer *Maddox* came under fire from North Vietnamese torpedo boats. Two days later, it was reported that the

Maddox and another ship had again come under attack. In fact, the second attack never took place, and the first occurred when the *Maddox* was within North Vietnamese waters (the territorial claims were disputed by the United States), after the United States had attacked two North Vietnamese islands on July 31.

40. Ibid., 15.

41. SDS had not sought coalitional endorsement for the march, but it did invite the other groups to attend. Liberal peace groups such as SANE objected to the SDS official policy of nonexclusion of communists and socialists—SDS had recently become independent of its initial organizational sponsor, the League for Industrial Democracy, over exactly this issue.

42. A. J. Muste, "The Movement to Stop the Vietnam War," *Liberation,* January 1966.

43. Lieutenant Colonel William R. Corson, quoted in Gabriel Kolko, *Anatomy of a War: Vietnam and the Modern Historical Experience* (New York: The New Press, 1985), 133.

44. Quoted in Halstead, *Out Now!,* 256–57.

45. Michael Bastedo and Patricia Gumport, "Access to What? Mission Differentiation and Academic Stratification in U.S. Public Higher Education," *Higher Education* 46 (2003), 341–43.

46. National Center for Education Statistics, "Table 175: Total Freshman Fall Enrollment in Institutions of Higher Education, by Sex of Student, Attendance Status, and Type and Control of Institution: Fall 1955 to Fall 1993," April 1995, http://nces.ed.gov/programs/digest/d95/dtab175.asp; National Center for Education Statistics, "Table 3 Enrollment in Educational Institutions, by Level and Control of Institution: Selected Years, 1869–70 through Fall 2016," August 2007, http://nces.ed.gov/programs/digest/d07/tables/dt07_003.asp.

47. See National Center for Education Statistics, Table 349, "Average Undergraduate Tuition and Fees and Room and Board Rates Charged for Full-Time Students in Degree-Granting Institutions, by Level and Control of Institution: 1964–65 through 2010–11," August 2012, http://nces.ed.gov/programs/digest/d11/tables/dt11_349.asp

48. David Karen, "The Politics of Class, Race, and Gender: Access to Higher Education in the United States, 1960–1986," *American Journal of Education* 99 (1991), 214.

49. Ibid., 220.

50. John Thelin, *A History of American Higher Education* (Baltimore: Johns Hopkins University Press, 2004).

51. Isserman and Kazin, "Failure and Success," 216

52. Advertisers were not blind to this emerging generational culture, first among the "beats" and the "folkies." Those marketing music, fashion, and other objects of consumption began to cater to the younger crowd in earnest. Such marketing further served to demarcate this generation and to increase the extent to which the disposable income represented by their capacity to consume such lifestyle paths marked them as relatively affluent.

53. Isserman and Kazin, "Failure and Success," 221

54. Clayborne Carson, *In Struggle: SNCC and the Black Awakening of the 1960s* (Cambridge, Mass.: Harvard University Press, 1982), 53.

55. Both Wini Breines and Clayborne Carson devote attention to these connections. Breines, *Community and Organization*; ibid. For a discussion of the evolution of organizational forms of the early New Left, see Francesca Polletta, *Freedom Is an Endless Meeting: Democracy in American Social Movements* (Chicago: University of Chicago Press, 2002), 37–54.

56. Isserman, "You Don't Need a Weatherman," 22–34. See also Polletta, *Freedom Is an Endless Meeting.* Many of the early most influential leaders and decision makers of the movement, such as A. J. Muste, Dave Dellinger, Norma Becker, Dagmar Wilson, Sidney Lens, Fred Halstead, Staughton Lynd, Benjamin Spock, and Richard Fernandez, were part of the pre–baby boom generation(s) of movement activists.

57. Isserman, "You Don't Need a Weatherman,"

58. For a brief related consideration of this point, see Small, *Antiwarriors*, 4.

59. Fred Rose first developed his analysis of the class cultures of social movements in the essay "Class-Cultural Theory," later expanded and incorporated in *Coalitions across the Class Divide*, 16, 20–23.

60. Mary P. Baumgartner, Melvin Kohn, Herbert Gans, and Lillian Rubin are some of the scholars whose work Rose draws on for theories of class and childhood. For a full discussion, see ibid., chap. 2.

61. Larana, Johnston, and Gusfield, *New Social Movements*, 7; Croteau, *Politics and the Class Divide*, 122.

62. John Lofland, Victoria L. Johnson, and Pamela Kato, eds., *Peace Movement Organizations and Activists in the U.S.: An Analytic Bibliography* (New York: Haworth Press, 1991).

63. Hans Morganthau, "We Are Deluding Ourselves in Vietnam," *New York Times Magazine*, April 18, 1965.

64. Quoted in DeBenedetti, *American Ordeal*, 102.

65. Ibid, 124; Gettleman et al., *Vietnam and America*, xii.

66. All of the early trade union antiwar activity included teacher locals. Even *über–* cold warrior Albert Shanker of the United Federation of Teachers briefly lent his name to the Trade Union Division of SANE advertisement, although he later regretted doing this and recanted it. See Letter from Shanker to TUD Sane, LLAP Papers, SANE Trade Union Division Records, Box 1, Folder 3, SHSW.

67. Dena Clamage, July 30, 1967, NCCEWV Papers, Box 1, Folder 16, SHSW.

68. Marcus Raskin and Bernard Fall, *The Viet-Nam Reader: Articles and Documents of American Foreign Policy and the Viet-Nam Crisis* (New York: Vintage, 1967); Marvin Gettleman, *Viet Nam: History, Documents, and Opinions on a Major World Crisis* (New York: Fawcett Crest, 1965).

69. Gettleman et al., *Vietnam and America*, xii

70. Quoted in Mitchell Hall, *Because of Their Faith: CALCAV and Religious Opposition to the Vietnam War* (New York: Columbia University Press, 1990), 30.

71. Quoted in DeBenedetti *American Ordeal*, 59.

72. NCCEWV Papers, Box 1, Folders 5 and 7; Peace and Freedom News Box 2, Folder 15, SHSW.

73. Irving Howe et al., "The Vietnam Protest," *New York Review of Books*, November 25, 1965.

74. Staughton Lynd and A. J. Muste each wrote replies to this liberal critique. In comparing the civil rights and antiwar movements, Lynd rejoined, "Isn't it the point that the nation had 'given its approval' to racial equality in just that insubstantial sense in which it might now be said to have 'given its approval' to the doctrine of loving one's enemies? In other words, isn't the effort in the one case as in the other to make the nation live up to concepts which it had endorsed in the abstract but which it had failed to practice?" Staughton Lynd, *New York Review of Books*, December 23, 1965. In a January 1966 article in the journal *Liberation*, A. J. Muste wrote a detailed critique of Howe et al.'s *New York Review of Books* article defending the need to make radical analyses and take radical positions and action, even if it meant alienating people today.

75. Muste, "Movement to Stop the Vietnam War," 35.

76. *New York Times*, September 7, 1965; August 27, 1966.

77. *New York Times* August 27, 1966; Nelson Lichtenstein, *The Most Dangerous Man in Detroit: Walter Reuther and the Fate of American Labor* (New York: Basic Books, 1995).

78. Jimmy Wechsler, "Labor in Retreat: The AFL-CIO Tragedy," *Progressive*, January 1967, 14.

79. Bert Cochran, labor analyst, attributed this gap between leaders and the rank and file to the following factors: "the membership knows little what its representatives are doing, does not view the union as an instrument of foreign policy, and has no ready mechanism to control these activities." He concludes, "In the absence of significant internal opposition groups, the labor officialdom, in this sphere, operates as a virtually sovereign power responsible to itself alone." Bert Cochran, *Labor and Communism: The Conflict That Shaped American Unions* (Princeton: Princeton University Press, 1977), 320. For a discussion of how elite and leadership positions shape public opinion, see Berinsky, *Silent Voices*, esp. chap. 6, 139–57). See chapters 4 and 6 for more discussion of the relationship between the rank-and-file members and trade union leadership during this period.

80. Quoted in Wechsler, "Labor in Retreat," 15.

81. Michael Foley, *Confronting the War Machine*, 89.

82. See Appy, *Working Class War*, chap. 2, 44–85, 220–23.

83. Andrew Levison, "Class and Warfare: Democrats and the Rhetoric of Patriotism," *American Prospect* 14 (September 2003): 26–29.

84. Quoted in Miller, *Democracy Is in the Streets*, 210. It is remarkable to contrast this faith in government with today's prevalent anti-government attitudes.

85. Edward Richer, "Peace Activism in Vietnam," *Studies on the Left*, no. 6, January–February 1966, 61.

CHAPTER 3

1. NCCEWV Papers, minutes from Standing Committee meeting, January 1966, Box 1 Folder 3, SHSW.

2. For a concise summary, see Small, *Antiwarriors*, 3.

3. Jack Barnes, SWP leader, cited the success of the first Mobilization to End the War (April 15, 1967) demonstration in New York City as evidence of the perspective that favored single-issue mass demonstrations: "Within the antiwar movement itself, April 15 was a blow against both our conservative opponents in the antiwar movement and the ultra-lefts, both of whom were swamped by the massive turnout. It was a vindication of a two-year fight for the line of single issue, non-exclusive, mass mobilizations as the main weapon of struggle against the administration policy in Vietnam." Jack Barnes, Antiwar Report, May 3, 1967, Halstead Papers, Folder 5, Box 2, SHSW.

4. Halstead, *Out Now!* 610–11.

5. Charles Chatfield, "The Antiwar Movement and America," epilogue in DeBenedetti, *American Ordeal*, 394.

6. The college rankings I use here are based on Cass and Birnbaum's *Comparative Guide to American Colleges*, which was used by David Karen in his research on working-class enrollment in schools in which he compared selective colleges with nonselective colleges. Lines of demarcation within the stratified college system "remain fairly constant" due to the combination of funding source, historical status, and mission. James Cass and Max Birnbaum, *Comparative Guide to American Colleges*, 7th ed. (New York: Harper & Row, 1975); Karen, "Politics of Class, Race, and Gender," 212.

7. Letter to Harsh Pittie, Swarthmore College, July 18, 1965, from Dena Clamage, SDS Papers, Box 8, Folder 14, SHSW. However, a week later, mailed on July 28, an SDS work list "carried a statement that disassociated SDS from the Washington assembly and discouraging attendance at it." Halstead, *Out Now!* 68. This statement "came too late to halt the work of the city committees [to end the war in Vietnam] and many SDSers simply ignored it, so there was a respectable enough turnout of five thousand on August 9; but the N[ational] O[ffice]'s gratuitous attempt to stifle the just-born

antiwar movement rankled many activists, and feeling ran high against its 'irresponsibility' and 'divisiveness.' Stanley Aronowitz, for one, was livid: 'He never forgave SDS for that,' Paul Booth said." Sale, *SDS*, 220. Every SDS letter from this period in its archives stresses the importance of the AUP Conference without endorsing it. This is probably due to some division in the office; Dena Clamage and Mel McDonald supported the idea of SDS working on Vietnam, whereas the official organization and many of its main leaders—Gitlin, Booth, Lee Webb, and Hayden—did not. Opposition to a Vietnam focus came from different quarters. ERAP-ers, who sought to create a SNCC-like "beloved community" in the North, found that it was not easy to adapt the SNCC organizational forms to the fight against the war. Others debated its reach; Paul Booth and Lee Webb wrote an article titled "The Antiwar War Movement: From Protest to Radical Politics," which argued, among other points, "the issue of the war in Vietnam cannot involve masses of people here in the United States." Quoted in Halstead, *Out Now!* 97. Gitlin later called this a "failure of leadership" on their part, whereas Booth looked back on his article with Webb and said, "It's an embarrassment to me." Booth and others later saw the SDS failure to lead on Vietnam as their greatest mistake. Sale, *SDS*, 214; Wells, *War Within*, 47.

8. The National Coordinating Committee to End the War in Vietnam is the group that, in one iteration or another, became the dominant antiwar organization of the period, usually known as the Mobilization or "Mobe"; its very name captures the impermanent nature of the organization.

9. Quoted in Anderson, *Movement and the Sixties*, 61–65.

10. Just listing the first dozen college chapters alphabetically gives a good sense of the rest: Berkeley, Boston University, Brown/Pembroke, Bryn Mawr, Carleton, University of Chicago, Cornell, Duke, Grinnell, Harvard/Radcliffe, Illinois. According to Kirkpatrick Sale, only "six of the chapters [were] west of the Mississippi, eight below the Mason-Dixon line." *SDS*, 161n.

11. SDS Papers, Box 8, Folder 14, SHSW; Sale, *SDS*, 247; Cass and Birnbaum, *Comparative Guide to American Colleges*.

12. Heineman, *Campus Wars*. Sale stresses the "thoroughly staid and unregenerately middle class nature" of the early organization throughout his discussion of the early years. *SDS*, 48; see esp. 22–23, 48–49. He then contrasts this to the 1965 group, who were "non-Jewish, non-intellectual, non-urban, from a non-professional class" (204).

13. For Hayden's discussion of his upbringing, see Tom Hayden, *Rebel* (Los Angeles: Red Hen Press, 2003).

14. Quoted in Heineman, *Campus Wars*, 82.

15. Sales, *SDS*, 204–6.

16. Heineman, *Campus Wars*, 81; Sale, *SDS*, 223–97; Gitlin, *Sixties*, 188–92. When writing about Kewadin, Gitlin emphasizes the entrance of Progressive Labor into the SDS scene and the changes to the exclusion clauses in the SDS constitution that facilitated the entrance of cadre organizations into the body.

17. Richard Flacks, "The Liberated Generation: Roots of Student Protest, a Revolt of the Advantaged," *Journal of Social Issues* 23 (1967), 52. Citations based on Google Scholar and JSTOR citation searches, March 27, 2007.

18. Milton Mankoff and Richard Flacks, "The Changing Social Base of the American Student Movement," *Annals of the American Academy of Political and Social Science* 395 (1971): 54–67.

19. Ibid.; Clarence Tygart and Norman Holt, "A Research Note on Student Leftist Political Activism and Family Socioeconomic Status," *Pacific Sociological Review* 14 (1971): 121–28; Roger M. Kahn and William J. Bowers, "The Social Context of the Rank-and-File Student Activist: A Test of Four Hypotheses," *Sociology of Education* 43 (1970): 38–55;

William S. Aron, "Student Activism of the 1960s Revisited: A Multivariate Analysis Research Note," *Social Forces* 52 (1974): 408–14.

20. Tygart and Holt, "Research Note," 127. See also Kahn and Bowers, "Social Context"; Mankoff and Flacks, "Changing Social Base"; Converse and Schuman, "Silent Majorities and the Vietnam War." The prevailing ideology of the previous decade undoubtedly helped shape the research inquiries of the first scholars who examined the nascent youth movement. For a bibliography of these early works, see Kenneth Keniston and Michael Lerner, "Selected References on Student Protest," *Annals of the American Academy of Political and Social Science* 395 (1971): 184–94.

21. Heineman, *Campus Wars*, 125.

22. Kahn and Bowers, "Social Context," 53.

23. Interestingly, at this point, the SDS leadership was once again a group of elites, many of whom in 1969 became the Weatherman faction. Students from very privileged backgrounds dominated this small group, only a few hundred strong. But the infamy of the Weatherman and Weather Underground helped to sustain the image of elite student protesters. In fact, Weatherman was an exceptional grouping, distinct from the diverse student movement as a whole.

24. Darren Sherkat and Jean Blocker, "The Political Development of Sixties Activists." *Social Forces* 72 (1994), 833. This article is interesting for the way in which it begins with the precise stereotypes I challenge here, which it never directly refutes, even though its findings do not support them: "In the late 1960's, the class participation of the student movement was abundantly clear: Participation was concentrated in the upper-middle classes. Movement activists have been shown to come predominantly from upper-middle class backgrounds and to have higher levels of education than non-participants" and "while the privileged students protested the war, the working classes fought the war abroad and the protesters at home" (824). Sherkat and Blocker set out to explore how "social class might structure participatory behavior through its influence on values, orientations, and social psychological dispositions" (825). In other words, because they initially accept the myth of significant class differentiation in social movement participation, they set out to explain why such a class differentiation exists, along the lines of: What makes these upper-middle-class kids different? They initially reject the idea that colleges themselves acted as mobilizing vehicles, instead hypothesizing that the more social psychological and network aspects of class acted indirectly through the colleges. Their study concludes that income has indirect effects on student activism that do not compare to the overall effect of college attendance (one indirect effect of income is that your kids are more likely to attend college, of course!).

25. NCCEWV Papers, Box 1, Folder 3, SHSW

26. Fred Halstead Papers, Folder 6, SHSW. The success of the SWP approach, as far as the actual involvement of working-class people in the movement was, however, mixed. For Halstead's assessment, see Halstead, *Out Now!* esp. afterward, 724–29. *Out Now!* is an outstanding reference for the movement as a whole, as well.

27. For a history of the local, see Jonathan Cutler, *Labor's Time: Shorter Hours, the UAW, and the Struggle for the American Unionism* (Philadelphia: Temple University Press, 2004). See also Koscielski, *Divided Loyalties*, 95–158.

28. Letter from Steve Fox to Paul Booth, and an attached flyer, "Why Are Americans Dying in Vietnam?", SDS Papers, January 15, 1966, Box 34A1 (Correspondence), SHSW. The attached flyer is the one written by the DCEWV. Despite the seeming naïveté of this particular project and the next one, the DCEWV was a long-lasting and seemingly effective antiwar presence in that city.

29. Koscielski, *Divided Loyalties*, 175.

30. Franklin, *Vietnam and Other American Fantasies*, 82–88.

31. Webb Papers, Box 3, Folder 15, SHSW. Emphasis in original.

32. Ibid.

33. Webb Papers, May 18, 1967, Box 3, Folder 21, SHSW

34. Lee Webb, "Viet Summer Shows What Can Be Done," *Vietnam Summer News*, August 27, 1967, 7. Box 1, A Collection of Materials About Protest Movements (Collection 550). Department of Special Collections, Charles E. Young Research Library, University of California, Los Angeles.

35. "War Not an Issue: Poor See Results on Local Issues," Vietnam Summer News, August 25, 1967, 11. Box 1, A Collection of Materials About Protest Movements (Collection 550). Department of Special Collections, Charles E. Young Research Library, University of California, Los Angeles.

36. "Mexican Americans Begin to Oppose War," "People for Peace: Corky Gonzales Leads the Chicanos," Vietnam Summer News, August 4, 1967, 8. Box 1, A Collection of Materials About Protest Movements (Collection 550). Department of Special Collections, Charles E. Young Research Library, University of California, Los Angeles.

37. Foley, *Confronting the War Machine*, 25.

38. Steve Hamilton, *New Left Notes*, July 1967, quoted in ibid., 88.

39. Foley, *Confronting the War Machine*, 66; Michael Ferber and Staughton Lynd, *The Resistance* (Boston: Beacon Press, 1971), 174.

40. Ferber and Lynd, *Resistance*, 112.

41. Foley, *Confronting the War Machine*, 97. Egleson's style, like much of SDS's public proclamations of the period, verges on grandiloquence, which might have been counterproductive to his stated aims.

42. Ibid., 67.

43. Ibid., 99.

44. Quoted in ibid., 69.

45. Jeffrey Alexander, "How to Beat the Draft Legally (and Illegally)," *Harvard Crimson*, February 12, 1968.

46. Foley, *Confronting the War Machine*, 73.

47. Herbert Hill, "The Problem of Race in American Labor History," *Reviews in American History* 24 (1996), 189. See also Noel Ignatiev, *How Irish Became White* (New York: Routledge, 1995); Robin Kelley, *Race Rebels: Culture, Politics, and the Black Working Class* (New York: Simon & Schuster, 1996); Lipsitz, *Possessive Investment in Whiteness*; David Roediger, *The Wages of Whiteness* (London: Verso, 1991); Bruce Nelson, *Divided We Stand: American Workers and the Struggle for Black Equality* (Princeton: Princeton University Press, 2001); Michael Goldfield, *The Color of Politics: Race and the Mainsprings of American Politics* (New York: The New Press, 1997); Steve Martinot, "The Racialized Construction of Class in the United States," *Social Justice* 27:1 (Spring 2000).

48. During those same years, to be sure, within black labor-organizing class identity did take on a primary role. And in the late 1960s, with the emergence of the Revolutionary Black Workers, the Dodge Revolutionary Union Movement, the Black Brothers, and other militant African American working-class organizations, class-based demands and struggle intensified in the black community. But, on the whole, from within and without, the collective identity forged among African Americans in struggle in this period was based in race before class.

49. Appy, *Working Class War*, 19.

50. Howard Zinn and Anthony Arnove, *Voices of a People's History of the United States* (New York: Seven Stories Press, 2004), 422–23.

51. Carson, *In Struggle*, 188. As if to confirm the SNCC analysis, the Georgia legislature denied Julian Bond, a SNCC member, his democratically elected seat a month later

for refusing to distance himself from this antiwar position. Bond's race and general politics were undoubtedly the main objections of the state legislature, and the U.S. Supreme Court, finding for Bond later that year, noted, "We are not persuaded by the state's attempt to distinguish between an exclusion alleged to be on racial grounds and one alleged to violate the First Amendment." Quoted in Taylor Branch, *At Canaan's Edge: America in the King Years, 1965–68* (New York: Simon & Schuster, 2007), 563.

52. Melvin Small, among others, notes the relationship between the nationalist turn of the SNCC and the movement of its white supporters into the antiwar movement. *Antiwarriors*, 5–6.

53. Though the AFL-CIO, shamefully, remained neutral.

54. Reeve Vanneman and Lynn Weber Cannon, *The American Perception of Class* (Philadelphia: Temple University Press, 1987), 225–51.

55. Hall, *Peace and Freedom*, 168.

56. John Herbers, "Rights Forces, After Wide Legal Gains, Grope for New Ways to Bring Negro Equality," *New York Times*, August 15, 1965.

57. Quoted in Branch, *At Canaan's Edge*, 286–87, 330.

58. Quoted in Gettleman, et.al., *Vietnam And America*, 315.

59. Branch, *At Canaan's Edge*. With tragic irony, King's death, in an immediate sense, constrained the warmaking abilities of the US government. As Colonel George L. Jackson detailed in the *Naval War College Review* in 1970, "[d]uring the fiscal year 1968, 104,665 National Guardsmen were called upon to quell civil disturbances, many of which were precipitated by the assassination" of Dr. King. See George Jackson, "Constraints of the Negro Civil Rights Movement on American Military Effectiveness," 1970. Reprinted in *Vietnam and America: A Documented History*, edited by Marvin E. Gettleman et al., 321–26 (New York: Grove Press, 1995).

60. Hall, *Peace and Freedom*, 33.

61. Derrick Morrison, "High School Students," *The Militant*, May 26, 1970.

62. Chicano Moratorium, "Chicano's and the War." Pamphlet, written sometime between August 29 and September 16, 1970, 2, Devra Weber Papers, Box 3 Folder 8, Chicano Studies Research Center, UCLA.

63. Lorena Oropeza, *Raza Sí! Guerra No!: Chicano Protest and Patriotism during the Viet Nam War Era* (Berkeley: University of California Press, 2005), 115.

64. Ibid., 141.

65. *The Militant*, May 22, 1970.

66. Quoted in "Chicano Leaders See Few Gains since Riot," *Los Angeles Times*, August 30, 1971, Devra Weber Papers, Box 3, Folder 5, Chicano Studies Research Center, UCLA.

67. "Chicanos' 3-Month March to Capital Reaches Salton Sea," *Los Angeles Times*, May 13, 1971, Devra Weber Papers, Box 3, Folder 5, Chicano Studies Research Center, UCLA.

68. Branch, *At Canaan's Edge*, 279.

CHAPTER 4

1. LLAP Papers, Box 1, Folder 1, SHSW.

2. Foner, *US Labor and the Vietnam War*, viii.

3. NALC was founded by A. Philip Randolph, President of the Sleeping Car Porters, in protest against racism within the labor movement.

4. Halstead, *Out Now!* 240–41; ibid., 54.

5. Quoted in John Fousek, *To Lead the Free World: American Nationalism and the Cultural Roots of the Cold War* (Chapel Hill: University of North Carolina Press, 2000), 183.

6. *Wall Street Journal*, September 21, 1970; Machinists, quoted in Foner, *US Labor and the Vietnam War*, 13–14.

7. Irving Bluestone, quoted in Koscielski, *Divided Loyalties*, 81.

8. *Wall Street Journal*, November 9, 1967, quoted in Foner, *US Labor and the Vietnam War*, 56.

9. Ronald Radosh, *American Labor and United States Foreign Policy* (New York: Random House, 1969), 383–93; 405–15; 424–34.

10. Quoted in Foner, *US Labor and the Vietnam War*, 25.

11. Fousek, *To Lead the Free World*, 186.

12. Foner, *US Labor and the Vietnam War*, 23. For a description of Tony Mazzochi's early successful and failed approaches to antiwar organizing, see Les Leopold, *Man Who Hated Work and Loved Labor: The Life and Times of Tony Mazzocchi* (White River Junction, Vt.: Chelsea Green, 2007), 197–223. For a discussion of the Detroit-based Trade Unionists for Peace, which became active in 1965, see Koscielski, *Divided Loyalties*.

13. *The Nation*, June 27, 1966.

14. LLAP Papers, Box 1, Folder 4, SHSW.

15. Letter signed by Murray Finlay, April 25, 1967, LLAP Papers, Box 1, Folder 4, SHSW.

16. LLAP Papers, Box 1 Folder 3, SHSW.

17. Sponsored by TUD-SANE, SANE, Working Families Party (WFP), Veterans for Peace, Women's International League for Peace and Freedom (WILPF) Midwest Faculty Committee, SDS, and Chicago Area Fellowship of Reconciliation, this was one of the last events that successfully united liberal and radical forces in this phase of the movement.

18. LLAP Papers, Box 2, Folder 10, SHSW.

19. "A Labor Leader Speaks for Peace," Fifth Avenue Vietnam Peace Parade Committee, Box 1, A Collection of Materials About Protest Movements (Collection 550). Department of Special Collections, Charles E. Young Research Library, University of California, Los Angeles.

20. The others were Patrick Gorman of the Amalgamated Meat Cutters, Al Hartung of the International Woodworkers, and Frank Rosenblum of the Amalgamated Clothing Workers. "Program for LLAP," LLAP Papers, Box 2, Folder 9, SHSW.

21. *Washington Post* November 12, 1967; LLAP Papers, Box 2, Folder 1, SHSW.

22. Meany, for his part, allowed the statement of the LLAP to be read by a lower state federation official at the AFL-CIO convention a month later in Miami but said, "he didn't have to read it for my benefit because I read it some time ago. I read it in the Sunday Worker two weeks before this meeting [of the LLAP] took place." Quoted in the *Madison Capital Times*, December 15, 1967, in LLAP Papers, Box 3, Folder 4. SHSW.

23. Quoted in Foner, *US Labor and the Vietnam War*, 56.

24. Foner's *US Labor and the Vietnam War* is a book dedicated to the antiwar efforts of labor. Koscielski's *Divided Loyalties* examines antiwar efforts in the UAW. Levy's *New Left and Labor* and Halstead's *Out Now!* both dedicate thoughtful, if intermittent, attention to it. Most histories of the period do not mention it, for example, Gitlin, *Sixties*; Anderson, *Movement and the Sixties*; Sale, *SDS*, or they do so in only in passing, for example, DeBenedetti, *American Ordeal* ; Wells, *War Within*.

25. LLAP Papers, Box 1, Folder 1, SHSW.

26. Stan Weir, *Singlejack Solidarity* (Minneapolis: University of Minnesota Press, 2004), 146.

27. Letter from Art Gundershiem to Robert Atkins, December 5, 1967, LLAP Papers, Box 2, Folder 10, SHSW. Atkins, a philosopher at Berkeley, had written in his letter to Gundershiem that "It has been the experience of Local 1570 . . . that a trade union can participate in political dissent without harming its economic interests." The preposterous projection of political and economic circumstances at Berkeley and those facing the labor movement as a whole was rather gently handled by Gundersheim, marking the nimble line

that many labor leaders walked negotiating their position between the labor and antiwar movements.

28. Halstead, *Out Now!*, 240.

29. Leopold, *Man Who Hated Work*, 203–5.

30. LLAP Papers, Drug and Hospital Employee Local 1199 Records, Box 1, Folder 1 SHSW.

31. Koscielski, *Divided Loyalties*, 169–70.

32. LLAP Papers, SANE-Trade Union Division Records, Box 2, Folder 2, SHSW.

33. Koscielski, *Divided Loyalties*, 208–10.

34. LLAP Papers, Box 2, Folder 10, SHSW.

35. Charles Hirshman, Samuel Preston, and Vu Manh Loi, "Vietnamese Casualties during the American War: A New Estimate," *Population and Development Review* 21, no. 4 (December 1995): 783–812.

36. Carton 4, Folder 6, Social Protest Collection, BANC Film 2757, Bancroft Library, University of California, Berkeley.

37. Bureau of Labor Statistics, average annual unemployment rates, http://www.bls.gov/cps/prev_yrs.htm; Andrew Levison, *The Working Class Majority* (New York: Coward, McCann, and Geoghagen, 1974), 81–82.

38. In the previous decade, over a million and a half unionized workers had lost COLAs in their contracts, and others, for example, auto and electric, had negotiated caps on their escalators. Inflation, therefore, was hitting workers hard. Richard Armstrong "Labor 1970: Angry, Aggressive, Acquisitive," *Fortune*, October 1969, 96.

39. Letter from Bob Weissman to Paul Booth, March 9, 1970, Paul Booth Papers Box 4, Folder 3L, SHSW. This letter was one of many exchanged among the older generation of SDS-ers who had become involved with the labor movement—they were working on a labor project at the time, attempting to create progressive networks among rank-and-file members and lower-level staff.

40. See Jefferson Cowie, *Stayin' Alive: The 1970's and the Last Days of the Working Class* (New York: New Press, 2010); Aaron Brenner, Robert Brenner, and Cal Winslow, eds., *Rebel Rank and File* (London: Verso, 2010).

41. "Business: The Hidden Costs of the Vietnam War," *Time* magazine, July 13, 1970.

42. Levison, *Working Class Majority*; Stanley Aronowitz, *False Promises*, 6th ed. (Durham: Duke University Press, 1993). For more a recent consideration, see Brenner, Brenner, and Winslow, *Rebel Rank and File*.

43. Foner, *US Labor and the Vietnam War*, 74; quoted in Armstrong, "Labor 1970," 94. For a detailed discussion of these fights, see Brenner, Brenner, and Winslow, *Rebel Rank and File*.

44. James Matles and James Higgins, *Them and Us: Struggles of a Rank-and-File Union* (New York: Prentice-Hall, 1974).

45. Stanley Aronowitz, "Opportunity for Left Seen in GE Strike," *Guardian*, December 6, 1969.

46. "GE Fiddles While Workers Burn," *Guardian*, December 17, 1969.

47. Minutes of Who Profits, Who Pays subcommittee, January 3–4, 1970, Paul Booth Papers, Box 4, Folder 3, SHSW.

48. Foner, *US Labor and the Vietnam War*, 74–76, 82.

49. *Guardian*, February 7, 1970.

50. Ibid., 82.

51. Lichtenstein, *Most Dangerous Man in Detroit*, 437.

52. Andrew Bornstein et al., *A Rich Man's War and a Poor Man's Fight: A Handbook for Trade Unionists on the Vietnam War* (Washington, D.C.: Labor for Peace, 1970), 2.

53. These are section headings from the pamphlet, also quoted in Leopold, *The Man Who Hated Work*," 278–79.

54. Foner, *US Labor and the Vietnam War*, 133–43.

55. Quoted in ibid., 152.

56. *New York Times*, May 27, 1970.

CHAPTER 5

1. Gwynne Dyer, *War: The Lethal Custom* (Basic Books: New York, 2005), chap. 2, 29–62; Neale, *American War*, 129.

2. Moser, *New Winter Soldiers*, 132; Cortright, *Soldiers in Revolt*, 24–25.

3. Movement for a Democratic Military, "Free the Fort Ord 40,000," pamphlet, 1970, Carton 2, Folder 5, Social Protest Collection, BANC Film 2757, Bancroft Library, University of California, Berkeley.

4. James Scott, *Weapons of the Weak: Everyday Forms of Peasant Resistance* (New Haven: Yale University Press, 1985), 29.

5. Ibid.

6. Brinkley, *Unfinished Nation*, 861. By associating My Lai with a breakdown of morale and discipline, Brinkley also implies that such a massacre was an exception to the normal operations of the war, an argument vigorously challenged by many soldiers and antiwar groups.

7. Robert D. Heinl, "The Collapse of the Armed Forces," *Armed Forces Journal* (June 1971), reprinted in *Vietnam and America: A Documented History*, edited by Marvin Gettleman et al. (New York: Grove Press, 1995), 327.

8. Appy, *Working Class War*, 18; Cortright, *Soldiers in Revolt*, 4.

9. For statistics, see Cortright, *Soldiers in Revolt*, 5.

10. Lawrence Baskir and William Strauss, *Chance and Circumstance: The Draft, the War, and the Vietnam Generation* (New York: Vintage Books, 1978), 281.

11. Appy, *Working Class War*, 51.

12. A couple of years before Vietnam, Paul Goodman observed, "the army has become the IBM of the poor boy." *Growing Up Absurd: Problems of Youth in the Organized System* (New York: Random House, 1960), 103.

13. Clyde Taylor, while listing many reasons for African American enlistment, relates, "Juvenile courts often make the alternatives clear: the Army or jail, a kind of modern Shanghai recruitment." Taylor, *Vietnam and Black America* (Garden City, NY: Anchor Books, 1973), 17.

14. Baskir and Strauss, *Chance and Circumstance*, 48.

15. Chicano Moratorium Committee 1970, Carton 1 Folder 22, Social Protest Collection, BANC Film 2757, Bancroft Library, University of California, Berkeley.

16. The Wisconsin Draft Resistance Union was active in Madison at the same time as the BRDG and had a similar philosophy of broad-based draft counseling. See Wisconsin Draft Resistance Union files, Robert Gabriner Papers, Box 22, F13–16, SHSW. Such unions existed in Cleveland, Oakland, and other cities as well; the Chicago Area Draft Resisters were active from 1967 to 1970.

17. Baskir and Strauss, *Chance and Circumstance*, 11.

18. Harold Jordan, "Whatever Happened to Vietnam Era War Resisters?" American Friends Services Committee, http://www.afsc.org/youthmil/conscientious-objection/Vietnam-war-resisters.htm (accessed July 28, 2008); Cortright, *Soldiers in Revolt*, 5.

19. Baskir and Strauss, *Chance and Circumstance*, 86, 91.

20. Appy, *Working Class War*, 44–50.

21. Baskir and Strauss, *Chance and Circumstance*, 91; David Sterling Surrey, *Choice of Conscience: Vietnam Era Military and Draft Resisters in Canada* (New York: Praeger,

1982); "Many Deserters Active in Sweden," *New York Times,* July 15, 1968; "For Some Deserters Canada Is Home, Other Exiles Hope to Return to the US," *New York Times,* February 4, 1973. Canada also had a large evader community—people who "dodged" the draft. Significantly, in the fights over amnesty, it was only occasionally recognized that the class base of deserters was predictably lower than those who overtly resisted the draft; President Jimmy Carter's amnesty in 1977 fully covered only the "dodgers" who had avoided the draft; deserters (those who were drafted but then left) received conditional clearance that depended on their own efforts to initiate it. Surrey, *Choice of Conscience.*

22. David Cortright, "GI Resistance during the Vietnam War," in *Give Peace a Chance,* edited by Melvin Small and William Hoover (Syracuse, N.Y.: Syracuse University Press, 1992), 117–18.

23. John Helmer, *Bringing the War Home: The American Soldier in Vietnam and After* (New York: Free Press, 1974), 51.

24. Interview in David Zieger, *Sir! No Sir!* Displaced Films and BBC documentary, 2005.

25. "Free the Fort Ord 40,000," pamphlet, Movement for a Democratic Military, Carton 2, Folder 5, Social Protest Collection, BANC Film 2757, Bancroft Library, University of California, Berkeley.

26. "Fort Knox Coffeehouse Firebombed," *Duck Power* 1, no. 6, October 9, 1969.

27. "Antiwar Show for GIs Has Receptive Audience," *Camp News* 2, no. 2, 1970.

28. As the ground war gave way to an air war (supported by naval aircraft carriers), the dissent, disobedience, and desertions shifted from their strongholds in the army to these other divisions of the armed forces.

29. Hunt, *Turning,* 68.

30. Foley, *Confronting the War Machine,* 309.

31. Cortright, *Soldiers in Revolt,* 33.

32. Zeiger, *Sir No Sir!*

33. Appy, *Working Class War,* 244–45.

34. Mike McFerrin, "Mike Company, 3rd Battalion, Fifth Marines," 1999, http://www.securenet.net/3rdbn5th/mike35/mike.htm (accessed January 6, 2009).

35. Heinl, "Collapse of the Armed Forces."

36. Appy, *Working Class War,* 222.

37. Cortright, 42.

38. Moser, *New Winter Soldiers,* 44–48.

39. Fragmentation grenades were used as threats—unpopular officers might find one on their pillow, for instance. Or they were used as actual weapons—tossed into an officers' mess or bunk, for instance, their provenance would be difficult to trace.

40. Heinl, "Collapse of the Armed Forces."

41. John Biewen, "The Movie in Our Heads: America Radio Works Revisiting Vietnam," part II of the *Revisiting Vietnam* series on American RadioWorks, American Public Media, April 2000, http://americanradioworks.publicradio.org/features/vietnam/us/movie.html (accessed February 16, 2008).

42. Joel Geier, "Vietnam: The Soldiers Revolt," *International Socialist Review* 9 (1999), 45–46. Geier quotes a soldier telling the *New York Times,* "The American garrisons on the larger bases are virtually disarmed" (46).

43. In Taylor, *Vietnam and Black America,* 203, 200–220.

44. Kimberly M. Phillips, "'All I Wanted Was a Steady Job': The State of African American Workers," in *New Working-Class Studies,* edited by John Russo and Sherry Linkin (Ithaca: ILR Press/Cornell University Press, 2005), 51. Blacks always had much higher rates of reenlistments than whites, however. The military was viewed as an opportunity for advancement, and despite the fights against internal racism, it was also a relatively

more equal-opportunity employer than many others available to young black men, both during Vietnam and today.

45. Neale, *American War*, 128.

46. The casualty rates in 1972 draw from a different phase of the war, when Air Force and Navy soldiers were being used more, and the ground troops from the Army in particular had been reduced. Differential racial composition of these different wings of the armed forced might also therefore account for some of the lower rates of African American casualties by 1972.

47. Ibid., 87; Cortright, *Soldiers in Revolt*, 43; "43 Black GI's Refuse Chicago Riot Duty," *The Ally*, no. 9, 1968.

48. Cortright, *Soldiers in Revolt*, 24–25.

49. Dave Grossman, *On Killing: Psychological Cost of Learning to Kill* (Toronto: Little, Brown, 1998), 29–36, 141–94.

50. Appy, *Working Class War*, 223.

51. Helmer, *Bringing the War Home*.

52. Hunt, *Turning*, 2. See also the discussion in Lembcke, *Spitting Image*, 67.

53. For first march of Barry and the other veterans, see Wells, *War Within*, 139–40. For the Communist Party story, see Halstead, *Out Now!*

54. John Kerry et al., *The New Soldier* (New York: Macmillan, 1971).

55. VVAW Papers, Box 13, Folder 10, SHSW.

56. VVAW Papers, Extension Kroll Box 1, SHSW.

57. Hunt, *Turning*, 85.

58. Hall, *Peace and Freedom*, 179.

59. VVAW Papers, Extension Boxes Cairo, SHSW; Hunt, *Turning*, 125.

60. Serving in 1968, Chitty was assigned shore duty patrol in San Diego the night that Martin Luther King was assassinated. "They gave me a .45, expected me to go out into the street against fellow citizens who were protesting what I also felt was a great injustice. . . . My heart was with the people . . . so I refused to go." The actions of Chitty and some of his friends led to a shipwide protest, a further example of the instability created in the armed forces due to the movement sympathies of active GIs (described in the first part of this chapter). Moser, *New Winter Soldiers*, 81–82.

61. Ibid., 130.

62. *Life* magazine, October 24, 1969, quoted in Hall, *Peace and Freedom*, 160; Halstead, *Out Now!* 473.

63. See John Herbers, "Vietnam Moratorium Observed Nationwide by Foes of the War; Opponents React, Many Show Support for Nixon by Flying Flags Full-Staff; Moratorium Is Observed Nationwide," *New York Times*, October 16, 1969; "October 15, A Day to Remember," *Newsweek*, October 27, 1969; Tom Seaver, quoted in Rick Perlstein, *Nixonland: America's Second Civil War and the Divisive Legacy of Richard Nixon, 1965–1972* (New York: Simon and Schuster, 2008), 425.

64. Quoted in Wells, *War Within*, 726.

65. "Military Moratorium Huge Success—1,000 Marines March in Oceanside," *Attitude Check* 1, no. 2.

66. Wells, *War Within*, 399; Small, *Antiwarriors*, 119.

67. Halstead, *Out Now!* esp. 563–81, 646–59; Wells, *War Within,* esp. chaps. 8–9.

68. Quoted in Hall, *Peace and Freedom*, 163.

69. The labels I employ here, *radical* and *moderate*, do not necessarily reflect the self-perceptions of those taking these different positions. The SWP, for example, did not consider itself a force of moderation, nor perhaps would many observers of the party. Yet in this debate SWP members aligned themselves with a single-issue focus and legally permitted rallies that I am calling moderate, even though they saw themselves as being

truly radical, as opposed to what they considered the juvenile and shortsighted notions of multi-issue radical action. See Halstead, *Out Now!* 522–25; Wells, *War Within*, 398–403: Hall, *Peace and Freedom*, 163–66.

70. Wells, *War Within*, 271–72.

71. Among others, see Anderson, *Movement and the Sixties,* 328–29.

72. Hunt, *Turning*, 144.

73. Halstead, *Out Now!* 611–12.

CHAPTER 6

1. C. Wright Mills, "Letter to the New Left," *New Left Review*, September–October 1960, http://www.marxists.org/subject/humanism/mills-c-wright/letter-new-left.htm (accessed June 2, 2007).

2. Some of the many books that have explored this topic include Werner Sombart, *Why Is There No Socialism in the United States,* edited by C. T. Husbands, translated by Patricia M. Hocking and C. T. Husbands (White Plains, N.Y.: International Arts and Sciences Press, 1976); Seymour Martin Lipset, *American Exceptionalism: A Double Edged Sword* (New York: W. W. Norton, 1996); Aristide Zolberg, *How Many Exceptionalisms?* (Philadelphia: Temple University Press, 2008); Kim Voss, *The Making of American Exceptionalism* (Ithaca: Cornell University Press, 1993).

3. We can trace the careers, writings, and speeches of Samuel Gompers and Eugene Debs as ideal types in the first set of debates, as Bill Fletcher Jr. and Fernando Gapasin do in *Solidarity Divided* (Berkeley: University of California Press, 2008), or we can read Selig Perlman's *A Theory of the Labor Movement* (Philadelphia: Porcupine Press, 1979 [1928]) against theorists in various Marxist camps or the Industrial Workers of the World (IWW) Manifesto in the other set. For a good overview of such academic debates within labor, see Simeon Larson and Bruce Nissen, *Theories of the Labor Movement* (Detroit: Wayne State University Press, 1987). See also Samuel Gompers, *Seventy Years of Life and Labor: An Autobiography,* Vol. 11 (London: Hurst & Blackett, 1925); Nick Salvatore, *Eugene V. Debs: Citizen and Socialist* (Urbana: University of Illinois Press, 2007).

4. For good discussion on the post-war boom as well as its limits, see Aronowitz, *False Promises;* Nelson Lichtenstein, *The State of the Union: A Century of American Labor* (Princeton: Princeton University Press, 2002); Lichtenstein et al, *Who Built America?*

5. Jack Metzgar, *Striking Steel: Solidarity Remembered* (Philadelphia: Temple University Press, 2000), 39.

6. Aronowitz, *False Promises*, 180.

7. Government and service workers were only at this time becoming unionized.

8. Metzgar, *Striking Steel*, 41.

9. David Johnson, John Rodgers, and Lucilla Tan, "A Century of Family Budgets in the United States," *Monthly Labor Report*, Bureau of Labor Statistics, May 2001; Levison, *Working Class Majority*, 31.

10. US Census Bureau Statistics, "Historical Income Tables: Families," http://www.census.gov/hhes/www/income/histinc/f01w.html (accessed June 30, 2008).

11. Levison, *Working Class Majority*, 32.

12. Quoted in George Lipsitz, *Rainbow at Midnight* (Urbana: University of Illinois Press, 1994), 230.

13. Aronowitz, *False Promises*, 248.

14. Art Preis, *Labor's Giant Step: The First Twenty Years of the CIO: 1935–55* (New York: Pathfinder, 1992 [1964]), 495.

15. Sugrue, *Origins of the Urban Crisis*, 325; Metzgar, *Striking Steel*, 101–8. See also chapter 4.

16. George Lipsitz, *Time Passages* (Minneapolis: University of Minnesota Press, 1990), 42.

17. Lipsitz cites television historian David Marc as pointing out, the opposite of "Hooverville," in ibid., 39.

18. Ibid.; Bodnar, *Blue-Collar Hollywood*, 136.

19. Michael Harrington, *The Other America: Poverty in the United States* (New York: Macmillan, 1962). Incidentally, Harrington's book, which proved inspirational in the New Left as well as Democratic Party policy circles, similarly divided the United States into "affluent" and "poor," with workers falling into either category, depending on their particular income and status. So, although the book served to open middle-class eyes to the persistent reality of economic inequality, it did so according to the same logic that largely erased the working class as distinct social group.

20. John Goldthorpe et al., *Affluent Worker in the Class Structure* (Cambridge, UK: Cambridge University Press, 1969).

21. Robert Alford, also finds that "class voting" had not in fact decreased in the early post-war period; "The Role of Social Class in American Voting Behavior," *Western Political Quarterly* 16 (1963): 180–94. Decades later, David Halle's ethnographic study, *America's Working Man*, found evidence to support both sides of this debate. Studying a higher-income and relatively skilled group of chemical workers during the 1970s, Halle discovered that their own sense of class was multifaceted—they attained a sense of being a "workingman" from the job while identifying with being "middle class" at home—and that their leisure behavior and political attitudes had elements in common with both traditional "working-class" culture and the more mainstream "middle-class" concerns and ideals. *America's Working Man: Work, Home, and Politics among Blue-Collar Property Owners* (Chicago: University of Chicago Press, 1984).

22. James W. Rinehart, "Affluence and the Embourgeoisement of the Working Class: A Critical Look," *Social Problems* 19 (1971), 157. In 1973, Gavin Mackenzie published *The Aristocracy of Labour*, which is about bricklayers, among others, in Providence, Rhode Island; in it he also challenges the embourgeoisement thesis. *The Aristocracy of Labour: The Position of Skilled Craftsmen in the American Class Structure* (London: Cambridge University Press, 1973).

23. Arthur B. Shostak, *Blue-Collar Life* (New York: Random House, 1969), 212. Shostak nevertheless maintains that a "distinct style of politics" exists that can be appraised "within these restrictions" (212).

24. Robert Nisbet, "The Decline and Fall of Social Class," *Pacific Sociological Review* 2 (1959),11.

25. As Ira Katznelson points out, this is also the period in which books such as Joseph Schumpeter's *Capitalism, Socialism and Democracy* (1942), Karl Polanyi's *The Great Transformation* (1944), and Friedrich Hayek's *The Road to Serfdom* (1944) all took on fundamental relations of political economy, which, he argues, later give rise to just plain "economics." Ira Katznelson, "Was the Great Society a Lost Opportunity?" in *The Rise and Fall of the New Deal Order 1930–1980*, edited by Steve Fraser and Gary Gerstle (Princeton: Princeton University Press, 1989), 191.

26. Milton Gordon and Michael Grimes both describe (the first approvingly, the latter critically) the typical post-war models as finding inspiration in both the newly translated Weber and the consensus frameworks offered by functionalism, emphasizing interdependence and differentiation over power and conflictual relations. Milton Myron Gordon, *Social Class in American Sociology* (Durham: Duke University Press, 1958); Michael Grimes, *Class in Twentieth-Century American Sociology: An Analysis of Theories and Measurement Strategies* (New York: Praeger, 1991).

27. Max Weber, *From Max Weber: Essays in Sociology*, edited and translated by Hans Heinrich Gerth and Charles Wright Mills (Oxford: Oxford University Press, 1946);

W. Lloyd Warner, Kenneth Eells, and Marchia Meeker, *Social Class in America: A Manual of Procedure for the Measurement of Social Status* (Chicago: Science Research Associates, 1949); Gordon, *Social Class in American Sociology*; Grimes, *Class in Twentieth-Century American Sociology*. Gerth and Mills' English translation of Weber had a tremendous impact on the US scene. But Joan Rytina, John Pease, and William Form, writing of the sociology that emerged from this time, point out that the frequent invocations of Weber by theorists eager to claim his authority for a status-based stratification model reflect a superficial (at best) and distorted (at worst) understanding of Weber's actual discussion of "class, status, and party": "Most American students of stratification simply use Weber's authority to assert that stratification is not simple and unidimensional (implying, incorrectly, that Karl Marx said it was) and that class and status are analytically distinct (implying, as Weber did not, that the two are therefore equally consequential in social life)." Joan Rytina, John Pease, and William Form, "Ideological Currents in American Stratification Literature," *American Sociologist* 5 (1970), 130.

28. Sociology stratification scholars also owed a large debt to the work Talcott Parsons, as well as to Kingsley Davis and Wilbert Moore, whose 1945 article "Some Principles of Stratification" became the touchstone for functionalist stratification studies; "Some Principles of Stratification," *American Sociological Review* 10, no. 2 (April 1945): 242–49.

29. See, for example Reinhard Bendix and Seymour Martin Lipset, *Class, Status and Power: A Reader in Social Stratification* (New York: Free Press, 1953); Walter Goldschmidt, "Social Class in America: A Critical Review," *American Anthropologist* 52, no. 4 (October–December, 1950): 483–98; Robert Staughton Lynd and Helen Merrell Lynd, *Middletown: A Study in Contemporary American Culture* (New York: Harcourt, Brace and Company, 1945).

30. Lynd and Lynd, *Middletown*.

31. Gordon, *Social Class in American Sociology*, 249.

32. Daniel Bell, *The End of Ideology: On the Exhaustion of Political Ideas in the Fifties* (Glencoe, Ill.: Free Press, 1960); David Riesman, Nathan Glazer, and Reuel Denney, *The Lonely Crowd: A Study of the Changing American Character* (New Haven: Yale University Press, 1961); John Kenneth Galbraith, *The Affluent Society*. Harrington's *The Other America* (1962) was a rebuttal to Galbraith.

33. Goodman, *Growing Up Absurd*, 159.

34. Kevin Mattson argues, "to a large extent, the book synthesized a decade's worth of social criticism." *Intellectuals in Action: The Origins of the New Left and Radical Liberalism, 1945–1970* (University Park: Penn State Press, 2002), 113.

35. Goodman, *Growing Up Absurd*, 160. Members of the Organization have bought into the need for, and rules of, the rat race. The poor and the independents, voluntary and involuntary exiles from the "center" of the metaphorical room, tend to be the groups that give the system some openness. Goodman's main concern is with the youth of this society, with an implicit focus on the youth of the Organization Men—the middle class—and their socialization within this "absurd" system. These youth were predictably disaffected (such as the beats), but possibly transformative.

36. Ibid., 161. Emphasis in the original.

37. Eric Hoffer, "The Negro Is Prejudiced against Himself; the Negro Is against Himself," *New York Times Magazine*, November 29, 1964; "Hoffer on Colleges: Strong Men Needed," *Washington Post*, May 10, 1969.

38. Shostak, *Blue-Collar Life*, 212.

39. Ibid., 213–14. Shostak later invokes working-class support for war and opposition to protesters as evidence of authoritarian values among workers. But, as James D. Wright points out, his support for these claims rests on the 1967 Cambridge, Massachusetts, antiwar referendum, in which little to no canvassing was done in key working-class districts,

and on a *Village Voice* article that anecdotally noted working-class antipathy to peace parades. Wright, "Working Class," 134–35n. 3.

40. Stanley Milgram, *Obedience to Authority: An Experimental View* (New York: Harper and Row, 1974).

41. Seymour Martin Lipset, "Democracy and Working-Class Authoritarianism," *American Sociological Review* 24, no. 4 (1959), 483, 482.

42. Among the more compelling critiques are Wright, "Working Class,"; S. M. Miller and Frank Reissman, "'Working-Class Authoritarianism': A Critique of Lipset." *British Journal of Sociology* 12 (1961): 263–76. The latter is an excellent overall critique of the piece. Among other points raised, these critics take Lipset to task for his notion of democracy, which they see as being particularly congenial to a middle-class liberal audience rather than a working-class one, for whom economic democracy was a precondition for many of the rights and freedoms associated with liberal ideals.

43. Seymour Martin Lipset, *Political Man: The Social Bases of Politics* (Garden City, N.Y.: Doubleday, 1960).

44. See Samuel Lubell, "Patterns of Government," *New York Times Book Review,* January 10, 1960, 6; Alexander Heard, "A Political Bookshelf for an Election Year," *New York Times Book Review* January 5, 1964, 38.

45. Gitlin, *Sixties*, 102.

46. Goodman, *Growing Up Absurd*, 55.

47. C. Wright Mills, *The New Men of Power* (Urbana: University of Illinois, 2001 [1948]), 269.

48. Douglas Kellner and Herbert Marcuse, *The New Left and the 1960s: Collected Papers of Herbert Marcuse,* Vol. 3 (New York: Routledge, 2005), 1.

49. Marcuse, *One-Dimensional Man*, xiii; Herbert Marcuse, "Socialism in Developed Countries," *International Socialist Journal* 2 (April 1965), 140.

50. Lipsitz, *Rainbow at Midnight*, 232.

CHAPTER 7

1. Homer Bigart, "War Foes Here Attacked by Construction Workers," *New York Times,* May 9, 1970; Homer Bigart, "Huge City Hall Rally Backs Nixon's Indochina Policies," *New York Times,* May 21, 1970.

2. Levy, *New Left and Labor*; Cowie, "Vigorously Left, Right and Center," 84; Barbara Ehrenreich, *Fear of Falling: The Inner Life of the Middle Class* (New York: Pantheon Books, 1989), 101.

3. Appy, *Working Class War*, 38.

4. Levison, *Working Class Majority*; Sexton and Sexton, *Blue Collars and Hard Hats.* For contemporary discussions, see also Edward F. Wehrle, "'Partisan for the Hard Hats': Charles Colson, George Meany, and the Failed Blue-Collar Strategy," *Labor* (fall 2008) 5: 45–66; Maria Graciela Abarca, "'Discontented but Not Inevitably Reactionary': Organized Labor in the Nixon Years," PhD dissertation, University of Massachusetts, Amherst, 2001.

5. Dorothy Sue Cobble, "'A Tiger by the Toenail': The 1970s Origins of the New Working Class Majority, *Labor* 2, no. 3 (fall 2005) 103–14.

6. Jefferson Cowie argues that Nixon's interest in the working class dated from his having read Pete Hamill's 1969 *New York Magazine* article about New York workers. "The Enigma of Working Class Conservatism: From the Hard Hats to the NASCAR Dads," *New Labor Forum* 13 (fall 2004): 9–17.

7. Strategically, however, opposition to the antiwar movement was not as powerful as the more serious wedge issues of the era proved to be for the Republicans—race, rights, and taxes, in the formulation of the Edsall and Edsall. Yet their success on those fronts was abetted by the campaign against the protesters in 1969–1970. Thomas Byrne Edsall

and Mary D. Edsall, *Chain Reaction: The Impact of Race, Rights, and Taxes on American Politics* (New York: W. W. Norton, 1992). Edward Wehrle calls Nixon's blue-collar strategy a "failed" one that had a momentary appeal due to the depth with which AFL-CIO leaders supported the war effort; "'Partisan for the Hard Hats.'"

8. Daniel Walker, "Rights in Conflict: The Violent Confrontation of Demonstrators and Police in the Parks and Streets of Chicago during the Week of the Democratic National Convention of 1968," National Commission on the Causes and Prevention of Violence, December 1, 1968, http://www.geocities.com/Athens/Delphi/1553/ricsumm.html (accessed January 28, 2008).

9. Anderson *Movement and the Sixties*, 235, 228; Converse and Schuman, "Silent Majorities and the Vietnam War."

10. Nathan Blumberg, "The Orthodox Media under Fire: Chicago and the Press," in *Mass Culture Revisited*, edited by Bernard Rosenberg and David Manning White (New York: Van Nostrand Reinhold, 1971), 277.

11. Quoted in Perlstein, *Nixonland*, 365. Here, Kraft anticipates the attacks on the media that were paired with the attacks on the protesters in the coming years, particularly from Vice President Agnew. He also paves the way for the conservative turn of the media, which were (self-)excused by reference to "systematic biases." Many later analysts point out that the media had not in fact been overly liberal in its coverage of the movements; Ehrenreich argues that the "discovery" by the media of a conservative white worker gave cover to the growing conservatism of media and political elites, a point I touch on again in my conclusion. Ehrenreich, *Fear of Falling*.

12. Ehrenreich, *Fear of Falling*, 97–143.

13. Richard Lemon, *The Troubled American* (New York: Simon & Schuster, 1970), 7; Hamill, "Revolt." Hamill used the term *lower middle class* because he was following the fashionable sociological assertion that everyone was now middle class, but he quickly sets the record straight: "Nobody calls it the Working Class anymore. But basically, the people I'm speaking about *are* the working class."

14. Hamill, "Revolt."

15. Ibid.,

16. Anderson, *Movement and the Sixties*.

17. Levison, *Working Class Majority*, chap. 4.

18. "Editor's Note," *Guardian*, October 19, 1968.

19. Much of the Left was also at this point looking for "a historical agent," having experienced the disillusionment of the student revolution. This does not mean that its interest in the working class should be written off entirely, just that this new working-class perspective should be taken with a grain of salt.

20. Paul Booth, Steve Max and Frank Goldsmith, SDS members, proposed a project the year before Nixon suggested his "Study of the Blue Collar Worker," called "Young White Workers: The Drift to the Right." They note that it was "not unreasoned" for such a shift to be occurring, if indeed it was. (The support for Wallace and Nixon in the 1968 elections was their evidence). Economic stagnation, perceived job competition with blacks, and the effects of integration on property values in neighborhoods all played parts in creating a Right-ward drift. Booth, Max, and Goldsmith wanted to study this transformation to see if the drift Right could "possible be transformed into a movement to the left if issues and solutions can be properly formulated." Booth Papers, December 1968, Box 4, Folder 3, SHSW.

21. For more discussion see Davis, *Prisoners of the American Dream*; Matthew D. Lassiter, *The Silent Majority: Suburban Politics in the Sunbelt South* (Princeton: Princeton University Press, 2007); Kevin Philips, *The Emerging Republican Majority* (New Rochelle, N.Y.: Arlington House, 1969).

22. John Judis and Ruy Teixeira, *The Emerging Democratic Majority* (New York: Simon & Schuster, 2004), 17; Bruce J. Schulman, *The Seventies: The Great Shift in American Culture, Society, and Politics* (New York: Free Press, 2001), 37.

23. See, among others, Edsall and Edsall, *Chain Reaction*; Paul Frymer and John David Skrentny, "Coalition-Building and the Politics of Electoral Capture during the Nixon Administration: African Americans, Labor, Latinos." *Studies in American Political Development* 12 (spring 1998): 131–61; Lassiter, *Silent Majority*; Robert Mason, *Richard Nixon and the Quest for a New Majority* (Chapel Hill: University of North Carolina Press, 2004); Jonathan Rieder, "The Rise of the Silent Majority," in *The Rise and Fall of the New Deal Order 1930–1980*, edited by Steve Fraser and Gary Gerstle, 242–69 (Princeton: Princeton University Press, 1989).

24. George Tagge, "Nixon: Here's What I'd Do," *Chicago Tribune*, May 5. 1968.

25. Wells, *War Within*, 311. Expanded wiretap and surveillance powers had recently been signed into law by President Johnson in the Omnibus Crime Control and Safe Streets Act of 1968.

26. Jeb Magruder, quoted in Halstead, *Out Now!* 483.

27. Anderson, *Movement and the Sixties*, 331.

28. Memo from Dwight Chapin to H. R. Haldeman, October 16, 1969, quoted in Halstead, *Out Now!* 493.

29. Harris polls, in the *Washington Post*, November 14, 1969.

30. Quoted in "11 Professors Bid Agnew Curb Tone; Speeches Drive Moderates 'into Arms of Extremists,'" *New York Times*, June 5, 1970.

31. The red-baiting of the Nixon administration and the Republican Party was extensive and deserves more space for a full explanation of how they sought to isolate the protesters. Here are some examples. On eve of the Moratorium, Hanoi sent a letter of support, "Dear American Friends," to the Moratorium. The day before the Moratorium was to begin (October 14, 1969), Agnew called on its leaders to "repudiate the support of a totalitarian government which had in its hand the blood of 40,0000 Americans." Earlier that week, then Governor Ronald Reagan of California said at a fund-raising dinner in Seneca Falls, New York, "We have a right to suspect that at least some of those who organize those parades are less concerned with peace than with lending comfort and aid to the enemy." Quoted in the *New York Times*, October 15, 1969.

32. See, among others, "Agnew Attacks War Protesters," *New York Times*, November 11,1969. See also a compendium of his quotations in "The Vice Presidency: Agnew's Pungent Quotient," *Time* magazine, June 29, 1970. The only group greeted with as much venom was the other side of that liberal elite—the mass media, or in the alluring alliteration of William Safire, speechwriter, the "nattering nabobs of negativism." The campaign against the media abutted the campaign against the college-educated and professionals, and undoubtedly reinforced their Rightward turn during the period.

33. "King's Taster," *Time* magazine, November 14, 1969.

34. Variations of this list were repeated in Wallace's stump speeches, including to the Associated Press in October 1968, and appeared in many papers around the country. See for example, "George Wallace, I Say What the People Want to Hear," *Sarasota Herald Tribune*, October 16, 1968.

35. Quoted in Eugene J. Dionne Jr., *Why Americans Hate Politics: The Death of the Democratic Process* (New York: Simon and Schuster, 2004), 91; Richard Scammon and Ben Wattenberg, *The Real Majority: An Extraordinary Examination of the American Electorate* (New York, Coward-McCann, 1970), 62.

36. "Agnew Scores War Foes; Rally to Hear Two Senators; Agnew Attacks War Protesters," *New York Times*, November 11, 1969.

37. See Rieder, "Rise of the Silent Majority," 173–74.

38. Paul M. Deac, quoted in "Man and Woman of the Year: The Middle Americans," *Time* magazine, January 5, 1970. In fact, some of "their boys" were doing all of these things, which perhaps contributed to the anger he describes here.

39. Adolph Reed, "Reinventing the Working Class: A Study in Elite Image Manipulation." *New Labor Forum* 13 (2004), 25.

40. Quoted in Anderson, *Movement and the Sixties*, 331. Nixon's approval rating in the aftermath of the "Silent Majority" speech was topped only once in his presidency—on the day he announced the cease-fire with Vietnam in January 1973. This indicates the centrality of Vietnam in US consciousness during the period and the extent to which the people of the United States wanted out of the war.

41. Wells, *War Within*, 409.

42. For a theoretical accounting of how the media both amplified and contained movement messages, see Gitlin, *Whole World Is Watching*, 249–82.

43. *Wall Street Journal*, May 11, 1970; quoted in Richard Rogin, "Joe Kelly Has Reached His Boiling Point: Why the Construction Workers Holler USA ALL the Way!" *New York Times Magazine*, June 28, 1970.

44. Quoted in Francis X. Clines, "For the Flag and Country, They March," *New York Times*, May 21, 1970; "Editorial," *New York Times*, June 7, 1970.

45. James M. Naughton, "Agnew and Student Leaders Hit Impasse in TV Debate," *New York Times*, September 22, 1970.

46. Quoted in "Workers Find Protest a 2-Way Street," *New York Times*, May 13, 1970.

47. Sexton and Sexton, *Blue Collars and Hard Hats*; Appy, *Working Class War*; Richard Sennett and Jonathan Cobb, *The Hidden Injuries of Class* (New York: W. W. Norton, 1993); Joshua B. Freeman, *Working-Class New York* (New York: The New Press, 2000); Levison, *Working Class Majority*.

48. Quoted in "For the Flag and Country" and "Huge March" *New York Times*, May 21, 1970.

49. Quoted in "Unionist Say War Protester Spark a Backlash," *New York Times*, May 17. 1970; quoted in "The Student as Hardhat," *New York Times*, May 31, 1971.

50. Sennett and Cobb, *Hidden Injuries of Class*, 23.

51. Quoted in Rosenberg et. al., *Vietnam and the Silent Majorities*, 69-70.

52. Quoted in ibid., 147.

53. Quoted in Appy, *Working Class War*, 303.

54. Quoted in Sennett and Cobb, *Hidden Injuries of Class*, 147.

55. Ibid., 69. The working-class activist quoted was John Welch, in "New Left Knots," in *Between Labor and Capital*, ed. Pat Walker (Cambridge, South End Press, 1979), 184.

56. Evidently, both My Lai and the killings at the end of *Joe* signified the death of innocents for John Avildson, the director; Peter Boyle interview, *New York Times*, August 2, 1970. But the disquieting comparison between the homicidal working-class Joe and the soldiers responsible for My Lai confirms the classist stereotypes that were employed by the filmmakers and that went unchallenged in the contemporary reception of the movie.

57. Ibid.

58. Reed, "Reinventing the Working Class," 23.

59. Boyle interview, *New York Times*, August 2, 1970.

60. Quoted in *New York Times*, May 17, 1970.

61. Frances Fox Piven, *Labor Parties in Postindustrial Societies* (Cambridge, UK: Polity Press, 1991), 236; Preis, *Labor's Giant Step*, 461–62.

62. Ruy Teixeira and Joel Townsley Rogers, *America's Forgotten Majority: Why the White Working Class Still Matters* (New York: Basic Books, 2000); Ruy Teixeira, "New Progressive America: Twenty Years of Demographic, Geographic, and Attitudinal Changes

across the Country Herald a New Progressive Majority," Center for American Progress, Washington, D.C., 2009

63. Quoted in Piven, *Labor Parties in Postindustrial Societies*.

64. Vesla M. Weaver, 'Frontlash: Race and the Development of Punitive Crime Policy," *Studies in American Political Development* 21 (fall 2007), 252–53.

65. Quoted in *Los Angeles Times*, August 16, 1970.

66. Levison, *Working Class Majority*, 234.

67. See full discussion in Cowie, *Stayin' Alive*, chap. 2, 75–124.

68. Rieder, "Rise of the Silent Majority," 256.

69. Lassiter, *Silent Majority*, 10.

70. Piven, *Labor Parties in Postindustrial Societies*; Nelson Lichtenstein, "From Corporatism to Collective Bargaining: Organized Labor and the Eclipse of Social Democracy in the Postwar Era," in *The Rise and Fall of the New Deal Order 1930–1980*, edited by Steve Fraser and Gary Gerstle, 122–52 (Princeton: Princeton University Press, 1989); Rieder "Rise of the Silent Majority," 258. The Democratic Party was not the sole bastion of liberalism during this period; "Rockefeller Republicans," of the John Lindsay variety, had long been socially liberal. In addition, the Democrats had recently been the party of Dixie and still had a strong presence in the South. But the parties were being reconfigured during this period. I therefore collapse the Democratic Party with the project of liberalism here because, by 1968, of the two, it *was* the party of liberalism, and particularly of the socially liberal brand of liberalism that the Republican Party was increasingly eschewing.

71. Levison, *Working Class Majority*, 233.

72. Sexton and Sexton, *Blue Collars and White Hats*, 258; Levison, *Working Class Majority*, 237.

73. Levison, *Working Class Majority*, 239.

CONCLUSION

1. "As Americans learn more about Occupy Wall Street, they are becoming more supportive of the movement's positions," reported CNN (11/3/11). A Pew Research Center Poll from December 2011, indicated that respondents with incomes under $100,000 supported Occupy by 12–14 points, those with incomes between $100,000 and $150,000 were nearly equally likely to support as to oppose (46 to 43), while those with the most income were more like to oppose. Further, more people at every level of education were more likely to support than oppose, with "some college" being the group with the widest spread, 50 to 33. The Pew Research Center for the People and the Press, "Frustration with Congress Could Hurt Republican Incumbents," December 15, 2011, 12.

2. Doug Fraser, resignation letter from the Labor Management Group advisers to President Jimmy Carter, July 17, 1978. Reproduced in full on the website History Is a Weapon, http://www.historyisaweapon.com/defcon1/fraserresign.html (accessed September 1, 2012).

3. Johanna Brenner and Robert Brenner, "Reagan, the Right, and the Working Class," *Against the Current* 2 (winter 1981), 29–31.

4. Doug Fraser, again: "Even if all the barriers to such participation were removed, there would be no rush to the polls by so many in our society who feel the sense of helplessness and inability to affect the system in any way. The Republican Party remains controlled by and the Democratic Party heavily influenced by business interests. The reality is that both are weak and ineffective as parties, with no visible, clear-cut ideological differences between them, because of business domination." History Is a Weapon, http://www.historyisaweapon.com/defcon1/fraserresign.html.

5. Ruy Teixeira and Alan Abramowitz, "The Decline of the White Working Class and the Rise of a Mass Upper Middle Class," Brookings Institution Working Paper, April 2008,

http://www.brookings.edu/papers/2008/04_demographics_teixeira.aspx (accessed January 6, 2009); Frances Fox Piven and Richard Cloward, *Why Americans Still Don't Vote: And Why Politicians Want It That Way* (Boston: Beacon Press, 2000); Brian D. Martin, J. Craig Jenkins, and Jeremy Forbis, "Party Mobilization and Working Class Voter Turnout: An Analysis of Non-Voting in Presidential Elections in the United States, 1972–2000," paper presented at the American Sociological Association Meetings 2004, http://www.allacademic.com//meta/p_mla_apa_research_citation/0/2/3/3/5/pages23356/p23356-1.php (accessed June 6, 2008).

6. Teixeira and Abramowitz, "Decline of the White Working Class."

7. Frank, *What's the Matter with Kansas?* 6–7.

8. Ibid., 245.

9. See Teixeira and Abramowitz. "The Decline of the White Working Class."

10. Whether or not they foreground this fact, many contemporary authors, writers, and people interested in working-class studies are in fact focused on the *white* working class. A recent outstanding contribution to this project is Jefferson Cowie's *Stayin' Alive: The 1970's and the Last Days of the Working Class*. To frame the story he tells of the decline of working-class power, culture, and self-identity, Cowie chooses as emblematic Dewey Burton, a white autoworker who was twenty-six in 1972 and whose political trajectory ran from New Deal Democrat to Reagan supporter. In the world outside Cowie's book, Dewey Burton was also made emblematic because the *New York Times* returned to interview him over the course of the 1970s, following his political transformation in its stories on working-class voting. Burton's story resonated with a narrative whose outer limits had been well-established when the *Times* selected him and continued to write follow-up reports. So there is a tautology at work in Cowie's selection of Burton: he well represents the story of the increasingly conservative white working class in part because the story of the increasingly conservative white working class was created through the mobilization of representations of Dewey Burton. And that is fine for a history that is really about the white male working class, as Cowie's book is—its culture, voting, institutions, as well as its representations in popular culture. Given the real and ideological limits to a broad, diverse working class that existed during the period, and given the clear focus on the white working class that most of the narratives of its decline and realignment have focused on, it is the white male workers' story that Cowie seeks to tell. This is an understandable limit to work within, and Burton's story is as good, if not better, than many others. Nevertheless, it is limited. One problem with sole focus on the conservatizing white working class is that the declensionist model does not allow for the extent to which other white male workers, along with black, brown, immigrant, and female workers, were writing another history at the same time. It is not the story that won out, but it is a story that—when we pull it into focus today—helps us understand the more recent political directions of workers and their institutions as a whole. The story of the "last days of the working class" puts an end to what could be otherwise be conceptualized as a longer process of change and transmutation within the working class and its institutions.

11. Hall, *Because of Their Faith*, 113–14.

12. Olick and Robbins, "Social Memory Studies," 122–34.

13. Quoted in Anderson, *Movement and the Sixties*, 394.

Bibliography

BIBLIOGRAPHIC NOTE

The sources for this book fall into three main categories: materials drawn from historical archives, newspapers and magazines contemporary to the period studied, and books. Because this book is a study of memory and discourse, many sources that might in other contexts be considered secondary sources have served as primary source material for my research; and to a limited degree, the reverse is true as well.

I made use of archives at the State Historical Society at Wisconsin (SHSW), reading material from individuals, Paul Booth, Lee Webb, Sidney Peck, and Fred Halstead Papers; and from organizations, the National Coordinating Committee to End the War in Vietnam (NCCEWV), the Labor Leadership Assembly for Peace (LLAP), Students for a Democratic Society (SDS), and Vietnam Veterans Against the War (VVAW).

At the Swarthmore Peace Collection, I made use of A. J. Muste's papers, as well as its Vietnam Summer Collection.

At the New York University Tamiment Archives, in addition to extensive use of the alternative-press microfilms (including the *Militant*, the *Guardian*, and *New Left Notes* for the entire period covered here), I used numerous collections that contained material covering the Trade Unionists for Peace, the GI movement, and high school antiwar organizing.

Berkeley's Bancroft library had recently committed its Antiwar National File to microfilm when I visited, and I was able to access its contents through both microfilm and, in some cases, hard copy.

I visited two archives at UCLA, reading the Devra Wagner and American GI Forum papers at the Chicano Studies Research Center, as well as a collection of materials about social movements (550) at the Charles E. Young Research Library.

I also made extensive use of contemporary articles from the *New York Times*, *Los Angeles Times*, *Washington Post*, *Chicago Times*, *Christian Science Monitor*, *Wall Street Journal*, and, to a lesser extent, *New York Daily News*. All citations from these sources can be found in the book text and endnotes.

PUBLISHED SOURCES

Abarca, Maria Graciela. "'Discontented but Not Inevitably Reactionary': Organized Labor in the Nixon Years." PhD dissertation, University of Massachusetts, Amherst, 2001.

Albert, Judith Clavir, and Stewart Edward Albert, eds. *The Sixties Papers: Documents of a Rebellious Decade*. New York: Praeger, 1984.

Alford, Robert. *The Craft of Inquiry*. New York: Oxford University Press, 1998.

——. "The Role of Social Class in American Voting Behavior." *Western Political Quarterly* 16 (1963): 180–94.

Ali, Tariq, and Susan Watkins. *1968, Marching in the Streets*. New York: Free Press, 1998.

Anderson, Terry H. *The Movement and the Sixties*. New York: Oxford University Press, 1995.

Appy, Christian. *Working Class War*. Chapel Hill: University of North Carolina Press, 1993.

Armstrong, Richard. "Labor 1970: Angry, Aggressive, Acquisitive." *Fortune*, October 1969.

Aron, William S. "Student Activism of the 1960s Revisited: A Multivariate Analysis Research Note." *Social Forces* 52 (1974): 408–14.

Aronowitz, Stanley. *False Promises*. 6th ed. Durham: Duke University Press, 1993.

——. *How Class Works*. New Haven: Yale University Press, 2003.

——. "Left May Have a Role in Unions." *Guardian*, December 23, 1967.

——. "Opportunity for Left Seen in GE Strike." *Guardian*, December 6, 1969.

Bailyn, Bernard, Robert Dallek, David Davis, David Donald, and J. Thomas. *The Great Republic: A History of the American People*. Boston: Little, Brown, 1992.

Baskir, Lawrence, and William A. Strauss. *Chance and Circumstance: The Draft, the War, and the Vietnam Generation*. New York: Vintage Books, 1978.

Bastedo, Michael N., and Patricia J. Gumport. "Access to What? Mission Differentiation and Academic Stratification in U.S. Public Higher Education." *Higher Education* 46 (2003): 341–59.

Bates, Milton J. *The Wars We Took to Vietnam: Cultural Conflict and Storytelling*. Berkeley: University of California Press, 1996.

Beamish, Thomas, Harvey Molotch, and Richard Flacks. "Who Supports the Troops? Vietnam, the Gulf War, and the Making of Collective Memory." *Social Problems* 42, no. 3 (August 1995): 344–60.

Beattie, Keith. *The Scar That Binds: American Culture and the Vietnam War*. New York: New York University Press, 1998.

Bell, Daniel. *The End of Ideology: On the Exhaustion of Political Ideas in the Fifties*. Glencoe, Ill.: Free Press, 1960.

Bendix, Reinhard, and Seymour Martin Lipset. *Class, Status and Power: A Reader in Social Stratification*. New York: Free Press, 1953.

Benford, Robert D., and David A. Snow. "Framing Processes and Social Movements: An Overview and Assessment." *Annual Review of Sociology* 26 (August 2000): 611–39.

Berinsky, Adam J. *Silent Voices: Public Opinion and Political Participation in America*. Princeton: Princeton University Press, 2004.

Bevington, Douglas, and Chris Dixon. "Movement-Relevant Theory: Rethinking Social Movement Scholarship and Activism." *Social Movement Studies* 4, no. 3 (2005): 185–208.

Biewen, John. "The Movie in Our Heads: America Radio Works Revisiting Vietnam." Part II of the *Revisiting Vietnam* series on American RadioWorks, American Public Media, aired April 2000,http://americanradioworks.publicradio.org/features/vietnam/us/movie.html (accessed February 16, 2008).

Blumberg, Nathan. "The Orthodox Media under Fire: Chicago and the Press." In *Mass Culture Revisited*, edited by Bernard Rosenberg and David Manning White, 276–90. New York: Van Nostrand Reinhold, 1971.

Bodnar, John. *Blue-Collar Hollywood: Liberalism, Democracy, and Working People in American Film*. Baltimore: Johns Hopkins University Press, 2003.

——. *Remaking America: Public Memory, Commemoration, and Patriotism in the Twentieth Century*. Princeton: Princeton University Press. 1993.

Bornstein, Andrew, David Eisen, David Elsila, Tom Gagliardo, Al Lannon, Tony Mazzocchi, Richard Prosten, Marvin Rogoff, Daniel Schulder, Patricia Schulder, Don Spatz, Katherine Stone, Patricia Strandt, and Frank Wallick. *A Rich Man's War and a Poor Man's Fight: A Handbook for Trade Unionists on the Vietnam War*. Washington, D.C.: Labor for Peace, 1971.

Bourdieu, Pierre. "The Forms of Capital." In *Handbook of Theory and Research for the Sociology of Education*, edited by John Richardson, 241–58. New York: Greenwood, 1986.

——. *Language and Symbolic Power*. Cambridge, Mass.: Polity, 1991.

——. *Practical Reason*. Stanford: Stanford University Press, 1998.

——. "What Makes a Social Class? On the Theoretical and Practical Existence of Groups." *Berkeley Journal of Sociology* 32 (1987): 1–18.

Bourdieu, Pierre, Claude Passeron, Richard Nice, and Tom Bottomore. *Reproduction in Education, Society and Culture*. London: Sage, 1990.

Branch, Taylor. *At Canaan's Edge: America in the King Years, 1965–68*. New York: Simon & Schuster, 2007.

——. *Parting the Waters: America in the King Years, 1954–63*. New York: Simon and Schuster, 1988.

Braungart, Margaret, and Richard G. Braungart. "The Effects of the 1960s Political Generation on Former Left- and Right-Wing Youth Activist Leaders." *Social Problems* 38, no. 3 (August 1991): 297–315.

Breines, Wini. *Community and Organization in the New Left, 1962–1968: The Great Refusal*. New Brunswick, N.J.: Rutgers University Press, 1989.

Brenner, Aaron, Robert Brenner, and Cal Winslow, eds. *Rebel Rank and File*. London: Verso, 2010.

Breslin, Jimmy. "One Way to End the War." *New York Magazine*, June 22, 1970.

Brinkley, Alan. *The Unfinished Nation: A Concise History of the American People*. Boston: McGraw Hill, 2004.

Burdick, John. *Blessed Anastacia: Women, Race and Popular Christianity in Brazil*. New York: Routledge, 1998

Burris, Val. "From Vietnam to Iraq: Continuity and Change in Between-Group Differences in Support for Military Action." *Social Problems* 55, no. 4 (November 2008): 443–79.

Bush, George H. W. "Inaugural Address." January 20, 1989, http://bushlibrary.tamu.edu/ research/public_papers.php?id=1&year=1989&month=01 (accessed on May 10, 2012).

Buzzanco, Robert. *Masters of War: Military Dissent and Politics in the Vietnam Era*. Cambridge, UK: Cambridge University Press, 1996.

Caldwell, Wilber W. *1968: Dreams of Revolution*. New York: Algora Publishing, 2008.

Carson, Clayborne. *In Struggle: SNCC and the Black Awakening of the 1960s*. Cambridge, Mass.: Harvard University Press, 1982.

Carter, Sandy. "Class Conflict: The Human Dimension." In *Between Labor and Capital*, edited by Pat Walker, 97–120. Boston: South End Press, 1979.

Cass, James, and Max Birnbaum. *Comparative Guide to American Colleges*. 7th ed. New York: Harper & Row, 1975.

Cawley, Leo. "The War about the War: Vietnam Films and American Myth." In *From Hanoi to Hollywood: The Vietnam War in American Film*, edited by Linda Dittmar and Gene Marchaud. New Brunswick, N.J.: Rutgers University Press, 1991.

Chávez, Ernesto. *Mi Raza Primero! My People First!: Nationalism, Identity, and Insurgency in the Chicano Movement in Los Angeles, 1966–1978*. Berkeley: University of California Press, 2002.

Chomsky, Noam. *Towards a New Cold War: Essays on the Current Crisis and How We Got There*. New York: Pantheon Books, 1982.

Cobble, Dorothy Sue, "A Tiger by the Toenail": The 1970s Origins of the New Working Class Majority," *Labor* 2, no. 3 (fall 2005), 103–14.

——. Cochran, Bert. *Labor and Communism: The Conflict That Shaped American Unions*. Princeton: Princeton University Press, 1977.

Cohen, Daniel J. "By the Book: Assessing the Place of Textbooks in U.S. Survey Courses." *Journal of American History* 91 (2005): 1405–15.

Converse, Philip E., and Howard Schuman. "Silent Majorities and the Vietnam War." *Scientific American* 222 (1970): 17–25.

Cortright, David. "GI Resistance during the Vietnam War." In *Give Peace a Chance*, edited by Melvin Small and William Hoover, 116–28. Syracuse, N.Y.: Syracuse University Press, 1992.

——. *Soldiers in Revolt: The American Military Today.* New York: Anchor Press, 1975.

Cowie, Jefferson. "The Enigma of Working Class Conservatism: From the Hard Hats to the NASCAR Dads." *New Labor Forum* 13 (fall 2004): 9–17.

——. *Stayin' Alive: The 1970's and the Last Days of the Working Class.* New York: New Press, 2010.

——. "Vigorously Left, Right and Center: The Crosscurrents of Working Class Life in the 1970's." In *America in the Seventies,* edited by Beth Bailey and David Farber, 75–106. Lawrence: University Press of Kansas, 2004.

Cox, Laurence, and Colin Barker. "What Would a Marxist Theory of Social Movements Look Like?" In *Alternative Futures and Popular Protest, Conference Papers II,* edited by Colin Barker and Mike Tyldesley. Manchester, UK: Manchester Metropolitan University, 2005.

Croteau, David. *Politics and the Class Divide: Working People and the Middle Class Left.* Philadelphia: Temple University Press, 1995.

Cutler, Jonathan. *Labor's Time: Shorter Hours, the UAW, and the Struggle for the American Unionism.* Philadelphia: Temple University Press, 2004.

Darnovsky, Marcy, Barbara Epstein, and Richard Flacks, eds. *Cultural Politics and Social Movements.* Philadelphia: Temple University Press, 1995.

Davidson, Carl. "Report from SDS Convention." *Guardian,* January 11, 1969.

Davidson, James West, William E. Gienapp, Christine Leigh Heyrman, Mark H. Lytle, Michael B. Stoff, and Brian DeLay. *Nation of Nations: A Concise Narrative of the American Republic.* Boston: McGraw-Hill, 2002.

Davis, Kingsley, and Wilbert E. Moore. "Some Principles of Stratification." *American Sociological Review* 10, no. 2 (April 1945): 242–49.

Davis, Mike. *Prisoners of the American Dream.* London: Verso, 1986.

DeBenedetti, Charles, with Charles Chatfield. *An American Ordeal.* Syracuse, N.Y.: Syracuse University Press, 1990.

Dellinger, David T. *From Yale to Jail: The Life Story of a Moral Dissenter.* New York: Pantheon Books, 1993.

Dionne, Eugene J. Jr. *Why Americans Hate Politics: The Death of the Democratic Process.* New York: Simon and Schuster, 2004.

Dittmar, Linda, and Gene Marchaud, eds. *From Hanoi to Hollywood: The Vietnam War in American Film.* New Brunswick, N.J.: Rutgers University Press, 1991.

Divine, Robert A., Timothy H. H. Breen, George M. Fredrickson, R. Hal Williams, Ariela J. Gross, and H. William A. Brands. *The American Story.* New York: Longman, 2006.

Dyer, Gwynne. *War: The Lethal Custom.* Basic Books: New York, 2005.

Edelman, Marc. "Social Movements: Changing Paradigms and Forms of Politics." *Annual Review of Anthropology* 30 (2001): 285–317.

Edsall, Thomas Byrne, and Mary D. Edsall. *Chain Reaction: The Impact of Race, Rights, and Taxes on American Politics.* New York: W. W. Norton, 1992.

Ehrenreich, Barbara. *Fear of Falling: The Inner Life of the Middle Class.* New York: Pantheon Books, 1989.

Elbaum, Max. *Revolution in the Air: Sixties Radicals Turn to Lenin, Mao and Che.* London: Verso, 2002.

Epstein, Barbara. "Rethinking Social Movement Theory." *Socialist Review* 20, no. 1 (January–March 1990): 35–65.

Fallows, James. "What Did You Do in the Class War, Daddy?" *Washington Monthly,* October 1975, 5–19.

Fantasia, Rick. *Cultures of Solidarity.* Berkeley: University of California Press, 1988.

Faragher, John Mack, Mari Jo Buhle, Daniel Czitrom, and Susan H. Armitage. *Out of Many: A History of the American People.* Upper Saddle River: Pearson, 2003.

Fendrich, James Max. "The Forgotten Movement." *Sociological Inquiry* 73 (2003): 338–58.

Ferber, Michael. "Why I Joined the Resistance." In *Against the War: Writings By Activists,* edited by Mary Susannah Robbins, 111–19. Syracuse, N.Y.: Syracuse University Press, 1999.

Ferber, Michael, and Staughton Lynd. *The Resistance.* Boston: Beacon Press, 1971.

Fink, Carole, Philipp Gassert, Detlef Junker, and Daniel S. Mattern, eds., *1968: The World Transformed.* Cambridge, UK: Cambridge University Press, 1998.

Flacks, Richard, "Knowledge for What? Thoughts on the State of Social Movement Studies." In *Rethinking Social Movements: Structure, Culture, and Emotion Lanham,* edited by J. Goodwin and J. Jasper, 135–53. Lanham, Md.: Rowman & Littlefield, 2004.

——. "The Liberated Generation: Roots of Student Protest, a Revolt of the Advantaged." *Journal of Social Issues* 23 (1967): 52–75.

——. "What Happened to the New Left?" *Socialist Review* 19 (January–February 1988): 91–110.

Fletcher, Bill Jr., and Fernando Gapasin. *Solidarity Divided.* Berkeley: University of California Press, 2008.

Foley, Michael. *Confronting the War Machine: Draft Resistance during the Vietnam War.* Chapel Hill: University of North Carolina Press, 2003.

Foner, Phillip S. *US Labor and the Vietnam War.* New York: International Publishers, 1989.

Foucault, Michel. *Language, Counter-Memory, Practice: Selected Essays and Interviews.* Ithaca: Cornell University Press, 1977.

Fousek, John. *To Lead the Free World: American Nationalism and the Cultural Roots of the Cold War.* Chapel Hill: University of North Carolina Press, 2000.

Frank, Thomas. *What's the Matter with Kansas?: How Conservatives Won the Heart of America.* New York: Metropolitan Books, 2004.

Franklin, H. Bruce. *M.I.A., or Mythmaking in America.* New Brunswick, N.J.: Rutgers University Press, 1993.

——. *Vietnam and Other American Fantasies.* Amherst: University of Massachusetts Press, 2000.

——. "Vietnam: The Antiwar Movement We Are Supposed to Forget." *International Socialist Review,* no. 22 (January–February 2002), http://www.isreview.org/issues/22/feat-franklin.shtml.

Fraser, Steve, and Gary Gerstle, eds. *The Rise and Fall of the New Deal Order.* Princeton: Princeton University Press, 1990.

Freeman, Joshua B. *Working-Class New York.* New York: The New Press, 2000.

Frymer, Paul, and John David Skrentny. "Coalition-Building and the Politics of Electoral Capture during the Nixon Administration: African Americans, Labor, Latinos." *Studies in American Political Development* 12 (spring 1998): 131–61.

Galbraith, John Kenneth. *The Affluent Society.* Harmondsworth, UK: Penguin, 1962.

Garfinkle, Adam. *Telltale Hearts: The Origins and Impact of the Vietnam Antiwar Movement.* New York: St. Martins, 1995.

Garraty, John A., and Mark C. Carnes. *The American Nation*. New York: Longman, 2000.

Geier, Joel. "The Soldiers Revolt." *International Socialist Review*, no. 9 (August–September 2000).

Georgakias, Dan, and Marvin Surkin. *Detroit: I Do Mind Dying*. Boston: South End Press, 1998.

Gettleman, Marvin E. *Viet Nam: History, Documents, and Opinions on a Major World Crisis*. New York: Fawcett Crest, 1965.

Gettleman, Marvin E., Jane Franklin, Marilyn Young, and H. Bruce Franklin, eds. *Vietnam and America*. New York: Grove Press, 1995.

Gitlin, Todd. *The Sixties: Years of Hope, Days of Rage*. Toronto: Bantam Books, 1987.

——. *The Whole World Is Watching: Mass Media in the Making and Unmaking of the New Left*. Berkeley: University of California Press., 1980.

Glazer, Nathan. "Vietnam: The Case for Immediate Withdrawal." *Commentary* 51, no. 5 (May 1971): 33–37.

Goldfield, Michael. *The Color of Politics: Race and the Mainsprings of American Politics*. New York: The New Press, 1997.

——. Goldschmidt, Walter. "Social Class in America: A Critical Review." *American Anthropologist* 52, no. 4 (October–December, 1950): 483–98.

Goldthorpe, John, David Lockwood, Frank Bechhofer, and Jennifer Platt. *The Affluent Worker in the Class Structure*. Cambridge, UK: Cambridge University Press, 1969.

Gompers, Samuel. *Seventy Years of Life and Labour: An Autobiography*. Vol. 11. London: Hurst & Blackett, 1925.

Goodman, Paul. *Growing Up Absurd: Problems of Youth in the Organized System*. New York: Random House, 1960.

Goodwin, Jeff, and James M. Jasper. "Caught in a Winding, Snarling Vine: The Structural Bias of Political Process." *Sociological Forum* 14, no. 1 (March 1999): 27–54.

Gordon, Milton Myron. *Social Class in American Sociology*. Durham: Duke University Press, 1958.

Graham, Hermann III. *The Brother's Vietnam War: Black Power, Manhood and the Military Experience*. Gainesville: University Press of Florida, 2003.

Gramsci, Antonio. *Selections from the Prison Notebooks*. New York: International Publishers, 1971.

Grimes, Michael D. *Class in Twentieth-Century American Sociology: An Analysis of Theories and Measurement Strategies*. New York: Praeger, 1991.

Grossman, Dave. *On Killing: Psychological Cost of Learning to Kill*. Toronto: Little, Brown, 1998.

Hahn, Harlan. "Correlates of Public Sentiments about War: Local Referenda on the Vietnam Issue." *American Political Science Review* 64, no. 4 (December 1970): 1186–98.

——. "Dove Sentiments among Blue Collar Workers." *Dissent* 17 (May–June 1970): 202–5.

Halbwachs, Maurice. *On Collective Memory*. Chicago: University of Chicago Press. 1982.

Hall, Mitchell K. *Because of Their Faith: CALCAV and Religious Opposition to the Vietnam War*. New York: Columbia University Press, 1990.

——. *The Vietnam War*. 2nd rev. ed. Upper Saddle River: Pearson Longman, 2008.

——. *Vietnam War Era: People and Perspectives*. Santa Barbara, Calif.: ABC-CLIO, 2009.

Hall, Simon. *Peace and Freedom: The Civil Rights and Antiwar Movements in the 1960s*. Philadelphia: University of Pennsylvania Press, 2006.

Halle, David. *America's Working Man: Work, Home, and Politics among Blue-Collar Property Owners*. Chicago: University of Chicago Press, 1984.

Halstead, Fred. *Out Now!* New York: Monad Press, 1978.

Hamamoto, Darrell Y. *Nervous Laughter: Television Situation Comedy and Liberal Democratic Ideology.* New York: Praeger, 1989.

Hamill, Pete. "The Revolt of the White Lower Middle Class." *New York Magazine,* April 14, 1969. http://nymag.com/news/features/46801/ (Accessed 8/11/2009).

Hamilton, Richard F. "A Research Note on Mass Support of Tough Military Initiatives." *American Sociological Review* 33 (June 1968): 439–45.

Handberg, Roger B. Jr. "The Vietnam Analogy: Student Attitudes on War." *Public Opinion Quarterly* 36, no. 4 (winter 1972–1973): 612–61.

Harrington, Michael. *The Other America: Poverty in the United States.* New York: Macmillan, 1962.

Harvey, David. *Spaces of Hope.* Berkeley: University of California Press, 2000.

Hayden, Tom. *Rebel.* Los Angeles: Red Hen Press, 2003.

Heineman, Keith. *Campus Wars: The Peace Movement at American State Universities in the Vietnam Era.* New York: New York University Press, 1993.

Heinl, Robert D. Jr. "The Collapse of the Armed Forces." *Armed Forces Journal* (June 1971). Reprinted in *Vietnam and America: A Documented History,* edited by Marvin Gettleman, Jane Franklin, Marilyn B. Young, and H. Bruce Franklin, 326–35. New York: Grove Press, 1995.

Helmer, John. *Bringing the War Home: The American Soldier in Vietnam and After.* New York: Free Press, 1974.

Henretta, James A., David Brody, and Lynn Dumenil. *America: A Concise History.* Boston: Bedford, 2006.

——. *America's History.* Boston: Bedford, 2004.

Hill, Herbert. "The Problem of Race in American Labor History." *Reviews in American History* 24 (1996): 189–208.

Hirsch, Arnold R. *Making the Second Ghetto: Race and Housing in Chicago 1940–1960.* Chicago: University of Chicago Press, 1998.

Hirshman, Charles, Samuel Preston, and Vu Manh Loi. "Vietnamese Casualties during the American War: A New Estimate." *Population and Development Review* 21, no. 4 (December 1995): 783–812.

Hitchens, Christopher. *For the Sake of Argument.* London: Verso, 1993.

Hoffer, Eric. "The Negro Is Prejudiced against Himself; the Negro Is against Himself." *New York Times Magazine,* November 29, 1964.

——. *The True Believer: Thoughts on the Nature of Mass Movements.* New York: Harper and Row, 1951.

Horowitz, Irving. *The Struggle Is the Message: The Organization and Ideology of the Antiwar Movement.* Berkeley: Glendessary Press, 1972.

Howe, Irving, Michael Harrington, Bayard Rustin, Lewis A. Coser, and Penn Kimble. "The Vietnam Protest." *New York Review of Books,* November 25, 1965.

Hunt, Andrew. *The Turning: A History of Vietnam Veterans against the War.* New York: New York University Press, 1999.

Ignatiev, Noel. *How the Irish Became White.* New York: Routledge, 1995.

Isaac, Larry, and Lars Christiansen. "How the Civil Rights Movement Revitalized Labor Militancy." *American Sociological Review* 67 (2002): 722–46.

Isaacs, Arnold. *Vietnam Shadows: The War, Its Ghosts, and Its Legacy.* Baltimore: Johns Hopkins University Press, 2000.

Isserman, Maurice. "You Don't Need a Weatherman, but a Postman Can be Helpful: Thoughts on the History of SDS and the Antiwar Movement." In *Give Peace a Chance,* edited by Mel Small and William Hoover, 22–34. Syracuse, N.Y.: Syracuse University Press, 1992.

Isserman, Maurice, and Michael Kazin. "The Failure and Success of the New Radicalism." In *The Rise and Fall of the New Deal Order 1930–1980*, edited by Steve Fraser and Gary Gerstle, 212–42. Princeton: Princeton University Press, 1989.

Jackson, George L. "Constraints of the Negro Civil Rights Movement on American Military Effectiveness," 1970. Reprinted in *Vietnam and America: A Documented History*, edited by Marvin E. Gettleman, Jane Franklin, Marilyn B. Young, and H. Bruce Franklin, 321–26. New York: Grove Press, 1995.

Jacobson, Julius, ed. *The Negro and the American Labor Movement*. Garden City, N.Y.: Anchor Books, 1968.

Jameson, Fredric. "Periodizing the 60s." In *The 60s without Apology*, edited by Sohnya Sayres, Anders Stephanson, Stanley Aronowitz, and Frederic Jameson. Minneapolis: University of Minnesota Press, 1984.

Janoski, Thomas. *The Handbook of Political Sociology: States, Civil Societies, and Globalization*. Cambridge, UK: Cambridge University Press, 2005.

Jasper, James M. *The Art of Moral Protest*. Chicago: University of Chicago Press, 1997.

Jennings, M. Kent. "Generation Units and the Student Protest Movement in the United States: An Intra- and Intergenerational Analysis." *Political Psychology* 23, no. 2 (June 2002): 303–24.

Johnson, David, John Rodgers, and Lucilla Tan. "A Century of Family Budgets in the United States." *Monthly Labor Report*, Bureau of Labor Statistics, May 2001.

Johnson, Paul. *A History of the American People*. New York: Harper, 1997.

Jordan, Harold. "Whatever Happened to Vietnam Era War Resisters?" American Friends Services Committee, http://www.afsc.org/youthmil/conscientious-objection/Vietnam-war-resisters.htm (accessed July 28, 2008).

Judis, John, and Ruy Teixeira. *The Emerging Democratic Majority*. New York: Simon & Schuster, 2004.

Kahn, Roger M., and William J. Bowers. "The Social Context of the Rank-and-File Student Activist: A Test of Four Hypotheses." *Sociology of Education* 43 (1970): 38–55.

Karen, David. "The Politics of Class, Race, and Gender: Access to Higher Education in the United States, 1960–1986." *American Journal of Education* 99 (1991): 208–37.

Karnow, Stanley. *Vietnam: A History*. New York: Viking Press, 1983.

Katsiaficas, George N. *Vietnam Documents: American and Vietnamese Views of the War*. New York: M. E. Sharpe, 1992.

Katznelson, Ira. "Was the Great Society a Lost Opportunity?" In *The Rise and Fall of the New Deal Order 1930–1980*, edited by Steve Fraser and Gary Gerstle, 185–211. Princeton: Princeton University Press, 1989.

Kelley, Robin D. G. *Race Rebels: Culture, Politics, and the Black Working Class*. New York: Simon & Schuster, 1996.

Kellner, Douglas, and Herbert Marcuse. *The New Left and the 1960s: Collected Papers of Herbert Marcuse*, Vol. 3. New York: Routledge, 2005.

Keniston, Kenneth, and Michael Lerner. "Selected References on Student Protest." *Annals of the American Academy of Political and Social Science* 395 (1971): 184–94.

Kerry, John, Vietnam Veterans Against the War, David Thorne, and George Butler. *The New Soldier*. New York: Macmillan, 1971.

Klein, Michael. "Historical Memory, Film and the Vietnam Era." In *From Hanoi to Hollywood: The Vietnam War in American Film*, edited by Linda Dittmar and Gene Marchaud. New Brunswick, N.J.: Rutgers University Press, 1991.

Kolko, Gabriel. *Anatomy of a War: Vietnam and the Modern Historical Experience*. New York: The New Press, 1985.

Koscielski, Frank. *Divided Loyalties: American Unions and the Vietnam War*. New York: Garland Publications, 1999.

Kovic, Ron. *Born on the Fourth of July*. New York: Pocket Books, 1976.

Kurlansky, Mark. *1968: The Year That Rocked the World*. London: Jonathan Cape, 2004.

Larana, Enrique, Hank Johnston, and Joseph Gusfield, eds. *New Social Movements: From Ideology to Identity*. Philadelphia: Temple University Press, 1994.

Larson, Simeon, and Bruce Nissen. *Theories of the Labor Movement*. Detroit: Wayne State University Press, 1987.

Lassiter, Matthew D. *The Silent Majority: Suburban Politics in the Sunbelt South*. Princeton: Princeton University Press, 2007.

Lembcke, Jerry. *The Spitting Image: Myth, Memory and the Legacy of Vietnam*. New York: New York University Press, 1998.

Lemon, Richard. *The Troubled American*. New York: Simon & Schuster, 1970.

Leondar-Wright, Betsy. *Class Matters: Cross-Class Alliance Building for Middle-Class Activists*. Gabriola, Canada: New Society Publishers, 2005.

Leopold, Les. *The Man Who Hated Work and Loved Labor: The Life and Times of Tony Mazzocchi*. White River Junction, Vt.: Chelsea Green, 2007.

Levison, Andrew. "Class and Warfare: Democrats and the Rhetoric of Patriotism." *American Prospect* 14 (September 2003): 26–29.

———. "Who Lost the Working Class?" *Nation*, May 14, 2001.

———. *The Working Class Majority*. New York: Coward, McCann, and Geoghagen, 1974.

Levy, Peter. *The New Left and Labor in the 1960's*. Urbana: University of Illinois Press, 1994.

Lewes, James. *Protest and Survive*. Westport, Conn.: Praeger, 2003.

Lewy, Guenter. *America in Vietnam*. New York: Oxford University Press, 1978.

Lichtenstein, Nelson. "From Corporatism to Collective Bargaining: Organized Labor and the Eclipse of Social Democracy in the Postwar Era." In *The Rise and Fall of the New Deal Order 1930–1980*, edited by Steve Fraser and Gary Gerstle, 122–52. Princeton: Princeton University Press, 1989.

———. *The Most Dangerous Man in Detroit: Walter Reuther and the Fate of American Labor*. New York: Basic Books, 1995.

———. *The State of the Union: A Century of American Labor*. Princeton: Princeton University Press, 2002.

Lichtenstein, Nelson, Susan Strasser, Roy Rosenzweig, Stephen Brier, and Joshua Brown. *Who Built America?: Working People and the Nation's Economy, Politics, Culture, and Society*. Vol. 2, *Since 1877*. 2nd ed. New York: Bedford/St. Martin's, 2000.

Lipset, Seymour Martin. *American Exceptionalism: A Double Edged Sword*. New York: W. W. Norton, 1996.

———. "Democracy and Working-Class Authoritarianism." *American Sociological Review* 24, no. 4 (1959): 482–501.

———. *Political Man: The Social Bases of Politics*. Garden City, N.Y.: Doubleday, 1960.

Lipsitz, George. *The Possessive Investment in Whiteness*. Philadelphia: Temple University Press, 1998.

———. *Rainbow at Midnight*. Urbana: University of Illinois Press, 1994.

———. *Time Passages*. Minneapolis: University of Minnesota Press, 1990.

Loewen, James. "Introductory Sociology: Four Classroom Exercises." *Teaching Sociology* 6 (1979): 221–44.

———. *Lies My Teacher Told Me: Everything Your American History Textbook Got Wrong*. New York: New Press, 1995.

Lofland, John. *Social Movement Organizations: Guide to Research on Insurgent Realities*. New Brunswick: Transaction Publishers, 1996.

Lofland, John, Victoria L. Johnson, and Pamela Kato, eds. *Peace Movement Organizations and Activists in the U.S.: An Analytic Bibliography*. New York: Haworth Press, 1991.

Lunch, William L., and Peter W. Sperlich. "American Public Opinion and the War in Vietnam." *Western Political Quarterly* 32 (1979): 21–44.

Lynd, Robert Staughton, and Helen Merrell Lynd. *Middletown: A Study in Contemporary American Culture*. New York: Harcourt, Brace and Company, 1945.

Mackenzie, Gavin. *The Aristocracy of Labour: The Position of Skilled Craftsmen in the American Class Structure*. London: Cambridge University Press, 1973.

Mailer, Norman. *The Armies of the Night: History as a Novel, the Novel as History*. London: Weidenfeld and Nicolson, 1968.

"Man and Woman of the Year: The Middle Americans." *Time* magazine, January 5, 1970.

Mankoff, Milton, and Richard Flacks. "The Changing Social Base of the American Student Movement." *Annals of the American Academy of Political and Social Science* 395 (1971): 54–67.

Marcuse, Herbert. *One-Dimensional Man*. Boston: Beacon Press, 1964.

———. "Socialism in the Developed Countries." *International Socialist Journal* 2 (April 1965):139–52.

Martin, Brian D., J. Craig Jenkins, and Jeremy Forbis. "Party Mobilization and Working Class Voter Turnout: An Analysis of Non-Voting in Presidential Elections in the United States, 1972–2000." Paper presented at the American Sociological Association Meetings 2004, http://www.allacademic.com//meta/p_mla_apa_research_citation/0/2/3/3/5/pages23356/p23356–1.php (accessed June 6, 2008).

Martinot, Steve. "The Racialized Construction of Class in the United States." *Social Justice* 27, no. 1 (Spring 2000): 43–60.

Marwell, Gerald, Michael T. Aiken, and Nicholas J. Demerath III. "The Persistence of Political Attitudes among 1960s Civil Rights Activists." *Public Opinion Quarterly* 51, no. 3 (August 1987): 359–75.

Marx, Karl, and Frederick Engels. *Collected Works of Karl Marx and Friedrich Engels, 1845–48*. Vol. 6, *The Poverty of Philosophy, the Communist Manifesto, the Polish Question*. New York: International Publishers, 1976.

Mason, Robert. *Richard Nixon and the Quest for a New Majority*. Chapel Hill: University of North Carolina Press, 2004.

Matles, James, and James Higgins. *Them and Us: Struggles of a Rank-and-File Union*. New York: Prentice-Hall, 1974.

Mattson, Kevin. *Intellectuals in Action: The Origins of the New Left and Radical Liberalism, 1945–1970*. University Park: Penn State Press, 2002.

Matusow, Allen J. *The Unraveling of America: A History of Liberalism in the 1960's*. New York: Harper & Row, 1984.

Mayer, Margit. "Social Movement Research in the United States: A European Perspective." *International Journal of Politics, Culture and Society* 4, no. 4 (1991): 459–78.

———. "Theoretical Assumptions of American Social Movement Research and Their Implications." Paper presented at International Sociological Association World Congress Madrid, July 1990.

McAdam, Doug. *Political Process and the Development of the Black Insurgency, 1930–1970*. Chicago: University of Chicago Press, 1982.

McAdam, Doug, Sidney Tarrow, and Charles Tilly. *Dynamics of Contention*. Cambridge, UK: Cambridge University Press, 2001.

McCarthy, Mary. *Hanoi*. New York: Harcourt, Brace & World, 1968.

McCormick, Anita Louise. *The Vietnam Antiwar Movement in American History*. Berkeley Heights, N.J.: Enslow Publishers, 2000.

McFerrin, Mike. "Mike Company, 3rd Battalion, Fifth Marines," 1999, http://www.securenet.net/3rdbn5th/mike35/mike.htm (accessed January 6, 2009).

Metzgar, Jack. *Striking Steel: Solidarity Remembered*. Philadelphia: Temple University Press, 2000.

Micklethwait, John, and Adrian Woolridge. *The Right Nation: Conservative Power in America*. New York: Penguin, 2004.

Milgram, Stanley. *Obedience to Authority: An Experimental View*. New York: Harper and Row, 1974.

Miller, James. *Democracy Is in the Streets: From Port Huron to the Siege of Chicago*. New York: Simon and Schuster, 1987.

Miller, S. M., and Frank Riessman. "'Working-Class Authoritarianism': A Critique of Lipset." *British Journal of Sociology* 12 (1961): 263–76.

Mills, C. Wright. "Letter to the New Left." *New Left Review*, September–October 1960, http://www.marxists.org/subject/humanism/mills-c-wright/letter-new-left.htm (accessed June 2, 2007).

———. *The Marxists*. New York: Delta Books, 1963.

———. *The New Men of Power*. Urbana: University of Illinois, 2001 (1948).

Moser, Richard. *The New Winter Soldiers: GI and Veteran Dissent during the Vietnam Era*. New Brunswick, N.J.: Rutgers University Press, 1996.

Muste, A. J. "The Movement to Stop the Vietnam War." *Liberation*, January 1966.

———. *Mobilizer*, December 19, 1966.

Mydans, Carl, and Shelley Mydans. *The Violent Peace*. New York: Atheneum, 1968.

Neale, Jonathan. *The American War*. London: Bookmarks, 2001.

Nelson, Bruce. *Divided We Stand: American Workers and the Struggle for Black Equality*. Princeton: Princeton University Press, 2001.

Nisbet, Robert. "The Decline and Fall of Social Class." *Pacific Sociological Review* 2 (1959): 11–17.

Nixon-Agnew Campaign Committee. *Nixon Speaks Out*. Campaign book of speeches, October 25, 1968.

Norton, Mary Beth, David M. Katzman, David W. Blight, Howard P. Chudacoff, Thomas G. Paterson, William M. Turtle Jr., and Paul D. Escott. *A People and a Nation: A History of the United States*. 6th ed. Boston: Houghton Mifflin, 2001.

Olick, Jeffrey, and Joyce Robbins. "Social Memory Studies: From 'Collective Memory' to the Historical Sociology of Mnemonic Practices." *Annual Review of Sociology* 24 (1998): 105–40.

Oropeza, Lorena. *Raza Sí!, Guerra No!: Chicano Protest and Patriotism during the Viet Nam War Era*. Berkeley: University of California Press, 2005.

Perlman, Selig. *A Theory of the Labor Movement*. Philadelphia: Porcupine Press, 1979 (1928).

Perlstein, Rick. *Nixonland: America's Second Civil War and the Divisive Legacy of Richard Nixon, 1965–1972*. New York: Simon and Schuster, 2008.

Peters, Cynthia. *Collateral Damage: The New World Order at Home and Abroad*. Boston: South End Press, 1992.

Philips, Kevin. *The Emerging Republican Majority*. New Rochelle, N.Y.: Arlington House, 1969.

Phillips, Kimberly M. "'All I Wanted Was a Steady Job': The State of African American Workers." In *New Working-Class Studies*, edited by John Russo and Sherry Linkin, 42–51. Ithaca: Cornell University Press.

Piven, Frances Fox, ed. *Labor Parties in Postindustrial Societies*. Cambridge, UK: Polity Press, 1991.

Piven, Frances Fox, and Richard Cloward. *Poor People's Movements: How They Succeed, How They Fail*. New York: Pantheon, 1977.

——. *Why Americans Still Don't Vote: And Why Politicians Want It That Way.* Boston: Beacon Press, 2000.

Podhoretz, Norman. *Why We Were in Vietnam.* New York: Simon and Schuster, 1982.

Polletta, Francesca. *Freedom Is an Endless Meeting: Democracy in American Social Movements.* Chicago: University of Chicago Press, 2002.

Polletta, Francesca, and James Jasper, "Collective Identity and Social Movements." *Annual Review of Sociology* 27 (2001): 283–305.

Poulantzas, Nicos. *Classes in Contemporary Capitalism.* London: New Left Books, 1975.

Preis, Art. *Labor's Giant Step: The First Twenty Years of the CIO: 1935–55.* New York: Pathfinder, 1992 (1964).

Przeworski, Adam. "Proletariat into a Class: The Process of Class Formation from Karl Kautsky's *The Class Struggle* to Recent Controversies." *Politics & Society* 7 (1977): 343–401.

Radosh, Ronald. *American Labor and United States Foreign Policy.* New York: Random House, 1969.

Raskin, Marcus, and Bernard Fall. *The Viet-Nam Reader: Articles and Documents of American Foreign Policy and the Viet-Nam Crisis.* New York: Vintage, 1967.

Reed, Adolph. "Reinventing the Working Class: A Study in Elite Image Manipulation." *New Labor Forum* 13 (2004): 18–26.

Richer, Edward. "Peace Activism in Vietnam." *Studies on the Left,* no. 6, January–February 1966.

Rieder, Jonathan. *Canarsie: The Jews and Italians of Brooklyn against Liberalism.* Cambridge, Mass.: Harvard University Press, 1987.

——. "The Rise of the Silent Majority." In *The Rise and Fall of the New Deal Order 1930–1980,* edited by Steve Fraser and Gary Gerstle, 242–69. Princeton: Princeton University Press, 1989.

Riesman, David, Nathan Glazer, and Reuel Denney. *The Lonely Crowd: A Study of the Changing American Character.* New Haven: Yale University Press, 1961.

Rinehart, James W. "Affluence and the Embourgeoisement of the Working Class: A Critical Look." *Social Problems* 19 (1971):149–62.

Roediger, David R. *The Wages of Whiteness.* London: Verso, 1991.

Rogin, Richard. "Joe Kelly Has Reached His Boiling Point: Why the Construction Workers Holler USA ALL the Way!" *New York Times Magazine,* June 28, 1970.

Rose, Fred. *Coalitions across the Class Divide: Lessons from the Labor, Peace and Environmental Movements.* Ithaca: Cornell University Press, 2000.

——. "Toward a Class-Cultural Theory of Social Movements: Reinterpreting New Social Movements." *Sociological Forum* 12 (1997): 461–94.

Rosenberg, Milton J., Sidney Verba, and Philip Converse, *Vietnam and the Silent Majority, A Doves Guide.* New York: Harpers and Row, 1970.

Rytina, Joan Huber, William H. Form, and John Pease. "Ideological Currents in American Stratification Literature." *American Sociologist* 5 (1970): 127–37.

——. "Income and Stratification Ideology: Beliefs about the American Opportunity Structure." *American Journal of Sociology* 75 (1970): 703–16.

Sale, Kirkpatrick. *SDS.* New York: Random House, 1973.

Salvatore, Nick. *Eugene V. Debs: Citizen and Socialist.* Urbana: University of Illinois Press, 2007.

Sayres, Sohnya. Anders Stephanson, Stanley Aronowitz, and Frederic Jameson, eds. *The 60s without Apology.* Minneapolis: University of Minnesota Press, 1984.

Scammon, Richard, and Ben Wattenberg. *The Real Majority: An Extraordinary Examination of the American Electorate.* New York, Coward-McCann, 1970.

Schneider, William. "The Vietnam Syndrome Mutates." *Atlantic D.C. Dispatch,* April 25, 2006.

Schulman, Bruce J. *The Seventies: The Great Shift in American Culture, Society, and Politics.* New York: Free Press, 2001.

Schuman, Howard. "Two Sources of Antiwar Sentiment in America." *American Journal of Sociology* 78, no. 3 (November 1972): 513–36.

Schwartz, Barry. "Memory as a Cultural System: Abraham Lincoln in World War II." *American Sociological Review* 61 (October 1995): 908–27.

Scott, James C. *Weapons of the Weak: Everyday Forms of Peasant Resistance.* New Haven: Yale University Press, 1985.

Sennett, Richard, and Jonathan Cobb. *The Hidden Injuries of Class.* New York: W. W. Norton, 1993.

Sewell, William H. Jr. *The Logics Of History.* Chicago: University of Chicago Press, 2005.

Sexton, Patricia Cayo, and Brendan Sexton. *Blue Collars and Hard Hats.* New York: Vintage, 1971.

Sherkat, Darren, and Jean Blocker. "The Political Development of Sixties Activists." *Social Forces* 72 (1994): 821–42.

Shostak, Arthur B. *Blue-Collar Life.* New York: Random House, 1969.

Small, Melvin. *Antiwarriors: The Vietnam War and the Battle for America's Hearts and Minds.* Lanham, Md.: Rowman & Littlefield, 2002.

——. *Covering Dissent: The Media and the Anti-Vietnam War Movement.* New Brunswick, N.J.: Rutgers University Press, 1994.

——. *Johnson, Nixon, and the Doves.* New Brunswick, N.J.: Rutgers University Press, 1988.

Small, Melvin, and William D. Hoover, eds. *Give Peace a Chance: Exploring the Vietnam Antiwar Movement.* Syracuse, N.Y.: Syracuse University Press, 1992.

Sombart, Werner. *Why Is There No Socialism in the United States?* Edited by C. T. Husbands. Translated by Patricia M. Hocking and C. T. Husbands. White Plains, N.Y.: International Arts and Sciences Press, 1976.

Stacewicz, Richard. *Winter Soldiers: An Oral History of Vietnam Veterans Against the War.* New York: Twayne Publishers, 1997.

Stinchcombe, Arthur L. *Stratification and Organization: Selected Papers.* Cambridge, UK: Cambridge University Press, 1986.

Stone, Isidor F. *In a Time of Torment.* New York: Vintage, 1968.

Students for a Democratic Society. "Port Huron Statement," 1962.

Sugrue, Thomas. *The Origins of the Urban Crisis: Race and Inequality in Postwar Detroit.* Princeton: Princeton University Press, 1996.

Summers, Harry Jr. *On Strategy: A Critical Analysis of the Vietnam War.* New York: Bantam, 1982.

Surrey, David Sterling. *Choice of Conscience: Vietnam Era Military and Draft Resisters in Canada.* New York: Praeger, 1982.

Tarrow, Sidney. *Power in Movement.* 2nd ed. Cambridge, UK: Cambridge University Press, 1998.

Taylor, Clyde, ed. *Vietnam and Black America.* Garden City, N.Y.: Anchor Books, 1973.

Teixeira, Ruy. "New Progressive America: Twenty Years of Demographic, Geographic, and Attitudinal Changes across the Country Herald a New Progressive Majority." Center for American Progress, Washington, D.C., 2009.

Teixeira, Ruy, and Alan Abramowitz. "The Decline of the White Working Class and the Rise of a Mass Upper Middle Class." Brookings Institution Working Paper, April 2008, http://www.brookings.edu/papers/2008/04_demographics_teixeira.aspx (accessed January 6, 2009).

Teixeira, Ruy, and Joel Townsley Rogers, *America's Forgotten Majority: Why the White Working Class Still Matters* (New York: Basic Books, 2000).

Thelin, John R. *A History of American Higher Education*. Baltimore: Johns Hopkins University Press, 2004.

Tindall, George Brown, and David E. Shi. *America: A Narrative History*. New York: W. W. Norton, 2004.

"The Troubled American: A Special Report on the White Majority." *Newsweek*, October, 1969.

Touraine, Alaine. *The May Movement: Revolt and Reform*. Translated by Leonard Mayhew. New York: Irvington Publishers, 1979.

Tygart, Clarence E., and Norman Holt. "A Research Note on Student Leftist Political Activism and Family Socioeconomic Status." *Pacific Sociological Review* 14 (1971): 121–28.

Tygart, Clarence E., Norman Holt, and Kenneth Walker. "Examining the Weinberg and Walker Typology of Student Activists." *American Journal of Sociology* 77 (1972): 957–70.

US Census Bureau Statistics. "Historical Income Tables: Families," http://www.census.gov/hhes/www/income/histinc/f01w.html (accessed June 30, 2008).

Vanneman, Reeve, and Lynn Weber Cannon. *The American Perception of Class*. Philadelphia: Temple University Press, 1987.

Voss, Kim. *The Making of American Exceptionalism*. Ithaca: Cornell University Press, 1993.

Walker, Daniel. "Rights in Conflict: The Violent Confrontation of Demonstrators and Police in the Parks and Streets of Chicago during the Week of the Democratic National Convention of 1968." National Commission on the Causes and Prevention of Violence, December 1, 1968, http://www.geocities.com/Athens/Delphi/1553/ricsumm.html (accessed January 28, 2008).

Walker, Pat, ed. *Between Labor and Capital*. Boston: South End Press, 1979.

Warner, W. Lloyd, Kenneth Eells, and Marchia Meeker. *Social Class in America: A Manual of Procedure for the Measurement of Social Status*. Chicago: Science Research Associates, 1949.

Wattenberg, Ben, and Richard M. Scammon. *The Real America: A Surprising Examination of the State of the Union*. New York: Putnam, 1976.

Weaver, Vesla M. "Frontlash: Race and the Development of Punitive Crime Policy." *Studies in American Political Development* 21 (fall 2007): 230–65.

Weber, Max. *From Max Weber: Essays in Sociology*. Edited and translated by Hans Heinrich Gerth and Charles Wright Mills. Oxford: Oxford University Press, 1946.

Wechsler, Jimmy. "Labor in Retreat: The AFL-CIO Tragedy." *Progressive*, January 1967.

Wehrle, Edward F. " 'Partisan for the Hard Hats': Charles Colson, George Meany, and the Failed Blue-Collar Strategy." *Labor* 5 (fall 2008): 45–66.

Weininger, Eliot. "Foundations of Pierre Bourdieu's Class Analysis." In *Approaches to Class Analysis*, edited by Erik Olin Wright. Cambridge, UK: Cambridge University Press, 2005.

Weinstein, Allen, and David Rubel. *The Story of America: Freedom and Crisis from Settlement to Superpower*. London: DK Publishing, 2002.

Weir, Stan. *Singlejack Solidarity*. Minneapolis: University of Minnesota Press, 2004.

Weiss, Philip. "How the Antiwar Was Won; The Ghosts of Vietnam Haunting the Iraq War Are Also Lurking over the Movement against It." *New York Magazine*, October 3, 2005.

Welch, John. "New Left Knots." In *Between Labor and Capital*, edited by Pat Walker, 173–88. Boston: South End Press, 1979.

Wells, Tom. *The War Within*. Berkeley: University of California Press, 1994.

Whittier, Nancy, Belinda Robnett, and David S. Meyer. *Social Movements: Identity, Culture, and the State.* Oxford: Oxford University Press, 2002.

Williams, William Appleman. *Contours of American History.* Chicago: Quadrangle, 1961.

Wright, Eric Olin, ed. *Approaches to Class Analysis.* London: Verso, 2005.

——. *Classes.* London: Verso, 1985.

Wright, Esmond. *The American Dream.* London: Blackwell, 1996.

Wright, James, "The Working Class, Authoritarianism, and the War in Vietnam." *Social Problems* 20, no. 2 (autumn 1972): 133–50.

Young, Marilyn Blatt. *The Vietnam Wars, 1945–1990.* New York: HarperCollins, 1991.

Young, Nigel. *An Infantile Disorder?: The Crisis and Decline of the New Left.* New York: Routledge, 1977.

Zaroulis, Nancy, and Gerard Sullivan. *Who Spoke Up?* Garden City, N.Y.: Doubleday, 1984.

Zerubavel, Yael. *Recovered Roots: Collective Memory and the Making of Israeli National Tradition.* Chicago: University of Chicago Press, 1997.

Zinn, Howard. *The Twentieth Century: A People's History.* New York: HarperCollins, 2003.

Zinn, Howard, and Anthony Arnove. *Voices of a People's History of the United States.* New York: Seven Stories Press, 2004.

Zolberg, Aristide. *How Many Exceptionalisms?* Philadelphia: Temple University Press, 2008.

Zweig, Michael. *The Working-Class Majority: America's Best Kept Secret.* Ithaca: Cornell University Press, 2000.

Index